appetites

BODY, COMMODITY, TEXT

Studies of Objectifying Practice

A series edited by Arjun Appadurai,

Jean Comaroff, and Judith Farquhar

APPETITES

food and sex in postsocialist china

JUDITH FARQUHAR

DUKE UNIVERSITY PRESS   *Durham & London*   2002

© 2002 Duke University Press

All rights reserved

Printed in the United States of
America on acid-free paper ∞

Designed by Amy Ruth Buchanan

Typeset in Scala by G & S Typesetters

Library of Congress Cataloging-in-
Publication Data appear on the last
printed page of this book.

For Jim

CONTENTS

Acknowledgments, ix

Introduction, 1

PART I. EATING: A POLITICS
OF THE SENSES

Preamble to Part I, 37
Lei Feng, Tireless Servant of the People

1. Medicinal Meals, 47

2. A Feast for the Mind, 79

3. Excess and Deficiency, 121

PART II. DESIRING:
AN ETHICS OF EMBODIMENT

Preamble to Part II, 167
Du Wanxiang, The Rosy Glow
of the Good Communist

4. Writing the Self: The Romance
of the Personal, 175

5. Sexual Science: The Representation
of Behavior, 211

6. Ars Erotica, 243

Conclusion, 285
Hailing Historical Bodies

Notes, 293

References, 323

Index, 337

Americans say thank you a lot. Those of us who speak Chinese in the course of everyday life in China find ourselves thanking people much more often than is necessary or expected. We translate our English-language manners into a Chinese situation and express our gratitude when someone passes a dish or holds a door or does his or her job by stamping a letter or calculating a bill. Certainly the words are available and easy to use. Yet we gradually become aware that we sound a little odd constantly saying "thank-you" for routine services and exchanges. A Chinese friend, hearing me murmur *xie xie* to a stranger for some utterly routine assistance, even asked me about this oddity once: "Don't people in your country ever help each other? These gestures are just part of everyday life—why do you have to say thank-you all the time?"

This is an interesting question, one that embodies some of the important differences between the life of apparent autonomy and self-reliance I lead in Chapel Hill, North Carolina, and the collective and interdependent lives that are being led at the same time in China. Perhaps thanking is one way in which we mark our many actual dependencies within a culture that has forgotten how to speak of the collective.

I wish I could mark all the gifts that have gone unthanked, not because they have been exceptional contributions to my life and this project but because of their very ordinariness. The chance remarks, the jokes, the suggested books or articles, the questions both naive and critical, the willingness to listen—these are the favors people do me every day and they are the seedbed from which much of this book has grown. This brief preface could never be a full catalog of the riches I routinely collect among my colleagues and students (especially in anthropology, cultural studies, and Asian studies at the

University of North Carolina) or of the kindness and intellectual stimulation of Chinese friends (especially in the world of Chinese medicine). But I here want to name some of the people whose insights about Chinese popular culture and ways of studying it have made my own thinking on the subject more effective. Each of them, usually unknowingly, has contributed to some worthwhile change in this project: Lisa Aldred, Cherine Badawi, Stuart Bondurant, Victor Braitberg, Tom Chivens, Galahad Clark, Cathy Davidson, Susan Dewar, Bruce Doar, Dan Duffy, Tom Farquhar, Peter Farquhar, Carleton Gajdusek, Alison Greene, Jacqueline Hall, Britt Harville, Hu Weiguo, Ann Jefferson, Yoshio Ikai, Bill Lachicotte, Bruno Latour, Li Xiumin, Ralph Litzinger, Donald Lopez, Tomoko Masuzawa, John McGowan, Christophe Park, Paul Rabinow, Randall Roden, Rafael Sanchez, Patricia Sawin, Hugh Shapiro, Susan Shaw, Lorann Stallones, Margaret Wiener, Terry Woronov, Yin Xiaoling, Zhang Jie, Zhang Qicheng, and Zhao Shuzhen. One could not wish for better people with whom to talk.

Early stages of this research were supported by funds from the Committee on Scholarly Communication with the Peoples Republic of China of the National Academy of Sciences, both as part of their Research in Rural China (Zouping County) program and in the form of a yearlong national research award in 1990–91. Over the last eight years I have received a variety of generous grants from programs at the University of North Carolina, including the Institute for the Arts and Humanities (which provides good fellowship along with research time), the Z. Smith Reynolds Foundation, the Arts and Sciences Foundation, the Triangle East Asian Studies Program (from a Chiang Ching-kuo Foundation Grant), the Institute for Research in the Social Sciences, and the University Research Council. Much of my daily life has been facilitated generously and efficiently by the staff of the Anthropology Department at the University of North Carolina; special thanks are due to Mrs. Suphronia J. Cheek, who always makes the office feel like home. I also wish to acknowledge the hospitality and fine colleagueship of staff members in the Beijing and Washington offices of CET Academic Programs, who helped to make semesters in Beijing with Study Abroad students in 1997 and 2001 both personally and intellectually rewarding. Institutional and financial support of this kind has translated into time in China and time to write, both essential forms of sustenance for which I am endlessly grateful.

Parts of this book were begun in the fall of 1993 while I was teaching in Montreal and enjoying the heady and supportive atmosphere of the Department of Social Studies of Medicine at McGill University. I am especially grateful to Margaret and Richard Lock, Mariella Pandolfi, Vinh-kim Nguyen, and Allan Young for the comradeship they offered then and the intellectual challenges with which they continue to sustain me. It was also delightful to spend time that semester with Ken Dean, Tom Lamarre, Robin Yates, and Grace Fong, whose ways of combining theoretical and historical literature with Asian studies are as serious as they are adventurous.

As will be evident in my endnotes, the brilliant work of Jing Wang and Gang Yue has been essential to my education and my own argument here. Their warm and stimulating friendship has been even more important, however; I feel very fortunate to live in the same part of the world they occupy. There are other friends whom I see less frequently whose work and conversation have also been an inspiration; these are Ann Anagnost, Tani Barlow, Nancy Chen, Huang Ping, Andrew Kipnis, Ralph Litzinger, Lydia Liu, Lisa Rofel, Volker Scheid, Louisa Schein, Nathan Sivin, and Angela Zito.

A very special group of graduate student researchers on Chinese medicine have helped and inspired me over the last few years. Jia Huanguang, Eric Karchmer, Lai Lili, and Wang Jun have offered willing labor as research assistants, sensitive insights as anthropologists, and delightful sociability. Alison Greene, Rebecca Schafer, and Zhao Hui also provided generous research assistance.

Ken Wissoker has expertly guided this book through its many stages, as editor, consultant, and dinner companion. I am most grateful to him, however, for having found two reviewers whose intelligent comments led to a revision that was a vast improvement over the first full manuscript.

Other readers of the book in its various incarnations have been Laurie Langbauer, Peter Redfield, Kathy Rudy, and Ann Stewart. Both their salutary criticisms and their encouragement to continue have been very important to me. But my greatest debt of this kind is owed to the members of my wonderful writing group, who have steadily worked their way through every draft, earnestly and imaginatively grappling with every problem from punctuation to grand theory. This is the one regular meeting I will never cancel, my golden hours with Jane Danielewicz, Marisol de la Cadena, Joy Kasson, and Megan

Matchinske. They have taught me how to write differently (better, I hope) and have kept me engaged with all our projects in a truly dimensional way.

Jim Hevia—scholar, teacher, editor, historical visionary, jokester, cook, gardener, and coconspirator—has been a part of the everyday life of this book from its earliest beginnings. How can I thank him?

食 色 性 也

shi se xing ye (Appetite for food and sex is nature.)

In the four words above, appetites for food and sex, important elements in the life of the body, make an appearance in philosophy only to disappear again immediately.[1] *Shi se xing ye* is an oft-quoted line from *Mencius* (fourth century B.C.E.), one of the earliest works that properly can be called Chinese philosophy. D. C. Lau translates the sentence as "appetite for food and sex is nature." Spoken by Gaozi, a disciple of the philosopher Mencius, the speech that begins "shi se xing ye" is preceded by a series of exchanges between Gaozi and his illustrious teacher in which Mencius questions the metaphors and logic of his student's rather facile pronouncements on human nature (*xing*). This opening is followed by a long and subtle conversation about the difference between benevolence (*ren*) and rightness (*yi*) and whether the former can be considered to be intrinsic to humans.[2] Thus, this remark would be more accurately, if rather freely, rendered in context as "[It goes without saying that] appetites for food and sex are innate. [But what about the less easily identified traits of benevolence and rightness?] Benevolence is intrinsic, not externally imposed, while rightness originates outside oneself; it is not intrinsic."

This assertion is followed by various proofs drawn from everyday life. Thus the appetites are invoked only to support an argument about less mundane human attributes. They stand in conveniently for those aspects of experience that can be taken for granted as natural, universal, and clearly innate. The self-evidence of appetites makes a nice contrast with the more difficult questions to which thinkers have devoted their critical intelligence; these involve intangibles like motives or styles of action, the nature of the good, and how such things can be known and evaluated.

I, too, am interested in these classic questions. But as an anthropologist I am reluctant to use everyday embodied life as a source of the metaphors through which we address such great philosophical problems. Writing in a tradition that has shown that social and cultural differences run very deep, and that has made it possible to imagine daily lives that are radically different from those of North American readers, the ethnographer cannot comfortably resort to many self-evident or common-sense presumptions about what people normally want or do.[3] Rather, it is self-evidence, common sense, and normality themselves that need to be interrogated and challenged.

So I cannot agree, exactly, with Gaozi (or, more properly, with translator Lau) when he remarks offhandedly, and with something else on his mind, that appetites for food and sex are natural.[4] Certainly, appetites are real experiences of actual bodies. But we become aware of desire only as it wraps itself around things (particular foods or bodily activities, objects we wish to hold, remembered or imagined situations); our wants draw specificity from the very conditions we have generated while pursuing, sometimes blindly, diverse goals. The things we desire need not be simple, immediately present to consciousness, or concrete: they can be abstractions like true love or true communism, complexities like protecting one's children (forever), or other impossibilities like writing the best book on China. Such variable ends give form to desires themselves. Once we admit the diversity of our wants, the historical slipperiness of goals, then all desires and objects of desire become complex. Food and sex, and our appetites for them, warrant detailed attention.

Postsocialist Appetites

"Shi se xing ye" is a line that is often quoted, but out of context and to quite different ends, in contemporary Chinese writing and conversation. In its modern uses, the sentence sounds more like, "Appetites for food and sex are *only natural*, after all." In other words, one can't expect people to forego their bodily pleasures even when a certain amount of self-sacrifice might be in a good cause. Moreover, the impeccable classical authority of this statement seems to support the universal common sense of human indulgence in personal appetites.

The point seems a truism, but its overt repetition in contemporary China is timely. Only a few decades ago it was not acceptable to introduce individual appetites, or their indulgence, into discourse. Within the culture of Maoism, which became well established in the 1950s and reached its greatest degree of ideological ambition in the late 1960s and 1970s, it was much more proper to speak of past suffering (in the old society), future utopia (when communism is achieved), and, in the present, work, production, and service. For at least two decades, the collective priorities of "building Chinese socialism" ruled all the surfaces of life. Although the everyday lives of quite material bodies persisted, of course, and wishes and discomforts could be spoken of casually and privately, the existence and indulgence of non-collective appetites were almost an embarrassment.

Nowadays, however, and in the roaring nineties of China's expansive and permissive reform economy, known (with considerable understatement and irony) as "socialism with market characteristics," the indulgence of appetites is a highly visible, even flamboyant, aspect of a growing consumer regime.[5] Except, perhaps, for the youngest consumers, relatively new forms of self-indulgence have a political and transgressive edge: 1990s individualism and consumerism are not at all socialist and are quite inimical to Maoism.

Some aspects of Maoist discourse have not disappeared, however. The moralistic rhetoric of the Communist Party, which urges collective service, public civility, and deferral of selfish aims, can still be found in all manner of official documents, from school textbooks to radio broadcasts to editorials in the official *People's Daily*.[6] In a sense, though, the sobriety of this rhetoric only makes it easier to note, in many mundane acts, the contrast between then and now, between Maoist asceticism and the modern middle-class enjoyment of capitalist luxuries. The best revenge, Americans like to say, is living well. Chinese consumers in the reform era (1976 to the present) appear to agree.

An Anthropology of the Mundane

This book explores the realizations over the last two decades of the shift from Maoist asceticism to capitalist boom in the everyday lives and embodied experiences of contemporary Chinese urbanites. My first goal is to capture a certain historical moment at the level of bodies and their appetites, phenomena that are often thought not to vary much either historically or culturally. I will not philosophize the body

One of the winners of the 1990 Chinese National New Year Painting Competition: "New Customer" by Zhang Dejun. Casual comradeship, relaxation, and apolitical hobbies like keeping goldfish have replaced the stridency of Maoist poster art.

and its capacities as much as historicize and pluralize embodiment.[7] Although Mencius and his students might have done well to devote a little more attention to the "natural" appetites, I nevertheless feel that philosophizing about bodies is as inconclusive as philosophizing about whether benevolence is intrinsic to human nature. The "problem" of human nature cannot be settled once and for all in theory; but bodies have histories, and with a little methodological creativity these histories can be told.

Methodological creativity, uniting an anthropology of the body and an anthropology of discourses and practices, is thus the second goal of this book. Having said that I wish to historicize and pluralize embodiment (as opposed to writing a philosophy of "the body"), I have committed myself to an account of some historical practices rather than a definition of a theoretical object—not the body but embodied, historical life. Conceived of as object, the body has been studied in languages of both anatomy and symbolism; understood as a general life process, embodiment has been elucidated in both physiology and phenomenology as if it were the universal substratum of experience.[8] Ethnography at its best has quite correctly refused to decide between these approaches, but its hybrid accounts have seldom been explicit about embodiment and anthropologists have always had to struggle against the perception that their topics are both local and remote.[9] If the object body is to be put in motion and the living, experiencing body is to be addressed in histories that go beyond area studies or "out of the way" places, the tool kit of ethnography must be expanded.[10]

One approach I have adopted in this study has been an increase in and a blurring of the boundaries between the genres of source material that can serve as an ethnographic text. Popular fiction and film, advertising, technical medical works, popular health advice, critical essays, and other media products—"reading matter"—take their place alongside accounts of my own fieldwork encounters and references to secondary works on China. Advertising and propaganda are not held apart from oral lore and those aspects of tradition that are kept alive in everyday practices; critical writing by Chinese scholars is not cleanly distinguished (as the words of "native informants") from my own speculations and interpretations. This is in a sense a kind of cosmopolitan or itinerant ethnography, but the itinerary really comes into existence only in the writing and reading of the book.[11] The route taken has not touched, much, on the burgeoning new ethnography of the People's Republic of China or on the lavish (and in some cases very thoughtful) journalism covering China's economic reforms or on the interesting and problematic genre of Chinese autobiographies written in English, though all of these could have been productively used.[12] Most such work has aimed at more comprehensiveness, a more total vision of some aspect of Chinese modernity, than this study does. In search of those resources that help to produce an ever-contingent embodiment—the bodiliness of modern Chinese people who have much to read in their environment—and keeping an eye out for those events that challenge bodily proprieties—especially illness and hunger—this book has wandered. It has tried not only to wander across the face of reform era Chinese popular culture and medicine but also to stray into "our" embodiment—my own and that of my readers. Reading, and the imagining that is an unavoidable part of it, is, after all, a bodily process; unlike "thought" (as in "Mao Zedong Thought" or the thought of John Dewey), it is tied to the particular site, the particular history and abilities of the concrete reader. One must always *claim* a reading: this is my interpretation, this is what I saw there. This study—a collection of readings—ranges far and wide looking for bodily particulars, hoping to invoke in readers a carnal imagination that acknowledges anew its own reliance on the particulars of everyday material and discursive life.

An anthropology of embodiment, then, and an exploration of an ethnographic technology of reading, these undertakings find their materialist precedent for me in some surprising places: in Marx, for example, who as historian and philosopher was no vulgar economic reductionist. In *The German Ideology*, in the course of critiquing the idealism of both Feuerbach and the young Hegelians, Marx insisted that human consciousness and human bodies themselves arise from the concrete "sensuous activity" of "really existing active men":[13]

> The production of ideas, of conceptions, of consciousness, is at first directly interwoven with the material activity and the material intercourse of men, the language of real life. Conceiving, thinking, the mental intercourse of men, appear at this stage as the direct efflux of their material behavior. The same applies to mental production as expressed in the language of politics, law, morality, religion, metaphysics, etc., of a people. Men are the producers of their conceptions, ideas, etc.—real, active men, as they are conditioned by a definite de-

velopment of their productive forces and of the intercourse corresponding to these, up to its furthest forms. *Consciousness can never be
anything else than conscious existence, and the existence of men is their
actual life-process.*[14]

Although *The German Ideology* refers often to the priority of human
productive processes, thus leading away from a general materialism of
the body and toward the economic emphasis of later works, in 1844
Marx had clarified (at least for himself) a fundamental significance
for this notion of a life process that is both contingent and productive:
"The transcendence of private property is therefore the complete
emancipation of all human senses and attributes; but it is this emancipation precisely because these senses and attributes have become,
subjectively and objectively, *human*. The eye has become a *human* eye,
just as its object has become a social, *human* object—an object emanating from man for man. The senses have therefore become directly
in their practice *theoreticians*."[15] And, finally, in a line that truly inspires this book, he writes that "the *forming* of the five senses is a
labor of the entire history of the world down to the present."[16]

With Marx, then, I wish to avoid the mystifications of an idealist
bias toward "consciousness." This study, by focusing on embodiment
in history, takes the concerns of the cultural anthropologist beyond
our classical interest in symbols, meanings, and social relations. As
will be clear from the amount of space devoted herein to writing and
subjectivity, this is not just a leap to the other side of a Cartesian divide between mind and body. Rather it is an insistence on the complexity of the activity that makes a life process real, that makes theoreticians of the senses. Bodies are far from inert or passive slaves to
the intentions of minds; they are inhabited by language and history
and ever-responsive to specific built environments. They also make
and are made by the local forces and temporal rhythms belonging to
particular lifeways.

It would seem that the contingency of bodies and the materiality of
discourse would hardly need to be stated in an anthropology informed
by materialists as diverse as Malinowski, Foucault, Evans-Pritchard,
Bakhtin, and Gramsci. But cultural anthropology has sometimes
been hasty in turning from carnal life to representations, from bodies and practices to symbols and meanings. At the same time, many
social anthropologists have sustained economic or biological reduc-

tions that too readily leave the life of speech and thought to one side. More troubling still, most anthropologists have continued to write (or at least teach) as if bodies and texts were two quite separate levels of being. Some critics of Foucault seek the "extradiscursive" dimension in studies of discourse (the "real, individual body" or "agent," as if this were a natural reality that Foucault somehow just failed to notice) and talk about how bodies are "inscribed" with "meaning," passively "suffering" the illegitimate force of a politics articulated in written words. These phrasings reveal a naive faith in the existence of material natures that are, in theory and essence, untouched by human history. This body and this material world are seen as prior to the violations and confusions of discourse. Yet, however much we may search for bodies innocent of discourse, we cannot know materiality except through the living of language-inflected social life.

Although I cannot claim to single-handedly rectify the deep-seated dualistic tendencies in anthropological writing, I attempt herein to treat bodies as formations of everyday life (temporal, dispersed, shifting) and everyday life as thoroughly suffused with discourses (collective, concrete, historical). Even the built structures, food, and clothing that make up any particular life—and there are no universal abstract lives, which was precisely Marx's point—take their nature from histories that are never nondiscursive. Meaning is not dualistic, it does not refer to a deeper ideal stratum of forms; rather, significance is intrinsic to material life. I have tried to write as if this inherency could be presumed.[17]

To this end, a wide variety of materials are invoked and discussed in these pages. Things that seem dissimilar and unrelated on the surface, such as medicine and banquets, eating and literature, and self-help books and movies, are presented and "read" for their historical and experiential import. In these readings, I pay special attention to a certain taken for granted dimension, the elements of everyday life that are made real more in their use than in their theorization. In anthropological terms, this involves reading for an assumed but seldom articulated habitus. Using (in part) Bourdieu, I understand habitus as a disorderly and inarticulate collection of "durable, transposable dispositions" informing routine practices, giving repetitive and predictable form to bodily life as "history turned into nature."[18] Many have read the concept of habitus as ahistorical and deterministic;

I consider this to be a misreading of Bourdieu's very careful prose. If the concept of habitus is to be useful for social anthropology at all, it must be seen as open to history and many unexpected variations. It cannot be mapped neatly over the conventional abstract categories of social science.[19] Habitus is neither culture nor psychological structure, role, or national character. It may vary by class, region, community, or family, but it cannot be reduced to either individual or collective behavior. Habitus, a structure of dispositions, is at once a kind of placement in a world that was always already in a state of play, a tendency to act, and a limited series of potentials that might be realized in action. It is quite different from the classic sociological and psychological notion of observable, quantifiable behavior; moreover, because habitus is always generated in collective social practice, it cannot ultimately be reduced to the pristine possession of an individual.[20]

The bodily dispositions and everyday practices that interest me usually go unnoticed in contemporary China's public debates. As a result, they slip through all manner of discursive gaps and quietly cross the borders between distinct social domains. In Bourdieu's terms, these dispositions "transpose" between and among diverse situations. They do not so much underlie discourses and practices as inhabit them. With a certain kind of attention, especially one informed by participation in the daily life of Chinese work units, cities, and provincial towns, the dispositions of people and things, times and spaces, can be read.[21]

Moreover, because habitus is made up of the mundane conditions of daily life and the practices of (broadly construed) bodies, a Chinese version need not be exotic. It is one of the arguments of this book, made in part through a style of writing that evokes familiar aspects of bodily life (hunger, touching, fatigue, breathing, and so on), that where material life is concerned there is no "Orient." The daily habits, attitudes, and strategic dilemmas described here are extremely contingent on the events and conditions of Maoist and reform China; even so, I believe they can connect through the mundane to the experiences that I share with my North American readers.

This simultaneous effort to achieve both specificity and commonality at least seeks to avoid any claim of universality or to trace the life of any singular or abstract "body." One cannot recover in ethnographic prose the phenomenal fullness of any bodily act, such as eating or sexual contact, much less claim to have thereby captured a generalizable "experience." The casual encounters, the banquets, the hunger, and the erotic activity described below are not identical either to events or my own memories or readings of them. It is not simply that words fail us; rather, reality is multifaceted and our points of view on it are partial. No event is simple enough to be pinned down in memory, in description, in writing.

I do not rehearse this axiom of phenomenology in order to claim that insights can belong only to particular unrecoverable events; this would be like shooting my own interpretive project in its clay feet. Rather than attempting to recover and record some illusory ethno-reality, then, I direct the ethnographic description and the interpretations that follow to the embodied reader, immersed in his or her own practical life. I speak of modern China while hoping to build an imaginative common ground on the shared pretext of bodies. In other words, bodies are no more simple than events, but they are at least a complexity to which we can all relate at times. On this very ordinary terrain, it will be possible to see how a wide variety of social and political purposes converge in particular embodied events, the reality of which always exceeds both analysis and experience.

Discontinuities

One of the principal arguments of this book is that everyday life in reform China is still inhabited by the nation's Maoist past. The three decades (1949 to 1978) of socialist construction, during which Communist Party rule under the leadership of Mao Zedong, "the great helmsman," came very close to making China a cultural (or at least ideological) unity, have not been forgotten by historians, but much work remains to be done before they will be well understood in either Chinese or Euro-American scholarship. I do not attempt a proper history of these decades. Rather, I will show some of the ways in which the projects and achievements of high Maoism were, and are, *lived* in mundane practices and embodied habits.

Because Maoism reached so deeply into the lives of so many people, and did so for such a broad sweep of the nation of China, at times in what follows I speak without apology of "China," though my own experiences extend to only some places and rather scattered readings. The hegemony of Maoism and the far from dead embodied memory of its programs allow this liberty for at least a few more years. Here, then, by way of orientation, I sketch a certain history of contemporary China with an eye to its usefulness for placing the mundane in a broader, more widely known, and decidedly national context. It is not a history of the modern Chinese body, but for the time being accounts like this can (and do) serve as a certain orientation toward that history.

As has often been argued, the ingredients and rhythms of everyday life change in a somewhat different manner than the highly visible institutions and state political relations that have made the history of events. Because alterations in mundane physical arrangements and the routines and rituals of everyday power are not usually found in official chronicles, social historians rely on memoirs, legal cases, business ledgers, birth and death records, letters, maps, and diaries, looking beyond the master narratives of the time in search of incidental details that reveal how ordinary people lived. The results of this kind of work often require an alternative periodization of history, one that shows fewer major ruptures (no revolutions, as Corrigan and Sayer have suggested) and dates the achievement of permanent transformations often long after they have been most noisily claimed.[22]

Although there is little doubt that China in the twentieth century experienced very rapid social change (and I for one still find the word *revolution* appropriate for one or two midcentury decades), some widely noted transformations occurred more gradually, unevenly, and incompletely than has traditionally been acknowledged.[23] I will discuss some of these gradual changes below, but first the usual periods of political history should be noted. The People's Republic was established in 1949, putting an end to civil war in most of the country. The early 1950s saw a period of land reform (which returned "land to the tiller" for China's huge rural majority), a rebuilding and development of infrastructures, and the nationalization of privately owned industries. At the same time the work unit (*danwei*) system was organized and expanded, extending government bureaucracy, socialist health and welfare services, and Chinese Communist Party management into the lives of most nonfarming citizens. Later in the 1950s, land was collectivized, following the Soviet model, and increasingly huge (and reputedly very inefficient) communes were developed. In 1958, the whole population was mobilized in the Great Leap Forward, a party-led movement in which rapid industrialization and intensified agricultural output were to be achieved through increased amounts of manual labor on the part of all citizens. After several bad droughts and little alteration in the intensification policy, much of the country experienced a disastrous famine. Many died of starvation or associated illnesses, and only a small proportion of the population, mostly highly placed urbanites, escaped periods of great deprivation.[24] By 1962, food supplies had mostly returned to (a rather ascetic) normal, but Mao Zedong's leadership had apparently been compromised by the failures of the Great Leap and its aftermath. Moves among other party leaders to sideline Mao resulted in 1966 in his direct appeal to the people, especially middle-school students, to make "cultural revolution." Youthful Red Guard organizations (or various cliques within them) attacked party members suspected of anti-Mao thinking as well as various representatives of the "bad classes" of landlords, capitalists, intellectuals, and rightists. The greatest chaos of the Great Proletarian Cultural Revolution lasted less than two years, and Mao himself was instrumental in restoring order in the fall of 1967. By calling on his popular support, however, Mao had regained unchallenged leadership of the country, and the party's extremely effective, nationwide propaganda apparatus (led, we are told, by Mao's wife Jiang Qing) insured that his image and his "thoughts" remained the central element of public culture.

The year of Mao's death, 1976, saw the deaths of several other top leaders and a disastrous earthquake in Tianjin. A relatively uncharismatic successor, Hua Guofeng, succeeded to party leadership, the Gang of Four (including Jiang Qing) were arrested and blamed for all the excesses and errors of the Cultural Revolution, and political maneuvering for deep political changes began. By 1978, Deng Xiaoping had ascended to power and had begun to establish economic reform policies. Over the next twenty years, these policies and an increasingly adventurous economic leadership would consolidate and vastly expand the forms of privatization that had been tentatively growing since the early 1970s.

This is, of course, only one way of telling the outline history of contemporary China. A history that emphasized democratization would find significance in the 1956 Hundred Flowers Campaign and the student movements that gained ground from 1976 forward. One that focused on international relations would mention the Korean and Southeast Asian wars and Richard Nixon's visit in 1972. All, however, would find a very significant break in history in the mid- to late 1970s, when China's leadership consolidated its decision to turn away from a totalizing state socialism toward capitalist-style participation in the world market.

None of these histories, however, would supply a very satisfactory account of how people lived through this transition or coped with the equally dramatic transformations that preceded it. Although I do not attempt to supply a full-blown bodily alternative to the standard histories—that would be far beyond the reach of a lone ethnographer—some of the materials discussed below actually do address this interesting problem. Among them are the fictional works of *Hibiscus Town, The Gourmet,* and *Love Must Not Be Forgotten.* These stories dwell on the life of the body in fascinating ways; indeed, they (and many other works of the 1980s and 1990s) make almost a fetish of the concrete and the mundane after decades of Maoist abstraction had produced a crisis of representation for writers. I discuss this language crisis at greater length in chapter 2, but I also rely on these works, authored by writers who lived through the early history of the People's Republic, to provide more detail than I can on the character of daily life within Maoism and after. (Of course, these authors had particular agendas in crafting their descriptions, of which I take due note below. But even purportedly objective historical accounts are not innocent of situated agendas, though these are sometimes less explicit.)

As an ethnographer of appetites, however, I can supply some observations about how life changed as Maoism receded. I arrived in China well after the crucial "turning points" of 1976 and 1978. Nevertheless, the work unit life I got to know in a medical school between 1982 and 1984 in some respects more closely resembled the daily life of the 1970s than that of the later 1980s. This was in part because of the continued public sway of what Li Tuo has called "Mao discourse."[25] Everyone I knew attended "political study" sessions on Thursday afternoons, every textbook was prefaced with paeans to the wisdom of China's laboring masses (sometimes reproduced in Chairman Mao's beautiful calligraphy), and a public address system instructed residents of every corner of the campus, morning and evening, with ideologically correct news and public service announcements. Although I lived in a very supportive and relatively open unit, it was still awkward for ordinary colleagues and fellow students to spend time with me, a foreigner, for fear of politically phrased criticism. (This situation did not deter all from befriending me, and

I also enjoyed the company of my "designated friend," a serious and intelligent party member who had been instructed to look out for me. I don't think she usually knew who my other friends were.) One woman with whom I often talked, who was in the almost unique situation of being divorced, was widely considered to be immoral (on no particular evidence as far as I could tell); social contact between the sexes had to be very carefully managed if one was to avoid this kind of unkind talk.

There was in this work unit no private space even for families lucky enough to be living together in a small apartment. A single living-sleeping-eating room often accommodated a couple and several children and/or an elderly parent, cooking and washing facilities were shared by groups of apartments, and walls and doors were thin. Many students and junior professors (and their counterparts in other kinds of administrative units) lived in dormitory rooms accommodating six or eight residents in a double row of bunks. Many married couples lived apart for years while struggling for permission for one or the other to shift to their spouse's work unit. Because it was inconvenient to shop (at free markets that were now quite legal but still few and far between) and there were no home refrigerators, university staff members often availed themselves of the simple and cheap food in the unit canteens; only on special occasions would most families bother to mount a full meal at home.

Everybody knew everybody else's business, and felt free to criticize it. Such criticism could and often did influence careers, despite the best efforts of some conscientious administrators to ignore idle talk. Certain public areas, at certain times, took on special significance since there were so few private spaces. In my work unit, the evening walk after dinner, when numerous groups of two or three would stroll around the circular drive in front of the main classroom building, was a chance to talk (quietly, so no one else would hear) with special friends during what might appear (at least the first few times) to be a mere chance encounter. Adventurous students, forbidden to become engaged or marry until after graduation, could slip out after dark to a nearby public park, but they would compete for space under bushes and behind buildings with huge numbers of other courting couples. No one was really invisible in these public places, but timing and location could be managed to insure that hardly anybody would be paying attention.

Village life offered even less privacy, it would seem. The space that could be devoted to housing was restricted by law (in many rural areas until the late 1980s) in order to maximize land for grain production. Until economic reforms began to produce greater wealth in the countryside (around the mid-1980s), few could afford to build houses with private rooms for sleeping. Families in Shandong Province, the place that I know best, shared one room, a kitchen shed, a privy, and a storeroom for all the indoor activities of everyday life. In the village where I have worked—which was a relatively early beneficiary of reform era rural development schemes—it was only in the late 1980s that families could get clearance to expand or replace their old houses. The first purpose of the many renovations that followed was to provide a separate single room for a married son and his incipient family.

I could go on, describing the sudden fashion shift in 1986 and 1987 that replaced the unisex trousers and jackets of the Maoist era with the ruffles and motorcycle jackets of markedly gendered clothing; the sexualization and gradual general acceptance of skirts for women (one village woman I knew in 1987 made herself a skirt to wear only in the evening after the outside door had been closed; I had the distinct impression that this was an erotic gambit); the diversification of local food delicacies, first seen in banquets among dignitaries and then, by 1990, in the emerging institution of the private department store and the supermarket (deep-fried scorpions was one impressive item in Shandong in 1988); and the emergence of personal hobbies (keeping fish and birds or carving carrots and turnips as garnishes, like one of my Beijing friends, who did so to enhance her delicious cooking). I could even (reminded by the memory of that good food) confess to a certain nostalgia for Maoist everyday life and to my fascination with watching new hedonisms emerge as Maoism receded. My point, however, is simply this: the asceticism of the Maoist period, and its attendant politics of political talk, mutual surveillance, and neighborly support-cum-criticism, did not suddenly disappear when Deng Xiaoping announced China's "opening" (kai-fang) to the capitalist world in the late 1970s. The 1980s was a decade that, at the level of daily life, saw a gradual but still contested movement toward individual control over wealth (and the downward spiral of some toward poverty) and gave an emerging middle class more opportunities to consume a few previously prohibited luxuries. At the same time, the volume and tenor of Maoist political language, with its high-minded (and to many still persuasive) demands that everyone "serve the people," only slowly changed. Down to earth habits of work, rest, talk, consumption, and erotic interaction evolved slowly and unevenly. As early as 1983, my barber expressed worries about the effect of decollectivization on women and children (would dependents be trapped in the patriarchal family form again?), and those who remembered the famine continuously deplored the waste and corruption of official banquets. Attitudes like these were accompanied by a million diverse strategies for forging new lives in the market economy, as the leadership of the party-state withdrew from work and family and praise for competition and entrepreneurship replaced the values and politics of collectivism.

By the mid-1990s, as citizens born at the end of the Cultural Revolution were reaching their twenties and beginning to form families of their own, a very noticeable generation gap began to be remarked. Young people, the "spoiled" children of the reform era, neither understood nor valued the asceticism and collective morality of their parents. One rural cadre, aged sixty, told me in 1996, "My son and I simply can't talk. There is absolutely nothing we agree about." He insisted that this was a common situation among his friends; certainly the "generation gap"—a term translated from American sociology—was often remarked in the newspapers. There is, in fact, a very clear cohort effect in contemporary China; I need only ask a new acquaintance how old he or she is to receive, unsolicited, a brief litany of the key personal facts that place him or her in the official history of the People's Republic. (A new collaborator in Beijing told me in the spring of 2000 that he had just turned forty-one and immediately mentioned that he tested into the college he now works for in 1977. This placed him in a legendary cohort, the "class of 1977," which was the first for a decade to enter college on academic merit. He would have been eighteen, about the age he would normally have graduated from upper middle school. I immediately asked him how many years of middle school he had missed and where he spent his time in the countryside. He was probably too young to have been a very active Red Guard.) The effect of Cultural Revolution disruptions on schooling, a period of time spent in the rural areas as a rusticated "educated youth," and participation in (or refusal of) official job assignment systems that have now almost disappeared—all these place the speaker in a whole history of values and practices that are entailed simply by chronological age. (In another conversation, a laboratory researcher I met far from her home city replied to my question that she was forty-five. She added that she went to college in the early 1970s as a student in the then approved worker-peasant-soldier category. We immediately turned to discussing the strategies by means of which she overcame the post-1976 stigma attached to this overly Maoist experience.) In such conversations, speakers know that much can be assumed about a modern Chinese life; once the timing is known, few circumstances need to be explained.

Neither the Chinese generation gap nor the relative gradualness of the changes that have produced it should surprise the anthropological observer, especially one interested in the nature of embodiment and the evolution of habitus. Bourdieu has noted the "hysteresis effect"—a kind of historical, bodily stutter marking the impossibility of feeling comfortable in the present—that arises when habitus is ill adapted to changing conditions. "This is why generation conflicts oppose not age-classes separated by natural properties, but habitus which have been produced by different *modes of generation,* that is, by conditions of existence which, in imposing different definitions of the impossible, the possible, and the probable, cause one group to experience as natural and reasonable practices or aspirations which another group finds unthinkable or scandalous, and vice versa." [26] Clearly, my retired cadre friend finds much of his son's life and interests scandalous, while the son (I only met him once, but I know many like him) finds his father's old Maoist commitments, and history of service, unthinkable. Their differences are rooted not so much in different ideals as in different bodily dispositions, inculcated by the conditions of everyday life in a postsocialist reform process that quietly evolved, beneath the hubbub of a much debated politics, over the course of a decade.

Ethnography of/as Reading

As I have suggested, bodies and the everyday life of which they are made up do not offer themselves directly to anthropological interpretation; they must somehow become legible through words and images. This admission is not a reduction of "real life" to the status of a textual representation (whose fixed and flattened status would then only invite a content analysis). Rather, it is an insistence on the inseparability of real human life from the life of language. Textuality in this approach is less useful as a source of metaphoric representations (those that stand for a nonlinguistic reality or concept) than as a process of metonymy, in which words and actions, discourses and practices interweave in syntagmatic strings or, more simply, in history. Much of what follows thus draws on particular techniques of reading and writing or, perhaps better, writing about reading. Even when I describe conversations, observations, or events from my own stays in China, I find myself dwelling on these things more as memories than as pieces of objective evidence recorded in systematic field notes. Though the rewriting of such memories requires that they be given at least the minimal form of a narrative, every narrative always offers more than one layer and can be approached from more than one perspective. I thus want to dwell for a moment on processes of reading and the ethnographic promise that they hold.

Seeing ethnographic descriptions as similar to other narratives, including fictional ones, offers me some very skilled ethnographic partners. I can claim as my allies in this undertaking film director Zhou Xiaowen (whose film *Ermo* is discussed in chapter 6), novelist Mo Yan (who contributes an essay on food and history discussed in chapter 3), writer Zhang Jie (whose famous story "Love Must Not Be Forgotten" I discuss in chapter 4), novelist Lu Wenfu (author of "The Gourmet," which is analyzed in chapter 2), and many others who live and work in the People's Republic of China. These writers offer, alongside other agendas in their carefully crafted and multistranded fictional works, important commentaries on broad collective dilemmas of reform Chinese culture. I do not always agree with the rhetorical implications of these analyses (my brief consideration of *Half of Man Is Woman* in chapter 5 and longer reading of *Hibiscus Town* in chapter 2, for example, suggest some of my problems with these works), but I do find all of them useful as responses to, and depictions of, certain broad national situations that trouble many contemporary Chinese people.

There are ethnographic riches in these works because they adopt the conventions of realism. Ethnography, like other nonfiction, is a realist genre. It posits the fabled anthropological "field" as a terrain of culturally specific activity in which the anthropologist has personally participated, the customary patterns of which he or she has carefully observed. Quite often in anthropological writing this field is treated as a context for some puzzling text. Much ethnography proceeds, for example, by identifying a cultural oddity that needs explaining—the cockfight of Clifford Geertz's famous essay is a classic example—and then placing it in historical, ideological, and practical context until it no longer seems odd.[27] In fact, more often than not ethnography succeeds in making unfamiliar cultural practices seem not only understandable but necessary. The familiar settings in which the *readers* of ethnography sit are thereby relativized, sometimes to such an extent that many of their own activities assume the appearance of cultural oddities in their own right.[28]

This rhetorical practice thus produces something real. In the present case, for example, ethnography posits a "China" that articulates with (while often contradicting) newspaper accounts, tour guide information, film images, travelers' anecdotes, and the everyday experience of living or traveling in the People's Republic. At the same time, it cultivates a reader, a subject who contemplates this China (or Chinese popular culture or Chinese medicine) from a great or little distance. Such readers may compare what they see on the page with all manner of other practicalities and textualities, allowing this text to modify, however slightly, their assessment of the reality in which they daily act. The general reading process in which ethnographic realism finds its (admittedly limited) powers is entwined with every aspect of modern life and contributes in manifold ways to the continuing production of complex realities.[29]

Ethnography exists alongside other genres of writing that perform this world-constituting work. Some of this parallel writing is Chinese. Because in this book I rely so heavily on modern Chinese writing (composed in the Chinese language and published in the People's Republic), it is important to identify in advance those points at which ethnography can coincide with the fictions and polemics of this particular time and place. In my readings below, for example, I have noted the critical rhetorical tendencies of the texts as part of more general historical situations (e.g., the state of Chinese nationalism after Mao). This is not an unconventional way to read modern literature, especially "third-world" literature,[30] and its usefulness will stand or fall on the persuasiveness of my particular interpretations. At times I have also used some tools of literary criticism, focusing particularly on language use and narrative form, in an effort to reveal the craft and per-

"Wintertime warmth," a well-known poster by Zhang Xinglong of the Maoist period. Workers throw themselves into collective labor under harsh conditions to open undeveloped northern lands to industry and agriculture.

formative power of the texts. But I have also relied on a more constitutive aspect of modern realist fictions, and that is their (limited but genuine) verisimilitude. This approach requires some historical background and explanation.

Let me begin this explanation with an "ethnographic" anecdote. A few years ago, in 1996, I taught a course to North Carolina undergraduates called "The Politics of Culture in East Asia." Among the American undergraduate students were two Chinese students, both in their thirties, who had recently entered graduate programs in other departments. They were just old enough to have been teenagers in China during the 1970s. In this course, we had occasion to view and analyze "propaganda" posters from the early 1970s. I chose a few images that depicted collective labor and relative gender equality rendered in that enthusiastic style known as revolutionary romanticism.[31] The paintings (Huxian "peasant" paintings, most of them) combined a "realistic" love of mundane detail with politically correct dispositions of healthy, active, committed bodies.

The American students, asking first about the "realistic" quality of the paintings, were all skeptical. "How can everyone be smiling with all that snow whirling around? They must be freezing!" "No sane person would dig in the bottom of that dank well for more than five minutes!" They were thus quick to denounce these images as propaganda in the classic, manipulative sense of the term. Their Chinese classmates were surprised and disturbed by the American students' responses, however. They protested: "But that's how it was! See that thermos bottle? It's just like the ones we used then. And those cloth shoes and padded jackets, those are exactly right!" And, "Yes, we did enjoy working together, it was much more fun than solitary study." These Chinese viewers were quite content to read the posters *as* realistic and to let the images bring back a certain memory of youth. The posters thus had a double efficacy for "native" viewers, one linked to their concrete verisimilitude and one deriving from their effectiveness in performing a more abstract social and cultural vision. There was both an "effect of the real" and an effective rhetoric.

Literary scholarship on fictional realism has long acknowledged that descriptive writing relies on an effect of the real. Roland Barthes's classic statement of this effectiveness has more to do with how certain genres claim plausibility than with theories of "world-constituting" linguistic productivity or performativity. But his acute observations about the function of "structurally superfluous notations" incorporate an understanding of literary reference that can lead in interesting directions when applied to anthropology.[32]

Discussing *Madame Bovary*, Barthes notes that certain signifiers (the classic example is the barometer atop a pile of cartons on Mme. Aubain's piano) are a collusion between signifier and referent, bypassing the narrative signified. In other words, rather than advancing the phantasmic project of the fiction, they produce a "reality effect, . . . that unavowed verisimilitude which forms the basis of all the standard works of modernity."[33] When he considers an aspect of the novel that approaches the domain of ethnography, "the description of Rouen (a real referent if there ever was one)," he points out that this description is subject to "the tyrannical constraints of what we must call aesthetic verisimilitude."[34] Its presence and function in the text "is quite irrelevant to the narrative structure of *Madame Bovary* . . . [but] it is not in the least scandalous, it is justified, if not by the work's logic, at least by the laws of literature: its 'meaning' exists, it depends on conformity not to the model but to the cultural rules of representation."[35]

Clearly, these cultural rules of representation constrain any text that places "real referents" in collusion with the signifiers of its descriptive language. The "tyrannical constraints of . . . aesthetic verisimilitude" go with the genre, and any author who mounts a realist narrative (be it ethnography, short story, news report, propaganda poster, or film) is subject to their dictates.[36] Description must seek plausibility for a community of readers, both recharging their prior "real world" with significance and offering new realities for incorporation into an evolving imaginary. The barometers and pianos, the thermos bottles and cloth shoes, of the fictional everyday world must connect as firmly with the lived context of the reader as with any broader purposes of the narrative.

This has been as true for modern Chinese literature, which has had at least two major realist movements, as for the classic realisms of Europe's nineteenth century. Marston Anderson and Jaroslav Prusek, among others, have shown how the writers of China's May Fourth movement studied and experimented in the 1920s with European-style realism and its forms of authorship. Like nineteenth-century European realist innovations, these were political projects inseparable from the nationalist and reformist concerns of the Republican period (1911–49).

> Realism was not primarily endorsed by Chinese thinkers for what Westerners associate most closely with it, its mimetic pretense, that is, the simple desire to capture the real world in language. At least in the early years of the New Literature movement, Chinese writers rarely discussed problems of verisimilitude—how the text works to establish an equivalence between itself and the extra-literary world—and little critical attention was given to the technical problems of fictional representation, a preoccupation of such Western realists as Flaubert and James. Instead realism was embraced because it seemed to meet Chinese needs in the urgent present undertaking of cultural transformation by offering a new model of creative generativity and literary reception.[37]

This model was thought of as individualist. Perhaps the most famous scholar of the May Fourth movement, Hu Shi, saw literary realism as a corrective to a traditional Chinese concern with matters of style. He emphasized writers like Ibsen, and recognized that "in Ibsen's world the positive effect of realist description is achieved by polarizing the individual and the social order; progress comes only through the lonely struggles of a few extraordinary people against society." [38] Thus, this realism was concerned with producing a new kind of Chinese reader, one who could take individual responsibility and would be embodied in a new way, cut loose from family and community ties and able to struggle against traditional authorities.

While these authors approved the capacity of realist writing to produce a heightened sense of contradiction between modern individuals and a troubled society, they ultimately rejected this style, seeing it as ineffectual against the chronic social problems and perceived cultural immobility of the Chinese nation.[39] Most of these authors, and their literary innovations, were eventually incorporated into a theory and practice of literature that married socialist realism to revolutionary romanticism. From the early 1940s to the early 1980s, under the sway of Maoist policies governing literature and the arts, writing sought to reach, serve, and instruct the masses, who were conceived of as disliking straightforward description. The moralizing tales of model workers (see the preambles to parts I and II) and the class-inflected narratives of the model operas (see my discussion in chapter 2 of *The White-Haired Girl*) in this period also made certain realist claims, of course. But they overlaid description of familiar concrete things, and the activities of everyday life, with a rhetoric describing that which should be, or soon would be, possible in socialism. (Thus, the rice crust that figures in the Lei Feng morality tale discussed in the preamble to part I is so familiar an object that even now I can feel and taste it in my mouth. But the point of the story is that this enjoyment was a stolen one for the naive Lei Feng. Here the "tyrannical constraints" of verisimilitude *oppose* the hard lessons of socialist morality.)

Revolutionary romanticism always involved a deferral, offering an image of what readers and viewers no doubt believed must be the case elsewhere in China, perhaps just down the road in the next village, though it had not yet quite been achieved in the here and now. This was a romantic realism that described a better world, highly recognizable but always ever so slightly deferred. Linking everyday life details (the slogans on red paper, the thermos bottles, the well-worn tools) to an image of a joyously cooperating collective, these works not only achieved a revolutionary plausibility but for a while they also collaborated in the building of a revolutionary world.

I find the works of the Maoist period politically seductive and technically fascinating. But as the regime that demanded and oversaw these artistic products lost credibility genres of representation changed and a more conventional realism once again gained a wide political appeal. Beginning in the late 1970s, after the death of Mao and the fall of the Gang of Four, the so-called literature of the wounded, populist reportage, and writers in search of national roots who experimented with "magical realism" forged a new encounter between a revalorized individual and a diversified, allegedly depoliticized reality.[40]

Emerging after forty years of a moralizing arts policy that had narrowed the themes of literature to those that "served the people," the fictional genres of the 1980s found inspiration in mundane detail and personal dilemmas. Chineseness and the nation—the political state of a very large collective—were still very much an issue, as I will argue in reading some of the fictional works that follow. But, unlike the writing of the May Fourth movement, realism after Mao was often more nationalist in the breach than in the observance. In other words, many writers presented humble lives with their unresolvable contradictions and idiosyncratic histories as allegories for a nation that now, perhaps, could not congeal.

This kind of writing presents an opportunity to ethnography, especially an ethnography that claims "reform China" for its field. If one is careful to keep the critical force and reflective complexity of these works alive while reading their necessary verisimilitude for subpolemical visions of modern Chinese everyday life, embodiment, and practical values, they make wonderful anthropological partners. The purposes of their authors are differently situated in history and the global order than mine are, though I am often in sympathy with their views. What we share is a technique of representation that is part of an existing world while seeking to modify it. Realism not only makes claims about reality, but it very often successfully performs it; it both responds to and modifies the conditions under which it appears. Realism is, moreover, the dominant genre of representation in the modern world; very little that claims to be truth escapes its stylistic grasp. In the ethnographic reading and writing that follow, I seek to participate in the play between, rather than purifying, the domains of the realistic and the real.

Interventions: Rhetorics of the Body in Chinese Medicine

If, as Marx said, history has made theoreticians of the five senses, we might suspect that in its long history Chinese medicine will have had a particularly good opportunity to articulate such a theory. Medical knowledge and its attendant clinical work offer particularly useful routes to the study of bodies in history, and I often turn to medical materials and practices in this book.[41] Illness is unpredictable; both a natural and cultural construction, and stubbornly complicated, it presents constant anomalies to knowledge and experience. Despite valiant nosological efforts in the last few hundred years of biomedical practice, it has not been possible to find adequate categories for a great many of the ailments that present themselves in clinics. Collectively, we continue to tinker with diagnosis, treatment, and classification in efforts to account for and bring under medical control many kinds of bodily experience. The anomalies, demands, and crises that inhabit medical writing, especially in the clinic, are not only the voice of the biological organism, though this is an important dimension to bear in mind; they are also (and always) the voice of the body as a site of cultural-historical intersections and a formation of everyday practice. We both suffer illness and respond, individually and collectively, to events like illness with new strategies, new languages, new culture.

This fertile, chaotic site is as active for biomedicine as it is for traditional Chinese medicine. In several respects, these two modern styles of clinical practice hold a certain body—when it is broadly enough defined—in common. Both locate disease processes within and immediately around individuals; neither has the time or resources, nowadays, to devote much attention to the more population oriented practices of preventive medicine or public health.[42] Moreover, disease (or at least disorder) is their common problem. Both approaches to the body devote most of their practical attention to the remedy of undesirable states, the relief of suffering, while admitting that it is sometimes necessary to induce disorder in the service of erasing it.[43]

Writers in Chinese medicine since the mid-1950s, when their field began to receive full government support, have justified traditional medicine as an integral part of a public health care system aimed at keeping the Chinese masses strong and productive. This has been a highly effective and at the same time deeply ethical strategy through which a (vulnerably "nonmodern") field sustained a place in the socialist structure of government support. But in practice the field does more than simply turn ailing bodies back into effective workers. Chinese medicine also offers a very personal kind of pleasure and a practical domain for the frequent exercise of discrimination between the desirable and the odious. The distinction is perhaps between a tool significant in terms of its results—health—and an intrinsically self-justifying practice, a regimen healthful in itself. The everyday techniques through which individuals, even if they are of modest means, comfort themselves, compensate for daily difficulties and frustrations, or build a life of reliable bodily satisfactions often include medical and exercise regimens alongside those of cooking, touching, and attire.

Thus modern "traditional" Chinese medicine is an especially fruitful site in which to consider the cultivation of enjoyment, the achievement of positive health, and even the aesthetics of life. In the burgeoning "self-health" (ziwo baojian) literature, television lifestyle programming, drug advertising, and hobbyist clubs that have appeared in the last fifteen years, for example, traditional medicine plays a very important role. Experts from this field work through these popular media to offer nutritional advice that relies on the logic and substances of the Chinese materia medica to explain ancient regimens of exercise and meditation and to emphasize the health benefits of a regular lifestyle.

Contributing to these popular genres has been a way for doctors attached to state work units, with their too slowly growing salaries, to cash in on the consumer wealth and individualistic hedonism of the reform era. The Chinese medical archive lends itself well to this interest in positive health; clinicians interested in translating their technical knowledge into the concerns of everyday (nondiseased) life have rich resources on which to draw. A constantly reiterated line from the second-century medical classic The Canon of Problems, "The highest medical work treats the not yet ill" (shang gong zhi wei bing), summarizes and authorizes traditional medical concern for illness prevention and the arts of everyday life.[44] But this is just the tip of a large premodern library of "life-nurturing" techniques (see chapter 6 for a discussion of *yang sheng*, the nurturance of life).

Whether for "preventive" or curative purposes, Chinese medical people are confident that they have effective technologies to intervene in the experiential life of the body. The very fact that herbal drugs are first and foremost classified by "flavor"—a technical concept that refers to more than actual taste—suggests the importance of the link between sensuous experience and healing in this field. These bitter-tasting but fragrant medicines are techniques for producing or maintaining pleasant, comfortable, gratifying, or interesting feelings in place of those that are painful, irritating, distressing, or dull. Both patients and doctors know "from experience" that these techniques work, often at levels of subtle subjective change that could not be detected by laboratory tests.

When one approaches the world of Chinese medical practice from the point of view of the sufferers of nonacute conditions who make up a significant portion of the patient load—infertile couples, balding or impotent middle-aged men, young people with acne or dizzy spells, women seeking to lose weight, men trying to quit smoking—traditional medicine can appear or develop as a connoisseurship of embodiment and a source of pleasure. A regimen of herbal treatment, especially if it begins to provide symptom relief and new feelings of control over recalcitrant daily experience, can even encourage an aesthetics of habitus with its own elaborate technology of self-transformation.

Thus, this book, which is about the pleasures and dilemmas of eating and sex, returns frequently to Chinese medicine, especially its recently growing popular side. The fact that traditional medicine has grown popular in the reform period far beyond the walls of clinics and hospitals is an important condition of the argument that follows. Part of the field's popularity derives from the specific efficacy of many herbal and acupuncture techniques, of course. Beyond this obvious observation, however, I wish to avoid understanding Chinese medicine (or new formations of eating or sexuality, for that matter) in functionalist terms. Too often in anthropology the mere existence of a cultural institution, such as a group of practices known as an "alternative medicine," is enough to persuade us that there must be some basic and universal human need that this set of practices functions to fulfill. Rather than suggesting that the users of traditional medical services in contemporary China *need* an indigenous form of psychotherapy, or *need* a mode of medical practice that is couched in "culturally appropriate" terms, I want to consider some of the pleasures that may be cultivated by those who (for whatever reason) seek traditional medical care. Although it may seem odd to think of medical services as objects of desire, as fulfilling wants rather than needs, perhaps in the case of Chinese medicine and its positive view of health this is not so far-fetched. By beginning with pleasure—the variable, contingent, and fleeting domain of subjectivity—rather than need—which a functional anthropology has tended to render as an inescapable and often unconscious feature of human nature and behavior—the body can be repositioned in history and the social.

Food and Sex

Appetites for food and sex belonged together for Gaozi and Mencius because both desires seemed so natural. Although this book shows that the forms of appetite are far from natural—in the sense of being ineluctable, everywhere the same, or determined outside of human history—food and sex still seem to have an inherent comradeship. As I searched for a title for this book, for example, I could not find a way to add medicine to the very short series "food and sex" in the subtitle, nor did any other master category of appetites suggest itself as necessary. Although a case could be made for including "health" as an object of some people's desires in modern China (or anywhere), the term on the face of it does not evoke the same questions of hedonism and history that *Appetites* seeks to address. And though medical materials are much used herein health as such is not really an object of this analysis.

I said above that I seek to capture a certain historical moment for modern China; this is a moment—not quite the present but not yet entirely in the past—in which pleasure counts for a great deal and not just for the young people who remember little of the Maoist moral order.[45] In fact, the materials presented here argue that much of the enjoyment available to those who do remember is the gratification of indulging in pleasures that were once forbidden, even unimaginable. It would be impossible to provide a full catalog of the new luxuries Chinese people pursue; popular desires change too quickly, and the list would be quite boring. Instead I have undertaken a series of topical studies that join the socialist past to the market-obsessed present; the life of the body to the seductive images of short story, essay, and film; and formal knowledge to elusive experience. Food and sex are useful domains for exploring all these dimensions of practice.

Appetites is divided into two parts. After a preamble that provides textual and anecdotal examples of how much has changed at the Chinese table over the last few decades, the first part, on eating, begins with the flavors of medicine. Chapter 1 shows how Chinese medicine produces a body that can be conceived of as a flavorful temporal formation. Medicine treats the vicissitudes of carnal experience with an array of herbal, mineral, and animal substances, bringing these two aspects of nature together through a systematic classificatory language. By way of the articulations of Chinese medicine and its strongly flavored decoctions taken by mouth, the body is thoroughly opened to history and all its occasions of eating (or not being able to eat). Chinese medicine, with its rich language and technology of flavors, mobilizes a kind of power that generates experience, acting on a body that, eating both medicine and food, is thoroughly informed by China's recent history of material duress and ideological profusion. Bodies marked by famine may need years of medical remediation; families that can finally eat well may need treatment for appetite disorders. All may gratefully turn to the (nominally politically innocent) domain of Chinese medicine for interventions in bodies that cannot forget politics.

One aspect of this political incarnation is the history of (always unevenly distributed) hunger. Chapter 2 thus reads certain fictional texts that have done much to inform historical consciousness about twentieth-century shortages as well as about the joys of the newfound wealth that began to appear in the reform period. This chapter shows, for example, how food was politicized in a particular Maoist formation in the 1945 opera *The White-Haired Girl*. Turning then to a reform era fictional representation of collectivist shortages and market plenty, *Hibiscus Town*, I use long extracts from this novel's descriptions of 1960s and 1970s eating to provide an impression of these earlier times that claims to be naturalistic. Both of these works attempt to tidy up the social and political world through rather markedly moral narratives. The Maoist work offers a tidier vision, with its emphasis on class struggle, while the reform novel eschews class politics but undermines some of its own most earnest clarifications. Neither work is able to banish politics.

Chapter 2 also includes a discussion of a much more comprehensive and ambiguous politicization of food, *The Gourmet*, a novella by Lu Wenfu. This is one of reform China's best-known fictional explorations of politics, eating, and modern history, addressing and weaving together many of the problems that still concern modern Chinese consumers. Which is preferable, scarce and bad food shared by all or civilized luxuries available only to the few? Can a class that only consumes be justified in a society that seeks to end the alienation of the producing classes? Understandably, *The Gourmet* concludes on an unresolved note, retreating from intractable ideological and bodily dilemmas with an aesthetic turn that its author shared with many other Chinese writers of the 1980s and 1990s.

Informed by the ambiguity Lu Wenfu is unable to resolve, chapter 3 returns to Chinese medicine and its historical body, explaining how theories of excess and deficiency in physiology and pathology can be figured in wider realms of memory, history, and practice. Thus, in this chapter medical theory is juxtaposed with an experience of banqueting—with all its micromaneuvering and well-lubricated eating—and the ironic nostalgia of Mo Yan, a writer who remembers famine and indirectly critiques its later appropriations. Problems of excess and deficiency link political and carnal domains from the most elevated to the most mundane, especially in the realm of eating.

Part II of the book turns to sex, not the act itself but certain discursive forays into the erotic domain in the Chinese popular culture of the last few decades. A preamble returns us briefly to the concerns of high Maoism in a consideration of one of the last classical stories of a model worker, the exemplary woman "Du Wanxiang" (Ding Ling 1988). Like her model soldier counterpart who opens part I, Lei Feng, Du Wanxiang is hardly ever caught in the act of eating or having personal desires. She does, however, offer access to a Maoist kind of collective erotics, a physical existence that had its own zones of sensitivity and excitement. Also in this preamble I recall my own sense of a heightened erotics in Maoist everyday life.

With this image of the erotics of the collective exemplar in mind, chapter 4 argues that after Maoism a certain individual had to be constructed before "modern" sexuality could be contemplated. To this end, I read a novella that in its day (1980) was immensely influential, *Love Must Not Be Forgotten,* by Zhang Jie. This story can be called sentimental only because it was the first to put sentiment—personal, private emotion—on the popular post-Maoist agenda. My reading explores the ways in which Zhang Jie's depiction of a secret love evokes much broader crises of politics, writing, and embodiment in the early years of the reform period. Juxtaposed with this story is a consideration of a series of autobiographical essays written by Chinese doctors. Appearing at the same time as Zhang Jie's story, and to almost as much acclaim (at least in the specialized world of Chinese medicine), these life stories make an issue of the self in a way that was then quite unprecedented. The chapter explores these early reform genres of popular writing as performative invocations—a calling into existence—of a certain modern self. Only after such personal selves had been constructed could sexuality—the subject of chapter 5— become a form of modern Chinese experience.

Sexuality became a hot topic in China a few years after the writings examined in chapter 4 were published. Chapter 5 considers the sex education and sexual liberation movements based in Shanghai, focusing especially on an ambitious and widely disseminated social survey of sexual behavior. Examining the rhetoric and assumptions of this sociological research, the chapter suggests that newly globalized forms of knowledge in China are no different from those we are familiar with elsewhere: they construct what they claim to describe. Thus, the sexual behavior polled by sociologists has become a form of experience under intensive construction for postsocialist Chinese consumers.

Yet sexuality cannot simply be seen as a discrete and unalterable modern formation diffusing smoothly into the newly privatized bedrooms of Chinese people. Chapter 6 considers a genre of literature that asserts the *national* character of "Chinese" sex. A recent wave of publishing on the ancient Chinese erotic arts offers some of East Asia's oldest writings, accompanied by vernacular translations and lavishly footnoted, for the delectation of modern readers. The texts that form the core of these "bedchamber arts," along with much of the work that followed in their train over two millennia, are simultaneously erotic and medical, carnal and metaphysical. They form an undeniably fascinating corpus, legible to moderns in many possible interpretations. I am more interested in understanding the contemporary reception of these texts in China, however, than in their historical or philosophical import. Reading commentaries and secondary bedchamber arts works, one can identify distinctly recent concerns with masculinity, expertise, and nationalism overlaid on the cryptic lines of the Han dynasty texts. In my own reading of these translations of the remote past into the heavily sexualized present, I explore the styles and politics of representing a national heritage and a historically specific body.

IN HIS FAMOUS ESSAY "Nietzsche, Genealogy, History," Foucault justifies a genealogical approach to history through a discussion of Nietzsche's trope of descent (*Herkunft*). Descent is a useful category because, among other reasons, "it attaches itself to the body":[46] "The body—and everything that touches it: diet, climate, and soil— is the domain of the *Herkunft*. The body manifests the stigmata of past experience and also gives rise to desire, failings, and errors. . . . The body is the inscribed surface of events (traced by language and dissolved by ideas), the locus of a dissociated self (adopting the illusion of a substantial unity), and a volume in perpetual disintegration. Genealogy, as an analysis of descent, is thus situated within the articulation of the body and history. Its task is to expose a body totally imprinted by history and the process of history's destruction of the body.[47]

Perhaps ethnography, too, can hope to "expose a body totally imprinted by history" and undergoing the steady and miscellaneous destructions of ideas and the passage of time. Like a genealogical approach that rejects the grand narratives of history, this would have to be an ethnography that turns away from the totalizing promises of "culture" and refuses the illusion of a substantial unity for the self. But like the "grey, meticulous, and patiently documentary" genealogist,[48] anthropologists can perhaps hope to perceive the ways in which collective experiences have been formed for certain people at certain times.

Experience can only be noted as such because it is in the past. Thus, it is always mediated by discourses and institutions, conforming to the sense-making images and tropes our histories have offered us. Experience is not present or singular, nor can it really serve as the foundation of a philosophy or a history. But its complexity, materiality, inarticulateness, and memoriousness—in short, its embodiment—continues to generate all manner of change and to challenge anthropological description. This is the challenge, and the history, this ethnography rises part of the way to meet.

PART I

eating: a politics of the senses

LEI FENG, TIRELESS SERVANT

OF THE PEOPLE

The story of Lei Feng, Chairman Mao's good fighter, conveys more clearly than any other text the cultural ambition of Maoism at its height. It shows how the lives of ordinary people were cast in the ideal light of socialist values, and its great range of influence exemplifies the scope and effectiveness of state hegemony in the 1960s and 1970s. These were the years when the motto "Serve the People" was emblazoned on every public surface from latrine walls to the gateway of the central government compound in Beijing. Building socialist civilization was every Chinese citizen's duty and, as often as not, a deeply felt responsibility. Although we anthropologists tend to place the culture of the people and the propaganda of the state in separate categories, the extent to which Lei Feng and his like were "models of and models for" a whole way of life suggest that there are settings in which the state and the people, culture and propaganda, are hard to distinguish.[1]

Lei Feng was a model soldier who died in a truck accident in 1962. After his death, his story was propagated through the state-controlled media, in which he was endlessly elaborated as an exemplar on which others should model themselves. This was shortly after the end of the famine known as "the three difficult years" (1958–61) and during a time when new mass education techniques (originating in the Central Political Department of the People's Liberation Army [PLA] but soon taken up by units under the party's Central Committee) were gaining national prominence.[2] First this model soldier and then other models (workers, mothers, farmers, and so on) were offered to the Chinese people not only through the mass media but in the then expanding institution of "political study" (*zhengzhi xuexi*). In small groups meeting several times a week throughout China, citizens met to "study Lei Feng" by reading and discussing documents sent down from the

A recently repainted portrait of Lei Feng on an alley wall in Beijing, photographed in 2000. The motto, in Chairman Mao's calligraphy, says "Learn from Comrade Lei Feng." Author photo.

party committees above them. Everyone was expected to take Lei Feng's good example very much to heart. In these documents, a certain politics of food (or at least hunger) was evident.

As Lei Feng's life was reported—not very consistently—in the officially sanctioned forms, he was an orphan who suffered much before the 1949 establishment of the People's Republic. His father, a worker and peasant wounded by Japanese invaders, died when Lei Feng was five, and his brothers succumbed to illness shortly thereafter. His mother took employment as a servant with an evil landlord. In this household, she was "not given enough to fill two bellies." The child Lei Feng "understood nothing but his own hunger."[3] His mother killed herself at Mid-autumn Festival, after making rich moon cakes for the landlord family while being allowed to eat only gruel herself. Some accounts state that land reform teams from the Communist army rescued Lei Feng from a similar fate shortly thereafter, sent him to school, and instilled in him a new idealism once he realized how the evils of the old society had been responsible for his family's suffering.

Lei Feng belonged to all the classes the Maoist administration marked as good. Born to a peasant family, he was a worker in a steel mill before he joined the PLA. (Workers, peasants, and soldiers were treated as privileged classes, especially during the Cultural Revolution.) After distinguishing himself in an army truck brigade, even his dream of joining the Communist Party was granted. Conveniently for the propaganda needs of the PLA, Lei Feng was frequently photographed—usually wearing his signature fur hat with earflaps—before his death in a truck accident at the age of twenty-two.[4] Even better, he left a diary. This book, full of earnest comments on selfless service and published in many forms, was a mainstay of political study sessions for years.

The diary reveals that the model soldier kept busy as a brigade leader who always went the extra mile, but he also found time to assiduously read, annotate, and memorize the multivolume complete works of Chairman Mao.[5] His daily entries are as much a record of this reading and its attendant ideological self-criticism as they are a record of his labor and service. When food appears in these day-to-day entries, it is not because Lei Feng eats but because he feeds others:

> Today after breakfast Company Commander Zhang gave us a job to do: go up on the mountain to cut grass and pull weeds. We worked until noon, then everyone got out the lunch boxes they had brought from the brigade canteen and gathered together to eat lunch. That was when I noticed that Comrade Wang Yantang was sitting off to the side watching everyone eat. I went over to take a look. He hadn't brought any food, so I got my own food and gave it to him to eat. Though I was a little hungry, my greatest joy was watching him eat his fill. I want to steadfastly remember those famous lines [of Chairman Mao]:
>
>> Treat your comrades with the gentle warmth of spring,
>> Tackle your labor with the fiery heat of summer,
>> Bring to individualism the leaf-scattering wind of autumn,
>> Treat enemies with the heartless cruelty of severe winter.[6]

Treating his comrade with the gentle warmth of spring, Lei Feng derives positive pleasure from service to others. At the same time, the incident gives him access via Chairman Mao's works to a broader vision of the national collective task, insuring that no amount of mundane labor, no small exchanges of kindness, will blind him to the scope and difficulty of the national task or lessen his steadfast desire to do his duty.

In another incident, one of the few in which the model soldier is caught in the act of eating, Lei Feng learns a lesson:

> At breakfast this morning, I noticed a lot of rice crusts in the mess hall staff's pot, and I grabbed a piece to eat as I was passing. Comrade X, one of the cooks, said, "Watch yourself!" When I heard these words, I was resentful. A piece of rice crust is no big deal! Feeling wronged, I put the crust back in the pot and left. Just then a newsboy gave me a copy of the daily paper, and as usual I turned first to the sayings of Chairman Mao. Chairman Mao said: "We are servants of the people; therefore if we have shortcomings we should not fear other people critically pointing them out. Don't concern yourself with who it is; anyone can point these problems out to us. All that is required is that you have spoken truly, and we will correct ourselves accordingly." I read this passage over ten times in one breath, and the more I read the more I felt I had been wrong; the more I read the more I felt that Chairman Mao was speaking these words directly to me; the more I read the more I suspected that I should not have felt wronged by that cook. I said to myself: How conceited you have been! When people's criticisms are a little heavy, you can't endure them! After thinking it over, I braced myself and ran back to the cook to confess that my taking that crust of rice had been wrong, and it had forced me to examine my own faults. Moved, the cook said: "You demand so much of yourself, you really are a good comrade."[7]

This incident highlights one of Lei Feng's particular obsessions, that of protecting the state's property. As a brigade leader and a driver in an army motor pool unit, it was of course part of his job to use state-owned goods to legitimate collective ends. But this anecdote about food reminds one that Lei Feng was also being faithful to the logic of agricultural collectivism. In the early 1960s, almost all food was the property of the people as a collective. Farmers produced food and turned most of it over to the state, which then redistributed it to soldiers, city dwellers, and other nonfarming citizens.[8] Although for three or four years there had been far too little to go around, the army had been among the better-fed and more thoroughly collectivized sectors of society. To directly appropriate food for oneself was not just selfish but potentially criminal. Thus, Lei Feng demonstrates how so-cialist theory teaches him that the act of taking a bit of leftover rice from a canteen cookpot, "no big deal" in a private domestic economy, is in a socialist economy a political, even a counterrevolutionary, act.

This can be seen as a sort of collectivist excess, and it has been easy to lampoon in later years and from far away. Nowadays it is easy to see Lei Feng as an unsophisticated busybody.[9] But some citizens even to-day—perhaps remembering still the egalitarian ideals of the revolu-tion or deploring the rise of consumerism—remember him as an ex-emplar of generous service and high moral seriousness.[10] At the same time, they are just as happy to forget the shortages and difficulties of the policies for which he stood. His was a morality that in fact de-pended entirely on the collectivization of all property, including even daily food rations. Because few in China are nostalgic for collective canteens or state production quotas, Lei Feng's image must take on a generalized moral message remote from the political programs he actually served. It is common indeed in today's Beijing for people of a certain age (over thirty-five, usually) to lament the passing of a more peaceful, less competitive, less selfish, and altogether more moral age. No one I have talked to, however, longs for a return to political infighting or Lei Feng–style guilt over crusts of rice.

Collective canteens still exist in the People's Republic, but I have seldom eaten in them. Not only is the subsidized food offered to ordi-nary workers in academic and bureaucratic work units not very good, but these are settings many people find less than convivial. More of-ten than not, people bring a container or two to fill with rice and a few vegetables, taking the food home or to the office or eating as they walk to their next task. A work unit dining hall is convenient for busy people, but unless it has been privatized and offers restaurant-style services it is not a place where one would often linger.[11] These days, in homes and restaurants, Chinese people are lingering over all man-ner of good meals.

Having arrived well after the abandonment of food collectivism, I have eaten marvelously in China. Having shared the pleasures of the table and the kitchen with friends and colleagues in Guangzhou in the 1980s and Beijing and rural Shandong in the 1990s, I have my own collection of favorite foods, stories about food, and culinary-linguistic skills. I recall teachers and doctors in the world of Chinese medicine enlivening meals with talk about the medicinal qualities of food and a farm wife who was teaching me how to make steamed bread arguing with a male visitor about how long dough should rest before steaming. I am grateful to dining hall chefs who helped me plan banquets to express my thanks to hosts and was amused by a chemical engineer friend who relied on his tastebuds and his small home kitchen to duplicate, successfully, Kentucky Fried Chicken. Every time I make a cup of tea I think of my academic adviser in Guangzhou punctuating our tutoring sessions on the medical classics with instructions about the different kinds of tea and the fine points of preparing it. Working in Beijing nowadays, I am as likely to meet someone for an interview in a MacDonald's—where some people say they enjoy the anonymity of the place—as in their home or clinic. And I have gratefully added conversations over restaurant meals to my fieldwork repertoire, taking advantage of a middle range of public etiquette introduced by a rapidly expanding restaurant culture between the casualness of street snacking and the formality of banquets.[12]

Returning to dwell on experiences like these and asking what of anthropological value can be found in them, I am persuaded of nothing so much as the intellectual clay feet of my research. Every little memory raises questions long after the fact. For example, early in my fieldwork years, a hostess urged me to rank the dishes she had served, declare my favorites, and explain why I liked them. Later I tried this approach to dinnertime conversation on other hostesses; meeting with apparent success, I could only wonder what I had thereby learned about Chinese foodways. Was my first hostess merely inventing an idiosyncratic game? Were subsequent hosts just being polite about my efforts to please? Would this sort of thing have worked as well in a working-class or rural household as it did in an academic work unit? An ethnographer eats his or her way through the field, finding the stuff of his or her own everyday life in settings that are always particular and never reliably typical.

During most of my years as an ethnographer, I have naturalized the mundane almost without noticing it. The cultural differences that usually interest ethnography quickly faded around Chinese dinner tables, and the fellow feeling that arose as food and drink were shared seemed to overcome barriers of language and etiquette. "Their" food became "my" food, and allowed me to focus my well-fed ethnographic energies on the "real" stuff of culture above the level of everyday sustenance.[13] Only lately have I begun to add eating itself to the categories through which I try to think about my social life in "the field."

This point can be illustrated with an example from my first year of research at a college of Chinese medicine. One hot summer day a woman friend came by my room to say that she had a lot of fresh lichees at her house and I would be welcome to come and help her eat them. She had also invited another woman of about our age; both of them were doctors as well as students in an English class I was teaching. The lichees—large, juicy, and delicious—had been brought to the city by a rural relative as a gift to the hostess, probably a gesture in a long-standing relationship of exchange and mutual assistance. The three of us sat at the table for hours, peeling and eating, talking about language and medicine and everyday life.

For me, this was one of those golden fieldwork opportunities. I learned a lot that afternoon about teachers, doctors, and women in an early 1980s work unit. My friends knew I was collecting information useful to my research, of course, but for them this was a different sort of occasion, one it has taken me some years to see in all its likely contours. Sharing this rural bounty with a foreign friend, for example, extended the chain of prestations of which the load of lichees had been part. To keep a gift of this kind within one nuclear family would have truncated the process of social relating, or *guanxi*, in which it had been offered; the generosity had to be passed on.[14] But the particular form of this sharing was not preordained. True, my hostess probably expected me and her other guest—a Communist Party member being groomed for an administrative position and also the "best friend" who had been designated to look after me—to be useful to her in the coming months and years. But she also knew she could expect to spend some pleasant hours with us, hours in which we all enjoyed the mild transgression of eating wonderful, unexpected food in vast quantities before any family members came home and demanded a proper meal. A few years before, this private gluttony would have been not only materially but politically impossible—fruit orchards were few and state owned, and excess food would have been minutely distributed in a much wider circle. There was, moreover, a gendered quality to this time: eating as a group of women, outside the family circle and the usual mealtimes, we found it easier to talk precisely because no particular form of talk was required. The lichees themselves were, after all, the point of our gathering.

The various cross-purposes that brought our small group of eaters together, the social networks that temporarily overlapped to accommodate fruit, a doctor, a foreigner, a party member, at least one farmer, and a number of people and agencies significant by their absence, could all no doubt be disentangled and sociologically analyzed. But something would be lost thereby. The cool flavor of those lichees, their rough skin yielding so easily to a fingernail, the translucence of their pale pink flesh around a smooth brown pit, are qualities inherent to my memory of the event. I want to persuade myself that these qualities may have been the only dimension that truly united the three of us while excluding everyone else. It is the lichees and the casual chat that I still remember; what has faded, or merged into a taken-for-granted knowledge, are the facts that I (may have) collected that day. I wonder what, if anything, my companions remember now.

Whatever the import of this lazy, well-fed afternoon, it stands in stark contrast to Lei Feng's hunger and his stolen crust of rice. I still suspect that one element of my lichee-eating companions' gourmandizing was a sense that a few years before such pleasurable excess would have been impossible. If I had had the wit to ask them, they would have both acknowledged the contrast and the historical specificity of their enjoyment. A forbidden crust of canteen rice does not taste anything like a luxury fruit that came unbidden, and almost entirely legally, into one's own home.[15] This is the difference, frequently figured in food and realized in acts of eating, that I want to explore in part I.

"China" is not, however, a totality that can be seen as having a special relationship to food, orientalist images and some recent ethnicity literature in the United States notwithstanding.[16] There is no doubt that China is strongly associated in the North American imagination with both desperate famine and sophisticated cuisine. It is therefore a particular challenge to write about eating in contemporary China without invoking traditional images of "starving masses" and "exotic delicacies." What must be emphasized is that there is nothing essentially Chinese about the unequal social relations that have produced a world economy of food maldistribution, nor is there anything ineluctably traditional about either starvation or connoisseurship. Both of these human conditions have emerged at various times in China, as elsewhere, as part of particular cultural, economic, and political conjunctures. Moreover, the conjoining forces that make Chinese history have long been global and have influenced other national situations in similar ways. I do not analyze these forces or explain their workings; instead I trace the contours of public discourses and institutional practices that have made hunger a cultural problem and eating a political practice in China's reform period.

chapter 1

MEDICINAL MEALS

This chapter is about mundane powers and the relationships between eating and medicine. People have some experience of eating—they don't just do it, they enjoy it or wish they could—day in and day out, in sickness and in health. Since these experiences are generated within asymmetrical systems of domination (both economic and epistemological), one can hardly imagine a life that is not pervaded by "the powers that be" (i.e., the powers that, while constantly under negotiation, keep turning up in similar constellations with boring but not entirely predictable regularity). A political economy of eating emphasizes the uneven distribution of nutritional resources, while a political phenomenology of eating attends to the social practices that make an experience of eating. Medical anthropology, with its political-economic and phenomenological branches and everything that ranges between these poles, is founded on a body that eats: both constructing and constructed, its experience arises from life within and among unevenly distributed, and thus contested, resources.[1] Its events, never really under control even for the most fortunate among us, present challenges to the naturalizations of power that make up common sense.[2]

This chapter is perhaps more concerned with medicine than any other, since it explores at some length the logics and practices of Chinese pharmacy. Yet therapeutic drug use is an aspect of medicine that at first seems particularly innocent of politics. In China, it is ancient, highly technical, and foundational in the sense that the powers of the materia medica are the most common and direct means by which medicine intervenes in illness processes. Chinese drugs have physiological efficacy, and Chinese doctors know "from experience" (two thousand years of it, they will remind you, speaking of the ancient and continuous archive of works on materia medica) how to combine them to maximize the benefits of this direct form of power. Surely this is a kind of power different from what we normally call political?

In theory, kinds and formations of power must be distinguished. In the practice of everyday life, however, they often get muddled. People may confuse the powers they wield by virtue of a long-standing social status—a teacher's structural ability to benignly co-erce undergraduates, for example—with the personal powers they micromanage in bodily life: fatigue and a self-critical mood impair a teacher's effectiveness in coercing undergraduates or at least one feels this is the case. Mastery of one's own experience is not always distin-guishable from one's degree of influence over others.

The disease of sexual impotence, a common concern in post-socialist China, offers a pertinent example (see also a more extended discussion in chapter 6). It is relatively easy to see common worries about sexual performance and self-diagnoses of impotence as a meta-phor for the receding powers of a certain class—party cadres, for ex-ample—or the weakness of a nation—China seen as a "backward" country.[3] The comparison mixes two rather different senses of the word *impotence*. A failure to achieve an erection in an intimate rela-tionship is not necessarily similar to the reform era reallocation of Communist Party and civil government responsibilities or to popular images of China as a country that still lacks a certain credibility and influence among nations. Why should all of these instances be linked to a failure of power? It is due in part to an accident of naming in En-glish, and perhaps we would all be better off if certain variations in male sexual activity had not been named with reference to power. The Chinese name (*yangwei*, or yang weakness disease) may not invite such a ready conflation of different types of power, but with its re-liance on the extremely adaptable and gender-marked yin yang rela-tionship, it still invites a certain generalization beyond the strictly medical domain.[4]

As analysts, we should be careful about positing a *theoretical* rela-tionship between the experiences of individual bodies and any na-tional or class body.[5] But when people themselves make this link, through some sense of identification with the nation or an explicitly named class (and aging cadres certainly are an explicit class in mod-ern China), they combine their own experience with a higher level of practice and a collective structure of feeling.[6] Here we are in the highly political domain of common sense and embodied experience.

Interventions at the level of the body are not distinct from efforts to exert power in the world. And eating is one of our most ordinary exertions.

It has often been pointed out that food and medicine are not radically distinct in China.[7] Chinese cookbooks and the new genre of books on herbal medicine cuisine emphasize the medicinal value of foods and the importance of nutritional therapies dating from earliest times; many of the vegetable and animal products decocted in Chinese medicines are used routinely in cooking.[8] The oral genre of grandmotherly advice on how to eat right for health thrives in daily conversations, and talk at banquets frequently revolves around the healthful properties of the foods being consumed. Although many doctors of traditional medicine are too busy to bother, nutritional and food preparation advice is supposed to be (and often is) offered in clinics along with herbal prescriptions. Modern periodicals ranging from daily newspapers to the most formal and conservative journals offer seasonal advice on adjustments of diet for health and well-being. Tonifying and qi-supplementing foods and drugs are often given as gifts to senior male relatives, teachers, and supervisors, and there are books aimed at a female readership that advise on how to eat right for beauty.

Perhaps eating everywhere is a "technology of the self" (i.e., of embodied historical experience), but in modern China this is perhaps a more extensively theorized and differentiated field of practice than in most other places and times. In keeping with the new cultures of consumption that have proliferated especially rapidly since the early 1990s,[9] those who can afford good food have many choices about what they will eat and many views about why they eat what they do. Both the things that are swallowed and the sources of information about them have been part of the explosion of commodities marking China's reform era. The food products available in markets are more diverse than they have ever been, thanks to rural truck farming industries, better transportation, and better information flow concerning new agricultural techniques. Supermarkets in urban areas are more and more common, as are their imported fruits and seafoods, shrink-wrapped or frozen, and their reputation for hygiene, which apparently justifies for some customers their high prices. Buyers who are still willing to wash their own food and prefer reasonable prices no longer need to rise at dawn to get to the street market before everything fresh is sold out. Markets are well stocked and stay open almost all day. All this convenience and diversity is the product of the rise of small entrepreneur agriculture in tandem with the vast increase in imports of food from Japan, Korea, Southeast Asia, and even the United States and Latin America.

In the case of Beijing, I date a certain turning point in food culture to the winter of 1990, when thousands of truckloads of state-subsidized Chinese cabbages, intended to provide a source of vitamins for urbanites during the winter, rotted at the depots for lack of customers. The work unit buyers, who in previous years had ordered large lots to be stored for the use of the workers in their agencies, simply didn't turn up. The Beijing residents for whom they once provided this nearly free food had recently seen the "chaos" of the student movement violently punished by their previously trusted army. They were, moreover, in an excellent position to quietly refuse this traditional form of nurturance from the state. The free markets were full of spinach, kale, snow peas, chives, bean sprouts, cauliflower, and root vegetables, offered at good prices by small entrepreneur farmers who had dotted the countryside around Beijing with cold frames and greenhouses. The monotonous routine of cabbage soup, pickled cabbage, and stir-fried cabbage that had once meant winter in northeastern China had been broken; families were cooking and eating meals that reflected, in great variety, the newly differentiated lifestyles of a growing middle class. Much less could be presumed about the "needs" of a population no longer organized into collective work units, no longer consuming only what the state provided. Even when it was offered free by government agencies—or perhaps especially when it was offered by a state that had lost some measure of legitimacy—cabbage in 1990 was not on the menu.

Speaking of menus, restaurant culture grew rapidly during the reform era, attracting people who were once accustomed to eating from the unit canteen or at home every night. As recently as the late 1980s, many of my friends hesitated to accept my invitations to take them to dinner in restaurants, as they didn't consider such places to be clean or safe. By the mid to late 1990s, I was often invited to restaurants myself by friends who were too busy to cook. Urban areas now boast restaurants of many kinds, offering not only the regional cuisines of China (which have themselves become much more numerous as they have been more clearly commodified) alongside various transnational fast foods and their local spinoffs but Buddhist-vegetarian, Korean, "Western," Muslim, medicinal, and imperial palace cuisines. There are one-food restaurants (hot pot, Mongolian barbecue, Beijing duck) and many neighborhood eateries offering "home cooking" (*jiachang cai*). Quite a few restaurants offer food in all price ranges, selling cheap (but sometimes famously good) bowls of noodles from a front window while hosting well-heeled parties in second-floor banquet rooms. And, although "modernizing" cities have recently been severely restricting mobile food vendors, in most places it is still possible to find cheap street food that is both sustaining and delicious.

This diverse field of alimentary practices and preferences is the setting in which health and food find their connection in reform China. In most mass market bookstores, for example, there are two places to look for materials on food, cooking, and eating. One is with the cookbooks, and the other is in the health section, labeled as "health care" (*baojian*) or "self-health" (*ziwo baojian*). The proportion of books concerned with food in this latter section has grown rapidly during the 1990s; works on nutritional therapy (*shi liao*) and medicinal meals (*yao shan*) are matched only by information on care of the aged in the number of publications filling the shelves. Books on the medicinal uses of food and the alimentary uses of medicines are of several main types: traditionalist works that link medicinal foods to a long history of "life nurturance" (yang sheng) and preventive medicine, cuisine-oriented works that emphasize elegant presentation along with the special powers of ingredients combined in certain ways, homely advice about the mundane use of herbals for better health, and lists of foods and recipes that address particular diseases (among them, tumor diseases, diabetes, high blood pressure, chronic heart failure, emphysema, acne, and the general debilities of aging). All of these sources are distinguished by a marked emphasis on the medical technique of *bu*, bolstering and tonifying the depleted or hypofunctional body.

One helpful work, *Seasonal Meals for Body Bolstering*, opens by defining the important verb *bu* as "a type of method that orally administers the food or drugs that function to build and supplement (*buyi*) or to regulate the yin-yang balance in the body, with the aim of strengthening the constitution, preventing disease, treating disease, and lengthening life. The word *bu* includes the meanings of repairing (*xiubu*), filling (*buchong*), supplementing (*buyi*), and nourishing (*zibu*)".[10]

This definition is not quite what would be provided by a Chinese medicine clinician uninterested in food therapies or by an acupuncturist (though the term *bu* would be key to their thinking), nor does it emphasize what would be obvious to an etymologist, that the roots of the written character suggest that it means "to patch," invoking a textile metaphor. It is clear, however, that the understanding of bu in *Seasonal Meals* is rather more committed to the idea of a basic yin-yang balance than many technical works on Chinese medicine might be. Although much of traditional medicine assumes the need to calibrate yin and yang processes, most practitioners usually find this level of analysis too general for elucidating actual clinical work. Yet it makes sense that authors explaining the uses of medicinal foods to a popular audience would posit the body's yin-yang balance as a fundamental aspect of their topic. Yang and yin are very broadly applicable as polar categories, making sense out of everything from the weather to the vicissitudes of history. As terms for passive (yin) and active (yang) states and incipient (yang) and developed (yin) processes, they can also figure in all manner of mundane experience. They classify things as well, including foods, in ways that are well known even to many who have never studied medicine. Yin foods can supplement the yin deficiencies of the body, and yang medicines can increase yang physiological functions. Thus, the usefulness of a yin-yang vocabulary for uniting the efficacies of food and medicine is fairly obvious; it suggests a body in motion, the activity of which can be influenced, and thus regulated, by the similarly classified efficacies of substances taken by mouth.

Although the notion of physiological balance seems obvious for a technique that makes medicine of food, the centrality of bu as a technique for maintaining this balance is suggestive. Why are there are so many more techniques for bolstering and supplementing an unbalanced system than for draining or depressing its functions? Is hypofunction a much more common disorder than hyperfunction? Are vulnerable or damaged bodies more prone to gaps, lacks, and failures of function than to excessive activity, redundancies, and proliferations? In Chinese medicine in general, the preponderance of bu methods relates to the inevitable decline that is human life. Gradually we use up our bodily resources, to the point that a good balance of yin and yang can no longer be sustained and death results.[11] This is also a popular way of conceiving of life in general: *sheng lao bing si* (Birth, aging, illness, and death—that's life!) people often say. This is no more profound a cultural principle than the sort of "death and taxes" remarks one might hear anywhere. But the fact that the body loses functional powers as it ages suggests that foods and medicines that bolster and supplement (buyi) would be more attractive to practitioners, patients, and connoisseurs than those that clear and drain (qingxie).

Food is, after all, nourishing. It remedies daily cycles of depletion and appetite. Medicinal food is distinguished in its capacity to do particular jobs on the foundation of the daily necessity and mundane gratifications of eating. Even the most general works on medicinal meals are organized for use by individuals with specific problems, and divisions of such books may be made in terms of Western medical diagnostic categories, Chinese medical syndromes, parts of the body affected, or Chinese medical treatment principles. These modes of organization make it easy for consumers to find the substances, recipes, and explanatory principles that pertain to their own conditions. Thus, these are reference works that allow individual experiences of lack and depletion to be met with foods that fill and nourish, each of them articulated in very focused ways that address a particular illness, a particular constitutional vulnerability.

This sounds quite individualized, but eating is generally a more social activity than medicine taking; people eat together, and Chinese food is famously organized for groups. Anyone who has lived single without a kitchen for long periods in China can attest to this. Eating alone in restaurants, it is not easy to get a balanced meal in quantities small enough to avoid waste. Even for families that usually cook, kitchens are too small and fuel too expensive to encourage the preparation of separate meals for those who have special needs. One friend of mine living in a county town ate bottled white asparagus from Japan every day for six months; she says it cured her throat cancer. Her husband ruefully recalls those months of asparagus at every meal because he and the children ate it as well. They still eat this expensive luxury food from time to time, although she has long been symptom free. The importance of this therapeutic commensality goes further, however. Food is a favorite form of prestation linking networks beyond the immediate family through gifts. Once my friend's relatives, neighbors, and coworkers learned of her dietary program, they took the opportunity to give her jars of asparagus on many formal and informal occasions. The expense for her family was reduced, and the problem of what to offer when a gift is expected was solved for many in this family's social circle. One person's throat cancer, along with the Chinese medical lore that suggested it could be treated with a food product, organized for a time a great deal of social activity.

The knowledge and practices on which this field known as medicinal meals is built is hardly new in China, and people in East Asia have shared much about the healing properties of food for many hundreds or even thousands of years. It almost goes without saying that the historical roots of such knowledge have been traced back to the nation's earliest records by specialists interested in nutritional medicine.[12] But I still think there is something recent about the new commodity forms of the linkage between food and medicine and consequently something historically important about the ways in which eating is now being done. Recall, for example, the changes in the meanings and uses of food discussed in the preamble to part I. The rice crust that Lei Feng almost stole in the early 1960s was a by-product of the collective cooking and serving of a plain staple food, but not everyone in the canteen would be able to enjoy crunching the crispy brown bits left at the edges of the pot. Implicit in Lei Feng's misdemeanor is the idea that he was not entitled—nor was anyone else, in theory— to a food that was not available to all.[13] By contrast, the lichees shared with me by friends in the early 1980s were delicious partly because we were not required to mete them out according to some rigorous principle of redistribution. Although Lei Feng lived at the height of food collectivism, which lasted only a few years, and my Guangzhou friends and I were eating lichees twenty years later, the differences between these two modes of food consumption are still remembered in the practice and experience of several generations of Chinese people.

It is also interesting that the plain staple foods that figure in memories of both the best and the worst years of high Maoism are seldom mentioned in contemporary discourses ranging from health writing to fictional literature. The gravel-riddled rice and coupon-bought flour, the occasional small piece of pork and the ubiquitous winter cabbage are foods that star in the writing and talk of a previous era. Nowadays we hear more about cuisines of the nation and the world, high-quality vegetables, exotic wild foods, and, of course, medicinal food specialties. Rice, flour, pork, and cabbage still appear in kitchens and on tables, but it is a more differentiated food economy and com-

Drug advertising on the side of a bus, Beijing 2001. The remedy is for depletion of the kidney visceral system, a condition associated with aging. Author
photo.

mensal situation that appears salient now, offering consumables that
address newly refined individual and class palates.[14] In its very discriminations and desires, the contemporary middle-class Chinese
body rejects the politics of the egalitarian Maoist past. This rejection
itself is a politics, but it is one that can often be forgotten in technical
elaborations of specialized knowledge and connoisseurship.

Chinese medicine, of course, in its use of natural substances that
bu bodily insufficiencies, offers many telling combinations of expert
knowledge and mundane things. Continuing, then, my argument
that control over the power to produce experience is a kind of politics,
I turn to some of the techniques by means of which medicine intervenes in the life of the body.

A Logic of the Concrete

What is the nature of the systematic knowledge used in medicinal
meals? This is an interesting question because in everyday life knowledge is not held apart from other kinds of experience. Far from being

a merely conceptual thing, knowledge has its own efficacies. One hardly needs to go further to understand this than to recall the clinical commonplace that diagnostic procedures often have therapeutic efficacy. An elderly but still fairly healthy relative of mine, for example, periodically develops chest and arm pains and begins to worry a great deal about heart disease. Thus far, his symptoms have been markedly alleviated by the administration of a full cardiac workup; the knowledge he thereby gains that his cardiovascular system is still in good working order holds his symptoms at bay for long periods of time. This is not just an example of psychosomatic medicine; it is also testament to the power that knowledge wields in experience.

In the early 1960s, Lévi-Strauss, continuing his investigations into the logic of the concrete, inaugurated his Mythologiques series with *The Raw and the Cooked*. Arguing that "there is a kind of logic in tangible qualities" (1; 9),[15] he justified his decision to "operate at the sign level" as follows.

> Even when very restricted in number, [signs] lend themselves to rigorously organized combinations which can translate even the finer shades of the whole range of sense experience. We can thus hope to reach a plane where logical properties, as attributes of things, will be manifested as directly as flavors or perfumes; perfumes are unmistakably identifiable, yet we know that they result from combinations of elements which, if subjected to a different selection and organization, would have created awareness of a different perfume. Our task, then, is to use the concept of the sign in such a way as to introduce these secondary qualities—on the plane of the intelligible and not only the tangible—into the operations of truth. (14; 22)

The way in which he then proceeded to introduce the "secondary qualities" of sense experience into the operations of truth performed the particular reduction for which structural analysis is well known: he treated the matter of the myths he analyzed (the cooked and rotten meat, the jaguars and maize trees) as "an instrument, not an object, of signification" (341; 346–47). For tangible qualities to have a logic, the analyst needed to show how myth narratives arranged concrete things in significant relationships; objects and qualities became operators reflecting more abstract contrastive pairs. Once the logic of this signifying arrangement was appreciated—promoted, as it were, to the cognitive level—the matter through which it had been made could be forgotten.[16]

But the tangible qualities of food, like those of perfume, are not so readily forgotten. Nor are they easily disciplined within the confines of a "logic." The analytic power and tidiness of structuralist analysis in the Lévi-Straussian manner gratifies me as an anthropologist even as it annoys the eater in me, for explanatory power about signification seems to be gained at the expense of the poetry—the flavors and pleasures—inherent in everyday reality. The structuralist analyst works through the concrete to reach the logical, leaving the charms of mundane experience far behind. The contradiction is not only Lévi-Strauss's; ethnographic description, with its local cultural commitments, often seems to work at cross-purposes with anthropological analysis, which compares and generalizes.

My point here, that there is a big difference between the mundane pleasures evoked by Lévi-Strauss and the cerebral gratifications of his structuralist reasoning, is neither original nor new: almost from its inception structural analysis stirred a "humanist" response in a debate that posed poetry against science, experience against cognition, politics against "mentalities," and even "body" against "spirit."[17] These dualisms may be impossible to overcome, but perhaps they can be made less foundational, less taken for granted, by noting the many ways in which everyday life mediates and muddles them.[18] In its detailed attention to the qualities of things eaten and sensed, Lévi-Strauss's project—and a few that have followed it in this respect[19]— still inspires my own reading of medicine and embodiment in contemporary China. If bodies are capable of imagining, we should be able to carnally imagine other life worlds, or sensory realms, through an ethnographic description that attends to the concrete and the everyday.

This description and reading are no simple transfer of the most "real" parts of one life world into the foreign context of another, however. (If you have never eaten lichees, you could hardly guess from my description what they taste like.) Rather, they resemble a translation process that must take the specificity of terms and entities in both the "source" and "target" languages very seriously.[20] Direct sensory experience, the material attributes of concrete things and mundane activities, can be invoked, and thereby imagined, but only by way of language and images and only in the context of times, places, and habitus that impose constraints on what can be experienced or imagined. If ethnography searches for a "logic of the concrete" or a "science of the tangible," then, it must always work on both sides of these somewhat oxymoronic terms. That is, both logical-scientific forms of knowledge and concrete characteristics of social life must be kept in play.

For this contradictory task, Chinese medicine offers much, assuming as it does a world, a consciousness, and a physiology that unite knowledge and experience, power and knowledge, in a single system of simultaneous understanding and action. Unlike those scientific empiricisms that seek to draw aside the curtain of (mere) appearances to reveal the (truer) underlying processes knowable only to the analyst, Chinese medicine relies heavily on many sorts of experience (*jingyan*). This experience is not a direct, naive immediacy but a heavily emphasized and ideologically fraught category that links a great many clinical and scholarly practices together. Nevertheless, even the act of positing experience as a central resource and authority for the field makes a strong contrast with experimental science. The perceived qualities of symptoms and drugs with which Chinese pharmacy often concerns itself would be extraneous factors—needing to be controlled before a clean study can be designed—in most laboratories.

Chinese pharmacy meets anthropology's science of the concrete with what appears at first to be an elaborate science of tangible qualities. Drug attributes such as flavor, warmth, directionality, and speed both classify (abstractly) medicinal substances and name (concretely) their sensory, material characteristics. Moreover, as I will show, the qualities of herbal drugs and bodily states are not mere passive reflections of hidden causes at work; these known and experienced attributes themselves have power. In this, they resemble the odors and colors that figure in the myths analyzed by Lévi-Strauss; at the level of the narrative or therapeutic process, the "hotness" or "sweetness" of a drug makes a difference. But unlike structuralist analysis of myths, Chinese medical theory does not abandon these manifest qualities in favor of an articulation of the abstract minimal contrasts through which they might signify. As will be seen, Chinese medicine does not even employ its "native" dualism of yin and yang to this end. Rather, doctors dwell on the concrete attributes of thousands of herbal, mineral, and animal drugs, weaving together known qualities into potent cocktails of flavor, heat, and positional tendency.[21] At the same time, the flavors of sweet, bitter, pungent, salty, and sour (and the attributes of warming and cooling and the positional tendencies that affect the five great visceral systems) offer classificatory rubrics from which principles of combination can be derived. Recall Lévi-Strauss's perfume example: a distinctive aroma produced from diverse elements by methodical combination is quite like a Chinese herbal prescription, except that the latter has the power to act directly on whole bodies. And this is an important difference.

Medical Meals in a County Town

Early in 1993, the brother of a doctor I knew opened a small "herbal medicine meals" (yao shan) restaurant in a county town in Shandong Province. At that time, there were very few indoor restaurants in town, though street-corner noodle stands had begun to appear to meet the needs of short-term visitors to town—truck drivers, villagers selling or contracting for agricultural products, purchasing agents for smaller communities or rural enterprises, and customers for the town's two periodic markets. A few formal restaurants had opened, mainly in hotels and guest houses; most of the trade for these establishments consisted of banquets for visitors hosted by county government officials or the town's few business leaders. (I discuss one such banquet in chapter 3.) Mr. Wu's Yao Shan Restaurant was somewhere between these two levels of public eating.[22] He and his wife, assisted by his brother, who had a small private Chinese medical practice, rented a shop-house and converted the front into space for two tables and four banquet rooms, each of which seated about eight. The living space in the back became the kitchen. Although the appearance of the place was not charming (it was quite low, dark, and cramped), the food was good and so was business. Mr. Wu attributed their success, especially during the lunch hour, to their proximity to the county's main Public Security Agency complex. Police and cadres often ate and entertained there.

In fact, Mr. Wu and his family were quite surprised—almost alarmed—when I walked in one evening with my friend Sarah, another foreign researcher. Their surprise was not attributable simply to the rarity of foreigners in town; it had more to do with our gender and our anomalous status as women unattached to any known household. The family members were very hospitable and happy to serve us an excellent meal, but they insisted we eat in a private room and they were glad that we had come for dinner rather than lunch.[23] They later suggested that any return visits be in the evening. They apparently did not like the idea of us mixing with their lunchtime clientele, middle-aged men who sometimes drank a great deal of white liquor and became rather rowdy at midday. (I didn't relish the idea myself.)

More puzzling was the fact that our waitress, Mr. Wu's daughter, did not see the point of serving us any medicinal foods, despite the prominence of the restaurant's specialty. (It was their large "herbal medicine meals" sign that had brought me to them, after all, not their relationship—which I learned later—with a doctor I had already interviewed.) She said that Sarah and I were not especially good candidates for this restaurant's herbal meals; the dishes they prepared daily were meant to improve (*bu,* or "bolster and tonify") the health of middle-aged men.

Dr. Wu, the proprietor's brother, later gave me a list of the herbal substances used most often in the restaurant: ginseng, astragalus, schisandra, chrysanthemum, fennel, hawthorn, and Asian cornelian cherry. Boiled in soups (*tang,* the same word used for Chinese medical herbal decoctions), these drugs show a definite tendency toward supplementing qi-energy, preventing the depletion of jing-essence (sometimes translated as "seminal essence"), and improving the functions of the visceral systems, of which the kidneys are the central locus.[24] (The Kidney Visceral System not only governs aspects of the fluid economy of the body, but it is central to sexual and reproductive functions.)[25] In other words—and somewhat oversimplifying— these were tonics for men, not quite aphrodisiacs but designed to improve the physiological basis for a fully functional masculinity. No wonder the Wu family's pokey little restaurant was such a hit with the Public Security Bureau.

I imagine everyone concerned understood the gendered character of these herbal medicine meals better than I did at the time. Although there must have been some conversation and explanation—when the restaurant was opening, for example—about the specific virtues of

the soups, much certainly went without saying. For one thing, everyone knows without dwelling on it what a tonic for middle-aged men
is; apart from the brothers Wu, I may have been the only person who
cared about the names and efficacies of the specific drugs in use. Still,
even while I remained ignorant of these details it was not hard to perceive the strongly masculine orientation of the service in this establishment. This quality was conveyed to Sarah and me from the moment we stepped across the threshold, especially in the family's
surprise and its kind but rather abashed service. (Being foreigners, of
course, we were accustomed to being attributed with—and forgiven
for—many small transgressions; it was only later that I began to
think about the reasons why this place was not for us.) No one really
explained it, but where spaces and practices are strongly gender
marked there is perhaps no need to explain. Several ill-assorted forms
of habitus confronted each other there, and we got the message.

Not all medicinal meals restaurants are so strongly gendered, and
this one was perhaps a little unusual in its insistence on specializing.
The particular soups served by Mr. Wu were not unlike the commercially packaged tonics and high-priced herbal drugs given by people of
both sexes to their male seniors. Despite their association with the
physiological substrate of sexual powers, these objects carry no im-
proper innuendo; they are no more embarrassing or unspeakable
than beauty products for women would be. Moreover, despite
Miss Wu's protests, I can find no suggestion in the materia medica literature that the soups she served would not also benefit my aging female physiology. As will be discussed in chapter 6, women, too, must
harbor seminal essence (jing), and nourishing qi and improving Kidney System function should be important for all aging bodies. Why
were the medicinal specialties at the Yao Shan Restaurant more appropriate for the bureaucrats from the Public Security Bureau than
for me?

Technically speaking, perhaps, they were not, but that is how they
were billed. Men who ate there regularly must have enjoyed the experience at several levels. One level is certainly that of a change in subjective bodily state. At least some of the substances used in the soups
reliably deliver noticeable effects, the stimulant activity of ginseng being only the most obvious. Especially if customers consumed these
things expecting a little energy boost, smoother digestion, and an im-

provement in mood, they would have walked away feeling stronger and more in command of at least a few things. At another level, it is worth bearing in mind that the early 1990s was not the best of times for many large government agencies. Many aspects of government in this Shandong county town had been removed from party control in the 1980s and assigned to a newly organized civil government. In parallel with this change, it was becoming clear that technical expertise was more valued in local government than the "redness" on which an older generation of administrators had built their careers.[26] Only a year or so later a national campaign for early retirement began, which aimed to banish men fifty-five and older from the offices (and chauffeured vehicles and midday banquets) where they had long served as loyal party members. At least some of Mr. Wu's patrons, I suggest, must have felt that their jobs were shaky, their loyalties outmoded, and their skills devalued. The physical boost of a medicinal meal—reaching both their mood and their masculinity—would have been a welcome addition to their daily lives.

Flavor Language, Flavor Experience

Most of the drugs used in Chinese medicine are not like ginseng, chrysanthemum, and hawthorn, for their physiological effect is not immediately noticeable. Their taste, however, is hard to miss. The languages of Chinese food and traditional herbal therapy share specialized terms that classify flavors and summarize elaborate technologies of cooking. Although considerations of appearance and texture, so important in the world of food, count for little in the preparation of medicine, both kinds of work are family affairs that can dominate daily life. Further, both cooking and herbal medicine draw on a wide variety of substances, which come to these domestic spaces bringing connotations of place, seasonality, and textual elaboration.[27]

Some of these connotations are carried by flavor words. Take *ku* (bitter), for example. The most common term in modern Chinese for suffering is *chiku* (eating bitterness). As Gang Yue argues in his discussion of Wang Ruowang's *Hunger Trilogy*, this ordinary word is strongly invested with a historical sense, and it is easy to solicit rueful comments from people about how much bitterness they or their family members have swallowed in the past.[28] And whatever personal bitterness they may be thinking of, to refer to this suffering as *chiku* is to link one's own difficulties to those of the nation.²⁹ *Ku* is widely used in other compounds as well, with a denotative scope ranging from the relatively literal referents of bitterness and pain to more figurative notions of earnest seriousness and painstaking effort. Hard work, for example, is often described as *xinku,* a compound translatable literally as pungent-bitter.

The technical uses of the flavor terms in Chinese medicine appear at first to be on the literal end of this range. Not only are these five commonly known flavor terms—sour (*suan*), bitter (ku), sweet (*gan*), pungent (*xin*), and salty (*xian*)—used to classify herbal medicines, but these words often (though not always) refer to the actual tastes of particular herbal drugs. It is often said among Chinese medical people that Shen Nong, the sage king and mythical founder of herbal medicine, "tasted one hundred herbs" and on the basis of this experience produced the first materia medica texts. When I began to study Chinese medicine, I assumed that the five flavors served solely as classificatory rubrics, so this use of the verb "to taste" puzzled me; why wasn't Shen Nong said to have used or tested or classified one hundred herbs? Once I turned to the concrete qualities of medicines that interest doctors and patients—encouraged more by the extensive descriptive information in pharmacopeia reference works than by the flavor terms per se—the word looked much more essential. Thus, although patients often complain that herbal decoctions are "too bitter," they also admit that they can detect the characteristically sweet taste of licorice root (*gancao*) in most prescriptions. A refined palate can no doubt also distinguish amid the bitterness some tastes that are more sour, salty, or pungent. Considering that individual drugs of diverse flavors are usually boiled together, it must be difficult to sort out all the tastes of a complex prescription. But there's no doubt, I think, that for a medicine to do anything very complicated it must assault the sufferer with a strong and complex flavor.³⁰

I am no Shen Nong, and my palate is not educated for discriminating Chinese medicine's "five flavors." Every herbal decoction I have ever swallowed has tasted simply horrid (i.e., ku) to me, and many Chinese patients I have checked with agree with me on this point. Still, the fact that drugs in the classic decoction form have flavor, that is, both an experiential quality and a classificatory function in a system of pharmaceutical effects, raises the question of what the efficacy of a "flavor" is. Isn't it rather odd, at least for those of us steeped in the subject-object divide of Euro-American common sense, to think of a personal experience such as a flavor acting directly on a biological condition? Lévi-Strauss, when he invoked the notion of a perfume, did not accord much power to the sensory qualities of aroma beyond, perhaps, the ability to invoke memories or set in train other more or less mental processes. When we think of the experiences that accompany therapies (the pain with physical therapy, the nausea with chemotherapy), we are more likely to think of them as side effects of a primary action that is—almost by definition—subexperiential. Muscles mend and bones knit, tissues or microorganisms die or proliferate, outside of our direct awareness.

In biomedical discourses, the causes of illness or healing certainly don't *need* to be perceived by the sufferer. This is why we consult a doctor, to learn the actual causes of our discomforts, which could never be figured out "for sure" from our experience. (It is not too many hours spent squinting at small print in archives that's causing our headaches but a pinched nerve, not a lack of vigorous exercise at the root of this back pain but a collapsing disc. The experiential reasoning with which we connect our ailments to the rest of our lives is more often than not dismissed or bypassed in biomedical diagnosis.) In addition, the metaphorical billiard balls of the standard materialist model of causation still bounce around in biomedical explanations of etiology and efficacy, and action at a distance—such as the effects achieved by acupuncture—remains difficult to explain. Muscles, tissues, and microorganisms are entities familiar to an anatomically based medicine of structures and can be invoked in etiological narratives that accord with a materialist logic of causes. But Chinese medicine cares little about anatomy. Rather, it has usually been characterized as a functional medicine that reads the manifestations of physiological and pathological changes without resorting to models of fixed structural relations.[31] Moreover, Chinese medicine is said to be "holistic"—it links manifestations of illness to causal narratives not with reference to an underlying anatomical field but in relation to temporal emergence. The appearance of symptoms in sequence or at the same time suggests that they are related phenomena, and the physician's job is to identify the process that could produce all these symptoms in precisely this temporal relation. Proximity in anatomical space counts for little in this holism. If these descriptions of Chinese medicine are correct at all, then some other form of causality—and efficacy, even power—must also be entailed.

The following excerpt from a 1978 pharmacy textbook indicates both how complex and how direct the relationship between drug flavors and drug powers is conceived to be.[32]

> The five flavors are the five types of pungent, sweet, sour, bitter, and salty. Some drugs have a clear or an astringent flavor, so in reality the types are not confined to five; but they are customarily still called the five flavors. The five flavors are also an expression of the roles of drugs, different flavors having different functions. . . . Generalizing from the historical experience of using drug flavors, their functions are as follows:
>
> *Pungent* has the function of spreading and disseminating, moving qi, moving blood, or nourishing with moisture. . . . *Sweet* has the function of replenishing and supplementing, regulating the activity in the Middle *Jiao,* and moderating acuteness. . . .[33] *Sour* has the functions of contracting and constricting. . . . *Astringent* has functions similar to those of sour drugs. . . . *Bitter* has the function of draining and drying. . . . *Salty* has the function of softening hardness, dispersing lumps, and draining downward. . . . *Clear* has the function of condensing Dampness and causing urine to flow.

The functions listed here (disseminating, constricting, and so on) are both technically inflected theoretical terms for normal physiological activities of the human body and words that could, with a little reflection, be readily applied to personal embodied experience. In other words, the logic that connects the flavors to the powers of medicines has room for the sensed responses of the lived body. What seems to require explaining, however, is the *connection* between the experience of a flavor and the experience of a bodily change. How can "sour" bring about a general contraction and constriction? Why does "bitter" cause fluids to drain? Although this passage introduces a textbook in which the classificatory functions of pungent, sweet, sour, bitter, and salty are emphasized, it also makes it clear that these are not entirely arbitrary rubrics. Shen Nong *tasted* one hundred herbs when he founded Chinese pharmacy. Pharmaceutical classification is presented as reflecting the actual tastes of substances in the materia medica corpus. That these tastes are then correlated with particular efficacies is a fact that requires no explanation in Chinese discourses beyond the usual reference to accumulated historical experience.

English does not offer a language for whole-body responses to tastes or a theory of flavor causation of this kind. Perhaps the closest we come is to the notion of "heavy" or "light" meals affecting our alertness, or learning that certain foods "disagree" with our stomachs. The idea that flavors could have powerful physiological efficacies is odd enough to have been politely ignored by most of the English-language literature on Chinese herbal medicine.[34] In North American nutritional lore, we tend to relegate tastes to that domain in which the (relatively isolated) human subject receives sensory input, registering pleasure or revulsion in response to food. We think of those forces and entities that actually alter our bodies as properties of the food that are quantifiable (e.g., fat, vitamin, or protein content) and inhere in the food whether we eat it or not. The body in question is a part of nature, while the cultural enjoyments of which it is capable don't really belong to a biological discourse. The rationally known efficacies of things cancel the relatively ephemeral experience of ingesting them, and our carnal tastes, when they are invoked, drift upward toward the cultural domain where subjective experience is stored. Apparently pleasure, when spoken of in English, has weak causal force.

In modern China, people who suffer from disease and seek relief in the use of herbal medicine tend to link the hungry or overworked, exciting or relaxing past experiences of their bodies to the present state of their pleasures and pains. This is a well-known feature of patients' subjective accounts of illness the world over.[35] But in the idioms made available by Chinese language and herbs, we can see bitter experiences rendered treatable with sweet drugs and pungent substances used to set the stagnant fixities of old pathology into more wholesome motion. This experiential side to Chinese medicine encourages a personal micropolitics, as patients seek to govern themselves and their immediate environment using techniques that fuse thinking and feeling, forming habits that make sense to their own senses.

The Chinese Medical Body in Practice

I have argued here that the direct efficacy claimed for the flavors of Chinese medicines involves a causal logic; flavors not only generate a fleeting aesthetic response, but they produce bodily changes that generate experience at a more lasting level. And this logic appears to be taken for granted in the classic works on which herbal medicine is founded. This situation is not simply a survival of an "ancient" craft, however. It is consistent with a particular form of experience, or mode of embodiment, visible in the lives of Chinese medicine's modern consumers. In order to lay a broader foundation for this book's argument that (modern Chinese) politics is embodied, I will present some basic features of the contemporary practice of Chinese medicine. Throughout the reform era, this practice has responded sensitively to broader social transformations and the changing desires of patients and their families. Through it, perhaps, a specific postsocialist Chinese medical body can be glimpsed.

In the early 1980s, it was common for theorists in institutions of traditional Chinese medicine to compare the body treated by Chinese medicine to a "black box." [36] This image borrowed from behavioral psychology and cybernetics lent a cosmopolitan and scientific aura to a set of ideas and practices that skeptics could too easily think of as flawed: Chinese medicine was not founded in anatomy. This condition of lack prevented any easy translation between Chinese medical knowledge and biomedical knowledge and (given the prestige of Western laboratory science) risked being interpreted as a mere oversight in the Chinese tradition. How could Chinese scholars have neglected to investigate the structure of the human body and thus failed to invent a Chinese version of modern medicine?

In those years, and to an increasing extent through the 1980s and 1990s, Chinese medical researchers and clinicians staked their careers on the essential scientificness of Chinese medicine, so they found it necessary to counter this fundamentally insulting question with concepts that could direct attention to the epistemological specificity of their field.[37] With the image of the black box, the functional body treated by Chinese medicine appeared as a site at which inputs and outputs were correlated in sophisticated classificatory abstractions. Although practitioners posit and discuss "illness mechanisms" of a particular Chinese medical kind, they ultimately can be agnostic about pathological anatomy as it is understood in biomedicine. As I have argued elsewhere, doctors of Chinese medicine don't worry much about the location and structural characteristics of a "lesion," nor do they bother to identify microbial agents of disease.[38]

What they are good at is fitting the therapy to the illness as it unfolds in time.

It would be a great simplification to suggest that the contemporary practice of Chinese medicine consists of matching symptoms with herbal treatments in a mere correspondence table.[39] But most patients and other outsiders to the field are strangers to its particular technical logics and skills. For them, this medicine cannot but appear as a matching process: details of the patient's reported history of discomforts and other symptoms are noted in a list, and an herbal prescription, a list of components with quantities specified, is generated in response. Quite often the only record about a case, for each clinic visit, is this list of symptoms and its corresponding list of drugs written in the outpatient case record booklet. Experienced doctors are able to interpret much from this minimal information with their "insiders' view" (neihang guandian), but patients see only notes on their illness and a skeleton of its treatment written down.

The herbs prescribed are carried home in a collection of paper parcels (one parcel for each daily dose). They must be boiled with water (and often some food additives such as red date or fresh gingerroot) in a partly closed receptacle for an hour or more; most households of my acquaintance have a special earthenware pot for the purpose. Many doctors instruct patients to boil the herbs down to half the volume of liquid, refilling with water twice or three times to extract the maximum efficacy. Thus, the decoction process can be very time consuming. Ideally, the earliest riser in the family (one pictures an old grandmother) should start the medicine cooking while preparing breakfast, and the first dose should be consumed by the sufferer at the start of the day. Subsequent doses on the same day can be warmed up in a steamer. As the drugs simmer on the stove, they produce an unmistakable odor; like the smells of garlic, ginger, and chili peppers that fill apartment buildings and household compounds later in the day, this aroma of Chinese medicine spreads through courtyards and back lanes, identifying the home of a sufferer.

Many contemporary Chinese consumers complain about the "inconvenience" of this process. Fewer families these days have extended family members handy to coordinate lots of elaborate cooking, and intensifying work and study schedules leave little time to prepare and "slowly sip" herbal decoctions. Some patients I've spoken with say they "can't swallow" Chinese medical decoctions, finding them too bitter. Thus, many who find uses for herbal medicine now prefer to consume "made up" medicines (*zhongchengyao*) in pill or infusion form; these can be bought in neighborhood drugstores and, if necessary, carried to work or social gatherings. Such patent medicines are "easier to swallow" and handier to take, but they are widely acknowledged to be less effective for stubborn complaints than custom-made prescriptions.[40] Hence, there are many who still seek out a classical form of "traditional" Chinese medical practice despite its inconvenience. Let us, then, turn to some of the basics of the clinical encounter so as to better understand Chinese medicine's appeal and powers.

The body at issue in the clinical encounter is a sensorily textured, collaborative product. Illness alters a sufferer's perceptions and practices of embodiment, and therapy, if it works at all, alters them again. For any style of medical practice, these transformations are played upon in every aspect of the daily work of healing. But Chinese medicine relies especially heavily on cooperation between patient and healer to work its effects. Certain relatively invariant features are suggestive for understanding how patient and doctor work together toward a better embodiment.[41]

1. *Medicine begins with discomfort on the part of the patient.* This observation is less obvious than it sounds. Doctors of traditional medicine in contemporary China deliver little primary care and operate outside most systems of public health screening of the general population. Users of traditional medicine tend to suffer from advanced chronic complaints (e.g., arthritis, migraines, chronic vertigo), stubborn debilities (e.g., fatigue and lassitude, constipation, impotence, poor digestion), or undesirable insufficiencies (e.g., infertility, baldness). These patients know they are ill because they feel bad, and they need to boost the efficacy of their everyday means of self-care.

In other words, patients have clearly identified complaints and have no difficulty saying on the basis of "subjective criteria" whether their treatment is working. In light of this fundamental feature of clinical work, it is telling that no "sufferer" (*huanzhe*) who presents a complaint at a clinic of traditional medicine goes away without a prescription or a treatment of some kind. Even if he or she consults a "modernizing" doctor who uses blood and urine chemistries, x rays and sonograms as part of his or her Chinese medical practice, and even if all these tests come out "negative," the patient is still deemed to be ill and a good candidate for treatment. Precisely because herbal prescriptions are so intimately tailored to symptomatic expressions, if the patient can name the symptoms (and I have never seen one who couldn't) the doctor can design an intervention. This is no quick, flavorless pill or injection but a whole technology of cooking, tasting, and timing as patients wait to feel the results.[42]

2. *The patient is able to report his or her condition in detail.* The naming of symptoms involves several complex vocabularies. The most important one, of course, is theoretically coterminous with modern spoken Chinese, the various local languages in which patients describe their worries and discomforts in clinical settings. But even the conventional medical language of symptoms is not really foreign. Unlike the Greek and Latin etymologies, which sometimes obscure commonplace notions in biomedical practice, symptom terms in Chinese medicine are mostly made up of words that are, or recently were, in everyday use. Language use in these clinics tends to reveal the medical nature of mundane discomforts more than it disguises within an esoteric vocabulary the mundane nature of medical concepts.

Symptom terms like aversion to cold, perspiration of the five centers (soles of the feet, palms of the hands, and center of the chest), reduction in appetite, and aches and pains that can be described as sharp (like a knife blow), dull (like aching), heavy, needling, twisting, scorching, icy, lurking, or tugging are defined in the authoritative dictionary of Chinese medical terminology and briefly explained in introductory textbooks.[43] Once one understands certain professional distinctions, however, such as the difference between chills and aversion to cold, such terms can function as a simple shorthand for patients' descriptions of their complaints. In clinics, where many patients return often for consultations and updates of their prescriptions, these terms are quickly adopted by all. In other words, patients may learn to focus on aspects of their conditions that their doctors find interesting, but this learning requires neither a new sort of experience nor a radically different language for it.

In effect, neither the patient's account of illness signs nor the doctor's record of medical symptoms seeks a very high level of generality.[44] If the patient has a number of miscellaneous illness signs to report, the record will show a rather long list of symptom terms. No one obsesses over achieving a one-to-one correspondence between patient narratives and case record inscriptions, but an oversimplification or too powerful abstraction of the patient's report could make it difficult to design a properly adjusted drug prescription. What both doctor and patient seek in the clinical encounter is not a powerful agent that penetrates to the core of a disease lesion but an intervention articulated to the many facets of the complaint itself. The notion of a hidden interior cause, knowledge of which relies upon technological visualization (microscopes, x rays, scanners, or tissue culture models), is not entirely foreign to contemporary Chinese medicine, but neither is it very important in clinical practice. The proverbial idea of a "magic bullet" that can quickly and insensibly eradicate disease has come only recently to the world of Chinese medicine, and many doctors and patients see this kind of medicine as only superficially effective. What traditional practitioners and their patients produce instead is a well-tailored garment of care that will fit the surfaces of the ailment and slowly but surely transform its manifestations.

3. *Doctor and patient collaborate in analyzing and monitoring an illness.* I have argued above that the symptoms addressed by a drug prescription are only slightly "medicalized" away from the patient's own account. These symptoms are then processed through higher levels of analysis, which arrive at a named syndrome and a closely matched treatment principle. There is no space in which to describe this more abstract and technical level of the clinical encounter here, but the process, and the continuing importance of the patient's reported symptoms, can be glimpsed in the following brief example.[45] This case of "amnesia" was published in a 1991 volume on disorders of the Spleen-Stomach System; the clinician was Lu Zheng.

> *Heart and Spleen Depleted and Weak.* Fang x x, male, age forty-six. Examined March 20, 1974. One year earlier, after he first vomited blood and then had bloody stools, he experienced severe memory loss. He has taken various patent medicines (e.g., danggui-chrysanthemum-foxglove pills, schisandra paste, and mugwort-tamarind tonic) without noticeable effect. At the time of the examination the patient was very forgetful, at the same time manifesting pale facial coloring, heart palpitations that interfered with sleep, listlessness and extreme fatigue, reduced food consumption, tongue pale with a clear thin

coating, and pulse fine and weak. The syndrome was classified as Simultaneous Depletion of Heart and Spleen Systems, with the seat of knowledge muddled and the vital spirit of the heart-mind unstable. Therapy ought to build spleen function and supplement qi in order to bolster the heart and regulate the qi-blood relationship.

Prescription:
Roasted astragalus root (huangchi), 45 gr.
Roasted codonopsis root (dangshen), 24 gr.
Roasted atractylodes rhizome (baishu), 12 gr.
Roasted angelica root (danggui), 12 gr.
Costus root (guang muxiang), 6 gr.
Tangerine peel (chen pi), 6 gr.
Roasted licorice (gancao), 6 gr.
Longan fruit (longyan rou), 15 gr.
China root (fushen), 15 gr.
Fresh ginger (sheng jiang), 3 slices
Jujube (hong cao), 8 pieces

After seven doses, the heart palpitations, insomnia, listlessness, and exhaustion had improved and the appetite was slightly stimulated, but the other symptoms had not yet changed for the better. The original formula was continued. After fifteen more doses, forgetfulness had lessened, facial color was visibly improved, heart palpitations were no longer interfering with sleep, tongue was light pink, and pulse image was small and moderate. I altered the formula by removing *costus* and *China-root* and adding *cassia twigs (guizhi)*, 6 gr.; *peony root (baishao)*, 12 gr.; and *refined honey (fengmi)*, 30 gr. After fifteen more doses, memory had returned and other symptoms had disappeared and tongue and pulse images were normal. Slightly modified the original formula and gave ten more doses. After this was finished, changed to use of Spleen Restoring Pills (6 gr three times a day) taken with warm water in order to maintain the therapeutic effect. (171)

Most of the symptoms in this case are known as a result of the history reported to Dr. Lu by the patient, Mr. Fang. Improvements in the illness condition are also noted as Mr. Fang monitors his condition from day to day and then reports changes to the doctor in follow-up visits. Facial color and tongue and pulse images are also important indices for the doctor, but in this case they would not have conclusively implicated the spleen system without the patient's report of loss of appetite and fatigue.

According to the classifications of the Chinese materia medica canon (standardized for more than three centuries), eight of the eleven drugs used in the original prescription are sweet, three are pungent, and eight are also warming. All affect the Spleen System. Interestingly, the quantities of the first three drugs used markedly exceed the recommended dosages. It is also worth noting that only two of the drugs, the longan fruit and China root, are known to be specifically for conditions like memory loss, spiritlessness, and insomnia; these two are used in normal quantities. All of these drugs make sense in the context of the stated therapeutic strategy, to build spleen function and supplement qi. Recall, for example, the functions of the flavors pungent and sweet: "*Pungent* has the function of spreading and disseminating, moving qi, moving blood, or nourishing with moisture. . . . *Sweet* has the function of replenishing and supplementing, regulating the activity in the Middle Jiao [i.e., the classificatory location of the Spleen and Stomach System], and moderating acuteness." Other aspects of the prescription reveal that Dr. Lu had a fairly complex interpretation of the pathological process, which I will not detail here. But perhaps it doesn't require too much guesswork to perceive the collaborative quality of the illness as it emerges in the clinical encounter: the patient's reported discomforts are addressed especially with the use of longan fruit and China root (both well known in popular lore for their efficacy in raising people's spirits). At the same time, Dr. Lu has analyzed this illness as a depletion rooted in the Spleen System, and he aggressively treats this root with a lot of drugs that feed and streamline the activity of this system. Presumably, Mr. Fang agreed with his doctor that his fatigue and loss of appetite were connected to memory loss; if he hadn't related his primary complaint to these symptoms before, he almost certainly began to do so after he had faithfully consumed his daily brew for a few weeks and began to feel his mental capacities return along with his energy and appetite.

4. *Subsequent visits reconsider symptoms as they change and adjust drug usage accordingly.* One characteristic of the contemporary practice of traditional medicine that is much valorized in contemporary Chinese debates is its flexible monitoring of illness changes. In the case of amnesia, for example, the published case history notes four

subsequent examinations, in each of which the improvement in the condition of the patient was encouraged and regulated with a new prescription.

However inattentive a patient may have been to his or her bodily state prior to seeking traditional medical treatment, once having entered into this therapeutic process he or she cultivates an attentiveness to symptoms and a willingness to report subtle changes. I have seen healthy and previously carefree young women who, having failed to conceive during the first year or so of marriage, became highly trained experts on their own bodily states when prompted by their doctors' questions. Slight feelings of chill or fever, headaches, periods of fatigue or irritability, the timing and colors of vaginal discharges, frequency and qualities of urination, and defecation are all monitored jointly by doctor and patient as they evaluate the effects of the drugs and work toward increasing reproductive capacity.

Similarly, patients living with a severe chronic illness such as asthma, arthritis, coronary heart disease, or migraines become microtechnicians of cause and effect. They note the timing of the appearance of symptoms in relation to daily demands, frustrations, and pleasures. They experiment with little disciplines and indulgences, monitoring responses in their conditions and weighing the costs and benefits of newly invented personal rituals. They may warn their families and coworkers not to upset them lest there be more frequent spells of heart palpitation or vertigo, or they may alter the family diet for months because some exotic food product tends to prevent painful flare-ups.[46] Even breathing has its therapeutic disciplines, as the Qigong craze that swept Chinese cities in the 1980s testifies.

Such responses to chronic illness are well known in North America as well. Here they can be seen at least in part as refusals on the part of patients to cede all expertise about the causes and management of their conditions to medical specialists. Creative self-regulation of medications and symptom flare-ups are sometimes classified as problems of "compliance" in the clinical literature of biomedicine. But Chinese sufferers have a responsive audience and a committed technical partner in their doctor of Chinese medicine. Evaluating the progress of the illness in regular clinic visits, he tinkers once a week, or every three days, with volumes and varieties of medicines. In response to the patient's regular report of his or her changing symptoms, the doctor produces an ever more specific herbal prescription, which is carried home and boiled up every day—requiring costly fuel and using scarce cooking space on two-burner gas stoves—with an aroma that wafts through whole apartment blocks and a taste that puckers the mouth and makes itself felt all the way down.

The Body as a Flavorful Temporal Formation

I do not want to create the impression that all modern Chinese people, or even all of those suffering from chronic illnesses, regularly use Chinese herbal medicine. Nor do I wish to claim that there is one modern Chinese form of embodiment (existing prior to any decision to use medicine) that would make Chinese medicine especially attractive. One need not subscribe to these totalizations to see the link between the forms of therapy discussed here and certain bodily habits that could be differentially distributed through Chinese, and to some extent non-Chinese, populations. Moreover, the forms of embodiment indicated here should not be held apart from the powers of therapy; Chinese medicine appeals to people who are already embodied, of course, but it also works on that embodiment and produces certain relatively inarticulate habits and preferences as it goes along.

All of these features of the clinical work of Chinese medicine, as well as of the domestic work undertaken by users of herbal medicine, place bodily experience (or its narration) at the center of attention. The puzzle posed above, how flavors can have causal force, appears less mysterious in this world. When the body itself is known as a flavorful temporal formation, its manifest qualities can be classified in the same nonbodily system of terms: sweet herbals build up our overworked spleens and pungent drugs mobilize energies that steady our fluttering hearts and clear the cobwebs from our flawed thinking. Yin foods build yin fluids and cool yang fire while yang medicines stimulate the functions of initiating systems and put slowed or static substances back into motion. This is a body that can both seek and enjoy positive good health beyond the mere absence of disease. The technical lore of Chinese medicine suggests that the refinements of such states of health can be aesthetic and effective at once.

I do not know the medical efficacies of Lei Feng's rice crust beyond its obvious capacity to nourish. But lichee is often listed as a food with medicinal properties. The fruit is classified as sweet and slightly sour, slightly warming, and especially efficacious for the Spleen, Stomach, and Liver Systems. It has the power of generating fluids, slaking thirst, bolstering (bu) Spleen qi, and supplementing Blood. Considering that those of us who were eating lichees together back in 1983 were women, it was no doubt good for us that our Blood was being supplemented (see "Blood is the Root of the Female" in chapter 6). Since we were all intellectuals, and thus prone to straining the reflective functions of the Spleen System and losing control of the emotional tendencies of the Liver System, we no doubt had a use for the warming and slaking juices of this food. And since we were located in a hot southern city where the approaching summer would surely tax body fluids, the lichees probably helped us store moisture and put it to work in a well-lubricated whole-body physiology. Like the soon to be superannuated policemen who availed themselves of Mr. Wu's medicinal meals, we found a highly sociable and palatable means of bolstering our normal lives with appropriate food. Perhaps this food even functioned for us as it did for those policemen, helping us maintain a physiology well suited for sexual life as women.

The technical medical knowledge that makes these meals appropriate for certain kinds of people at certain times in their lives need not be made explicit, though nowadays it very often is. But the fact that such knowledge exists, disseminated through medical school textbooks, popular health education tracts, and orally transmitted lore, indicates that there are guides to eating that target particular bodies in particular ways. Though until recently I was mainly ignorant of how complicated this knowledge could be, I am sure my medical friends knew better than I and would not have shared their lichees with me had they not been good for all of us. We were eating for the sheer pleasure of it, but we were also participating in a gendered structure of knowledge and practice, one that placed our bodies in history and social life in a specific way.

I have argued that Chinese food and medicine, and especially the domain called medicinal meals that they nowadays share, offer powers that can be mobilized to produce specific kinds of experience. This argument puts a certain notion of power together with a certain historicization of experience to reveal a body that can be, in a sense, "made to order." This is not a body that is manning the barricades for a cause much greater than itself. Rather, it is an embodiment that maintains a more intimate relationship with power, cultivating through food and medicine certain powers to act, powers to feel well. It need not wait for true communism to be achieved, for life to be good for all, before it can enjoy some parts of life in its own way. In fact this body rejects the Maoist vision in which power can only derive from service to the collective. But, as I will show in the remainder of part I, amid the pleasures and the efficacies of late-twentieth-century market-mediated eating worries and doubts also proliferate.

chapter 2

A FEAST FOR THE MIND

Is eating and drinking a mere trifle? No. Class struggle exists even at the tips of your chopsticks.

—*Red Flag*

The question above, and its answer, offer a thoroughly Maoist image of the intimacy of class struggle.[1] In 1970, this may have been a fresh phrasing, but ideas linking food and politics were not particularly new in China. For most of the twentieth century, modernizing nationalists had been founding their arguments for change on the hunger of the masses and the gluttony of the powerful. Writers of fiction and essays had deployed a complex oral imagery to figure social and political relations of domination and victimization.[2] Farmers and eaters had fought over who would control the land and its produce in China's "peasant revolution."[3] And Mao Zedong frequently used food metaphors as he expanded the reach of his polemic voice over the whole nation and into every part of daily life. In keeping with his well-known remark that "revolution is not a dinner party" (in his "Report on an Investigation of the Peasant Movement in Hunan"), he also famously argued that "if you want to know the taste of a pear," or have reliable knowledge, you must bite into it ("On Practice") and described "political synthesis" as akin to eating crabs: "eating one's enemy" involves absorbing the nourishment and expelling the waste ("Talk at the Hangzhou Conference").[4]

Throughout the history of the People's Republic, the leadership has offered constant reminders that political change has direct consequences at the dinner table. At the same time, it has insisted that politics cannot be banished from eating. Socialist egalitarianism should be materially evident in the production, distribution, and consumption of food, and the basic needs of the people should be met in an evenhanded manner. When inequalities emerged, rectification might be required. Although the more thoroughly socialist rhetoric requiring state control of production and consumption was discredited and abandoned between the late 1970s and mid-1980s, much of the rationale for "market socialism" had to do with food as well: private control of the land and entrepreneurship in distribution would "liberate the enthusiasm of the people for labor" and thus be more efficient in meeting the nation's needs.

The public discourse on food shifted dramatically in the reform period, but it did not disappear. I was reminded of this fact recently when I met an émigré artist who had left China for New York in the 1990s. He inquired about my research, and I told him the title of this book. "Food and Sex in China," he mused. "Ah, food is so political in China." When I asked him why he thought so, he said that Chairman Mao had always insisted that eating was an important aspect of political struggle and no one has been able to forget this. "Everyone notices what everyone else is eating; no one can avoid being moralistic about food."

How food got to be so political in China can be observed in three works of popular literature, one written in the 1940s (and revised for the Cultural Revolution) and two published in the 1980s. Not only were these works widely read and admired, each in its own time, but they also address certain social problems and historical contradictions that many writers and thinkers agreed were central to the Chinese national situation. These works are quite different, and their conceptions of the politics and ethics of food reflect distinct political stances, state projects, and aesthetic strategies. One is an opera-ballet and the other two are novellas; each adopts an accessible and evocative writing style to clarify for its readers the ways in which class struggle can exist at the tip of your chopsticks.

The first literary work considered here, *The White-Haired Girl*, became a model theatrical work—the preferred, and at times almost the only, genre of arts made available by Cultural Revolution leaders—and thus it is generally thought of as straightforward party propaganda. The second text discussed, *Hibiscus Town*, is often seen as part of popular resistance to government programs, although, as we shall see, its depiction of early reform era market changes is consistent with the Deng Xiaoping economics of the time. These first two pieces of literature define basic human needs and outline the distribution of social responsibility that should meet those needs. They do not leave these fundamental definitions to chance. Both answer recurrent twentieth-century Chinese questions: what forms and levels of sustenance do the people need and who shall remain in power by seeing that they get it? And both locate eating in broader narratives that have very clear political agendas. They sort and re-sort the confusing plenum of the social world into categories that distinguish producers from consumers, needs from wishes, exploiters from victims, good humans from evil monsters, and the hopeful present from the abysmal past. In doing so, each naturalizes a tidied-up social world.

The third work to be taken up in this chapter, *The Gourmet*, although it appeared only a few years after *Hibiscus Town* and shares some of *The White-Haired Girl*'s leftist commitments, pointedly destabilizes the politics of food embodied in these two works. In this history of antagonism between a conscientious Communist restaurant manager and a self-indulgent "specialist in beautiful food" (*meishijia*, the name of the novella translated as *The Gourmet*), no equilibrium between culinary pleasure and political justice can be found. One can only enjoy good food, it seems, at the expense of someone else's labor. The contradictory politics of eating that is meticulously outlined in this work informs my reading of all three texts: food itself realizes the intractable inequalities with which we must somehow live.

A Brief History of Hunger

As I suggested in chapter 1, in the contemporary People's Republic both Chinese food and Chinese medicine offer their delicacies as commodities and some of them are expensive. The enjoyments they offer can command ever higher prices from an emerging entrepreneurial class. But few contemporary consumers of elegant cuisine and expensive medicines have been able to indulge their newly refined palates throughout their lives. Many who now pick and choose among national and transnational commodities understand their recent pleasures in contrast to their memories of a simpler, poorer, or hungrier past.

In many parts of China these days, and in the national media as well, acute hunger is usually depicted as a thing of the past. With a few exceptions, the truly hungry have seldom written of their experiences

while they were living them or in the present tense.[5] Hunger remembered and inscribed into a historical narrative has, however, taken on
great importance in genres ranging from the historiography of Maoism to the consumer-oriented mass media of the 1990s. In this connection, there are at least three modern historical episodes to which
Chinese chroniclers readily refer. The first is the era of poverty and
food shortages associated with the widespread social chaos of the war
years between the early 1930s and 1949. This is the period often referred to as the "old society." The second is the famine that followed
the development programs of the Great Leap Forward, which began
in 1958. These "three hard years," as they are widely known, led to an
estimated 30 million deaths from starvation (perhaps 5 percent of the
population) between 1959 and 1962.[6] Shortages reached even into the
elite compounds of the capital city's highest cadres.[7] The third period
in which a significant part of the population regularly experienced
hunger was the Great Proletarian Cultural Revolution of 1966–76.
Those who remember the food shortages of this period are a minority,
but they are influential. They are mostly "educated youth" (*zhiqing*)
who were "sent down" to parts of the countryside where food supplies
were scantier than in the cities and a smaller number of intellectuals
and cadres who were sent down to labor reform camps where they
were sometimes pointedly starved. It is members of this sent-down
group, some of whom turned to writing after returning home or being rehabilitated, who have most clearly thematized Cultural Revolution hunger in contemporary literature and journalism. Their narratives of hunger both place shortages firmly in the past (although there
are plenty of people in China today without enough to eat) and privilege the phases that have been especially important to intellectuals in
a public discourse that is easily dominated by the educated and the
powerful. Thus, writing about the suffering of a limited number of intellectuals between 1966 and 1976 has always been much greater in
volume than literary reflections on the disastrous famine of the late
1950s. It is worth noting, however, that the earlier Maoist genre of
"speaking bitterness" (suku), in which peasants and workers addressed public meetings with harrowing accounts of their suffering
before the Liberation of the late 1940s, may have established many
conventions that have informed all genres of writing about hunger
and oppression.[8]

Not everyone in China can remember personal starvation, however, and not all memories accord with the official periodization of hunger in China. Many born after the nationwide famine of 1959–61 have never had to skip a meal, and others date their current good fortune from a much later time than the economic recovery of the early 1960s. Residents of the village in central Shandong where I have spent time, for example, say they were desperately poor until well after the famine was over; finally a government expert helped them successfully reorganize their farming practices in the early 1970s. There are regional differences as well; many farmers in the well-watered south did better as private small farmers before Liberation than under collectivization and are now reported to recall the years before 1949 as fatter than any since. (This difference in productivity and rural standard of living between southern and northern areas explains some of the differences between two of the works I discuss in this chapter. The White-Haired Girl describes, polemically, the near starvation of northern villagers in winter; Hibiscus Town depicts the population in the years before the national famine as fairly well fed.) In the coastal plains further north, where the land is flat and the weather dry but fairly predictable, there are still benefits to collective agriculture, and some villages have clung stubbornly to the organizational forms they learned from socialism. At the same time, rural planners have noted the reemergence of poor villages and families in areas where local leaders have abdicated all collective responsibility. These struggling farmers thus include some who see the years of socialist agriculture as fat and the current regime of sink-or-swim entrepreneurism as very lean indeed.

Despite these local and individual differences, the broad history of hunger in China is widely agreed-upon. It is still a civic duty to remember the bitterness of the old society before the 1949 establishment of the People's Republic. School textbooks, state-sponsored films, and television documentaries reinforce the standard trajectory from the bitterness of the old society to the more hopeful and well-fed times of party-led socialism. More recent works have moved on to glorify the new wealth and cosmopolitan consumption of the reform period, but many still sort out the good guys from the bad guys along class lines.[9] The sufferings of today's poor—migrant workers, farmers trapped on poor land in the interior, members of minority communities in underdeveloped parts of the country—are no longer made part of a progressive historical narrative; rather, they are depicted as the pitiable and unfortunate casualties of a capitalist economic order that is essentially good, natural, and permanent. Insofar as hunger is systematic, policymakers agree that adjustments must be made to equalize the rate and rewards of development throughout the country and the population. But, unlike previous historical periods in which the people ate a lot of bitterness but their suffering could charter a revolution, hunger is now a problem not for political morality but for development science.[10]

A distinction between a national, essentially state-economic history of China and the particular narratives of ordinary people became important in the 1980s, especially in the hands of memoir writers and muckraking journalists who collected the personal stories of ordinary people.[11] Although the voices of the common people collected by journalists resembled the speaking bitterness narratives, nominally they were not a state-sponsored genre. These new kinds of narrative were thought of as a second liberation, giving scope to the voices of ordinary people who had suffered from the errors of an overzealous party and its representatives. Thus, it was tempting to see these stories of eating bitterness as part of the "depoliticizing" cultural tendency of the reform era.[12] Many of the stories in this genre oppose the political and the personal, seeing bitter experiences as a personal dimension in an overpoliticized world. Along with everyone else—as the stories tend to go—the protagonist was oppressed by the Maoist politics that penetrated into every corner of daily life; he or she was afraid *not* to think and act politically. When the Gang of Four fell, it was possible to "return" to a natural (i.e., newly naturalized) order in which everyone could look after his or her own affairs and seek happiness without the interference of the (new, reform, pragmatic) state. As we shall see, *Hibiscus Town* fits this mold in many ways. But I should point out in advance that I cannot consider this narrative convention, with its important shift toward the personal, to be a form of depoliticization. Rather, it represents a reconfiguration of the political field, reinventing the domestic and the personal as new domains of politics separate from power struggles at the level of state leaders. The intensity with which Chinese people of the 1980s turned toward "seeking their own happiness" (*zhaole*) strongly suggests a kind of political movement; this insistence on private lives bespeaks (despite itself) a resistant self-positioning in a power-infused public field.

Remembering Bitterness: The White-Haired Girl

The initial version of classic 1940s opera *The White-Haired Girl* was written in the "Liberated Areas" as a way of educating rural people about the land reform goals of the Chinese Communist Party. The play combined most of the elements of the old society that would define historical bitterness for subsequent generations: crushing debt, oppression of women, superstitious delusion, and hunger. The story is simple: A tenant farmer is forced to sell his daughter Xi'er to the landlord to settle a twenty-five dollar debt and kills himself in shame. (Later versions have Old Yang dying from a beating administered by the landlord's thugs after he had refused to turn over his daughter.) Xi'er, raped and pregnant, is eventually hounded out of the landlord's household and takes refuge in the caves outside the village. There she and her infant daughter subsist on scanty raw food offerings stolen from the local temple. Nutritional deficiency turns her hair white, and, glimpsed occasionally late at night, she comes to be feared as a powerful ghost. Eventually the Eighth Route Army, which is liberating the area, finds her and "turns her back into a human being" by exposing her story and prosecuting the landlord and his clique. The people are dissuaded from their superstitions and throw themselves wholeheartedly into land reform.

The opera was performed throughout the country from the late 1940s onward. It was later rewritten as a ballet in the Cultural Revolution period and joined a few model theatricals (*yangbanxi*) as one of the few sources of cultural representation between the mid-1960s and the beginning of the reform period in the late 1970s. Theater of this kind was a genre useful to the ambitious propaganda goals of the Maoist regime. There were public stages and traveling performers active in many parts of China in the 1940s and 1950s, and it was relatively cheap for local governments to provide new material for actors and singers and to find places for them to perform even in the smallest villages. (Something had to be done with these people, as all forms of livelihood had come under the sway of government management.) Thus, for a time, before television became common in rural areas (and this was not until the late 1980s even in relatively developed areas), the itinerant theatrical was an important medium for the voice of the state.[13] Those who didn't see the plays onstage saw them in film versions mounted by government projection teams or broadcast on televisions that were collectively owned, one per village. As a result of the state monopoly over the arts (which is only now really breaking up), works like *The White-Haired Girl* were extremely influential. People above a certain age tend to know at least a few model operas by heart. This has been remarked in some of the English-language auto-biographies of Chinese émigrés, but it became especially evident to me when, watching *The Red Lantern* on television in a Beijing dormitory common room in 1997, the building's custodial staff gathered around to sing along with their favorite arias. They were obviously enjoying themselves.

The White-Haired Girl demonstrates how natural it was, in the Chinese socialist context, to think social inequality in terms of eating and drinking. At the beginning, when the rich are celebrating the New Year in grand style and the poor join forces to scrape together a few steamed dumplings, this difference is complacently noted by Landlord Huang and his family.[14]

> Glories in the sky, libations on earth
> Bespeak a rich harvest;
> Lanterns are hung and banners unfurled
> Celebrating this night of plenty.
> All in the household laughingly make joyous offerings;
> It's not so much wine as complacency that intoxicates us. (22)

In the next scene, as snow blows around the stage, a poor peasant sings a parallel aria:

> High winds and heavy snow fill the air,
> Lamplight shines from only a few houses;
> We too celebrate the New Year with everyone else
> But a poor people's New Year is not like the holiday of the rich.
> In the lordly houses there is wine and meat,
> In the homes of tenant farmers there is neither rice nor flour! (31)

In fact, flour has been painfully acquired, a pound at a time, by several local families; one lucky youth even gets hold of a pound of pork. Thus it is that these humble peasants, demonstrating their spontaneous collectivism, can gather together for a New Year's Eve meal of dumplings. Constantly demonstrating their affection for and trust of each other, and forgetting for a while the depredations of the land-lord's debt-collecting steward, they are even able to dream of the day when Xi'er and her young neighbor might marry.

This scene of eating makes a strong contrast with the only eat-ing actually witnessed in the landlord's house. Poor Xi'er, sold to the wealthy Huang family and working as a serving maid, is constantly scolded and beaten for bungling the preparation of sweet lotus seed soup for her mistress. Madame Huang, reclining alone within her bed curtains with her opium pipe, cannot be satisfied; the soup is too hot, too cold, or too bitter because the lotus has not been properly cleaned. Xi'er, of course, is a nervous wreck, trying to anticipate the whims of this picky eater. Another servant comforts her, "[It tastes bit-ter] because smoking too much opium makes a bitter taste in her mouth" (68). Madame Huang's alimentary habits are thus at the other end of the scale from those of her son's tenant farmers: eating an exotic (and not very filling) food alone, she cannot enjoy it because of her overindulgence in an even more expensive luxury, opium. Un-like the poor, who "eat bitterness," Madame Huang only imagines that her lot in life is hard. Not only has the landlord class gained con-trol of all the food, it has lost touch with the simple human enjoy-ments that eating brings in train. The ritual, filial, and reproductive riches enjoyed by Xi'er and her neighbors, despite their extreme pov-erty, render them naturally human, while their oppressors have clearly become monsters who cannot distinguish the bitter from the sweet.

A clear distinction between necessities and luxuries underlies the political trajectory of the play. As the abuses of the tenant-farming sys-tem progressively remove all the ingredients of a decent livelihood from the homes of the peasants, it becomes more and more difficult for the people to sustain human life. The play opens with Xi'er wor-ried that her father, Old Yang, who has fled the village to avoid the end of year collection on his debt to the Huangs, will not return from his hiding place in time for the holiday. The ritual calendar according to which social ties are re-affirmed through commensality is in danger of being violated; poverty puts humanity itself at risk. Although Xi'er and her father are able to pass New Year's Eve eating dumplings with neighbors, when Old Yang dies by his own hand that night, mortified by the ravages inflicted by his debt, it becomes clear that not even physical life can be sustained under these conditions. Grain and meat—simple, sustaining food—are necessities; lotus seed soup and opium are the unnecessary food of monsters.

Of course, the landlord class gets what is coming to it. By the end of the opera, Liberation has reversed the situation that was so advantageous to Landlord Huang and his family. As representatives of the new Eighth Route Army government convene a mass meeting to criticize the landlords, repossess the grain collected in their granaries, and reduce the rent, a jubilant chorus of peasants sings:

> The crimes of a thousand years must be punished,
> The injustices of ten thousand years must be rectified!
> Once forced to become a ghost,
> Xi'er can now become human again!
> Crushing rents must be reduced,
> The grain we have paid must be reclaimed!
> Those who have known bitterness all their lives
> Will stand up and rule with dignity (*shenfan*) today! (149)[15]

Like other works of official literature produced in the service of the Chinese revolution, *The White-Haired Girl* emphasizes class struggle and revenge. The wisdom of the people, we are told, is to materially support each other while never forgetting who their enemies are. The model theatrical works of the Cultural Revolution period provide many examples, but the much earlier *The White-Haired Girl* already shows the relationship between comradeship figured in food exchange and antagonism toward those who made life so bitter. When the landlord's house servant, Aunty Chang, helps Xi'er to escape, for example, she advises the girl, "Here are some rolls, mind you only drink running water while you're on the run. Never forget how they have harmed your family, Child, never forget!" (95). The right that finally triumphs in the end is a marked reversal of the poles; the power to dominate is (apparently) transferred to a different social bloc. The closing words of the opera find sweetness not in the promise of more food and less drudgery for all but in a reversed political hierarchy and the promise that the guilty will be severely punished.

> Landlord Huang, you have bowed your head!
> You quake with dread!
> Age-old feudal bonds

Today are cut away!
Crushing iron chains
Will be smashed to bits today!
We who suffered in days bygone
shall be our own masters from this day on! (97) [16]

In this political logic, living well is not revenge enough. Apparently, past bitterness was to be remembered, and present sweetness reflected on, not simply to produce sentiments of gratitude and satisfaction among the people. Those guilty of greedy exploitation must be punished. Until the end of the Maoist cultural regime, this structure of memory served to advance the continuing revolution and keep the nature and necessity of class struggle clear. Enemies in the bad classes were monsters, while the common people displayed a spontaneous solidarity and eminent humanity. At the same time, works like *The White-Haired Girl* asserted the primacy of socialist rationality over unruly senses and desires by using narrative to translate the people's material needs into a state-sanctioned structure of rule. The party's intervention would be needed if all the hungry were to be fed. In this politics, every pang of hunger, every bite of food, every catty of stored grain had a class character and an almost martial significance. [17] Distinct forms of eating separated the Chinese people from their old society exploiters; in popular consciousness, dumplings came to be a figure for the sustenance to which the people had a natural right. Wrapping into one rounded parcel the grain, vegetables, and meat that were in hard times so difficult for poor people to gather together, in Maoist China dumplings often functioned as a code for a human minimum guaranteed by the revolution. "In the old society we didn't see meat from year to year, but now we can have dumplings whenever we want"—this is the sort of thing people would say in summing up the achievements of the People's Republic. Meanwhile, for several decades elite luxury foods like lotus seed soup disappeared from public view completely.

A Feast for the Mind: Hibiscus Town

Speaking bitterness, along with "remembering bitterness while reflecting on [present] sweetness" (*yiku sitian*) was a technique through which the Maoist regime tried to keep the naturalized dualities of Liberation and the land reform era (1949 to the mid-1950s) alive among the people. Bitterness needed to be blamed on evil exploiters and sweetness credited to the goodness of the party-state. But memory is tricky; it can paradoxically evoke experiences that work against official historical narratives. Times of shortage have often led people to remember in the "wrong" direction, savoring *past* sweetness and reflecting critically on *present* bitterness.[18] *Hibiscus Town* plays with this slippery temporality.

When terms drawn from the everyday life of the body are used to figure vast collective histories, everyday experience can be appropriated in unexpected ways. In hard times, the authority of one person's history may be invoked to insist that present bitterness cannot compare to past, even to pre-Liberation, sweetness. Although the whole history of China after Liberation has been officially sweet compared to the bitterness of the old society, by the early 1980s it was no longer a political requirement that ordinary people sustain this simplified account of (what was supposed to be) their own experience. Not only had the compulsory mass campaigns receded in importance; the beginning of the reform period saw numerous literary and journalistic attempts to re-remember the flavors of good times and bad and to recast them as individual rather than national experiences.

Bodily imagery in these writings is sometimes a metaphor for broad social change and sometimes an indictment of the excesses of Maoist politics, which distorted the down to earth wisdom of the people. The most powerful writings of the early years of the reform period were excruciatingly concrete in their descriptions of violations of bodily health and dignity, showing how class struggle became very literal and material for some during the Cultural Revolution. But by rewriting history as a chronicle of personal, bodily events this literature also produced a new and seductive idiom for the memories of those who read it. In many different ways, the new fiction and reportage used the language of embodiment to privatize what had been a thoroughly public everyday life. In the same gesture, the realistic genres of the early 1980s appeared to depoliticize the private life of Chinese citizens.

Gu Hua's 1981 novel *Hibiscus Town* is a fairly typical example of the genres of popular literature that appeared after 1979.[19] Widely read at a time when novels were immensely influential,[20] it was quickly made into a film that remained in distribution for a long time. Telling an ideal-typical early reform story, the book was an important influence on the new structures of memory that emerged after the fall of the Gang of Four to recast the politics of everyday life. Less starkly moralistic than its model opera predecessors but still clear about the distinction between good and evil characters, it develops a cast of sympathetically drawn workers and peasants whose lives are nearly destroyed through the machinations of a small group of corrupt ideologues.

In a southern river town, the fortunes of rice and bean curd vendor Hu Yuyin and her customers rise and fall in response to various national and regional government campaigns. Hu Yuyin early falls afoul of an ambitious party cadre who manages the state-run restaurant in town. Resenting the competition of both the bean curd stand and its attractive proprietress, this frustrated spinster turns every political campaign against Yuyin and her honest, hardworking friends. Yuyin suffers the death of her first husband early on, and then the imprisonment of her lover, as well as the regular humiliation of being struggled against as a "new rich peasant," one of the "five bad categories." The town becomes an oppressive place, rife with suspicion, everyday talk silenced in fear of political reprisals for any ill-judged remark. Eventually, of course, after the arrest of the Gang of Four, the abuses of the evil cadre Li Guoxiang and her opportunistic allies are rectified and the people of Hibiscus reemerge as honest, trusting souls who help each other and willingly share the necessities of life. The town's most vocal ideologue is hustled off to an asylum, clearly insane because he won't stop shouting "Never forget class struggle!"

Some of the conventional oversimplifications of this novel are obvious even from this brief summary: the sexually frustrated single woman who sets all manner of social destruction in motion; the rapid political reversal through which rhetoric that yesterday persuaded, or at least struck fear into the hearts of ordinary people, today comes to sound like madness; and the simple goodness of the townsfolk, which requires only the removal of the oppressive hand of government to flower again. These are narrative elements that need not surprise us. Perhaps more interesting, however, is a parallel narrative at the level of descriptions of everyday life, the naturalistic ground from which the more dramatic events of the story spring. At the outset of the novel, for instance, Hibiscus Town is depicted as a convivial place where a full ritual calendar is marked by all manner of special meals and food exchanges. It also has a lively periodic market where people and products of many kinds mix freely and everyone—even the dung dealer who collects his goods after the animal market closes—depends on the profits from this relatively unregulated commerce.[21] The heightened state activity brought to the countryside by the Great Leap Forward (1958) severely restricts this market activity, however, and those who would sell the products of their own labor on private plots or in the mountains have to do so warily, looking out for confiscations or extra taxes. Partly as a result, the people go hungry. The happy conclusion of the novel, as we shall see, returns free markets to the town with even more variety and liveliness than before.

This trajectory, from free market to free market via state repression and hunger, is completely consistent with the economic policies of the early reform period. State controls over production and distribution were removed first in the countryside, and the "household responsibility system" that returned land to the farmers on long-term contracts also encouraged them to make a profit on their produce in whatever ways they could. While the government continued to buy its quota of mandated grain, prices were significantly increased and many entrepreneurial opportunities were suddenly open to rural producers. *Hibiscus Town*, submitted to the censors in 1981, was rapidly approved for publication no doubt in part because of its final lyrical invocation of the rich and earthy culture of rural markets and its acknowledgment that "to get rich is glorious."[22] Like the slogans being propagated through official channels in 1981, the novel presented direct market exchange between producers as natural and state cooptation of the market function as a historical deviation. A fictional work thus contributed to the reform era's economic revisionism by presenting a morality tale that could vividly demonstrate the cost of national policy errors in the lives of the common people.

Hibiscus Town directly addressed the lives of its readers in its use of food and drink to figure the social problems of various years, decades, and campaigns in the People's Republic. Hu Yuyin serves her bean curd soup on market days with a smile and a joke, while the employees of the state restaurant are surly and uncooperative; an honest northerner endears himself to the townspeople by learning to eat their many kinds of hot peppers and their local favorites of snake, cat, and dog meat. When yet another directive for the inspection and regulation of peddlers comes down from higher administrative levels, people complain about the cadres in cities and towns who receive grain coupons, a system that institutionalized a classic distinction between producers and consumers: "Those people on state salaries, eating state grain, still think they should control whether the [farming] people have oil, salt, firewood, and rice, whether the people's bellies are empty or full!" Moreover, the functionaries who patrol the few remaining markets often confiscate choice goods for politically motivated bribes to more powerful cadres; thus, food figures corruption as well as honesty. In secret, it also still cements social ties: a surreptitious wedding feast between two illicit lovers is blessed by the visit of a friendly older cadre; a drinking bout between discredited old friends leads to an episode of noisy truth telling in the middle of the night; and a shared roast chicken launches the rather disgusting love affair of two cynical cadres. In all of these vignettes, food signifies something beyond nourishment and pleasure, and a history of the nation is told as one small town's eating is chronicled.

Gu Hua thus uses novelistic methods to rewrite history in broad strokes. This new version of the meaning of the People's Republic was straightforwardly populist and deliberately opposed to "class struggle." It is worth noting, for example, that one important difference between the structures of The White-Haired Girl and Hibiscus Town is that the latter eschews class revenge. The female cadre who put so much viciousness into motion in the end is merely banished into marriage with a party official in a faraway city while her sloganeering henchman is sent off to hospital. It is enough, apparently, simply to remove the worst abusers of the people's trust from the everyday life of the town. By the time the novel appeared, most of those demonized by one faction or another during the Cultural Revolution had been rehabilitated and their property and (usually) positions restored. The ranks of the forgiven included people of all political persuasions who might themselves have had some difficulty forgiving those who had betrayed them. This situation was a source of some anxiety for years after the reform period began. The first step toward historical rectification was to scapegoat a few leaders, the Gang of Four, and depict them as master manipulators of public opinion. But in the longer run only the complete abandonment of the Maoist idea of class struggle and the state's eventual cancellation of all class labels in the late 1980s could slowly assuage the guilt and rage of the people. This fundamental shift in state policy promised much for the future;

at the same time it had important implications for how the past was to be remembered. What had once been revolutionary Liberation could now be "recalled" as class pathology.

The practice of remembering itself is sensitively explored in *Hibiscus Town* in a passage called "A Feast for the Mind." Here the author both deplores and laughs about hunger in a way that productively muddles the standard categories.[23]

> Remember that expression "a feast for the mind" (*jingshen huican*)? It was a local joke, a product of eating in the communal canteens in 1960 and 1961. For months the comrades (*sheyuanmen*) in the Wuling Mountains had seen no oil or meat; in fact for more than a year their teeth had rarely bitten anything solid (*yinian nan da yici ya ji*). The vegetable diet was nothing but fiber, and there was almost no fat or protein: the more you ate squash leaves the skinnier you'd get. Bellies stuck to backbones, and gullets stuck out their hands to beg. Of course, this was blamed on the imperialists, revisionists, and counterrevolutionaries as well as Old Man Heaven. Old Man Heaven had become one of the Five Bad Categories, maliciously stirring up trouble for the people and the communal canteens. Later [the famine] was blamed on the Peng Dehuai, Liu Shaoqi, and Deng Xiaoping line because those leaders opposed the red flag "all eat from one big pot" program.

Looking back twenty years, Gu Hua here reminds his readers of some of the slogans that had ruled their lives during the famine years. He allows the passage of time to lump all of these political values into one slightly ludicrous category despite the fact that two quite separate phases of policy are referenced. Clearly (we gather), these ideas must have been mistaken. At the time of writing, Deng Xiaoping was already hard at work engineering China's economic reform policies. Moreover, it is a joke on the arrogant ambition of the revolution, now visible after the fact, that Old Man Heaven is classified with "the five bad categories" of class enemies. As the passage continues, this satirical tone continues to maintain a historical perspective on the ways in which, during the commune years, dietary shortages were mixed up with political contradictions: "What was wrong with those meals from one big pot, anyway? Well, it was a steady diet of greens and turnips without oil, served up with a big dose of remembering and comparing, recalling past bitterness and reflecting on present sweetness (yiku sitian). 'If you think this is hard, just remember how hard it was for the Red Army on the Long March.'" Thus, eating and remembering go hand in hand in a commune that hopes the people will swallow both its famine rations and its preferred account of history. In theory, linking the provision of food to a narrative of the past should be a very effective method of nation building. But what if the food is terrible? The more one eats the skinnier one gets; eventually the contradictions of the situation will emerge. The connection no longer makes carnal sense.

> I wonder how those first heroes who sacrificed their lives in snowy mountains and grassy steppes for the liberation and well-being of the Chinese people would have seen it? Damn it, do you think they ate the bark from trees and the roots of the grass so people could sit like idiots in communal canteens eating "ragout of squash leaf"? The commune members in the hills couldn't understand the abstruse metaphysics expounded in lofty pavilions and vast palaces. For ordinary people, food is all, and the comrades only knew that their stomachs ached from hunger and their mouths were watering for food. After eating fernroot sweetcakes, your stools would be as hard as iron, jam up in the rectum and make it bleed; you'd have to poke with a little stick or dig it out with a finger—life really sucked (*huo zuo nie*)!

Hard times, indeed! Even the ordinary enjoyment of a bowel movement was apparently out of reach! Here Gu Hua satirizes the idiocy of calling famine foods by elevated names ("ragout of squash leaf"), and sees the practice of "remembering and comparing" as incomprehensible "metaphysics" emanating from "lofty pavilions and vast palaces," that is, the government above. Still, the presumption remains that the revolution was, or should have been, about simple bodily well-being, something the people apparently know all about. The residents of Hibiscus Town, hungry as they are, presume that the achievement of a normal digestive life for all is the obvious cause for which their revolutionary heroes sacrificed so much. Even within this satirical critique, some close relationship between political language and everyday eating is still imagined.

The feast for the mind goes on to weave speech and food, thought and the senses, still more closely together.

> The daytime was not too bad, but at night people couldn't sleep. So
> they devised a way to make up for their short rations. They would
> trade recollections, telling where and when, with whom and on what
> occasion, they had had the richest feasts: whole chickens and fish, fat
> meatballs and crispy-skinned legs of pork, chunks of fatty meat al-
> most too big to get their chopsticks around. Of course, what these
> mountain people most loved to eat on snowy days was dog. If one
> family made a meal of dog, the aroma would entice all the neighbors.
> Dog meat is deliciously greasy—every belch brings up some of that
> good oily flavor—and very filling; it warms the whole body. Dog is
> usually thought of as tasty but crude, hardly the sort of thing for
> fancy banquets. But it moistens yin and strengthens yang; especially
> for working men on the street, it makes a great snack and keeps them
> going for long hours. Thus, for both storytellers and their listeners
> [as they spoke of such things] it was as if their eyes were beholding a
> delectable vision and their noses could smell the aroma of meat; it
> had everyone drooling! Well, life is long, and they'd get their chance
> later: they fixed their hopes for full stomachs on the days to come.

This hope for full stomachs in the future is of course the standard
deferral typical of progressive state ideologies and especially Chinese
Communist rhetoric. As propaganda frequently promised in the early
years of the People's Republic, the achievement of true communism
would be accompanied by food for all. The imaginary banquets recounted in Hibiscus during the darkest nights of the famine are
an even more satisfying vision than that of the state, however: meat
that "warms the whole body" and "keeps [one] going for long hours"
will eventually be available again in "the days to come." The party
may confine its ambitions to feeding all at a minimal level, meeting
their needs for survival alone; ordinary people, however, when they
dream of an end of hunger, have higher hopes. They remember and
desire not only satiation but pleasure, not only a meal but long days of
strength, health, and enjoyment.

Promises about the future naturally recall the national political situation, and as the passage continues a certain down-home patriotism
and faith in the state emerges.

> Now that more than ten years had passed since Liberation, a few

people in this mountain town had had some schooling and knew a thing or two about language, so they fixed on this genteel expression, "a feast for the mind." It wasn't popular for very long, maybe six months to a year in a few villages and towns. In our five thousand years of history and ten million square kilometers of territory, haven't many famines occurred? There have been times when destitute people and starved corpses were all over the place. So, looked at in the vast stream of Chinese history, what did this little "feast of the mind" really amount to? You have to distinguish the old empire from the new People's Republic; they're as different as night and day. After all, the new China had only been in existence for eleven or twelve years; we had to start from scratch and feel our way along. If we wanted to learn how to be a modern society, the nation and the Chinese people would have to pay some tuition fees. In the end, it would be up to posterity to judge our achievements and our mistakes.

In these last few lines, the author adopts official phrases in a slightly more sympathetic tone. The image of the people shifts a bit. No longer are they hapless victims dominated by an irrational politics from above. Instead they are wise survivors who know how to use an imaginative deferral to get through times of hardship. Whether present hunger is displaced via memory into a better-fed past or contemporary political disaster is seen as "tuition fees" paid for lessons about the future achievement of "a modern society," the point is that present suffering is not as important as it sometimes seems. Moreover, people remember both politics ("those heroes") and food, and they hope for both material well-being and a sound national society.

Insofar as the dominant recollection that frames the text is one of a famine that took place after the establishment of socialism, Gu Hua reperiodizes modern Chinese history, placing the most important bitterness in New China rather than the old society. This is a strong critique typical of the scar genre with which Hibiscus Town can be classified. It is entirely in keeping with the political tenor of much early 1980s writing, moreover, embodying a critique centered on "extremist" abuses without directly challenging the Communist Party regime or socialist principles. The image that may come closest to a fundamental critique is the "stew of greens and turnips without oil," a nasty food in a paragraph fragrant with culinary delights. Ladled out in the commune canteens, this is the form in which the official historiography of recalling bitterness is fed to the people; readers in the reform 1980s are expected to respond "never again," rejecting a watered-down ideology at the same time as they refuse a flavor-less food.

The passages quoted above appear near the beginning of *Hibiscus Town*. By the end of the book, which chronicles the cruelties visited upon townsfolk in the name of ideological mass campaigns during the Cultural Revolution, the reform period is beginning and state propaganda has receded as free markets reopen. There has, moreover, been a significant change in the significance of food. The connections between ideological and material food, past and future, that characterized the feast for the mind are obliterated in this orgy of rural consumerism. The passage begins by reminding readers of Maoist market regulation.

> This spring saw a great change in the Hibiscus market. In the past when people from the hills had gone there to peddle furs, herbs, and other mountain products, it was like a black market, they had to have eyes in the backs of their heads and be aware of which way the wind was blowing. It was forbidden to sell grain, tea, oil, peanuts, soybeans, cotton, lumber, pigs, cows, and goats because they were among the "three types of commodities" on which the state had a monopoly. As for pork and beef, even those who raised animals rarely tasted meat from one end of the year to the other, being forced to sell even their suckling pigs to the state. Only if a pig died from disease could they take it to market and sell it as "adversity pork" (*zai zhurou*). As for the townsfolk, their meat ration was half a pound per head per month, sometimes only obtainable illegally through a back door.

Adversity pork is one of those small historical jokes typical of the reform period: when state redistribution was strong, it was not a joke at all but a sort of technical term, like "USDA Prime." Maoist language was full of such terms, marking the socialist state's intention to unify thought, economy, and sustenance in its role as mother and father of the people. After free markets reemerged, any such euphemism that united a revolutionary-romantic word like *adversity* with a down to earth word like *pork* or *meat* could raise a smile. One might wonder, adversity for whom? The state? The producers (who after all made an opportunity out of the illness of their pig)? Perhaps it was really only adversity for the pig itself. Encapsulated in *adversity pork* was a whole revolution in language and everyday life; once the revolution was over and politics and eating had been sundered (so convenient for a market economy not to be hindered by political moralisms!), such terms became an ironic little snack for the mind.

The list of state-controlled agricultural products in this passage— grain, tea, oil, peanuts, soybeans, cotton, lumber, pigs, cows, and goats—offers a convenient catalog of everyday needs. Along with fuel and green vegetables, and the three chickens each household was allowed to raise, these are the things people needed to get by.[24] They are also the things they would not be allowed to supply directly to each other. There are no luxuries and little variety on this list. One sacrifice that had been made for the revolution was the little differences in daily cuisine that had once marked Hibiscus Town's social life.[25] But all this is about to change.

What amazing tricks time can play! A little over two years after the fall of the Gang of Four, it was like a different world for the townspeople; they had entered a fresh new era. Now Hibiscus had a market fair six times a month. To it flocked Yao and Zhuang girls in their colorful clothing and sparkling silver trinkets, Han youngsters all spruced up, bike riders with a laughing girl perched on the back, householders and their wives beaming with satisfaction, bulging purses at their waists. People came in couples or small groups, carrying loads of tender shallots or crisp fresh cabbages, lugging crates or baskets full of speckled hen's eggs and pale green duck's eggs, or pushing a handcart full of wriggling live seafood from their brigade's new sideline business. People came to market along the highways and byways from the townships all around, converging on the new streets and old alleys of Hibiscus Town to buy and sell, each taking a few feet of space to show his goods amid the buzz and confusion of the market in this big mountain town. What drew everyone's eyes the most were the newly opened rice and meat markets. There were white rice, red rice, coarse rice, and polished rice in rows and rows of baskets or piled up in heaps, the vendors eager to measure it out and haggle over the price. The new policies allowed commune members who had fulfilled their grain quotas to sell their surplus grain and oil in this market. The meat market was an even more impressive sight, with plank tables arranged in two long rows, as if it were a contest, allowing people to compare and assess the pigs raised by different commune families, seeing which had the fattest sides, the thinnest skin, the tenderest flesh. Even on off days, pork was on sale from dawn to dusk. A new contradiction faced the Supply and Marketing Cooperative: the shops couldn't move as much pork as the commune members could produce, especially since a small town like this had no cold storage. Private citizens couldn't unload all of their pigs, and the cooperative didn't know where to put the butchered meat. The relationship between supply and demand had certainly changed in the last couple of years! These mountain folks didn't know much about "The Four Modernizations," but they had already seen the benefits for themselves and had begun to taste the sweetness of plenty.

Apparently there is now no need for nostalgic or utopian deferral. The heady excitement of the periodic market and the meat glut has stimulated very immediate appetites, even implying that not entirely proper glances might be exchanged between Han youngsters and their Yao and Zhuang neighbors. Culinary variety has returned, figured most powerfully in the old category of needed foods: no more poor quality rice with gravel in it but white rice, red rice, coarse rice, and polished rice, along with pork that could be distinguished according to "which had the fattest sides, the thinnest skin, the tenderest flesh." This is enough to make any good cook's heart sing; it even invokes the visual beauty of bustling street markets with their arrays of colorful produce and crowds of many kinds of people. Certainly a choice among types of rice and pork implies many more specialized choices nearby in the market as well. Where there are "tender shallots [and] crisp fresh cabbages, . . . crates or baskets full of speckled hen's eggs and pale green duck's eggs, . . . handcarts full of wriggling live seafood," housewives can go back to doing what comes naturally, cooking good (and distinctive) meals for their families. The food egalitarianism of the communal canteens, with their uniform ragouts of squash leaf, has been left far behind.

These "mountain folk" are still depicted as not able to comprehend national policy, but nowadays they can afford to forget politics— almost. A few scattered doubts remain: "Although there was now less to feel sad about, still people felt some concern about the future. Old shadows had not completely withdrawn from their hearts. They still worried and wondered about whether the Left Extremists would suddenly some night find a way to come back and douse these fragile flickers of hope. Could all the slogans and theories, struggles and movements, become important again, ruining people's lives and replacing the things that are necessary for life like oil and salt, vegetables and rice?"[26]

By this (concluding) point in the narrative, food has been rescued from overpoliticization and "all the slogans and theories, struggles and movements." The fear that ideology could replace (*daiti*) "the things that are necessary for life" presumes a clear distinction between material sustenance and political ideology. The Maoist state stands accused of having tried to feed the people on insubstantial ideas; the reform regime provides a delightful new material plenty. The recent abundance of food in Hibiscus is contrasted with the shortages that once accompanied a discursive glut and a state-controlled redistribution system. The real needs of the people, once again redefined after the fall of the Gang of Four, are posited as a foundation for a simpler and less ambitious state politics. The state should withdraw from daily life and productive activity, allow markets and people to regulate themselves, and keep its politics to itself.

The concept of "the things that are necessary for life," so well illustrated by the list of staples (oil and salt, vegetables and rice) that accompanies it, is seductively self-evident. With it, *Hibiscus Town* simplifies history (the most pervasive mass campaigns were developed several years after the national famine, but here these periods are collapsed) and economics, naturalizing the present, market-driven order. The "need" in question is that of natural human bodies that require sustenance and should not be shortchanged even in the service of shared ideals. But the images of plenty and conviviality associated with the free markets at the beginning and end of the book have already established that the food supply cannot be separated from the quality of communal life. People need not only staple foods but community, not only nutrition but the special delicacies that can support a ritual life and be exchanged among townspeople. Only with a return to free markets are the citizens of Hibiscus able to return to fully human status.

This idea of humanity does not imply an entirely simple or "natural" relationship with history, however; as the quote above suggests, people must engage in the work of remembrance through which they make their history. In particular, Gu Hua would have his reader recall the Maoist period as a time when the state's intention of meeting the needs of the people through socialist management was perverted into a "cultural" and continuing revolution that hopelessly muddled eating and thinking, the mundane and the political. The tidy division of the material from the ideological preferred by early reform writing like Gu Hua's is like a limited return to Marxist historical materialism in that it replaces the economic base in a foundational position.[27] Political mobilization will no longer be relied upon to transform China. The only revolution anyone desires (anymore) seems confined to mode of production, leaving relations of production to evolve as they will in a global order that is capitalist. Whereas once the state sought to serve the people right down to the level of their quotas of grain, their conversation at meals, and their historical memories, now it is content to let the market self-regulate and allow thinking (on the whole) to take care of itself. Those who have some control over the means of production will presumably flourish; those who don't will have to find a way to pay the going price for their (newly diversified) needs.[28]

A Feast for the Body

The glowing vision of abundance offered by the market vignettes that conclude *Hibiscus Town* disguises a problem that the book, despite itself, cannot resolve. Apparently there is something worse than starvation, even in the view of these mountain folk, for whom food is supposed to be everything. Gu Hua's narrative suggests that the darkest hours before reform were those that introduced social chaos and moral confusion. The extremist politics of class struggle precluded even the small pleasures of laughing together at a ragout of squash leaf.

The feast for the mind indulged in during the hard years of collectivism had, after all, certain genuine satisfactions, even in the depths of a famine. Shared thoughts of food cannot fill empty bellies, but they can help people while away the long nights together. And hope for a better future is bolstered by a continuing engagement with the drama and promise of the Chinese revolution. Mixed with the bitterness of the famine there had been hope that could be sustaining, thoughts that could be a feast, and food that, however nasty, could be a political statement. By the time *Hibiscus Town* brings us through horrific tales of class struggle and betrayal among neighbors to a restoration of free markets, the novel appears to have achieved a clarification of values in relation to eating. Food is found to be the foundation of communal human life. Free markets, moreover, are good because they allow people to feed each other directly, without interference from above. Not politics or ideology but food and people are what counts.

This is an oversimplification in that it attempts to reduce the needs of simple folk to food (and its usual partners, clothing and shelter) alone.[29] Moreover, as the text admits, "old shadows had not completely withdrawn from [people's] hearts." Whether it is the Left Extremists who are imagined to haunt the future or some less familiar ghost of an emerging and unprecedented global capitalism, the new market order does little to exorcise them. Chairman Mao had at least been willing to sketch the contours of a communist future, and there is little doubt that this vision captured the imaginations of ordinary people throughout China. The market, however, while filling people's stomachs more effectively, in Hibiscus Town offers too little food for thought. In the reform period, a feast for the body has replaced the mental feasts that once filled the long hungry nights of the famine years. The duality is intentional, informed by a populist idealism that presumes that "for ordinary people, food is all."

But some collective situations are worse than hunger. The three famine years were lightened by jokes and memories, but what can be said of those darkest days of the Cultural Revolution when even the most enthusiastic ideologues were brought low? Townspeople who had suffered at the hands of local politicos are shocked when Red Guards from the north arrive to struggle against their more familiar Hibiscus oppressors.

> These rough and impetuous Red Guards with their northern accents, their heads swollen with power, used their leather belts to thrash that self-professed "True Leftist," Li Guoxiang, into silence, unable to plead her case.
>
> What kind of times were these? Times when everything false, evil, and ugly took the place of everything true, good, and beautiful; the unreal uncannily displaced the real, red became black. These were times when cow's liver and pig's lung, wolf's heart and dog's stomach, were all fried and stewed in one pot, when justice was vilified

and humiliated, people plodded through a pathetic existence, and factionalism was rife, its firestorms raging out of control.[30]

This is a political situation that calls reality itself into question, conjuring up images of unthinkable food and an unlivable Armageddon. No one wastes any sympathy on Li Guoxiang, who had long ago alienated all the right-thinking people of the town. But how can ordinary people swallow the confusion of this unexpected development? It was difficult enough, the narrative suggests, to live with the excesses of the town's True Leftists in the name of party ideals; these abuses at least left the moral order of the world intact. When Red Guards arrive— they might as well be from Mars, with their northern accents—and turn everything upside down, existence becomes pathetic indeed, an inedible stew of ghastly combinations. The opposed kinds of leftists, performing political contradictions with direct bodily domination, are like wolf's heart and dog's stomach: whoever thought they could be cooked up together in the same horrifying pot?

The White-Haired Girl is much tidier, of course, in effecting its neat reversal of oppressors and oppressed. The extraordinarily vengeful closing of the play is perhaps best understood as a cleanup operation; if the revolution is to be complete, the landlord class must suffer exactly as much death, hunger, and humiliation as the peasants did in the old society. They must be deprived of the grain they have stockpiled so it can be redistributed to the poor. And some, in parallel with Old Yang at the beginning of the play, must pay with their lives the debt they owe to the tenant farmers. Only after this revenge has been accomplished can a future free of oppression, because it is classless, be imagined. *Hibiscus Town,* appearing forty years later, with its easily classified good and evil characters and a structure that neatly moves us from a free market through compulsory politics and back to the free market again, also performs a significant clarification. The people of Hibiscus are depicted as simple producers and consumers meeting their needs through exchange both in markets and on ritual occasions. As these activities return to prominence, the human and the natural are redefined for the reform period. Or perhaps I should say "for the moment" because ambiguities remain and both the past and the future are haunted by politics.

The final words of the book make this clear: the town's True Leftist sloganeer, now demoted to ordinary citizen, had been disturbing and upsetting his former victims with his shrieks and howls about class struggle. Finally, he is banished "for the cure" to a mental hospital and Yuyin's husband, Hibiscus's intellectual, pronounces a valediction: "Doesn't every city and town now have a few wandering, raving madmen? They are the last word of a pitiable, regrettable era." [31] This remark seems to put a firm cap on the damage done by ideologues: political enthusiasm has become mere raving and historical error naturalized as madness. Yet every city and town has a few of these "last words" roaming its streets, unsettling the memories and disrupting the hopes of moderate, cautious citizens. Hibiscus town has temporarily banished its slogan-shouting activist, but it is more difficult than Gu Hua imagines to banish politics from the dinner table.

Beyond Need

Perhaps this difficulty arises partly because eating is a pleasure, constituting one of the great goods of human existence. This, at least, is what Lu Wenfu's novella *The Gourmet* suggests, as it grounds its subtle repoliticization of food on the persistence of an aesthetics of eating. In this story, the questions raised by the appeal of beautiful food refuse to disappear even in society's darkest hours and even against all the best efforts of Chinese "asceto-Marxism" to banish luxury from the people's desires. [32] In this respect, it resembles Gu Hua's feast for the mind, in which gustatory pleasure is especially figured with reference to dog meat, that "deliciously greasy" local specialty that "moistens yin and strengthens yang" and "warms the whole body" on wintry days. This is a food that is strongly class marked: "especially for working men on the street, it makes a great snack and keeps them going long hours." [33] By confining his story to one small town in which nearly everyone belongs to the same social stratum— earnest leftist classifiers are only able to find twenty-some members of the Five Bad [Class] Categories—Gu Hua was able to depict the entire social world as composed of those who, in effect, enjoy eating dog. But in more class-differentiated urban places, and in the hands of authors who are less comfortable with a simplistic populism, tastes vary a great deal.

    The Gourmet, a novella set in Suzhou and written in 1984, only a few years after *Hibiscus Town*, develops an aspect of the political problem of eating that is mostly avoided by the two works discussed above.

Refusing to reduce the question of food to any simplistic definition of basic human needs, this narrative constantly invokes and complicates the pleasures that eating brings, showing that commensality is almost by definition riven by the displacements of discourse and the antagonisms of an asymmetrical social world. Can carnal pleasure be separated from material exploitation in today's world? This is the problem that *The Gourmet* takes up and, understandably, fails to resolve. In the process, however, the story traces the unsettled moral habitus, as it were, of postsocialist Chinese eaters.

Early in this delicious novella, the idleness of a pre-Liberation landlord is described as follows.

> Once Zhu Ziye had settled himself in a room [in the bathhouse after lunch], he was like an invalid in the hospital; he did nothing whatsoever under his own power. Waiters brought and poured tea, masseurs drew water; he didn't even have to remove his own shoes. Zhu was unwilling to lift a finger because he witlessly preferred to concentrate all his efforts on that stomach of his. He felt that since eating was a pleasure digestion was also an inexpressibly refined beauty; one should devote oneself to knowing it experientially and not allow externals to disperse one's attentive powers. The best way to concentrate this power was to soak in warm water, evacuating all thoughts, stilling all memories, just feeling the delicate movements of the stomach, such that the whole body had an unspeakable ease and sweetness. This was as wonderful as tasting fine food, though the two experiences could not be exchanged.[34] (6)

Throughout the story, the world of food, cooking, and eating is evoked in this sort of vivid prose. Lu Wenfu succeeds in stimulating the senses while at the same time examining the politics of production and consumption in everyday life. Thus, his description of Zhu Ziye's after lunch routine in the bathhouse exemplifies the dual tone of the whole story: while indicating his narrator's contempt for the landlord class, he also, and in the same words, evokes the reader's carnal identification with these hedonistic parasites.

The narrator, old Gao, is the manager of a state-owned restaurant and a conscientious socialist cadre; his nemesis, Zhu Ziye, a distant relative, is a gourmet and an idle member of the former landlord class. Gao hates Zhu with a righteous passion. He claims to despise the food business and the parasitic eaters who take it seriously, yet in

Street food. The vendor is selling a spicy soup made with pork viscera, a Bejing winter favorite. Author photo, 1993.

his account a whole history of the revolution and the People's Republic is told through images of oral consumption. The narration is stuffed with food words, and the eating, cooking, buying, and transporting of food accompanies every step as the plot develops. Hostile actions are phrased as swallowing, roasting, and slicing; pain is sour, pungent, or searing; and emotions and events are reported as bitter or sweet. Bodily pleasure is especially sweet, and detailed sensory images are constructed to articulate it. At the same time, an intimate portrait of the old city of Suzhou is accomplished through a minute rendering of its local cuisine, and the action takes place in streets and lanes full of food vendors and the sounds and smells of cooking.

This is realistic writing in which an experiential quality is fused to the coordinates of time and space. Zhu Ziye must get up early to catch the first batch of "over the bridge" noodles at a certain Suzhou shop, justifying this obsession with the sententious remark, "The art of eating is just like the other arts; one must firmly control the relationships of time and space." He even hires the narrator, Gao, when still a youth, to run all over town collecting snacks for him and his cronies to eat while they relax in a tavern. Thus, he turns the boy into an expert on the food map of pre-Liberation Suzhou. Years later, when Zhu has become an "expert in beautiful food," he lectures on this aesthetic of time and space.

> The east is sour and the west is pungent; the south is sweet and the north is salty. Everyone says (*renjia kou zhidao*) that Suzhou dishes are all sweet, but this is a misconception. In addition to Suzhou's sweet dishes, what we emphasize most meticulously is the adding of salt. Salt enhances all the flavors. If you forget to add salt to fish lung soup, for example, it is bland, utterly tasteless. The moment you add salt everything happens: the fish lungs freshen and the ham becomes savory, the water shield smooth, the bamboo shoots crisp. Although the salt brings out all the flavors, it is not itself noticeable. . . . The adding of salt is not rigid; it depends on the people and the timing (*yih shi, yin ren*). At the beginning of a banquet the people's mouths crave salt; subtle flavors would be wasted on them. When people have just begun eating their mouths are still plain tasting but their bodies need salt. As dish follows dish, though, each should have a little less salt; if the banquet has forty dishes, the last soup should be entirely without salt. People will still find it tasty; after consuming so much food and drink, they have met their needs for salt, and what they need at that moment is water.

This argument is reminiscent of one that is frequently made in teaching Chinese medicine: the administration of therapy should be flexible, responding to the specific character of place, time, and person. (In fact, the same terminology is used: yih shi, yin ren.) Clearly, in keeping with the argument in chapter 1, this gourmet wants to demonstrate how food, artfully managed, can mobilize those powers that produce pleasurable experience. But Lu Wenfu is not content with this kind of intimate body politics; he insists that food is also political at the level of societal production and consumption.

The morals and politics of production and consumption, collective duties and personal desires, can be infinitely extended through the allegorical form of eating. The exploitation of bathhouse workers noted in the quote above—everyone should at least be required to remove his own shoes—is only one of the many ways in which Zhu Ziye's pleasures are depicted as riding upon the labor of the masses. At one point, the gourmet's wife, who is laboriously cooking to serve his pretentious guests, says of him that "this man is nothing but

a gilded chamber pot; all he can be is a mouth" (84). This is an eloquent image of the consumer as moral cipher. Rather than earning
his food and drink by participating in some form of production, the
landlord Zhu Ziye is a parasite. Even after the new government has
confiscated his properties, he receives a stipend to compensate him
for the loss of that income. Like a chamber pot, he has no place in any
work process. His sole function is to receive. The gourmet affronts
the sober egalitarian morality of the narrator by eating for pleasure,
not for health or even to cement social ties. Rather than producing a
sound socialist citizen who serves the people, his eating produces
only the private ephemera of bodily pleasure for a person who doesn't
know how to work.

Worst of all, he and his like are so besotted with the fetishized
values of food—flavor, presentation, physiological effect—that they
cannot perceive the exploitation that is inherent to its existence. A
labor theory of the value of cuisine would at least acknowledge the leg-
work of an errand boy, the chopping and frying done by a wife or
mother. Zhu Ziye's wife points out, while she is hard at work in the
kitchen, that restaurants cannot produce food as well as good cooks
working at home for special occasions because the best food requires
weeks of planning and preparation. Her husband never sees the
labor-intensive side of his obsession, but Old Gao is reminded of the
everyday asymmetries of the working world when he wants to enter-
tain a friend from out of town. He asks his wife to get some food and
prepare it for them, though it is usually his mother who does the cooking. His modern young wife retorts, "What, have you forgotten your
own advice? You said that if a young person wasted all her time in the
kitchen she'd never have any prospects. . . . This young woman with
prospects doesn't even know where the oil bottle is!" (39). With all of
his commitments to the working classes and yearning for a communism beyond exploitation, Gao has forgotten how much he depends
on his mother.

Zhu Ziye displays a similar but more extreme form of gendered
selfishness at the nadir of the Cultural Revolution, when he and Old
Gao have been linked in the imaginative accusations of a disgruntled
waiter.

> The neighborhood committee could hardly fail to make some ges-
> ture. . . . It was pretty easy for them to make me stand at the doorway

to their offices in the morning, confessing my crimes along with Zhu Ziye and [his wife] Kong Bixia. It had come to this, that Zhu Ziye and I were standing up together!

Standing in front of the neighborhood committee wearing a placard—the taste of this was harder to bear than [my previous experience of] being made to stand on a stage as a criminal. . . .

Kong Bixia couldn't stew for long like this, standing there with her head half-shaved, and wearing a placard saying "female special agent"; she was a person who liked to dress up and who valued her dignity. . . . In addition, that blasted Zhu Ziye had the effrontery to volunteer the confession that he had seen Kong Bixia peeling the paper labels from foreign canned goods [received from her ex-husband in Hong Kong] and pressing them in the glass-topped table; then he said he saw her burn them at the time of the campaign against the "Four Olds." . . . The "secret messages" were supposed to have been on the back of the labels! Kong Bixia blushed, then glared, then became agitated; after standing for less than half an hour, she toppled to the ground, her face flushed, unconscious. (55–56)

As those thought to be guilty of crimes against the people cook slowly in the heat of distasteful attention, often seriously contemplating their own errors (50, 54), the gourmet can only seek to shift the blame to his own wife and devoted cook. The idea that cans of food should be the bearers of a counterrevolutionary code draws attention to the way in which political purposes also reside in everyday necessities. But from the point of view of the narrator this conflation of food and politics offends the Maoist sensibility he has long cultivated (assisted perhaps by fictional works like *The White-Haired Girl*). As far as Old Gao is concerned, there are no coded messages outside the desperate imagination of the gourmet. In a politically sensible world, he seems to think, food does not speak and eating should just be eating.

Shortly after this denunciation, the narrator and his whole family are sent to the countryside, where they eat tough old hens and drink bad liquor for some years; Zhu Ziye continues his old life relatively undisturbed, "still living [with Kong Bixia] at No. 54" and eating relatively well. Unlike *Hibiscus Town*, this Lu Wenfu novella is uninterested in extreme hunger, relying instead on the differences through which social distinctions can be figured in everyday life. At one point, for example, Gao persuades his worker friend A'er to give up the degrading but profitable work of pulling a rickshaw; but since the only work A'er can find to replace his old job is canal dredging his family eats and drinks less well—"the roast goose and bottle of wine disappeared"—for a time, and old Gao learns his first lesson about the practical disadvantages of ideological correctness.

Even the "three hard years" are not described in the apocalyptic language some authors have favored; instead this period of famine provides an occasion to once again differentiate the honest cadre narrator from the self-indulgent aesthete Zhu Ziye. Thus, old Gao is offered a cartload of pumpkins—not exactly a gourmet food in China—that has come as a windfall to his loyal friend A'er; the two of them hope that the cooked pumpkin will help nourish Gao's wife, who is suffering from malnutrition-induced edema, back to health. The gourmet Zhu begs for a few pumpkins for himself and is enlisted to help push the cart. His nemesis having become rather pitiful in these hungry times, Old Gao wonders whether his old landlord might have finally realized the value of labor and the folly of his parasitic ways. The words they exchange while moving the pumpkins prove otherwise: all Zhu can talk about is food, as he narrates his own feast of the mind, describing both past and future delicacies to his unwilling listener. Even in the depths of a national famine, he still thinks like a gourmet, fantasizing the humble pumpkin into an implausible "Eight Treasures Pumpkin Cup" stuffed with unattainable goodies.

Figures like this remind us that not only have amounts and styles of food varied in modern Chinese history and been unevenly distributed among China's people, but so have daily acts of eating built and rebuilt the asymmetrical connections among people. Just as we have never finished eating and must always return to the social relations of the table, so *The Gourmet* constantly reassesses the relationship between the gourmet and the moralist, the landlord and the cadre. Food flows between them, repetitively raising the possibility of commensal fellow feeling and then reasserting the inequalities that divide them. Perhaps it is important that this is not a power differential: Zhu Ziye is richer than Gao throughout most of the story, but he is always on the margins of real social power. Old Gao takes responsibility, wielding power in the context of his socialist work unit, the state-run restaurant, and suffering the consequences as the revolution continues. Throughout the story, he claims to shoulder the burdens of administration reluctantly, but we must presume that the life of the communist cadre, especially when it was informed by revolutionary fervor, had its own pleasurable rewards. Still, Old Gao repeatedly gnashes his teeth in frustration: the one person over whom he has no control is his parasite kinsman, Zhu Ziye, the unredeemable, essential consumer who always seems just beyond the reach of reforming power.

This problem of power is made very clear as *The Gourmet* ends. The still dutiful cadre, now known as Director Gao rather than Comrade, is trapped into a banquet at Zhu Ziye's house, where a group of ideologically suspect cronies of the gourmet urge Gao to hire their "bloodsucker" host as a consultant in the state restaurant. Our narrator manages to leave before he is required to commit himself (a serving of "three-in-one duck" intervenes at the crucial moment). With all his old animosity toward Zhu Ziye revived, he hurries off to a wedding party at A'er's house.

At the wedding, all is as it should be: "This was a joyful world, no false courtesies, no hypocrisy, no talk of extravagance. The courtyard was full of people cracking melon seeds and eating wedding candy." Gao's one-year-old grandson is there, being spoiled by all the adults, who offer him the best tidbits and goodies. But he won't eat ordinary Chinese hard candy. Someone finds a chocolate bar, an expensive, foreign-style sweet, which the baby takes to instantly, much to the delight of the adults: "This baby's really clever, he knows how to eat good things!" This is too much for old Gao.

> My head suddenly began to explode. When he grew up he, too, would be a gourmet! Though all my life I had been unable to control that Zhu Ziye, I could still control this little creature! I reached out and took away the chocolate and forced a piece of hard candy into his little mouth.
>
> The child started to scream. . . .
>
> Everyone there was stunned; they must have thought that this old guy had gone completely crazy. (85)

And there the story ends. The evil of exotic pleasures has made its way even into the bosom of the narrator's family, corrupting the future that the little grandson figures. The formal powers enjoyed by the conscientious socialist cadre are shown to be helpless against a stubborn bodily coding of inequality, one that inhabits taste buds and appetites even more than hearts and minds. It appears that from the

beginning the gourmet has been drawing on deeper and more permanent sources of human significance than his idealistic revolutionary kinsman has perceived. Ideals, we are led to think, can at times
become insanity; down-to-earth eating, however, only produces garden variety gluttons and beggars. This ending, then, is not unlike that
of *Hibiscus Town*. Maoist ideology has become a form of madness, but
food—even the difference between cheap hard candy and expensive
chocolate—is only natural.

But the text as a whole is more complicated. Reading Lu Wenfu's
novella *as* gourmets, vicariously (and perhaps guiltily) enjoying the
delicacies consumed by Zhu Ziye—first-batch noodles, a fish fillet
fried in the shape of a squirrel's tail, snowflake chicken balls, crab-
meat with cabbage hearts, rice flour balls in osmanthus broth, a fresh
tomato stuffed with stir-fried shrimp—we have participated in a certain pleasure of the text, recovering the genteel daily life of an earlier
Suzhou and relishing the imagined tastes of its many local delicacies.
Reading in league with Old Gao, the narrator, we have rejected the
self-indulgent and exploitative implications of "knowing how to eat
well," and we have shared his hope for a future China in which no one
will be able to use others in the service of such ephemeral pleasures.
Reading from a position outside the text's own voices (are we reading
along with the author or along with the broader conditions under
which he writes?), we weep for a China suspended between the
"chocolate" of a rapacious global capitalism (a system and a language
that relentlessly separate the economy that must feed the people from
a politics that might heal their social divisions) and the three-in-one
duck of a "feudalism" that will not die, partly because it offered such
refined pleasures to the few.[35] The gratifications attendant on high political purpose now appear ludicrous, having been replaced by the
undignified but "natural" scramble to consume. If there were subtle
gratifications that accompanied the regime of asceto-Marxism, they
have now been overwhelmed in a frenzy of consuming new pleasures.
Between these poles, neither the mass line of Maoist practice nor the
simple rewards of family and community life offer stable answers to
the question of how to eat both ethically and with pleasure, that is,
how to "eat well."

Old Gao himself appears pathetic at the end. The revolutionary
ideals for which he tried to stand for thirty-five years have long
ago gone sour; he has repeatedly been accused of making ideological

mistakes, while his old enemy Zhu has almost entirely "escaped reformation." While A'er's proletarian family wedding celebrates a modest prosperity achieved since the revolution, the gourmet at his banquet down the street is indulging his unproductive and exploitative appetites more excessively than ever. Most unbearable is that such appetites have themselves become a kind of expertise, worthy of a monthly stipend at the state restaurant and worthy of praise in an infant gourmet.

Typical of Lu Wenfu's gustatory tropes, the three-in-one duck that distracts banqueters at Zhu Ziye's house, allowing Old Gao to slip away, is an eloquent materialization of reform era social difference. This labor-intensive dish is a game pigeon stuffed in a chicken stuffed in a duck, then put back together to resemble a whole duck and surrounded with quail eggs arranged to look as if the duck had just laid them. No wonder these gourmets paused a moment in their politicking to wonder at this apparition! Three-in-one duck is remote indeed from the meat dumplings that had for decades been the good-times food of the common people: it takes a true expert to make this dish (though dumplings are made at home by the whole family), it incorporates mostly exotic materials (no mere pork, flour, and cabbage here), and it is all protein, eschewing any leavening with staple grains or vegetables. It both recalls and in its splendor occludes those social hierarchies in which bigger fish eat smaller ones and rich people drink the life's blood of the poor. Dumplings were a food that the Liberation era government could promise (and at times almost deliver) to all; three-in-one duck was never meant for anyone but gourmets.

An aesthete of the body, Zhu Ziye has slipped through, under, and around all the labels, evading the ideological entrapments that affected the lives of so many during the Cultural Revolution and the antirightist campaigns that preceded it. Never attempting anything beyond the bounds of his own sensations (he doesn't even know how to cook!), Zhu Ziye can never be held responsible for anything dangerous; he can be accused of nothing worse than being a "bloodsucker," a mere mosquito on the transforming body of the masses. His story figures the excess that pleasure is for the historical analyst; neither Old Gao nor the party theoreticians above him can figure out how to control a human who lives only to eat.

As the ambiguous ending of *The Gourmet* suggests, the opposition of the aesthete to the ideologue cannot be resolved; both figures

A hostess awaits her guests for a special meal in a neighborhood restaurant. Author photo, 2001.

appear ridiculous in their excessive emphasis on one aspect of alimentary practice. Zhu Ziye's obsession with his stomach, which enjoys abundance, and Old Gao's concern for the people, who require austerity if all are to eat, are forever incommensurate and always coexistent. The strength of Lu Wenfu's writing is that he offers a more complex text for our delectation than either of his main characters could ever produce. *The Gourmet* serves up history, suffering, and morality along with imagination, enjoyment, and beauty. It is not only *about* eating, but it performs it, leaving the reader with both tingling taste buds and a few indigestible lumps. The text is at once political and aesthetic, satisfying the senses and unsettling the intellect; it truly performs a "feast for the mind." The reader becomes an embodied guest at this feast of images and memories, just as likely to enjoy flavors and companionable talk, to suffer hunger or anxiety, as the characters in the story. In this respect, Lu Wenfu undermines all the oppositions that drive his narrative, producing instead a polyglot mix of enjoying, sociable, antagonistic, desiring, political bodies.

Lu Wenfu's strategy in *The Gourmet* is in keeping with the "aesthetic resistance" mounted by writers in the mid-1980s to protest the

Maoist politicization of literature.[36] The resistance in question opposed itself to the thorough politicization of all language, and thus all
experience, by the state; as the reform period advanced, writers experimented with ways of using language that could infuse new
significance into a modern Chinese language that had become thoroughly imbued with nationalism, Marxism, and class struggle. Words
needed to find new referents; this required writers to build a context
within which texts could mean something besides what the state had
for decades been saying. *The Gourmet* participates in this aesthetic resistance at two levels: Zhu Ziye is parodied as an aesthete, but Lu
Wenfu also redeems the bleakness of his social vision with an overtly
aesthetic writing style. By invoking intimate experiences of alimentary pleasure for the reader, *The Gourmet* interpellates a body and self
that in the early 1980s was just beginning to appear. (This argument
is much expanded in chapter 4.)

Lu Wenfu's rejection of the excesses of a state-led political logic is
especially evident in the episode in which a Red Guard restaurant
worker cooks up ludicrous conspiracy charges against the narrator.
This "mystery story" scenario involves the labels on cans of food sent
from Hong Kong and the gift of pumpkins during the hard years). But
Lu's story, while it seems to share with its readers a desire for an escape hatch, a place where eating is just eating, offers no space for a
meal that can really be free of the political. He can only retreat toward
a use of language that distracts us with its nostalgic and gustatory
beauty and an idiom that, while still invoking power and inequality,
stands in contrast to the ponderous moralizing of Maoist propaganda.
Like Gu Hua, who used *Hibiscus Town* to dramatize a reform era opposition between material needs and political idealism, Lu Wenfu,
along with many authors who lived through the latter decades of the
Mao years, sought to remove the life of the body from the oversimplifications of state politics.[37] But beautiful prose is not enough to answer the questions posed by the revolution and incorporated into eating itself by generations of Chinese citizens.

In fact, Lu Wenfu appears to realize that it is not just food but
beauty itself that comes at a considerable social cost. After all, his
home town of Suzhou is known as a beauty spot throughout China
and the world, "a Heaven on earth" (*renjian Tiantang*). Its extraordinary gardens and parks, when I visited it in 1983, just about the time
that *The Gourmet* was being written, had suffered from years of ne-

glect and misuse. But restoration was under way, mobilizing the skills of master woodworkers to rebuild pavilions and arcades and organizing gardeners into societies to cultivate rare plants and relandscape miniature vistas. The work required, and the expense, were everywhere made obvious in signs explaining the renovations; many sites had collection boxes for donations. Lu's novella itself refers to an earlier stage of labor in the service of Suzhou's beauty when A'er gets a job after giving up his rickshaw: "This work involved dredging Suzhou's narrow canals. It was very hard work but also very significant. The old society had left us with sludgy, clogged waterways; the sludge needed to be changed into clear, flowing water in order to make this Venice of the East live up to its reputation and to make this Heaven even more beautiful. This was an aspect of our revolution" (20). A'er, however, must work much harder in his new job of beautifying Suzhou than he had when he facilitated Zhu Ziye's eating by pulling a rickshaw, and he brings home only three catties of rice a day. The production of lasting beauty, in other words, is a much bigger job than the service work that makes life easier for a consuming class. The "inexpressibly refined beauty" of Zhu Ziye's very private digestive processes is quite a different thing, socially, than the loveliness of a town and the peaceful gardens, well-kept streets, and clean waterways that help to sustain life for its residents.

Perhaps for a time in the 1980s writers like Lu Wenfu, and their vast numbers of readers in a reforming China, thought that beauty was enough. But the history that had led readers and writers (i.e., cultural China) to this apparent solution had not disappeared, nor could it. The deep satisfactions offered by *The White-Haired Girl*, in which an oppressed and silent majority of rural producers at once finds voice and power (but opts for a continuing, and vengeful, class struggle), and the desperately desired material simplifications worked out in *Hibiscus Town* (while nevertheless failing to banish ambiguous memories), are incorporated into the aesthetics of *The Gourmet*. This last book's various characters and their adventures say much about a specifically Chinese sense of the past and its capacity to haunt everyday life. Old Gao, for example, came into existence as a moral being with the New China and the Communist Party (his youthful studies show as much [9]), and some of his most carefully crafted descriptions as the narrator are devoted to the desperate poverty of Suzhou's pre-Liberation beggars and workers. The text makes it clear that he speaks from the early 1980s perspective of a still loyal communist, so he does not wish to forget how dreadful the old society was. Although he has seen the error of certain leftist excesses where the restaurant business is concerned, he cannot let go of an ingrained Maoist egalitarianism.

The Gourmet also offers us less vocal characters with an even firmer hold on morality, A'er the willing worker and Kong Bixia the hardworking (and beautiful) cook married to that "gilded chamber pot" Zhu Ziye. These characters, unlike the book's protagonists, do not theorize food or eating; they simply get by, offering services or performing the productive tasks essential to eating. In a sense, both Gao and Zhu are "eaters of state grain"; although the more incidental characters of A'er and Kong Bixia are not producers of staple foods, they nevertheless earn their keep. Thus, the latter two conclude the story on the sidelines; they hold the only viable moral authority on offer, but theirs is a silent voice.

Most interesting, of course, and most problematic, is Zhu Ziye. This gourmet emerges by the end of the story as quite a talker, though from the point of view of Old Gao his words are empty. But this is the only change his character undergoes. As an eater, Zhu is always there, always the same. His very existence forges an equivalence, at the level of the body and desire, between the old society before Liberation and the reform era in which it is glorious to "get rich." Lu Wenfu thus treats him as expressing an inherent tendency in human social nature; his selfish approach to oral pleasure is built into the problem of eating itself. This trope suggests yet another naturalization: greed is natural, and ultimately it is madness—"they must have thought that this old guy had gone completely crazy"—to try to control it for the sake of the collective and in the name of an idealistic politics.

MY GRANDFATHER, a high school Latin teacher, always used to resolve battles among his young grandchildren by saying "De gustibus non disputandum est" (concerning tastes there can be no disputing). His technique was brilliant, no doubt the result of his classical education. He would sophistically reduce our antagonisms to mere questions of taste and then pronounce the ultimate adjudication, "there can be no disputing." The materials discussed in this chapter have presented many disputes about taste, expressing deep-seated historical antagonisms that admit of little adjudication, at least in theory.

But these arguments have tended to leave taste itself untouched. When bodily experience is thus naturalized, historical difference is occluded. The many and changing ways in which lived bodies have come into existence cannot be perceived when pleasure, desire, and greed are seen only as the inevitable and unchanging conditions for any politics. In practice, pleasure and greed undergo profound alteration as circumstances change.

As we shall see in the next chapter, and as was suggested in chapter 1, the politics within which these carnal realities are produced has been very explicit in postsocialist China. The bodily and social idioms that charged food with collective values far beyond the nutritional have been well and variously explored by writers in several eras. Although the fictional works I have explored here almost completely ignore it, we also saw in chapter 1 that there is a theoretics of flavor and power—in other words, a language for historically contingent pleasures—available in the techniques of Chinese medicine. What connects these two idioms of embodiment? What links the social or critical dimension of post-Maoist thought to the therapeutic or phenomenological aspects of a medically theorized life? In chapter 3, it will be possible to bring together the reflections of the great fiction writer Mo Yan and some of the theoretical resources of Chinese medicine to explore these connections. This conjunction does not, however, resolve the contradictions addressed, and in a sense heightened, by *The White-Haired Girl, Hibiscus Town,* and *The Gourmet.* Despite all efforts to make peace on the terrain of taste (and *pace* my grandfather), all that can be seen in China, as elsewhere, is continuing battles.

chapter 3

EXCESS AND DEFICIENCY

The question is no longer one of knowing if it is "good" to eat the other or if the other is "good" to eat, nor of knowing which other. One eats him regardless and lets oneself be eaten by him. . . . The moral question is thus not, nor has it ever been: should one eat or not eat, eat this and not that, the living or the nonliving, man or animal, but since *one must* eat in any case and since it is and tastes good to eat, and since there's no other definition of the good (*du bien*), *how* for goodness sake should one *eat well* (*bien manger*)? And what does this imply? What is eating? How is this metonymy of introjection to be regulated? And in what respect does the formulation of these questions in language give us still more food for thought? In what respect is the question, if you will, carnivorous?
—Jacques Derrida

"How, for goodness sake, should one eat well?" This question from an interview with Jacques Derrida echoes the ethical and political concerns explored by the fictional works discussed in chapter 2.[1] We have seen that the ways in which Chinese writers have articulated this question have been strongly influenced by the history of the People's Republic. Lu Wenfu, in particular, despite his efforts to aestheticize eating through writing, demonstrated the intractability of the moral dilemmas faced by people who have learned all too directly that one's own sustenance depends upon the exploitation of others. While Derrida raises the question of eating well in the context of the chronic ambiguities of drawing a line between self and other (the "calculation of the subject," as the interview title announces), Chinese authors have tended to seek a clarification of the problem of eating by charting a middle way between excess and deficiency. They have sought to regulate the "metonymy of introjection"—the relationships between eaters and what they eat that determine the very identity of eaters and eaten—along *economic* lines. How much blood and sweat may be extracted from producers so that consumers may eat? How much enjoyment or bulk is justifiable for the fortunate in a world where starvation is all too real for some of their neighbors? Is there value in "high" civilization (gourmet food, for example) if many of the socially "low" have no access to its sophisticated pleasures? Can past famine justify indulgence in present and future gluttony?

Chinese medicine parallels these twentieth-century concerns with a rich vocabulary and logic of excess and deficiency figured as the pathological processes of repletion and depletion. Many illnesses take the form of a depletion in crucial body substances (fluids, Blood) or insufficient functioning of key systems and active entities (Spleen System depletion, qi depletion). Repletions, in not quite parallel fashion, tend to be malfunctions that allow substances to become excessive, collecting and stagnating in one place. Thus, a functional depletion can cause a state of substantive repletion. Both medical and economic notions of excessive and deficient function predate the Marxist and capitalist economisms of the nineteenth and twentieth centuries, drawing on very old market and agricultural metaphors. Nevertheless they are important in recent history because they have offered an idiom for modern experience of many kinds. In clinics, individuals suffer from depletions and repletions that are deep seated and can be remedied only with long periods of technically complex therapy. At the same time, the national body of which sufferers of illness are a part has been ravaged by famine and uneven productivity while pockets of wealth and privilege have proven hard to control. Recent claims, for example, that sybaritic banqueting took place in the central Communist Party compound in Beijing at the height of the national famine of 1959–61 have not so much shocked citizens as impressed them with a sense of symbolic appropriateness: the chronic "Chinese" problem is one of deficiency and excess at the same time.[2]

As we have seen, the economic goals of the Maoist state, with its egalitarian rhetoric and revolutionary concern to rectify old wrongs, were pursued through a minute accounting of wealth and resources. Everything from the granaries of the landlords mentioned in *The*

White-Haired Girl to the mountain products sold in the streets of Hibiscus Town counted as a form of potentially pathological excess subject to redistribution in a state project that kept class struggle at the tips of everyone's chopsticks. In a pointedly "nonpolitical" and parallel discourse of its own, Chinese medicine also took account of states of repletion and depletion and operated an "economic" rectification in the form of therapies for the imbalances afflicting individual sufferers.

In this chapter, I will examine some of the parallels and linkages between Chinese medicine and the ethics and politics of food that have concerned contemporary writers, especially novelist and essayist Mo Yan, a writer well known in China for his interest in food, drink, and mundane bodily functions. There is a striking mirror effect between Mo Yan's descriptions of deficient and excessive eating and Chinese medicine's diagnoses of functional depletions and repletions. Also in this chapter I introduce observations about the practice of a form of eating—official banqueting—considered by many to represent an unacceptable form of social excess. To see these disparate elements as sharing a logic will also necessitate returning to the ethical issues taken up by Derrida in the interview from which this chapter's epigraph is drawn. Derrida *can* comment on these Chinese issues precisely because the discourses and practices that link the domains of Chinese medicine, critical writing, and social customs like those of banqueting share a broadly economic logic that would seek to regulate states of excess and deficiency. As Derrida has perceived, beyond the quantitative issues of redistributing unevenly allocated resources there are questions of the agent: who eats whom; how shall the eating self and the eaten other be understood and how shall their relations—this "metonymy of introjection"—be regulated; can a broader and more ethical commensality be achieved; and on the basis of what experience should ethical discriminations be made?

Among the many economistic discourses in modern China, Chinese medicine stands out as a field that offers answers to these questions and suggests ways to get beyond the dilemma of an impossible egalitarianism, an implausible dream of redistribution that would eliminate all pockets of shortage and wealth, all distinctions between consumers and producers. Steeped in a therapeutic logic that refuses to abandon a vision of positive good health for whole systems, practitioners and patients in the practical world of clinics *must* seek some resolution for the pathologies of uneven distribution. The resolution they sometimes achieve is not necessarily egalitarian, nor is it inherently progressive. Read in a certain way, however, there are interesting political and ethical allegories in the practical logics of Chinese medicine. Just as Derrida elsewhere in his interview speaks of "determining the best, most respectful, most grateful, and also most giving way of relating to the other," Chinese medical theory offers a physiological vision of circulation and networks that can remedy impacted repletions and chronic depletions. These widely separated discourses may be speaking on quite different topics, but they both move beyond the problem of appropriation and exploitation that has occupied so much ethical attention in both North America and China.

Medical writers seldom apply the insights of their field to "social" or "political" problems. There are good reasons not to; bodies are not societies, and individuals have requirements and capacities different from those of communities. Nevertheless, if economic excess and deficiency are persuasive tropes for understanding modern national dilemmas in China, then bodily repletion and depletion cannot help but comment, from a short distance and "apolitically," on the heterogeneous terrain of the nation. Before turning to this commentary in disguise, however, I want to clarify the ways in which popular discourse in the reform era has figured the broad social problem of excess and deficiency for modern China.

When We Reach Communism

One of Marx's most unforgettable passages in *The German Ideology* offers a utopian vision of everyday life in communism. He writes, "In communist society, where nobody has one exclusive sphere of activity but each can become accomplished in any branch he wishes, society regulates the general production and thus makes it possible for me to do one thing today and another tomorrow, to hunt in the morning, fish in the afternoon, rear cattle in the evening, criticize after dinner, just as I have a mind, without ever becoming hunter, fisherman, shepherd, or critic." [3] Like many utopias, this vision is framed in the context of a critique; the argument Marx develops involves the alienation produced by the fixed social roles of an increasingly complex and rigid division of labor. He may have been referring more to "primitive communism" than a vision of what might be possible under the communism to come. But perhaps visions like this have played a role in the futurist imaginations of many socialist movements. The apparent contradiction between a society that "regulates the general production" and individual workers who can engage in various productive activities "just as [they] have a mind" can be resolved if we see consciousness as arising from human productive activity. (This is, after all, the central argument that opens *The German Ideology*.) A fully collectivized individual who recognizes the immediate benefits of laboring for the general good will "have a mind" that wholeheartedly accepts social "regulation." But other possible difficulties with this vision are simply elided in its seductive pastoral imagery. Hunters, fishermen, and shepherds are not on the whole large-scale producers whose goods can be widely distributed to help support all the economic activities of a twenty-first-century nation. The only imaginable modern economy that could enable the lifestyle of Marx's famous "critical critic," with his forests, streams, and flocks, would be one that enjoyed great plenty.[4] Social regulation of general production should produce so much surplus that its management would require no hard decisions; effort could be readily shared among amateurs, and no individuals would have to exert sustained labor of any one kind. This is a society beyond the exploitation of producers by consumers and the distinction between eaters and eaten. Surplus itself allows such a system to work.

The utopian logic of Marxism in China has conflated social wealth with socialist regulation. The party promised an eventual end to the chronic excesses and deficiencies of Chinese history by unifying policies of state-directed modernization with images of wealth "when communism comes." When there is enough for all, socialism can become communism and people can do "just as [they] have a mind." In one of his earliest manifestos (1919), for example, Mao Zedong wrote:

> What is the greatest question in the world? The greatest question is that of getting enough to eat. What is the greatest force? The greatest force is that of the union of the popular masses. . . . We must act energetically to carry out the great union of the popular masses, which will not brook a moment's delay. . . . Our Chinese people possess great intrinsic energy. The more profound the oppression, the greater its resistance; that which has accumulated for a long time

[presumably, a state of pathological excess controlled by the oppres-
sors] will surely burst forth quickly. The great union of the Chinese
people must be achieved. Gentlemen! We must all exert ourselves,
we must all advance with the utmost strength. Our golden age, our
age of brilliance and splendor, lies ahead.[5]

Since the greatest question is that of getting enough to eat, the golden
age would presumably incorporate this very concrete satiety. The pre-
diction, that goods that had accumulated for a long time would "burst
forth quickly," appears to have been fulfilled during the land reform
period thirty years later; the party-led redistribution of privately held
wealth during this period resulted in a few years of immediate prosperity for many farmers. The "golden age" of the early 1950s is remembered as a period of good harvests, family control over production, and enough surplus to enable savings accounts for many who
had previously been desperately poor. Though land reform itself had
involved painful calculation and manipulation of the excesses and
deficiencies in every administrative unit no matter how small, once it
was accomplished there appear to have been a few years in which
people simply enjoyed their new access to resources.[6] What had been
static and unproductive excess controlled by the few was converted
into a modest prosperity and even a little surplus for many.

Chairman Mao's optimism did not entirely disappear as his leadership responsibilities grew.[7] On the eve of the founding of the
People's Republic, he said: "Of all things in the world, people are the
most precious. As long as there are people, every kind of miracle can
be performed under the leadership of the Communist Party. . . . We
believe that revolution can change everything, and that before long
there will arise a new China with a big population and a great wealth
of products, where life will be abundant and culture will flourish. All
pessimistic views are utterly groundless."[8]

The promises of the party and its great helmsman became well in-
tegrated into popular consciousness during the Maoist period. In an
essay by Mo Yan to which I will shortly return, for example, a soldier's
father travels in the 1970s from the family's impoverished village to
his son's army base for a visit, finding the army reorganized: "Because
the livelihood in the companies of the new army had been somewhat
lacking, the companies had just been divided into new work units,
and these units were like heaven on earth. Our unit only had eleven

or twelve men, and we farmed about 50 *mu* [8.2 acres] of land. Each
year we planted two crops, one season of wheat and one season of
corn. The wheat was milled into white flour and the corn was used to
raise pigs, so you can just imagine how great our life was in that unit!
My war veteran father came and ate at the unit for several days and
could hardly believe it. He said, What is communism? This is!"[9]

The referent for *communism* in this epiphany is not so much the
new administrative structure as the plentiful pork and steamed bread
Mo Yan's father found himself eating. Around the same time it was a
common joke to observe that "for Russians, communism must be
beef and potatoes."[10] Clearly, the remark compares national palates
more than the political theories of the socialist world.

The Maoist idea of a communism to come kept promising an end
to shortages "before long." Mao's very public predictions meant to
speed up the process through which China was to catch up with Great
Britain in industrialization were a well-known component of the politics of the Great Leap Forward. Filmgoers will recall two scenes referring to the communist utopia in Zhang Yimou's *To Live,* a production that includes a realistic (i.e., conforming to a current mainstream
perception of historical realities) image of commune life in the Great
Leap Forward period.[11] In the first of these scenes, during the height
of the mobilization to produce steel in local blast furnaces, a father
diverts his tired son Youqing with a just-so story.

—Does Youqing like to eat dumplings?
—Yes.
—Does Youqing like to eat meat?
—Yes.
—That's good. If Youqing does as Daddy says, our daily life will
get better and better. Our family now is like a little chicken. As
it grows it will become a goose, then become a sheep; when the
sheep grows up it will become an ox.
—After the ox?
—After the ox comes communism, and we'll eat dumplings and
meat every day.

Some years later, after the reform period has begun, the same father
has a parallel exchange with his grandchild Mantou as they find a
place to keep some baby chicks they have just bought.

—This chest is bigger than the cardboard box; they'll have more room to run around. The more they run around the more they'll eat; the more they eat the faster they'll grow.

—When will they grow up?

—Very soon.

—After they grow up?

—When a chicken grows up it becomes a goose, when a goose grows up it becomes a sheep, when a sheep grows up it becomes an ox.

—And after the ox?

—After the ox, Mantou will grow up.

—I want to ride an ox . . .

—Mantou won't ride an ox; he'll ride trains and airplanes, and life will get better and better.

Obviously, the contrast in these two scenes between future communism and future modernity is meant to mark a shift in values between the Maoist and the reform periods. The substitution of an apolitical life of comfort and mobility, Mantou's future, for the ideal political order Youqing was encouraged to dream of may not be much of a leap; after all, if communism always meant, for many Chinese, whatever utopia contrasted most sharply with their present reality (e.g., eventually being able to eat dumplings and meat every day), then market socialism, with its less regulated markets and entrepreneurial opportunities, might seem like just a different path to the same end. This relation of means to ends, in which a market economy is supposed to lead to a more communist state in some sense, continues to inform the official economic policy of the Chinese Communist state. The assumption that great plenty will resolve stubborn economic inequalities is common to both these social visions. But writers like Mo Yan call that assumption into question.

Mo Yan's "I Can't Forget Eating"

If Chinese national dilemmas are thought of as problems of excess and deficiency, history can be cast in a rather simple narrative. During the last years of China's twentieth century, the most convenient and common way of thinking about the past was to criticize the revolutionary excesses of the first few decades of the People's Republic while at the same time seeing all past hardships as forms of deficiency, hunger being an especially privileged instance. In the reform era, there is a double-entry bookkeeping air about this, a politics of restitution in which people are intent on "getting rich" (*facai zhifu*) and "enjoying themselves" (*zhaole*) as a way of making up for the poverty and misery many associate with their collective history. But as any doctor of Chinese medicine could tell you, excess and deficiency are not so easy to sort into discrete temporal cubbyholes. Following material lack with material gluttony is far from healthy, nor can dangerous tendencies toward unevenness be safely relegated to the past. Depletions develop even in people who have food: lack of appetite is a sure (and common) sign of pathology, as is eating without feeling full or maintaining weight. Many states of repletion, moreover, are accompanied by, and even attributable to, simultaneous states of depletion in an adjacent system. Depletion conditions can be treated with carefully judged forms of nourishment brought from places where there is plenty (the outside world of materia medica or the surplus energies from elsewhere in the body's systems of circulating qi), but careless use of bolstering (bu) treatments can produce dangerous repletions. When repletion appears, not only must it be dispelled but its causes must be understood so that local excesses do not recur.

Thus, when history is simplistically periodized and whole eras are denounced as pathology—when Maoist China is seen as a uniformity of material lack and political excess—the social and economic dynamics that link deficiency to excess become difficult to perceive. In Mo Yan's "I Can't Forget Eating" (Wangbuliao Chi), it is precisely these dynamics that the author seeks to illustrate by remembering the history of the Maoist period differently.

Mo Yan is a well-known fiction writer whose career has spanned the reform period. Author of the book on which the film *Red Sorghum* was based and of a more recent novel variously translated as *Liquorland* or *The Republic of Wine*, he has often written of food, drink, and cannibalism.[12] Judging from the sarcastic tone of the opening to "I Can't Forget Eating," his persistent use of bodily imagery and his focus on the cycles of eating and excreting has been called vulgar by some critics. Thus, the essay counters with a series of "scraps and shards" (*jiling gousuide poshi*) of description that elevate all sorts of unusual things—insects, extruded turnip leaves, tropical fish—to the status of food.

Insofar as they are food, however, these things participate in the problem of too much or too little. Satirizing a certain rage for elegance among other writers, for example, he begins with a paean to the potato: "You can go right on eating white-flour cakes if you wish, but personally I eat potatoes (*shanyaodan*). Potatoes are one of those beautiful foods that pleases common people and elite types alike, the emperor and Old Hundred Names [i.e., *baixing*, the Chinese people], both love to eat them. They're good roasted or boiled, fried or stewed—oh, potatoes, your name is Beauty! Oh, potatoes, how many insults have been heaped on you, as if you were a mere 'dirt bean' (*tudou*, a more common name for potatoes). Speech has two ends [high and low]—I think we should discard this word *tudou* and not use it for a while" (93). Thus, even language has its extremes, and elevating the humble potato—always less valued than rice and wheat in China, as the joke about the Russian communists reminds us—to a beautiful food for emperors is only part of Mo Yan's satiric task; he also sarcastically proposes aestheticizing the name of this food, reminding fellow writers of the social class implications of a speech that "has two ends."

The essay then proceeds to re-remember the famine of 1958–61 as Mo Yan (born in 1955) claims to have lived it. Beyond nostalgia, this account demonstrates again and again how quickly deficiency can turn to excess and vice versa. But first Mo Yan grounds his discussion on the fact of hunger, saying, "as long as I could remember, my stomach had rumbled with hunger. To say this may sound like I'm trying to be a crowd pleaser, adopting a pose that would 'blacken the name of socialism.' But it really was like this—hunger is neither beautiful nor brilliant, why lie about it? But does hunger have to be melodramatically vaunted as 'bitter hardship'? Apparently it does, at least this is what I've learned from you guys" (93).[13] Addressing his critics and fellow writers, Mo Yan here identifies a sentimentalizing tendency in the many works that have remembered the national famine and the Cultural Revolution as pure deficiency. (Recall, for example, the sermonizing tone on the subject of food in *Hibiscus Town*, a depiction that was quite consistent with the book's "blacken the name of socialism" pose.) Mo Yan's ironic critique is made more explicit a few paragraphs later, and throughout the essay, as he reflects on the wild plants, fish and insects people used to forage during the three hard years: "Many essays paint the three hard years as pitch black, lacking all enjoyment, but this isn't right. For children, at least, there were some pleasures. When you're hungry, every pleasure has to do with food. In those days, children were demons for foraging, we were like the legendary Shen Nong [founder of herbal medicine], we tasted a hundred grasses and a hundred bugs, making our own contribution to broadening the diet of the human race.[14] Children then had swollen bellies and legs like sticks, and their brains were enlarged with queer ideas. I was one of them" (93).

The very picture of a false excess due to an underlying deficiency! Yet as the essay develops its anecdotes on foraging unexpected pockets of pleasure and abundance emerge. Not only are there seasonal gluts of "fat locusts," "both nourishing and delicious," which "turned bright red when roasted," but there are delicious crabs and fish to be found in the puddles of a nearby bottomland. Insects especially are described in mouth-watering detail. In addition to crickets with "an unusual aroma," there are grub larvae that fly toward lantern light (hence they are popularly called "blind crashers"). "This kind of bug was plentiful," Mo Yan writes: "Strung on a twig or a blade of grass, they looked like ripe grapes. Every night after dark we would collect 'blind crashers'; you could fill a pocket full in one evening. Roasted, their flavor was entirely different from locusts and crickets. There were also bean worms, which would come out of hibernation after Mid-autumn Festival. The abdomen of this bug was full of a white leaf fat, solid protein!" (94). In the bean worm, then, the inedible leaves that during the famine had been found unsatisfactory as human food could be converted into an abdomen full of solid protein. The digestive processes of a lowly insect could mediate between nonfood and human hunger. The kind of short-lived bounty Mo Yan describes here never really slaked people's hunger, though it may have kept them alive. Still, the less concrete rewards of comradeship, ingenuity, and humor were also in good supply at times: "We formed little bands and roamed around the village looking for food. Just outside the village was a sort of bottomland, which stretched farther than we could see. In it were many small pools of murky water where dry grasses grew. That bottomland was our larder and our playground. There we gathered weeds and the roots of grasses, eating as much as we collected, singing as we went. We were part cow or goat, part balladeer; we were the singing farm animals of the time" (93–94).[15] If the essay had confined itself to these relatively innocent rambles, it might itself be

seen as sentimentalizing. But more disturbing events are also discussed at length. A shortage of coffins, for example, means that those
dead of starvation will be eaten by dogs; thus, a humiliation for humans becomes a feast for animals. Mo Yan writes: "The best thing to
do when someone died was to drag him out and let the dogs first eat
him and then shit him out. This was a golden age for dogs; once
they'd started to eat the dead, they all went mad, and whenever they
saw a living person they'd attack" (95). How quickly a golden age
turns into the repletion disease of madness! Cadres who have guns
avoid the meat of carrion-eating dogs, preferring to shoot wild game
such as rabbits. And everyone else, too weakened to run, fears for
their lives as the feral canines terrorize the village. Thus, there are no
readily available corrections for this dangerous state of deficiency for
humans and excess for dogs.

In another incident, an official effort to remedy the people's hunger by distributing carefully judged amounts of simple food quickly
goes sour.

> Probably it was at Spring Festival in 1961 when the government is-
> sued each person half a pound of soybean cake for the holidays.
> When we collected our bean cakes, the scene was truly one of joy and
> festivity. Some people stashed their cakes in their clothes and stuffed
> their mouths with them as they walked home. Our neighbor Papa
> Sun ate his whole family's allocation even before he reached his
> house. When he got home, he was surrounded by his wife and chil-
> dren crying and cursing him, wishing they could rip open his belly
> and take out the bean cakes. Apparently love among the starving is
> heavily discounted. Papa Sun lay on the ground, his face ashen, tears
> filling his eyes, not making a sound as he suffered the blows of his
> family. Papa Sun died that night. Having eaten too many bean cakes,
> he got thirsty and drank a whole jar of water; so he died from the
> swelling. By that time our stomach linings had become as thin as pa-
> per, even a little distention would burst them. When Papa Sun died,
> his wife and children shed not a tear. Even many years later when you
> bring it up Old Lady Sun has no hesitation talking about it. She
> blames her old man for eating all the food himself, says he lacked any
> flavor of humanity and dying was too good for him. (95)

Half a pound of soybean cake per person was more than these villagers had been able to eat for quite a while, and yet it could hardly be

deemed an excessive amount of food. In the hands of hungry people, however, a little food does not necessarily go a long way. Mo Yan reports that seventeen people died in the village from bellies swollen by those bean cakes. And if death is not an excessive price to pay for eating what is?

"I Can't Forget Eating" provides, then, a highly nuanced picture of hunger, one that is full of flavors and variations, not all of them pleasant. Mo Yan is also good at describing glut, as when he joins the army in the early 1970s.

> It was only after I joined the army that my stomach really got full; this would be beneath the dignity of some to mention, but personally I don't dare lack affection for the army. Just before I went to join up, a few retired soldiers in the village came to give me the benefit of their valuable experiences in the military. They told me, when you're eating noodles, only fill your first bowl half full because they cool very fast. When you've finished that bowl, go fill up another bowl and eat your fill. If you fill the first bowl right up, by the time you've finished it and gone back for more, there will only be broth left in the pot. If you're eating rice, never delay by chewing it, or all the soldiers from the south will laugh at you. When I got into the army, I discovered that those retirees were really full of it. . . . These [army] units were like heaven on earth. (96)

In other words, the complex strategies by means of which those accustomed to hunger manage to eat as much as possible when they have the chance become unnecessary when there is enough food to go around. As the narrator's father declares on visiting his son's unit, "What is communism? This is!"

But the alimentary plenty the narrator encounters in the army quickly turns to a form of excess. Once the unit commander realizes what a great capacity for food his new recruits have, he orders a pig feast, stating: "Soldiers who eat can get things done; those who don't eat can't. Besides, we have plenty of food. Tomorrow kill a pig for me so I can give these kids some greasy guts."

In the small "communist" system of the army, and where food is concerned, apparently no one needs to worry about remedying deficiencies or preventing the emergence of excess. The image of the greasy guts of the pig appeals particularly to prototypical Chinese ideas of surplus and its generative virtues. The New Year is the time

at which surplus is celebrated and redistributed through social networks. In parts of South China, pure white pork fat, deep-fried in a
batter shell, is served as a New Year's dish, signifying the surplus of
the pig and thus of the social body itself. Thus the communism of the
army finds itself on the leading edge of utopic progress toward a society in which surplus will be general, usable, and thus wholesome.

Mo Yan's narrative continues, however, suggesting once again that
long-standing lack tends to produce pathological excess.

> Sure enough, the next day a big fat pig was slaughtered and the
> meat was taken off in big handfuls, some of which was cooked in red
> sauce in a big wok. Wheat-flour buns white as snow were freshly
> steamed, and the pork was cooked to where it just melted in your
> mouth. Wasn't this good fortune? Didn't this just move us to grateful
> tears? Didn't this drive us mad with joy? Absolutely! At this meal, we
> new recruits danced with joy; we were drunk with eating pork. My
> stomach felt very full and heavy, as if I were carrying a litter of piglets
> in it. The meal was really a lifelong craving finally satisfied. For the
> first time in twenty years, I felt I could die content. But the after-
> effects were massive. I spent the whole night walking on the athletic
> field, every whiff of lard was like a little snake creeping up my gullet,
> and my throat and eyes felt like they'd been cut with a knife. The next
> day we still had big steamed buns and red-cooked pork, but we began
> to bashfully pick and choose the leaner meat, which would go down
> more easily. Our commander ribbed us: "We thought we had some
> real tough mountain guys here, but it appears they're only sissies
> after all." (96)

From the point of view of the hungry, no amount of food can be too
much, but it takes only a few hours for this narrator to realize for himself—though he might have known better after seeing Papa Sun die
from hogging government-issue soybean cakes—that excessive consumption has its costs.

Even insects and wild grasses can, with the passage of time, be
rewritten as instances of excessive consumption. A man who grew up
foraging in the bottomland with Mo Yan, and who as a child distinguished himself in his willingness to lick spilled gruel from the bare
ground, has gotten rich from insects: "That boy is now our village's
richest man. He got rich from insects. He raises scorpions, cicadas,
and bean worms, selling them at high prices to big restaurants and

official guest houses. He saw clearly that the mouths of people with money and power would become more and more picky and their appetites more and more cagey. They would refuse big fish and real meat, preferring like adorable little birds to pick at 'strange magic and ancient sages.' His vision turned out to be solid gold. He says the next step is to train the upper ranks to eat boll weevils" (93). The boll weevil, bane of the existence of cotton growers everywhere, is a well-known pest in the Shandong countryside where Mo Yan grew up. Cotton is often planted after the first wheat harvest on part of the wheat land, along with corn and peanuts. The women of cotton-growing households almost daily walk the rows of plants with a heavy tank of insecticide strapped to their backs, operating a hand pump to spray the cotton bolls as they develop. Men do not usually contribute to textile-related agricultural production, and women consider chronic back pain to be one of the common problems resulting from their productive and reproductive lives. Even with all the spraying, it is often necessary to pick boll weevils off the cotton by hand. This is a bug, in other words, that requires people to eat much bitterness (chiku) and contributes actively to the support of a strongly gendered social order. What an amusing vision it is, then, to imagine "people with money and power" turning boll weevils into high-priced exotic food commodities! What effects would such an unlikely turn of events have on the excesses and deficiencies of rural everyday life? The idea that pathological excess could be turned to the purpose of remedying deficiency is unfortunately only a satisfying joke for Mo Yan; he offers no suggestion that anyone has yet found a way to do this in real societies.

Mo Yan makes his own distaste for the cagey and picky appetites of the rich clear in the concluding paragraph of his essay, where he summarizes problems of hunger and enjoyment, starvation and gluttony. Writing in the midst of the consumer frenzy that has gripped China especially since the early 1990s, he denounces the extremes of excessive consumption along with the deficiencies of recent famine: "Having now lived a few more decades and become a so-called writer, I have been at banquets where locusts, crickets, bean worms and other insects were served. I have once again eaten [as delicacies] the foul-tasting weeds and grasses we hated in the hard years, while everyone at these banquets ignored the chicken, duck, pork, and fish that also filled the table. And that rich guy in the village has become an expert

at raising insects. No wonder the sages said that poles are interconnected: both extreme hunger and extreme gluttony eat grass, wood,
insects, and minnows; both the North Pole and the South Pole are
frozen wastelands" (96). A Chinese doctor could not have put it more
succinctly. Because poles are interconnected, there are many qualitative possibilities along the space between them and no absolute division between them; as we shall see below, "major excesses have states
of shortage; advanced deficiencies have times of overabundance." [16] At
the same time, the extreme points of any polarity are, to say the least,
uninhabitable.

This essay by Mo Yan, with its ironic "scraps and shards" of memories, comments on consumption as an issue that is central to the
ethical, political, and cultural life of contemporary China. While
scrupulously avoiding the explicitly political language of Lu Wenfu's
narrator in *The Gourmet*, the essayist of "I Can't Forget Eating" nevertheless makes no secret of his moral rejection of the excessive indulgences of the nouveau riche. He implies that some of the unthinking
greed that is visible everywhere in China's booming economy may be
implicitly legitimated by a simplistic idea of the past: only if the
people periodize and displace hunger and shortage, placing these
deficiencies firmly in the past of a discredited state socialism, can they
indulge in today's voracious consumption with a clean conscience and
a strong stomach. But it is precisely this periodization that doesn't
work, historically or personally. Mo Yan's evocative writing about experiences that were, after all, shared by many of his generation, works
to produce a common sense of the historical and social field—and the
personal habitus—that must now be negotiated. Even famine had
its delightful flavors, and people sometimes tasted triumph even in its
depths; hidden within gluttony, however, there are deathly states of
a deeper depletion.

Systemic Depletions, Local Repletions

Discourses and practices of Chinese medicine are particularly rich in
insights about such paradoxical states. The pleasures and dangers of
ever-shifting relationships between excess and deficiency are figured
in a medical language of depletion (*xu*) and repletion (*shi*), which is
constantly deployed in the everyday work of clinics. Although depletion and repletion have many technical ramifications, the basic ideas

and experiences these terms denote are also well understood by non-specialists. Thus, a practice like Chinese traditional medicine can reveal some features of local bodies, and thus—as I argued in chapters 1 and 2—local politics.

In Chinese medicine, the relationship between excess and deficiency is an abstraction, or a different realization, of the same poignant dyad that inhabits the world of eating: too little is hunger, and too much is indigestion. Or, in the case of banquet drinking, which I will take up below, too little toasting is ungenerous but too much drinking is ridiculous. *Hibiscus Town* argues that a scarcity (of food) should not coexist with an overabundance (of ideological language), and "I Can't Forget Eating" shows how quickly pathological deficiency can turn into pathological excess. Whatever the domain of material life, these sources suggest, the logic of excess and deficiency can accommodate and clarify a wide range of experiences. Further, because this dyad is of special concern in Chinese medicine, one can read the social from a foothold in medical practice. Rather than understanding medicine as a figure that *expresses* the form of a broader contextualizing society or social structure as *analogous* to the biological body—medicine and society are not separate entities like text and context or map and territory—what I seek is a certain level at which Chinese medicine shares forms of habitus and common sense with other, parallel yet overlapping domains of the social, in this case eating and writing about eating.

Medicine, like other social practices in the 1980s and 1990s, is infused with popular anxieties in an everyday life that has been importantly transformed since the death of Mao. So is eating. But, unlike some of the writers I have presented here, virtuosos of traditional medicine cannot simply stand to one side and make ironic observations about the history of repletions and depletions; as medical practitioners, they must intervene. Depletion states must be brought back to active wholesome fullness, and stagnating repletions must be both drained and prevented from recurring. Fatalism, detachment, and mea culpa hand-wringing are not allowed. In any comparison, then, between the economies of food distribution in China or the world and the dynamics of substance and energy circulation in ailing bodies, Chinese medicine has a special edge: it must test its analysis of systematic inequities with therapy, and it must keep doing so until a substantial and lasting improvement has been wrought. Lurking within the technical language and accumulated wisdom of the field are insights about the techniques by means of which chronic pathologies of uneven distribution might be rectified.

As was evident in the case of amnesia discussed in chapter 1, Chinese medicine is particularly good at identifying areas of deficiency, which it figures as functional debility or depletion. Diagnosis traces depletions to their systematic roots, and therapy intervenes to nourish these roots and gradually eliminate the state of depletion. In the case of amnesia, the depletion in question was "simultaneous depletion of Heart and Spleen Systems, with the seat of knowledge muddled, and the vital spirit of the heart-mind unstable." By building Spleen function and supplementing qi, which would in turn bolster Heart System function and regulate the qi-blood relationship, the doctor in this case worked on two roots at once. But these two sites are interacting systems governing various whole body functions; as Spleen function improves and qi circulation strengthens, the Heart System (of which "the seat of knowledge" is an aspect) begins to return to healthful activity as well.

A somewhat more problematic (both technically and philosophically) parallel interest of Chinese medicine is states of repletion; this term can refer to excessive function, but it is more commonly descriptive of local accumulations of substance. Depletions quickly ramify throughout the whole system; states of repletion, in contrast, tend to be static and localized, leading to the stagnation and corruption of crucial substances that should, by their nature, circulate. An edema of the abdominal region, for example, would first be explained with reference to the Spleen System. But since it is the function of this visceral system to move fluids and other substances through the body (sending clear fluids upward and turbid substances downward) it stands to reason that most Spleen "repletions" would be interpretable as an underlying depletion of Spleen *function,* probably along with several other interacting visceral systems.

Repletion and depletion form one of the four key sets of contrastive terms used in the diagnostic method called the eight rubrics (the others are Hot-Cold, Inner-Outer, and Yin-Yang). Most clinicians use some version of eight-rubrics categories to classify reported and elicited symptoms and develop a picture of the general tendency of the disease process.[17] Table 1 suggests the range of symptoms that can be thought of in these terms; it also indicates the secondary

Table 1 Symptoms Resulting from Depletion or Repletion

Type/Site	Depletion	Repletion
Qi	*Lung qi depletion:* short and hard breathing, spontaneous perspiration, spiritless speech. *Middle jiao depletion:* weak and cold extremities, intermittent abdominal swelling, aching eased by hand pressure, no appetite, diarrhea. *Source qi depletion:* depletion yang floating upward; cheeks splotchy red-and-white, and tender; ringing in ears and deafness; dizziness and palpitations; hand tremors; irregular breathing.	*Lung qi repletion:* stuffy chest, dizziness, blurry vision, excessive mucus, difficult breathing when reclining. *Stomach qi repletion:* abdominal fullness, heartburn and upset stomach, foul-smelling eructations, sour taste when swallowing, nausea, vomiting. *Intestinal qi repletion:* lower abdomen distended, umbilical area pain, constipation or excessive urination (urine reddish or clear), hectic fever and delirium. *Liver qi repletion:* headache and dizziness.
Blood	*Blood depletion:* Lips pale, face white, agitation and instability, weak nerves, depleted fluids, night fevers and sweats, muscular twitching and cramps, limb convulsions in extreme cases.	*Stasis in muscles and tendons:* local swelling and pain. *Stasis in circulation tracts:* body aches and clenched muscles. *Stasis in upper jiao:* pain on rotating trunk. *Stasis in middle jiao:* acute abdominal pain. *Stasis in lower jiao:* distension and acute pain in lower abdomen. In all these blood stasis conditions, location of pain unstable, black stools.
Five Visceral Systems	*Heart depletion:* tendency toward melancholy. *Liver depletion:* blurry and reduced vision, contracting testicles, cramps, anxiety. *Spleen depletion:* reduced use of extremities, poor digestion, full abdomen, sorrow and worry. *Lung depletion:* short breath, shallow breathing, lusterless hair and skin. *Kidney depletion:* dizziness and blurry vision, lower back pain, constipation, irregular urination or dysuria, nocturnal emission, early morning diarrhea.	*Heart repletion:* personality abnormalities, hysterical laughter. *Liver repletion:* aching sides, anger. *Spleen repletion:* abdominal fullness and distension, constipation, edemas. *Lung repletion:* cough, difficulty breathing. *Kidney repletion:* blockage of lower jiao, aching or distension.

categories—qi, Blood, and the Five Visceral Systems—that must be considered in order to make clinical sense of an otherwise overgeneralizing dualism. Thus, depletion and repletion are expressed differently in different visceral systems of function and in relation to the activities of Blood and qi: a Blood depletion may produce "agitation and instability," while a depletion in the Heart System results in a "tendency toward melancholy." Moreover, it might take a careful clinical analysis to distinguish between the agitation and instability of Blood depletion and the "personality abnormalities" or "hysterical laughter" of Heart System repletion.

Although the categories of depletion and repletion are logically symmetrical (and appear especially so when their affiliated symptoms are arranged in a table like the one I have translated here), in practice depletion states are much more commonly found. In fact, textbooks argue that a great many repletion symptoms are traceable to an underlying state of depletion. Deng Tietao, for example, in a practical guide to diagnosis, quotes an unnamed classical source to advise that "major excesses have states of shortage; advanced deficiencies have times of overabundance." He urges clinicians to "penetrate through" the symptomatic manifestations of the illness in order to draw out the "true character of the disease changes."[18] The symptoms most often classified as repletion are swollen and aching abdomen and a strung pulse. (This is both stated in the textbooks and consistent with my observations in Chinese medical clinics.) When this can be treated as stemming from a state of depletion, the image is one of bodies enlarged, overstressed, and laboring under a burden of too much matter because one or more of their five visceral systems has become too weakened (its function too depleted) to smoothly process all the stuff of bodily life. To put it in more immediately recognizable experiential terms, what looks like fat—so positively valued in traditional Chinese folklore—may in fact be unhealthy bloating. In a slightly less common but still plausible situation, hysterical behavior indicating Heart repletion might result from a Kidney depletion in which the watery Kidney system has failed to operate its cooling and moderating influence on Heart Fire.[19] The clinical task is to discern the root of the illness process; until the underlying functional inadequacy has been identified, there will be no telling the difference between true and false symptoms.

Excess is more often found outside bodies than in them. Excessive heat, wind, or humidity, especially at unseasonable times, can easily act as a pathogen for people who are already suffering some kind of debility.[20] (And most Chinese medical doctors can identify some tendency toward depletion or—more rarely—repletion in even the most healthy feeling person. A perfect harmony of natural forces is rare indeed.)

I, for example, have been told since the early 1980s, when I first got involved in Chinese medicine, that I have a tendency toward depletion of Spleen System function. "Be careful," my Guangzhou friends would say, "being so far from home, in this tropical climate, and longing for your family, you may be harming your Spleen." Knowing the rule of thumb that "the Spleen hates damp" and recalling that both the Spleen System and the emotion of "thought/longing" (si) belong to the five-phases category of Earth, this made sense even as it amused me that a tendency toward excessive thought should be a potential pathogen. I enjoyed thinking of Spleen depletion as an occupational hazard for academics. After decades of indomitable health (periods of homesickness aside), in 1998 an unusually long spell of "summer heat" (shu) in muggy North Carolina got to me, producing some of the symptoms listed in table 1 for Spleen depletion. Although I could attribute my discomforts to other causes (normal aging, stress, carpal tunnel syndrome, and so on), I quickly grew to enjoy blaming the awful weather for my aches and pains; it was so delightfully externalizing and free of guilt! Moreover, a course of acupuncture focusing on bolstering the Spleen System and the muscles (for which Spleen functions provide nourishment), as well as controlling Heart Fire by bolstering Kidney Water, quickly began to provide significant relief.

Like states of the weather, emotions can be pathogenic. Some are more dangerous than others—anger, for example, which harms the Liver System if it is allowed to get out of control. Patients are often warned, in fact, not to get angry. Once, after spending some days in a gynecology clinic, I asked the doctor why he so often told his middle-aged female patients to avoid getting angry; how could they control these feelings anyway? I wondered. He explained that, in the particular cases concerned, anger would only make their symptoms worse and delay their return to good health. Yes, anger is hard to control, he admitted, and he added that middle-aged women have a lot to be angry about, what with demanding husbands, parents, and children and jobs to worry about, too. But further damaging their health by succumbing to anger was not going to make their situation any better.

Contemporary Chinese medical textbooks love to decry excesses of many kinds. Too much rich food and drink, overwork, and sexual overindulgence are all bad. (All of these sins against good health, incidentally, are much more associated in practice with the reform period than with full-scale state socialism.) By far my favorite form of pathological excess, however, is that of the emotions, especially the classic Chinese medical maxim that "too much joy harms the Heart." Some of the reasons why this is so are discussed in a 1989 textbook of "theoretical foundations."

> Because emotional factors can make people ill, Chinese medicine strongly emphasizes conserving good health through the principles of "detachment and nondesiring" and "inwardness of spirit." As the *Plain Questions, juan* 1:1, says, "It is from calm, indifference, emptiness, and nondesiring that true qi arises; if the spirit is harbored (*bao*) inside, whence can illness arise? When the will is at rest and wishes little, when the heart is at peace and fears nothing, when the body labors but does not tire, then qi flows smoothly from these [states], each part follows its desires and the whole gets everything it seeks. Thus it is that [the wise and healthy person, the lord] is able to savor his food, shoulder his responsibilities, and take pleasure in his passions; high and low do not envy each other, so the people of his domain are called simple and honest (*pu*). Compulsive desires cannot engage his gaze, and the evils all around him (*fu xie*) cannot afflict his heart. Thus it is that he can live to be one hundred years old and nothing he does can weaken him.[21]

In a typical juxtaposition of up-to-date scientistic phrasing ("emotional factors" and the need to place ancient philosophic terms in quotes) with the epigrammatic style of Chinese medicine's first classic (compiled in the first century C.E.), this passage conflates arts of personal cultivation, classic Confucian concerns with rulership, and modern psychology. The promised payoff is immensely attractive: if we cultivate detachment and refuse to be slaves to our emotions, only then can we savor our food, shoulder our responsibilities, and take pleasure in our passions. This is the explicit or implicit promise Chinese medical doctors make when they advise "don't get angry" or "don't worry."

Although in my observations of clinics I have seldom seen an illness that was primarily explained as caused by excessive joy, or any other emotion, many such cases are published; nowadays they are often collected in anthologies as instances of Chinese medicine treating psychological disorders.[22] But even in clinics where feelings are not easily spoken of between patients and doctors the heights and depths, the sudden shifts and settled moods, of emotional life are seldom forgotten. Precisely because the "seven emotions" can be powerful pathogens, attacking particular physiological systems in particular ways, doctors are able to discern the operations of strong feeling in the pulse, in the changes in color and surface quality of the tongue, and in the patterns of symptoms reported by their patients. And they build the resulting perception of the whole physiological situation, including the threat of the powerful pathogens of anger, worry, or even joy, into their herbal prescriptions or acupuncture strategies, seeking to strengthen the person's most vulnerable systems against the assaults and frustrations of an imperfect everyday life.[23]

Medicine's superior ability to clarify the dynamics of excess and deficiency in bodies and their environments relates to the experiential elements of the clinical work of Chinese medicine discussed in chapter 1. Aiming at a "political phenomenology" that could consider together pleasure and efficacy or experiences and powers, I argued there that Chinese technologies of oral consumption, including both food and medicine, could be used to exert some control in the world. Eating well and dosing irregularities with medical flavors could draw on collective experience to produce an individual experience of heightened efficacy for those whose social powers are on the wane. But as critical writers Gu Hua, Lu Wenfu, and Mo Yan have suggested, eating well is no simple task. The flavorful temporal formation embodied in the practice of medicinal meals is one that must be alert to the pathologies of excess and deficiency. How is one to know when a depletion is sapping one's powers? How do we recognize a pathological state of repletion? Medically, these discriminations are not so hard to make. Socially, there may be more confusion.

Social Repletion?

Mo Yan in *The Republic of Wine* argues as much. Near the beginning of this 1992 novel he describes a disturbing banquet held in Liquorland, the provincial town where detective Ding Gou'er has gone to investigate allegations that local leaders are raising human babies to be roasted and served at banquets. Faced with Diamond Jin, the probable ringleader of this horrific scheme, Ding Gou'er is awed by Jin's capacity for liquor.

> He picked up a cup of liquor and drank it down, noiselessly and without spilling a drop; his simple yet elegant style showed that he was no ordinary drinker. His pace quickened with each succeeding cup, but with no effect on accuracy or results—cadenced and rhythmic. He held out the last of the thirty cups and described an arc, like a bow moving across violin strings; the soft, elegant strains of a violin swirled in the air of the dining hall and flowed through Ding Gou'er's veins. His caution began to crumble, as warm feelings toward Diamond Jin surfaced slowly, like water grasses budding atop a stream during a spring thaw. He watched Diamond Jin bring the last cup of liquor to his lips and saw a look of melancholy flash in the man's bright black eyes; he was transformed into a good and generous man, one who emanated an aura of sentimentality, lyrical and beautiful. The strains of the violin were long and drawn-out, a light autumn breeze rustled fallen golden leaves, a small white blossom appeared in front of a grave marker; Ding Gou'er's eyes became moist, gazing at the cup as if it were a stream of water bubbling up past a rock and emptying into a deep green lake. There was love in his heart for this man.[24] (51–52)

Moments later, Ding Gou'er is offered "a large round gilded platter in which sat a golden, incredibly fragrant little boy" (52).

This amazing—and for me experientially correct—description of banquet drunkenness takes us back to the problem of aesthetics discussed in chapter 2. There we saw that Lu Wenfu, after clarifying the moral dilemmas of excessive consumption in an economy of systematic deficiencies and local excesses, turned to beauty—beautiful writing, beautiful food—as his only answer to the social contradictions narrated in his story. In *The Republic of Wine*, Diamond Jin is above all an elegant drinker, and Ding Gou'er's perception of him, made more susceptible to sentiment by wine, allows the beauty of Jin's actions to slide into the domain of ethics. By virtue of being a beautiful banqueter, he becomes "a good and generous man" worthy of uncritical love. The criminal nature of this love object immediately surfaces, however, when the "incredibly fragrant" evidence of the town's sideline industry is ceremoniously presented to the special investigator. And the lovely feelings that Diamond Jin and his liquor had stimulated must suddenly be transformed back into suspicion.

Mo Yan's hallucinatory novel continues, calling all beauties and crimes into question; the actual humanity of the roasted "baby" becomes questionable along with the human intentions and critical capacities of all the narrators and characters who appear. His book amounts to an exploration of the possibility of truth, goodness, or beauty in Liquorland, the terrain of excess.[25] Liquor itself, as the distilled essence of agricultural products that would otherwise be food, is both a figure for and a producer of excesses. Truth, goodness, and beauty are terms that were frequently used by Chairman Mao, and Mo Yan is nothing if not post-Maoist in his continuing interest in the problems they present; in this book, however, he satirizes Ding Gou'er the (sometime) idealist and makes Ding's concern with the truth appear weak, ridiculous, and deluded. Further, Ding's susceptibility to beauty—especially beautiful food and wine—continually proves to be his downfall. His ethics are unable to withstand the onslaught of the pleasure seeking he encounters among almost all the residents of Liquorland, including, eventually, himself.

Ultimately, Mo Yan takes no position on the criminal excesses he describes (or hallucinates) in Liquorland. In the banquet scene noted above, he demonstrates his understanding of some of the reasons why it is difficult to do so. We are all, after all, under the influence. As drinkers and eaters, it is not easy to decide for ourselves where the line between enough and too much really lies, especially when we attempt to calculate the social ramifications of consumption and especially when so many banquets are on offer.

This is certainly the case in contemporary China. In the 1980s, banqueting—in restaurants, conference centers, rural courtyards, and village and township meeting rooms—became a central technique for building and maintaining social relationships under the new entrepreneurial order. A great many newspaper articles have appeared since the mid-1980s to both document and denounce the

corrupt tendencies exemplified by subsidized formal meals in business and government settings. A 1995 newspaper article noted by
Andrew Kipnis, for example, estimated that cadre spending on banquets amounted to twelve billion U.S. dollars annually. This expenditure is generally seen as wasteful at best and usually as leading to private enrichment at the expense of publicly responsible progress.
(Thus, the criticism can be directed against business and government
at once, especially since these domains are much less oppositional
than they once were.) Kipnis also notes, however, that periodic central
government directives intended to limit or ban official banqueting
and numerous critical editorials in state media organs had almost no
effect on the local practices of food and liquor exchange he observed
in early 1990s Shandong. Mayfair Yang has argued that exchange
practices like those involved in banquets tend to bypass government
economic priorities and can build networks that work outside the
"proper channels" through which party leaders think things should
be done.[26] This alone might account for the expansion of the practice
in the reform period. But banquets are not just a strategic site where
deals get made; although they are in a sense an acquired taste, they
can also be a source of pleasure that might be rather hard to forego.
Here I will show that some of the enjoyment involved in ritual eating
on special occasions derives precisely from the process in which
eaters negotiate social pathways through an asymmetrical field; excess at the table is accompanied by deficiencies that are lived by the
parties to this game. Banquets may not collapse all inequalities, but
they do work to alter the dispositions of the diverse resources brought
by eaters to the table.

Local customs of banqueting vary quite a lot, but they share some
principles of propriety. In what amounts to a ritual space, guest lists,
menus, seating hierarchies, and the order of courses and toasts all signify. Like other rituals, this shared eating is both constrained by many
"traditional" (but inarticulate) expectations and traversed by the em-
powering possibility that anything can happen and the results may be
irremediable. Almost always facilitated by strong drink, these complex encounters manage to be both high-stakes social games and
enjoyable occasions for the cultivation of fellow feeling. Everyone is
required to keep the work of maintaining and revising the pertinent
hierarchies in mind, but they are also expected to enjoy themselves
and—above all—feel affection for their dinner companions (this is

the *ganqing,* or "sentiment," so richly explored by Kipnis). This impossible-sounding balancing act can become almost second nature to habitual banqueters, but it takes some time and practice to learn, partly because to banquet well requires something beyond good intentions, a political sense, and a strong stomach. It requires a disposition for social relations (the famous Chinese skill of "doing guanxi") that is thoroughly embodied. Let me illustrate with some of my own experiences.

In 1987, I returned to China to begin field research in rural Shandong.[27] I had last been in China in 1984, and though I had attended my share of banquets during the early 1980s everything was different when I went back. Going as a professor to a nonacademic environment hundreds of miles north of my original fieldwork home in Guangzhou, I was required to both assert my status and negotiate the necessary connections in a political climate in which the role of banqueting had been rapidly expanding. In other words, I could not escape banqueting precisely because I had to bring my contribution (research fees as well as possible connections to the wealthy and modern United States) to the table while trying to exact support for my research from local leaders: their contribution to the relationship was information and relationships with the doctors and patients I wanted to interview. I had (more or less) learned to cope with one form of banqueting at a medical college in Guangzhou, but this newer Shandong style was less comfortable for me. First of all, it was male dominated. The men with whom I frequently found myself eating and drinking were diverse collections of county, township, and village cadres who occupied several ranks and represented networks of power and influence I didn't understand. Without the shared professional domain of Chinese medicine that had made talk in Guangzhou so rewarding, conversation was often quite difficult. To me, the table talk seemed to be an incomprehensible (and pointless) series of boasts, teases, and challenges. I tended to remain tense and watchful throughout these meals, fearing that I would make a fool of myself and wishing there were a potted plant nearby into which I could pour my white liquor.

Eventually I learned some of the rules and managed to invent a compromise in which I made toasts to senior people often and to each of my table mates at least once. I learned to fear white liquor a little less and also learned to avoid the heaviest drinking obligations by claiming the weakness of my gender. Women are not supposed to be as practiced at drinking as men, and I was happy to hide behind that presumption. There were a few female cadres who had gained a reputation as drinkers; they apparently had earned the ungrudging respect and cooperation of male colleagues partly through their capacity to drink with the men. Unfortunately, I didn't feel physically able to follow their example. As I banqueted on, my tolerance for the standard jokes (sexist and classist as they often were) and my understanding of the usual little contests grew, but it was a long time before behaving properly at banquets felt at all natural to me. I still don't consider myself to be very good at it.

In this, I am like most other Americans who have feasted socially in reform China. The central problem often seems to be the 120 to 150 proof *baijiu*, or "white liquor," around which so much polite activity focuses. Baijiu is central to the basic task of banqueting: to avoid getting drunk while acknowledging others by toasting as well as responding to the toasts of others. Given that the words of the most common toast, *gan bei*, or "empty the glass," urge amounts of consumption beyond the polite sip, and that people constantly examine and comment on the amount of liquid in each other's glasses, remaining in command of one's faculties is a strategic challenge. Those who are good at it are praised for being able to hold their liquor; they can do guanxi through numerous courses of food without collapsing or becoming rowdy. (I recall a six-table banquet in Guangzhou where a Korean doctor present became very excited, walking around and demanding that everyone sing with him. He was quickly hustled off to his room.) As long as civil talk is maintained, the amount of alcohol consumed is not thought of as excessive. But it is polite, and strategic, to act as if even one glass might be too much for you. Those who admit to having a large capacity for liquor (*jiuliang da*) will surely be pushed to their limit with competitive toasting. But if they remain functional they will be admired.

For me, there was a turning point in my attitude toward banqueting. What I had long seen as an excessive demand on my time and a waste of government money suddenly began to look like an essential enjoyment. During a visit to Shandong in the early 1990s, after spending several summers in the area, I was invited to a small banquet concocted more or less in my honor by two cadres in the county health department. I dreaded this occasion because I knew

who would be there: the two functionaries hosting the meal, whom I
didn't know very well and who had arranged the occasion as a duty; a
semiretired doctor of Western medicine who had often been assigned
to accompany me on my visits to patients and doctors and whose company I had never enjoyed; the medical director of the local hospital of
Chinese medicine, an interesting person whose abrupt speaking style
and local dialect nevertheless made him hard for me to talk to; the associate director of the county Foreign Affairs Office, whom I liked
very much; and the middle-ranked cadre from the foreign affairs
office who always looked after me, an ex-soldier whose chief qualifi-
cation for his job was his capacity to drink a lot at banquets. All were
men, and almost all had given me reasons to avoid their company in
some previous context.

We met in a private room at one of the town's larger restaurants. We
took our seats after the usual jockeying—"oh no, I wouldn't presume
to sit there, please, you take this [higher] seat"— and began to nibble
on the cold dishes while making small talk. This occasion probably
wasn't the most consequential banquet any of them had been to that
week; it did not, for example, include the local exotic specialty of deep-
fried scorpions, and there was a particularly jocular and casual quality to the chat. Moreover, it appeared that my hospital director acquaintance was not a usual member of this group and perhaps not
even very accustomed to official banqueting (though he later hosted
a few small and jolly meals for me in a room attached to the hospital
kitchen). Certainly, he was the least influential person present, and his
daily work consisted in trying to keep a relatively devalued health institution afloat with almost no help from the very department that was
hosting this banquet. His awkwardness was palpable, and at the beginning of our meal everyone made an effort to put him at ease, calling him by some rather old-fashioned honorifics, for example, but
with a smile, acknowledging that these forms of address were not
quite usual or appropriate. As the meal progressed and one fragrant,
colorful hot dish followed another, a minialliance developed. Those of
us interested in clinical medicine and research (the hospital director,
the doctor of Western medicine, and me) began to talk about things
we found interesting: recent disease patterns in the county, unusual
patients seen in clinics, and strategies for providing health care to
farm women.

This sort of conversation was not suitable for a banquet, as we well knew, and the administrators present began to tease us about our seriousness. We three, emboldened by our brief collusion, teased them back about their paper-shuffling working lives. This line of conversation began to separate the Foreign Affairs Office personnel from the Health Department men, who did do some desultory medical work from time to time. Moreover, much of this jockeying for conversational position was accomplished through tongue-in-cheek toasts directed by one drinker to another or to a category of one's fellow drinkers. It was thus easy to tell who was on which "side" at any given moment, even as we (I?) became too inebriated to care a great deal.

Eventually, the cadres hit upon the strategy of comparing Chinese and Western medicine in order to break the solidarity of the medical faction. It worked. Faced with an attack on his specialty, my hospital director friend found himself dragging out all the old jokes about how clumsy, narrow, and expensive Western medicine is compared to China's nuanced indigenous treasure of traditional medicine. Of course, the senior doctor of Western medicine couldn't take this lying down; he jokingly countered with a little science and a little alarmist rumor. Even I managed to get in a (hackneyed but sincere) word or two in support of the indigenous "treasure house" of Chinese medicine. I most clearly remember violating the (more or less proper) order of toasts to direct a special one to the hospital director, expressing (more by gesture than in words) my sense of comradeship with him as someone who knew the value of traditional medicine. He discerned my intentions, and everyone else at the table mustered a kindly chuckle as well. For the space of time we were together, this embattled administrator of a resource-poor unit had gained the support of the wealthy, foreign guest of honor. His deficiencies had become a valued asset in the Health Department's efforts to cultivate a good relationship with me.

By the end of the evening, I had drunk more liquor than ever before. I felt quite lucid, though not entirely in command of all my limbs, and I loved these men. I especially loved the hospital director. But I also loved everyone else for being good allies and opponents, for drawing me into the circle of men, for respecting me and the hospital director enough to challenge our commitments to Chinese medicine, and for simply being there with us as this game was played. When I saw some of them in subsequent days and years, the memory of that evening was still with us. We did not necessarily have more interests, ideas, or abilities in common than before, but we were linked by something more substantive, a pleasantly shared moment in our lives. This comradeship (ganqing) existed (and for some of us still exists, I think) as a real foundation for continued negotiations that would match our respective offerings and requirements (excesses and deficiencies) in working relationships.

This sense of commonality, inclusion, and affection is what is supposed to emerge at Chinese banquets. There is a voluminous literature on guanxi work in modern China that often presents the "networking" accomplished through banqueting as cynically instrumental; the relationships that eaters and toasters forge and deepen are in such analyses reduced to the means by which (more or less selfish) utilitarian ends will be achieved. Andrew Kipnis, in his study of rural guanxi production in the same area, has thoughtfully critiqued the utilitarian reading of the Chinese art of social relationships. He not only emphasizes the ceremonial production of sentiment (ganqing), but his study demonstrates that these ritual practices do more than reflect existing hierarchies. They produce social subjects: "subjects constructed in magnetic fields of human feeling are pulled by the remembrance of specific, past *ganqing* exchanges." [28]

Of course, I cannot be sure that my experience was anything like that enjoyed by Chinese banqueters. Perhaps my wine and talk-induced feelings of affection are unlike the ganqing that develops at "real," thoroughly "Chinese" banquets. Still, after that evening I felt differently about banqueting. I could understand why many different kinds of people enjoy this sort of social labor; why some people do the unpaid work of (for example) matchmaking just because they love wedding banquets, suffused as they are with local kinship politics; and why cadres in retirement often say they miss banqueting more than any other part of their working lives. [29] The enjoyment of occasions like this is partly due to the special occasion food and it is certainly assisted by the drinking, but a capacity to enjoy banquets really stands or falls on an ability and willingness to appreciate and engage with one's fellow eaters.

As Kipnis has pointed out, in discussing a fundamental doubleness at the heart of the institution of banqueting, "toasting materialize[s] respect, while drinking deconstruct[s] the boundaries that distinguish . . . guests from hosts, thus allowing *ganqing* to flow. [30] One must raise one's glass to show respect for one's companions, and one must actually drink the liquor to find carnal, emotional, and spiritual commonality with them. The technique is a social gesture combined with a bodily practice of consumption, but the stakes are political since they both dissolve and revise hierarchies of power and influence. And these double, or multiple, tasks are accomplished simultaneously in a practice of eating and drinking that is at its best when experienced as spontaneous, needing no theories and no rulebook. Even to narrate a feast, as I have done, is to misrepresent its lived immediacy, fascination, and anxious consequentiality.

The banquet I have described would rest in my memory as an entirely positive recollection if it weren't for Mo Yan's pressing reminder that certain necessary ethical discriminations are hard to make while we are eating and drinking. Perhaps all we were doing that evening was reproducing a structure of elite privilege. Perhaps my dining partners were luring me into a corrupt system of unequal distribution and unjust appropriation. Or perhaps I was similarly corrupting them or at least wasting their time. I cannot decide because I no longer stand at a distance from the banquet itself. Banquets are precisely about transcending the interests and judgments that divide eaters from each other. By eating and drinking, I had joined the club.

The experience of banqueting described here is a formation of eating and social relations particularly characteristic of the reform era. These round tables in small air-conditioned rooms that are often noisy and smoke filled far into the night are a new hybrid space, neither public nor private, neither collective nor individual. They are criss-crossed with a fluid but pervasive sense of hierarchy and charged with potentials for political maneuvering, all inseparable from the material qualities of the food, and especially the drink, consumed there. Careers are advanced, and deals are made (though the details are generally worked out later); newcomers are acknowledged and seniors are placated; insider information is exchanged, and new plans are hinted at; subtle insults and oversights do not go unnoticed; and (when things work as they should) everyone goes away a little changed. This is not quite the kind of state-driven, ideologically articulated politics that filled everyday life for ordinary Chinese before the 1980s, nor is it simply the politics of manipulative network building required by a new business class. Rather, banqueting is a ritual practice in which people are repositioned (and thus remade) even as their shared and idiosyncratic perceptions of the field of play are revised. New inequalities are produced at these tables even as old ones are undermined. Can one speak of gustatory-political pleasures or, perhaps, a carnal-hierarchical romance?[31]

Drawing the Line

Is the well-lubricated love of banquets—love of the play of relationships, love of one's playmates—just another form of immoral excess? How would anyone know when these pleasures cross the line into social pathology? Who can be relied upon to tell us, considering that no one is outside the reach of consumption and its uneven distributions? As Derrida points out in the epigraph that opens this chapter (and as Mo Yan echoes in the amoral glossolalia that ends *The Republic of Wine*), "it is and tastes good to eat, and . . . there is no other definition of the good" ([1989] 1991:115). Well, there are in fact other definitions—Christian, Marxist, and humanist—but all of these appeal to transcendent values and ideologically delimited essences. The love and judgment of God authorizes a Christian conscience, while the notion of man as producer informs the utopic visions of most of the world's Marxisms. At the same time, the quasi-sacred individual recognized by Euro-American common sense underpins both liberal ethics and liberatory politics. Anthropology, however, has made it more difficult to universalize the definitions of gods and humans that have anchored our ethics and our politics, and the poststructuralist critique of metanarratives has withdrawn any sense of natural priority for the universal values on which we have attempted to found our morality. As attention has turned back to history, with its play of interests, antagonisms, and political blocs, theoretically engaged scholarship has found it increasingly difficult to separate ethics from politics or virtuous goals from interested projects. It is now hard to find timeless values or a priori criteria for "the good."[32]

Still, the fact that it tastes good to eat has seldom, in our debates, led directly to either moral *or* political conclusions: the two senses of the good (pleasure and virtue) have been held apart, and good-tasting experiences must sometimes be seen as bad.[33] My enjoyment at the banquet table, it must be acknowledged, might sometimes blind me to the fact that back in the kitchen babies are being cooked. But how can I know when? And on the basis of what *other* experience (e.g., political economic analysis, historical study, or spiritual insight) could I know?

Contemporary Chinese eaters once had recourse to the ethical clarity of a Maoism that took food to be a central political problem and proposed state-socialist solutions to the unevenness of its distribution. The story of Old Gao, the self-righteous food service cadre of *The Gourmet*, shows how Maoists tried to find a middle way between famine and glut. His efforts attest to the dream of moral clarity that inspired him and many nonfictional people of his revolutionary generation. The willingness of the "mountain folk" in *Hibiscus Town* to see their hunger as similar to the sacrifices made by revolutionary heroes, as all Chinese strove to produce a future world of plenty and equality—"communism"—testifies to the characteristic troping of time within Maoism: we will be good (virtuous) now so as to generate goodness (pleasure) later. The relationship between these two senses of goodness was, during the first three decades of the history of the People's Republic, both carefully maintained and strategically collapsed. While Mao and Party theorists found ever more refined ways of distinguishing "the (good) people" from their (evil) class enemies, and making sure that the latter group suffered, a revolutionary-romantic propaganda apparatus represented the process of building socialism as both correct and pleasurable at once. The goodness figured in the rosy cheeks and cheerful smiles of the model workers and farmers seen on billboards, posters, and handbills was double. These upright citizens were enjoying well-fed good health, adequate clothing, the comradeship of their fellows, and a warm bed at the end of the day, but their smiles were also lit from within by the knowledge that they were serving the people in a cause greater than themselves.

For better or for worse, that inner glow—once quite real even for many who would never have passed for poster children of socialism—has faded in contemporary China. The structures of time and feeling characteristic of Maoist teleologies have decomposed into the small goals of many modern lives with many private trajectories. Yet, as we have seen in the materials discussed above, public denunciations of excesses and deficiencies remain visible at the level of the nation. Social differences have only grown more marked as economic life has been increasingly deregulated. In relation to problems as diverse as population, the rural-urban divide, and ideology, an economic model of excess and deficiency is constantly invoked to explain pathologies of circulation in a national system. Urbanites and villagers alike, in my experience, echo the government stance that there are too many Chinese people and there will soon be too little food to go around. (There already is, but that's a separate question for those who complain of overpopulation.) Writers in the new liberal magazines note the asymmetries of China's chronic rural-urban divide: there are too few schools and hospitals in the rural interior, while expensive privatized services offer choices to those living in cities and towns. And acquaintances of mine ranging from language teachers to storefront tailors confide that China's greatest problems are spiritual: there is too much hypocritical posturing and too little honest truth. This logic of too little in general, with pockets of too much, inhabits the comments on China's domestic affairs one can collect from any neighborhood store owner or taxi driver in Beijing: "we are a backward country, with too little wealth to go around, but everywhere we look we see selfish fashion plates who hide in their luxury apartments and clog the streets with their air-conditioned cars." There is more than a hint of nationalist thinking in observations like these. "China" is here perceived as a single, whole system, and people complain because they feel it must be somebody's responsibility to see that the nation's process of economic development is even and just. Although the political path to more even development is now seen to involve indirect government regulation rather than direct state ownership of productive resources, the basic sense of the national problem remains the same: China's poverty must be remedied and wealthy exploiters (especially the corrupt and the criminal) should be curbed.

This popular perception of China as a national system suffering from deficiencies and excesses leads me irresistibly back to Chinese medicine, with its perception of the body as a system in which functions can be strong or weak and substances can pile up or thin out, producing pathological symptoms. My own Spleen depletion disorder, for example, was treated within this framework. Diagnosis generates a narrative that locates depletion (xu) and repletion (shi) in time and space and at the same time indicates the herbal medicine or acupuncture techniques that would target these deficiencies and excesses.

Where food and its distribution are concerned, the circulatory vision of Chinese medicine is a seductive allegory. Recall the textbook

passage cited in chapter 1, for example, which generalizes the efficacies of medicines by using the five flavor categories.

> *Pungent* has the function of spreading and disseminating, moving qi,
> moving blood, or nourishing with moisture. Usually refers to drugs
> that treat disorders of the outer parts of the body . . . or drugs that
> treat blockages of qi and blood. . . .
>
> *Sweet* has the function of replenishing and supplementing, regu-
> lating the activity in the Middle Jiao, and moderating acuteness; usu-
> ally refers to the moistening, bolstering, and strengthening drugs
> that treat depletion disorders, drugs that soothe acute pain, and those
> that regulate the functions of other drugs. . . .
>
> *Sour* has the functions of contracting and constricting. In gen-
> eral, drugs that have a sour flavor are used to treat depletion disorders
> and excessive excretion . . . for example, excessive perspiration and
> diarrhea. . . .
>
> *Bitter* has the function of draining and drying. Its draining capaci-
> ties are many, including the treatment of constipation, of coughs re-
> sulting from the reverse flow of lung qi [bitter drugs would turn the
> flow downward again], of heart system agitation due to excessive heat
> that needs to be cleared and drained; as for its draining functions,
> these are mainly used in dampness syndromes. . . .
>
> *Salty* has the function of softening hardness, dispersing lumps,
> and draining downward; much used in treating scrofula, phlegmy
> cough, abdominal lumps, and heat-knotted constipation.[34]

Reflecting on these drug efficacies, it is hard for me to imagine a bodily state of excess or deficiency that could not be addressed by some
combination of these powers. One is tempted by this list to start analyzing everyday discomforts as fleeting states of particular excess or
deficiency in order to custom design a diet of "flavors" that would immediately address and smooth out every creaky joint, every case of
hiccups, pimples, or flyaway hair. There is an immediate experiential
appeal to this image; how gratifying it might be to have an articulate
analytical vocabulary, not for the lesions and diseases that can be
structurally identified by biomedicine but for the ephemera of bodily
life, the things that, though they may change of their own accord, still
constantly draw our sometimes unwilling attention.

Of course, in practice considerable technical expertise is required
to mobilize this vision in both diagnosis and therapy. Determining

where there is blood or qi that should be set in motion by pungent drugs, what subtle hungers can be reached by sweet drugs, and which inner swamps can be safely drained by bitter drugs is a complicated task. Educated and experienced judgment is required to ensure that each drug of each flavor targets the specific region and function that requires intervention without harming neighboring regions or functions. Yet looked at overall and as a kind of allegory—a structure that is perfectly real and effective in itself but is also a complex model that can bring meaning to other domains of experience—Chinese medicine offers an emphasis on circulation and dynamism that is immensely attractive.

This is a dynamic that is directly experienced. The patients who use Chinese medicine understand what it means to live a body that is appropriately active. Their idea of health involves a state in which digestion is working well, energy is available as needed, and appetite and fatigue pleasurably and predictably mark the times of the day. In clinics, of course, I have mainly heard patients complain of failures to achieve these ideal states of activity and watched through many repeat visits as their doctors worked to regulate the bodily economies of energy circulation to achieve satisfying eating, effective labor, and sound sleep.[35] All of these mundane satisfactions are figured in Chinese language and medicine as processes that, if they are to work well, must keep various forms of circulation active.

In the same way, social life is flawed if it is not actively caught up in networks of circulation. Just as the Spleen System and Kidney System can develop states of depletion, families, villages, and regions can suffer from chronic deficiencies. If bodily depletions can be remedied—as in Chinese medicine—by stimulating a relationship with a site "upstream" from the system that displays the most obvious symptoms, then local deficiencies in the social world can be remedied by strengthening functional relationships between sites that have a surplus and those that are in need. Marriage strategies in the Shandong countryside offer an example: residents of poor villages there seek to marry their daughters to men who live in wealthy villages or in the townships where there are industrial and bureaucratic jobs. This is not only to ensure that the daughter will be well fed and will bring goods home to her natal family from time to time. Rather, there is a much more long term, functional logic that is quite explicit in the politics of marriage. An alliance with a stronger village and a richer family, if it works well, can develop as one of those "upstream" relationships along which benefits will continue to flow to make the originally deficient site more active. Since marriage alliances are often initiated through affinal ties, other connections can be made in the future; since news of job openings or good deals on agricultural supplies can travel by way of women just as well as men, there will be a working pipeline to wealth and opportunity. Hence, it is often the case that the poorer family in a marriage negotiation contributes more material wealth to the engagement and marriage process than the wealthier family does. This is an investment that, while it may lead to even greater deficiency—a certain amount of belt tightening and a lot of borrowing—in the short run, builds a relationship that might gradually cure the original poverty by altering the dynamics of the family's (and village's) relationships.[36]

Since the Chinese medical language of depletion and repletion applies just as well to nonbodily states of excess and deficiency (and is paralleled by Mo Yan's anecdotal warnings in "I Can't Forget Eating"), it is also worth noting that depletions have many ramifications. A few days of depleted Lung function could easily lead to disorders in the fluid economy and disrupt the flow of fluids through the system; as a result one would not only see spontaneous perspiration and lusterless hair and skin (see table 1) but also quickly experience compromises in the functions of other visceral systems. The Kidney System would, perhaps, receive less systemic fluid and begin to deplete its own reservoirs of more fundamental water to make up the difference; the Liver System, unguided by the dominant flow control of qi usually provided by the breathing lungs might begin to overproduce qi, which could rise upward and produce the repletion symptoms of aching sides or anger. As Mo Yan knew from experience, "poles are interconnected," deficiency quickly becomes excess, and both are pathological states. Lasting hunger made Papa Sun and his family vulnerable to food itself, as "stomach linings . . . as thin as paper" could not handle the state distribution of surplus soybeans. Viewed from the perspective of Chinese medicine, neither the invisible hand of the market nor the more visible hand of the socialist state can redress economic inequality merely by shuffling goods around. This would be an endless losing battle, for new arenas of depletion and repletion would open up even as old ones are briefly closed.

The Maoist economic vision presumed that deficiencies resulted from an unjust distribution of resources that with the proper effort could become bountiful: if some were starving, it was because others were consuming too much, more than their fair share. At the international level, this logic was of course quite plausible; if the world *is* a system, there are indeed pathologies of distribution that have made some nations rich and kept others "underdeveloped." Nationally, the land reform and collectivization of the 1950s significantly leveled consumption patterns; all citizens of underdeveloped China became relatively poor, and although there were many kinds of poverty (rural, minority, salaried, and so on) there were relatively few who enjoyed the privileges of wealth. Campaigns like the Great Leap Forward (1957–59) relied for their persuasiveness on the typically Maoist idea that China's resources were underutilized and could be newly appropriated for national use through mass mobilization. Harder work on everyone's part would short cut slow trajectories of industrialization and modernization. China would catch up with Great Britain in fifteen years. Communism would involve plenty of dumplings and rice for all. As a socialist country, China would resolve its chronic deficiencies without reproducing the patterns of exploitation that had divided other countries. As long as the laboring classes remained in charge, no class of privileged exploiters would emerge to eat the livelihood of the poor. Class cannibalism would be kept at bay.

Of course, excesses and deficiencies continued to emerge even during the Maoist period. After the famine, there were the venal crimes of the Cultural Revolution, and along with massive displays of national well-being staged in the urban centers of the coast gritty problems of economic survival continued to trouble people of the rural interior. As long as the state was aggressively involved in economic redistribution, individual citizens were not implicated as exploiters. Moreover, continuing class struggle kept a ready supply of scapegoats at hand; every work unit and agricultural collective had its standard group of former landlords, capitalists, or Old Rightists to struggle against when a public ritual of social sorting out was required. These individuals were the exploiters, now safely relegated to positions of powerlessness as symbols of a banished past. As long as food was directly or indirectly provided by the socialist state, people could comfort themselves that class struggle was *not*—for the time being—at the tip of their own personal chopsticks. Even as vouchers and subsidies, famine relief and state quotas purged all flavor of exploitation from the act of eating, a vigorous propaganda insisted on the moral and political significance of food.

This combination of distributed responsibility and heightened moralism was profoundly altered by the privatization of production and distribution that quickly developed in the late 1970s and 1980s. Food industries and markets were the first to change. In the early 1970s, many villages and townships were already beginning to experiment with small, quasi-private, food production industries; the Shandong village I know best had a privately operated steamed bread plant and a flour mill under contract to the village committee even before the death of Mao in 1976. "Free markets" in the late 1970s became an important figure for liberalization and, as *Hibiscus Town* reminds us, the focus of many ardent hopes. But as the provision of food was slowly turned over to the invisible hand of the market and as social inequalities reemerged as obvious pathologies of public space (beggars, shantytowns, endless rows of marginal vendors) economic excesses and deficiencies became evident in a way that they had not been for three decades. Did people of the reform period presume, as inequities of distribution escalated, that those who were growing more comfortable were doing so *at the expense* of those whose suffering was all too patent? Considering the tightness of the link Maoism (drawing, of course, on much previous economic logic both Marxist and liberal) had forged between excess/deficiency and exploitation, and recalling Mo Yan's sarcasm on the subject of the rich, it is not surprising to find that for many Chinese people the moralisms of the socialist period were not discarded in quite the same way that its economic policies were. Instead the politics of Maoist discourse was privatized to become a seldom articulated form of personal morality, a conflicted habitus of anxious consumption.

Thus, some kind of social struggle has returned to the tips of the chopsticks of those who consider themselves ethical. People notice and resent what others are eating; they criticize official banqueting and decry rising food prices. In Beijing, many of my acquaintances in the academic world and Chinese medicine are salaried workers. Thus, they reserve a special kind of outrage for the businesspeople (vendors on the street as well as the CEOs of supermarket chains) who cheat the ordinary consumer by charging what the market will bear and thus driving up prices. These people, they believe, are getting rich at the expense of consumers and taking unethical advantage of the government's laissez-faire market policies. A great deal of everyday talk among the teachers and staff of the Beijing academic institutions where I worked in the 1990s centers on good food and where it can be obtained most cheaply. Shopping goes on all the time, and no talk of shopping is complete without a careful enumeration of prices. But encoded in every report of an especially cheap or annoyingly inflated price is an obscure suspicion that some people are accumulating surplus without working for it while others are having to work harder just to make ends meet. It is also common knowledge that many are able to get the best delicacies without paying for them at all. Although eating well—that is to say, enjoyably—seems to be a widespread popular avocation, little talk of food proceeds without being accompanied by resentful hints of inequality and the complications of managing it.

As an allegory of reform era excesses and deficiencies, Chinese medical approaches to depletion and repletion could be treated as a fund of strategies that are quite pertinent to the problem of eating well. Therapeutics demands that vital substances be kept in motion, that all functional sites be maintained in good working order to both generate qi, blood, and fluids and to receive nourishing input from neighboring and linked sites. Lungs must send qi to the Kidney System, Kidney Water must cool Heart Fire. Food and breath entering from outside the system of the body will be useless (or worse, will form a repletion) if the Spleen and Lungs are unready to transform and transmit them. More to the point, no visceral system is autonomous; the very nature of these organ-centered networks of whole body activities is to transform and transmit substance and force in a profoundly circulatory system that is selectively open to the outside. The Kidney System "eats" qi that the Lungs have transformed from breath; in other words, the Lungs "give" transformed qi to the Kidneys to eat. The Kidney System in turn gives its coolness to the fiery Heart while imparting strength to the bones and moist health to the hair. Physiology works not only by consuming air, food, and drink from outside the body but by using the Kidney System's seminal essence, from which many kinds of qi are transformed. One could go on at length tracing the sustaining practical connections between and among the subsystems of normal Chinese medical physiology. This body can be seen as a banquet where all diners act only to feed others and receive food from them. No site can supply its own needs; no visceral system can cease its activity of transforming and transmitting.

The result of any such deficient activity would be pathological repletion. And when such repletions and depletions develop the flavors of herbal drugs can provide their diverse stimuli to restore not substance but function to wholesome activity.

Of course, I oversimplify drastically for the sake of the metaphor. Still, when we consider the ethical stances available to those of us who eat in a world we have analyzed as both excessive and deficient there are some useful commentaries in Chinese medicine. They accord, I think, with Derrida's observations in the interview cited at the beginning of this chapter. As he points out there, "one never eats entirely on one's own: this constitutes the rule underlying the statement, 'One must eat well.' It is a rule offering infinite hospitality."[37] Just as the visceral systems offer infinite hospitality to each other and the outside world, just as they continually transmit while transforming, we must recast our position as consumers, seeing our "selves" as contingent sites in an active network. Whatever our needs may be, they cannot be met solely from within ourselves. We must eat. Further, if the network of functional relationships that is at once a body and a society is to be sustained in good health, we must feed others. Consumption takes place in heterogeneous fields, where sites of excess and deficiency are intertwined and dependent; the needs that develop within systems of distribution and consumption are contingent on these relations of dependency. As Derrida and Chinese medicine in this discussion have jointly insisted, "no one eats alone." We are charged with determining "the best, most respectful, most grateful, and also most giving way of relating to the other and of relating the other to the self."[38] Self and other are sites in active networks of exchange; no self or other is possible unless our ethics goes beyond that logic of appropriation in which individuals have presumed they could "take in and grasp" sustenance itself. Rather, an ethics of eating would seek to "learn and give to eat."[39]

Perhaps none of the writers or events I have analyzed in part I of this book would agree with Derrida or me on this question of generosity and circulation. Perhaps there seems to be little difference between the not quite forgotten party-state demand that all Chinese citizens "serve the people" and any concept of "learning and giving to eat." But there is no doubt that in the reform era food has remained political in China long after the death of the dictum of class struggle (*The Gourmet* showed us as much) and that many continue to be appalled by the implicit cannibalism of emerging social and economic inequalities. Mo Yan, with his blind crashers and roasted baby boys, is only one among many in his generation who have raised their voices to criticize the frozen poles of excess and deficiency and to seek some generous national solution to the parallel problems of hunger and greed. Their evocative writing about experiences that were shared by several generations of Chinese people are not simply historical memoirs. Instead they produce the common sense of the historical and social field—and the personal habitus—that must now be negotiated. Even famine had its delightful flavors and sometimes tasted of triumph; hidden within gluttony are deathly states of a deeper depletion. Between these poles, if we can find our way along a path of generous moderation, it might be possible to learn to "savor our food, shoulder our responsibilities, and delight in our passions."

PART II

desiring: an ethics of embodiment

DU WANXIANG: THE ROSY GLOW

OF THE GOOD COMMUNIST

In a story first drafted in the mid-1960s and revised and published in 1978, woman author Ding Ling presents her heroine, Du Wanxiang, as quite sexless.[1] On the day of her marriage at thirteen, for example, little Wanxiang is simply happy that her new family, better off than her own, is able to provide the newlyweds with a warm bed and a fresh blanket. Her husband is not even mentioned, except as the youngest son of his family, and apart from the birth of a daughter in a subordinate clause late in the story there is no direct evidence that little Wanxiang ever had sex. The most intimate moment of her marriage appears to have occurred when her husband, returning from the Anti-American (Korean) War, announces that he has joined the Communist Party. Du Wanxiang "nearly died of happiness. She no longer thought of him as just her daily helpmate, but as an utterly reliable partner in a sacred relationship founded on shared ideals and a common language."[2]

In Ding Ling's story, Wanxiang gradually becomes a model worker of the sort familiar in the Chinese literature of the 1960s and 1970s. After being summoned by her husband to "the Great Northern Wasteland," where she has no proper job but is merely a "dependent" keeping house for him, Du Wanxiang begins to serve the people on a volunteer basis.

> The hastily thrown-together facilities housing the thirty dependent families started to change. The filthy latrine no one had ever bothered with before was suddenly immaculate, swept out daily, spread with a surface layer of lime so that people no longer gagged on the stench when they used it. Thresholds sparkled without the coal chips, garbage, and cigarette butts. . . . Some of the women who had lots of kids and found buying grain and oil bothersome, seeing that

A poster entitled "New Household in a Mountain Village." Like Du Wanxiang, this woman serves the people joyously (she has a barefoot doctor kit in the house) while remaining domestic. Her home offers the basic comforts together with the right-thinking slogans of Mao Zedong thought. Poster courtesy of the International Institute of Social History Stefan R. Landsberger Collection.

Wanxiang had no children, prevailed on her to pick things up for them or to mind their children. Gradually more and more people sought her help. . . . When they found her making cloth shoes for herself they asked her to make a few pairs for their children. Or seeing that she was doing her mending, they'd drag their husbands' things out and bring them over to her. Some even borrowed grain coupons or a few coins, which they never repaid. Wanxiang never faulted them.[3]

The tasks that our heroine takes on in this excerpt are strongly gender marked, not only because they are domestic in character but because they are performed for no pay and involve many associations of lowliness and pollution. By quietly taking responsibility for the dirt of the collective, Wanxiang adopts a position as a "daughter of the party," consolidating the communist state's position as father and mother to the people.[4] (Every "family" has its dirt to deal with, and daughters, or junior women, are there to clean it up.) As Tani Barlow has emphasized in comments on this story, Du Wanxiang's labor is a political transcendence of gender, subordinating all personal considerations, including her occasionally remarked desire for a happy marriage, to love of the state. But it is also an expansion of gendered responsibility, for Du Wanxiang now nurtures and serves China itself and derives deep satisfaction from doing so.

This is not just an ideal transcendence; it is constantly figured in earthy, physical terms.

Caught up in the joy of labor [on the threshing ground], Du Wanxiang felt neither fatigue nor hunger. When everyone else rested she kept on, and even when they all stopped to eat, her hands and feet were still busy. Some of the dependents laboring on the threshing ground got paid by the hour, some by the piece. Only she worked for no pay at all. Everyone on the threshing ground gazed in amazement at the short, slender, serene young woman, a little smile always on her face. They wondered at her inexhaustible energy, at the lofty, solemn, and virginal glow that shone from her otherwise ordinary face. It was impossible to keep one's eyes off her.[5]

The story is replete with nationalist language that is even more lyrical than this. Much of it takes the form of paeans to China and the Communist Party that are either transcriptions of Du Wanxiang's "private" thoughts or outbursts by others who are inspired by her simple and undemanding service. In passages like this, the body of the worker is inseparable from the body of the state. From the point of view of this kind of Maoist writing, loyalty and labor alone were not enough; service to the people was also expected to produce a "lofty, solemn, and virginal glow" in citizens whose patriotism suffused their whole bodies.[6]

Wanxiang's body found its life force and its meaning in the body of the collective. The culmination of this model's story takes the form of a speech she delivers to the workers who had left their comfortable homes farther south to open and develop The Great Northern Wasteland. The workers are extraordinarily moved by her "simple speech," with its hymns of praise for the struggling workers and the difficult terrain on which they labor. Her example inspires them.

> Du Wanxiang had not recited the classics like a pendant, but the maxims and wisdom of those classical works were diffused throughout her simple speech. Just as crops absorb sunlight, rain, and dew, good people, good works, and good precepts had slowly saturated her very soul, worked into her blood, and made her a living thing with deep roots and abundant foliage, able to resist all contagion. Du Wanxiang did not have a superior, bigger-than-life spirit. She was simple and affectionate. No matter how much people looked up to her and were guided by her, in the end she remained the same amiable, straightforward, simple and honest, modest, incandescently fervent Du Wanxiang so familiar to all of them. . . . A thunderous round of applause swept through the Great Audience Hall. Waked from their revery, the farm employees, as though discovering a ray of light in the dead of night, felt a surge of limitless hope in their hearts. They accepted Du Wanxiang completely. Du Wanxiang is our frontline soldier. We must learn from her. We must go forward with her.[7]

The Maoist logic of the model, in which exemplary people emerge from the masses and embody in their persons the political purity of the masses, is here offered as an extraordinarily passionate consummation. This is a world that imagines love and sexuality together in a general and diffuse eroticism oriented first toward the collective. Both "amiable" and "incandescently fervent," Du Wanxiang offers herself as an obliging love object within the national imaginary. At the same time, for readers who identify with Wanxiang she encourages a fantasy of receiving perfect love and affection from all sides unalloyed by any of the frustrations that afflict merely mortal love relationships. Glowing quietly at the center of a vast collective project, this model woman exhibits a very pure form of pleasure, one that only the collective can generate.

This story, published on the verge of a decade known for its many anticollectivist literary works, may be the last prominent fictional statement of Maoist ideals of gender, sexuality, and personhood. When it appeared in 1978, radically different works were already on their way to press. In the chapters that follow, I will discuss some of these reform era works, beginning with narrative materials that rejected the logic of the model to explore the inner lives of individuals (in chapter 4) and then turning to nonfiction writing about forms of sexual activity that little resemble Du Wanxiang's "virginal glow" (chapters 5 and 6). I will argue that the reform era works that turned toward the individual soul and the private bedroom are not a return to natural human preferences after decades of collectivist distortions. Rather, I suggest that private love and sex were constructions, laboriously formed as a reaction against the regime that had made such a success of collective love. Doubtless many frustrations and hypocrisies were experienced by those who attempted Du Wanxiang's kind of passion, and certainly the socialist world that cultivated that passion lost its hold on the public imagination. Still, with all its lyrical excesses, its implausible realist narrative, and its complicated historical positioning, Ding Ling's story testifies to the possibility—even the reality—of a love that can be broad and diffuse while offering deeply personal rewards.

Passion in Public

This style of desire, so clearly articulated by Ding Ling in 1978, was soon to be forgotten. But it was perhaps a bit slower to dissipate in the habitus of post-Mao Chinese people than has been believed. Du Wanxiang's collective fervor was well adapted, for example, to living and working conditions that offered almost no space for private activities. Public commitment to collectivism changed rapidly after 1978, but the actual conditions that would enable private lives were slow to emerge. When I lived in Guangzhou in the early 1980s, for example, educational and structural reforms were well under way in my academic work unit, but individuals and families had not achieved much privacy. Nor had their working lives been significantly decollectivized. Many married couples were living apart in remote work units, and those who were living together were often crammed into tiny rooms subdivided from larger apartments, with shared kitchens and toilet facilities. Offices, laboratories, and dormitory rooms were always shared by at least six people, and the only space available for studying was public. Moreover, marriage regulations were more stringent then than they are now; college students were not allowed to marry, and courting was discouraged. The job assignment system made it very possible that best friends in college would end up working far from each other, perhaps even in different provinces. Many students argued that it was wiser to find a marriage partner after moving to the work unit that (it seemed at the time) would be their home for life. As a consequence, many claimed to be avoiding romantic entanglements while clearly taking great pleasure in deep bonds among classmates of the same sex.

Of course, people had special friendships. Secret meetings were common among us at that time, though they were complicated to arrange. I did my share of sneaking around to find some private time with Chinese friends during those early years. It was still not entirely proper for academics to fraternize with foreigners, and men and women also had to be careful not to give the wrong impression by spending time with each other apart from others. I spent many late night hours with a few friends, both male and female, and one at a time, in offices or laboratories left empty after working hours. And the winter months were welcome because perfectly respectable evening walks could be conducted in darkness and in whispers.

It was an institution at the time for many who lived in my work unit to take a stroll after dinner. Among the elderly people and families on the oval drive in front of the campus's main building, one always saw some very small groups of college students, looking nonchalant but nevertheless seeking to stay far from the largest crowds and keeping their voices low as they talked. Sometimes one of three students would casually depart, leaving, as if by accident, two people together to continue their private exchange. All of this, I feel sure, was carefully planned.

Foreigners like me faced certain special challenges in the conduct of a secret life; unlike my local friends, I lived in a compound with a gate that was locked at about 11:00. At times, I would spend a long evening with a friend in a laboratory building directly adjacent to my dormitory. Leaving there in time to get through the gate before it closed, I would slip out the door that faced in the wrong direction, hugging the shadows, and make a large loop so that I could stroll toward the foreign students' compound looking as if I had just come from downtown.

I sometimes saw others returning home through the main gate at that time; perhaps they were returning from late hours at a hospital affiliated with the school or from a visit to relatives elsewhere in the city. It also occurred to me, though, that they might be returning from a secret rendezvous in a public park. Parks stayed open in the evenings, were only spottily lit, and were well known as places of privacy. I think the people who frequented parks after dark learned to look the other way; no one went there for exercise or to enjoy the flowers, so everyone kept their attention focused on their own companion and avoided noticing who else might be present.

Thus, any direct sexual activity was hard to arrange and consequently rare except for married couples who lived together in a private room. This situation led to a significant eroticization of the surfaces of everyday life. I felt that the most exciting encounters with my secret friends came unexpectedly in the course of daily work in the classrooms and gathering places where we were always part of large groups, getting work done. We shared metaphorical double entendres, exchanged covert looks just a bit more sober and sustained than usual, and achieved apparently casual touches of shoulders and hands. These acts of intimacy are well known to lovers, but within the social conditions of the Maoist period work unit they were in many respects the central acts of many kinds of love. And they were sexual, or at least they seemed so at the time.[8]

It took me a while to accustom myself to this mundane and inconclusive eroticism. The passionate quality of everyday collective life went beyond my heightened interest in a few work mates who especially attracted me. It seemed that everyone had their reasons for giving something extra in group activities. In the English class I taught, these special investments contributed to the joy we took in spirited wordplay, startling revelations, and hilarious language hybrids. In the classes I audited with middle-aged doctors of biomedicine who had been assigned for two years to the school, the sense of cohesion we developed in the group led to an especially lively and erotically freighted buzz between classes.

Having eventually learned to enjoy the subtleties of these exchanges (rather than longing for impossible consummations), I have also come to miss them. In the academic and clinical settings I now visit, many more people have private lives, to which they return as soon as work is done. Work units have decomposed and no longer guarantee that groups of coworkers will be friends and neighbors for a lifetime. It is no longer necessary to send signals of love through the public air of meetings and classes. I am sure the many changes that have led to private lives and better conditions for sexual activity are much appreciated by most of those who were my companions at that time. But, I wonder, do they still remember how passion was once distributed across their most mundane public activities? Would they still recognize in Du Wanxiang, as I can, an object of love, glowing quietly at the heart of collective life?

chapter 4

WRITING THE SELF: THE ROMANCE
OF THE PERSONAL

Chinese medicine is a great treasury; this is an objectively existing reality. We seek to cherish and research this treasury with all the proud daring of our people, with a no longer restricted field of vision, and with liberated thinking, taking Natural Dialectics as our weapon. We should truly recognize that Chinese medicine and pharmacy are sciences rich in content, accumulated in practice over the last several thousand years by the Chinese people as they struggled against nature and disease. Our finest scholars, both ancient and modern, often relied on a naive materialist point of view to observe the phenomena of human life and disease, to link these phenomena to certain macroscopic principles of all nature, and to continually deepen [their knowledge and abilities] through the therapeutic experience gained in long years of practice. In this way, they gradually formed a Chinese medicine and pharmacy that have a unique theoretical system and a high level of systematicity and scientificity. Of this, we, the Chinese people, ought to be justifiably proud.

—*Paths of Renowned Senior Chinese Doctors*

We have from the very inception of this [autobiographical] project cherished a pressing sense of urgency. . . . News [of deaths] has made it impossible for us to rest and has led us to handle the revered authors' manuscripts as if we were protecting a flame. An unspoken imperative urged us to hasten the process of editing, making fair copies, and bringing this volume to the world; rescuing the work and realities of senior Chinese doctors' experience can brook no delays!

—*Paths of Renowned Senior Chinese Doctors*

This chapter is about writing and experience and about the emergence in the early reform period of writers who made individual experience and private memories a public concern.[1] Practices of the self and intimate exchange changed profoundly after the fall of the Gang of Four. For understanding reform era cultural life, these transformations are at least as important as the much more widely noted introduction of free market economic activity and government policies of "opening" (kaifang) China to the capitalist world. Some writers have been tempted to see new forms of subjectivity and intimacy in reform China as a reappearance of something that was always hidden there, a liberation in which the natural individual throws off the yoke of an oppressive collectivism. I think this is a mistake. The simplistic idea of a natural individual with universal needs and capacities cannot explain for me the considerable labor that reform era writers devoted to the task of producing new forms of experience, selfhood, memory, and discourse.[2] This notion of a natural individual is also dangerous in that it offers itself as a ground for a liberal ethics that conveniently forgets its debt to vast political changes.

The ethico-political labor of producing and reforming personal experience through narration is not confined to China in the late 1970s and early 1980s, of course. Wherever realistic writing is widely distributed and read in the contemporary world it is an important part of the generative labor that produces plausible people and worlds. What is special about China is the rapidity with which all sorts of things— personal and collective, textual and otherwise—changed after the Cultural Revolution. In what follows, I track the emergence of new forms of experience, arguing that they are both intimately connected to realist discourses and elude direct representation. I also wish to suggest, without really arguing the point, that new experiences drew on a new national order that was not so much a withdrawal of the state from private life as it was a reorganization of governmentality to suit an emerging market regime.

The passages quoted above, which are drawn from the prefatory matter introducing a collection of autobiographical essays by senior doctors of Chinese medicine, exemplify something important about the transformation that concerns me here. Between these two extracts there are only a few pages but a great difference in emphasis. The first repeats a formula that in 1981 had been obligatory for publications in traditional medicine for many years. The thousands of years of struggle on the part of the people as a whole were repeatedly credited with the accumulation of an undifferentiated "treasury" of medical knowledge and techniques. The text adopts a certain defensive tone. For decades, Chinese medicine had been faced with a dual problem of legitimation. Writers in the field felt they had to justify their profession to both bourgeois modernizers who emphasized science and Marxists who emphasized secular rationality, cultural evolution, and the centrality of the common people. Some of the formulaic language here was (by 1981) a time-honored way of asserting the political and empirical value of the field of traditional medicine. It also adopts a reform era optimism with its reference to a "no longer restricted field of vision" and "liberated thinking" while sticking with a Maoist structure of memory: medicine is a treasury "accumulated in practice over the last several thousand years by the Chinese people as they struggled against nature and disease." This is one of the official forms of memory of the Maoist nation: its temporality runs in the thousands of years, it emphasizes the continuity and creativity of the people, and it imagines forward progress in human struggle.

The second extract concerns itself with particular people, not the people as a whole. It refers to those senior Chinese doctors who had practiced (or at least studied medicine) before the establishment of the Peoples' Republic and had since worked hard to establish the national profession. As the same source points out, by 1981 these worthies had become "as scarce as stars at dawn." The particular "work and realities" of the field's senior doctors constituted a fragile kind of experience, which, rather than accumulating smoothly into a single huge treasury, was in danger of irrevocable disappearance with their deaths. It was an act of devotion to both respected individuals and the heritage of the field to "rescue" individual experience. The task must have seemed both daunting and dangerous at the time because only a few years before it would have been counterrevolutionary to single out individual "experts" for attention and praise.

This chapter considers several kinds of personal, embodied experience that emerged in the early reform period. For better or worse, the mass of "the people" was in eclipse and the particular "paths," or personal stories, of individuals offered a fresh appeal. I will return below to a more extended reading of the *Paths of Renowned Senior Chinese Doctors* project; but most of the discussion that follows focuses on a path-breaking short story, first published in 1979, that has nothing to do with medicine. This story by Zhang Jie nevertheless accomplishes something significant: it centers private experience, narrates an intimate subject, and recasts memory as individual and therefore infinitely variable. All of these were moves that many writers in many fields had come to believe were important in the reform era.[3]

"Love Must Not Be Forgotten" was both topically innovative and massively popular during the opening years of the 1980s. In keeping with its date of appearance in a nationally distributed literary magazine, the narrative is a reflection on issues that were both private (even secret) and widely salient in the few years just after the death of Mao and the fall of the Gang of Four. Writing of romantic love between individuals, a subject that had been absent from published works for many years, Zhang Jie with this story opened up a domain in which people could explore the possibilities of a personal life within the broader social transformation that was just beginning. She wasn't the only author working along these lines at the time, but this story was almost certainly the most prominent example of the new love stories. For some years in the early 1980s, it was a must read for everyone literate, reaching a huge audience in a nation that had extended primary and middle school education to most of its vast population, and the collection of Zhang Jie's works to which this story lent its name came to have an iconic value far beyond its particular content. Passed from hand to hand, it was an unobtrusive signal of shared values or reciprocated love.

Zhang Jie's story appeared just as several other genres of writing that emphasized individual experience were emerging. One well-known group of essays and stories common in the late 1970s was "scar" literature or "the literature of the wounded." These were narratives in which the authors told of their suffering during the Cultural Revolution, often in lurid detail. The predominant tone was sensational, it was mainly events that were narrated, and many stories expressed the rather self-righteous belief that in the reform period the world had been turned right side up again. I mention scar literature here because it incorporated a highly conventional form of memory. In these stories, the years before the 1976 death of Mao were very very bad; now that this era of dogmatism and extremism is safely in the past, they suggested, it is the writer's sacred duty to remember those bad years and report them unflinchingly so that they will never be repeated. Thus, a certain fixed notion of recent history made this genre what it was. Partly as a result of these writings, the Cultural Revolution came to be seen publicly as a discrete historical period that lasted a tidy ten years and incorporated a vast national "error" and a (suddenly obvious) affront to common sense.[4]

This historical tidiness and moral certainty was not new to the discourses of memory in China. Only a few decades before, everyone had been encouraged to "speak bitterness" in public meetings, on the radio, and in newspaper articles. Like scar literature, speaking bitterness periodized history in a straightforward way: for thousands of years the old society had produced widespread suffering for the vast majority of Chinese people. Liberation (in 1949) had changed all that. But the bitter old days had to be remembered as graphically and as long as possible to prevent younger and more fortunate citizens from forgetting the reasons why the struggle had to continue. Both of these forms of narrating the past, speaking bitterness in the 1950s and 1960s and writing the literature of the wounded in the late 1970s and early 1980s, participated in a broadly shared, officially recognized, historical vision. This vision was, moreover, morally simplistic.

After this first outbreak of remembering Maoist crimes, however, writing on the complexities of political and moral experience in the Cultural Revolution period became more nuanced, often inspiring authors to reflect on their own collusion in unjust accusations and ideological excesses. But scar literature marked that important moment when Mao's widow, Jiang Qing, and three of her close associates were being successfully scapegoated for the political errors of the Cultural Revolution and everyone else could be seen as an innocent victim of their manipulations. Perhaps more effectively for the general Chinese population than the often ambiguous statements issued by the national leadership, these writings accomplished an unequivocal turn away from cultural Maoism.

As this literature of the wounded was enjoying its brief popularity, however, other kinds of writing were embarking on the more difficult, longer term, historical labor of decollectivizing subjectivity and pluralizing memory.[5] As I have suggested, realist fiction like that of Zhang Jie played a role in privatizing experience and producing a more autonomous subject in the early reform era. It was one of the first pieces of popular writing to ignore and even violate the neat divisions of official history, suggesting that individuals had their own, differently organized stories. This sort of personalizing gesture was not confined to fiction alone. The problem of individual experience began to develop in numerous other discursive domains as well, such as the autobiographical essays by senior doctors collected in *Paths of Renowned Senior Chinese Doctors*. Like "Love Must Not Be Forgotten," these medical works were passed lovingly from hand to hand for a few years, taking on iconic value as evidence that traditional medicine also could have its heroes and heroines, dramatic moments, and elegant figures of speech that pushed beyond the Communist Party rhetoric of taking health care to the people.

In this chapter, I focus on these two types of writing. "Love Must Not Be Forgotten" is important here because the text sensitively addresses the problem of subject (re)formation. In it, Zhang Jie pursues with particular rigor the work of making imaginable private experience and personal (even selfish) goals. She also presents several models of remembering (or not), recasting (several times over) the relationship between the past and the future. At the same time, the story addresses the problem of whether subjective experience really can be represented in language while thematizing a broader language crisis that afflicted many forms of writing practice at the time. I admire this story, and wish to share it here, because it refuses to oversimplify the individual subject and it has such an interesting viewpoint on the relationship between writing and experience. In other words, the story effectively decouples writing and experience at the level of representation while fundamentally linking them in relation to performance or efficacy.

The autobiographies of senior Chinese doctors address a somewhat different but no less important question, that of the experiential authority of individual medical experts and their relationship with a historical archive. This was a problem in the aftermath of the "Red vs. Expert" dichotomies of the Maoist period; during this time, individual authorship and professional seniority were completely eclipsed by committee documents and politicized professional hierarchies. Medical experts were lying low, and hospitals and schools run by party cadres were full of "worker, peasant, soldier" trainees. I suggest that the emergence of personal essays in this medical field—essays that emphasized experience and revalorized a debt to the past—meant a great deal to Chinese medical people as they faced an uncertain professional future at the end of the Cultural Revolution. Autobiographies of the field's oldest teachers and practitioners helped many in the field, people of all ages, to invent themselves as individually responsible healers and founders of a future. This project, too, I think, was driven by a love that must not be forgotten.

Speaking of Love

Zhang Jie's story focuses on the secret and unconsummated love between a man and a woman (both good revolutionaries, both now dead) and on the present dilemma of the woman's daughter. The daughter, Shanshan, is a young woman of thirty, "the same age as our People's Republic," who narrates her thoughts as she reads the diary her mother, Zhong Yu, kept throughout her life. As she considers whether to marry a handsome young man she does not love, Shanshan is haunted by thoughts of her mother's disappointments in a life that included a short and unloving marriage. At the same time, Shanshan tries to understand her mother's secret love, revealed in her diary, for a married man whom she rarely saw and never touched. Zhong Yu's passion was founded on shared political values; her lover was an upright cadre whose dutiful marriage had been an act of revolutionary class feeling. Despite her loneliness, she apparently loved her remote cadre partly because he was morally and politically incorruptible.

But Shanshan already belongs to the reform era; she wants no part of the idealistic deferrals, political or romantic, that structured her mother's life. Still, she must decide whether to marry her vapid "Greek god" of a suitor, who is, after all, present and available, or wait for a more perfect love to enter her life. She does not know what a relationship with "that one who calls out to one's very own soul" (*neige huhuanzhe zijide linghun*) would bring, and she fears that such a love is impossible. Ultimately, she decides to resist all pressures and live single in the hope of someday finding a love worthy of the name.

At the most general level, then, this is a story of a young woman achieving greater autonomy and more confident (or deliberate) selfhood through reflection on the mistakes and miseries of a loved one's experience. This is hardly an unusual scenario in twentieth-century fiction, and, although it was a bold move to publish this kind of story in China in 1979, there was plenty of precedent in an earlier world of Chinese letters.[6] Zhang Jie herself, for example, in a biographical essay, attributes most of her values and commitments to her reading of "classic literature," especially eighteenth- and nineteenth-century European novels.[7]

Realist fictional writing translated from European languages was an important influence on all twentieth-century Chinese writing, in fact. In the 1920s and 1930s, the May Fourth movement of intellectual radicals placed great emphasis on the liberatory potential of realist writing in the vernacular. Although some of the political values associated with literary realism went into eclipse after Mao Zedong's 1942 "Talks at the Yan'an Forum on Literature and Art" (which sought to discipline Chinese writers into a form of socialist realism that was later called "revolutionary romanticism"), by that time many of the naturalistic devices of Western fiction had been incorporated into the heart of the modern Chinese written language.[8] Moreover, during the thirty-plus years of Communist Party cultural hegemony, there were only a few years, perhaps ten, when those who had access to collections of world literature were strongly discouraged from reading it.

Thus, "Love Must Not Be Forgotten" could be read as a mere import from overseas, translating themes of self-realization and romantic love into a Chinese historical situation but only revealing a story that is universal: that of the autonomous natural individual who throws off the shackles of social control in the name of deeper, more authentic forms of experience, selfhood, and freedom.

I wish to read the story otherwise, however. Shanshan's dilemma is, after all, only the framing device for Zhong Yu's story, which takes up much more space and is the occasion for the text's most appealing writing. It was the older woman, not the younger narrator, who was in love and unable to forget. Shanshan, in contrast, has trouble remembering anything, although she eventually justifies her own choice as a way of commemorating her mother's sacrifice and commitment. In considering the reader's point of view, and bearing in mind the extraordinary popularity of this story, one can only conclude that something beyond a conventional decision about whether or not to marry must have animated interest in this work.

I think the greatest pleasure of this text lies with the figure of Zhong Yu, who builds and sustains a life of private experience in a daily practice of simultaneously writing and concealing a love affair. For Chinese readers immediately after the death of Mao, this character combined both verisimilitude (secrets remained important) and new possibilities (deep romantic love). This subject was not free to reorganize her life in accordance with her desires, and the public autonomy she enjoyed as a divorced writer on a government stipend was experienced as an unwelcome loneliness. Moreover, she makes the central decision of her life, to avoid all contact with her lover, out of consideration for the old cadre's wife—neither of these lovers is willing to cause a third person pain. This is not, in other words, quite the individual who plays the central role in a universal drama of self-realization. The appeal of Zhong Yu's condition lay elsewhere. But to understand the way in which "Love Must Not Be Forgotten" reached (and altered) the imagination of personal experience in the early re-form period requires a closer reading of the text.

Soul Mates

In the story something happens for Shanshan. She undergoes a transformation, makes a decision, and resolves her relationship with the past in her determination to remember her mother's love affair. But almost nothing happens for Zhong Yu. The story provides no origin point for Zhong Yu's love affair, nor does this love ever end—it survives the death of the virtuous cadre and in a sense even that of Zhong Yu herself. This is perhaps because the romance never existed except as writing. The secret diary addressed to the mostly imagined lover is written in the first and second person: an I addresses, end-lessly, a you. Couched as one side of a conversation between two indi-viduals, this writing can be sustained for years in the absence of any real referent for *you*. Changes in a publicly recognized reality need not alter this idealized secret world.

To write a secret love could be seen as dangerously unrealistic given the context of the times. Few intellectuals dared to commit their private thoughts to paper during this time, the Cultural Revolution, when the thinking of scholars and writers was a heavily disciplined public concern. The perilousness of this diary keeping is even noted in the story when Shanshan expresses amazement that her mother, who had been the target of frequent political attacks, should have kept on writing in private (116; 10).[9] Perhaps this one-sentence remark in the story is a signal that Zhong Yu is very much an after the fact con-struct, a person capable of sustaining a kind of experience that only became imaginable in 1979 and was then projected back into a past that had made this kind of love almost impossible, if not downright dangerous. Thus, the unreality—and also the appeal—of the story lies not only in how Zhong Yu writes to her remote cadre but in the implausible but inspiring figure of Zhong Yu herself.

Writing in the late 1970s, Shanshan's idealistic approach to love is a bit more understandable. As she reads, she thinks of her mother's relationship as one between two "souls" (*linghun*): they "meet" when her mother takes solitary walks in the lane where she and her lover once strolled (119; 13), and they merge after death, as "the wrinkled skin and grey hair of these two old people are transformed from mere carbon compounds into some other element" (120; 13–14). This way of imagining a great love accords with Shanshan's favorite expression for a true lover, "the one who calls out to one's very own soul."

Zhong Yu admits to being an idealist, too, telling her daughter at one point that "those who know their limits are always happy" because their needs are adjusted to actual conditions. But "I will never enjoy that happiness," she adds ironically, as "I'm only able to be a suffering idealist" (107; 4). In general, though, she avoids abstract and romantic language, preferring to write as if her interlocutor were fully present in her life, perhaps just gone out of town for a few days. Only at two points in her diary does she adopt a more spiritual idiom. The diary entry marking her lover's death begins: "You have gone. It seems as if a part of my own spirit (*lingxing*) has followed you"(117; 11). The word she uses here, *lingxing*, is difficult to translate; dictionaries suggest rendering it as "intelligence" (the sort that clever animals can have) or "natural gifts." *Ling* is a word that combines notions of magical efficacy, protean complexity, and embodied specificity. Shanshan describes Zhong Yu's eyes as *lingxiu*, which might be translated as "beautifully expressive." Gods (and their images) have their own ling, and gestures are ling when they are especially graceful and appropriate to the task.[10] The second character, *xing*, is a very flexible word. As a noun, it means "character," "nature," or "disposition" (in a relatively unconnected usage, it also means "sex"). Appended after a qualitative word like *ling*, it functions like the English suffixes -*ness* or -*ity*. Thus, part of Zhong Yu's "lingness," her specific personality, her particular abilities (as a writer, too, perhaps?), has followed her upright cadre into death.

The final entry in Zhong Yu's diary, written just before her own death, addresses the issue of idealism more directly: "I am a person who believes in materialism. But now I hope there is a Heavenly Kingdom (Tianguo). If there is a 'Heavenly Kingdom,' I know you are there waiting for me. All I want is to go there and meet you, we will be together forever, never parting. Never again will we have to sacrifice ourselves (*geshe women ziji*) for fear of spoiling someone else's life. Wait for me, darling, I am coming" (24; 13). Here, too, there is no talk of souls per se, but the old Christian word for *heaven* is contrasted with the Marxist materialism that has characterized Zhong Yu's lifelong commitments. In a sense, the relationship between these two lovers remains the same: a deathbed turn to a religiously marked space only changes the country in which the relationship lives. Personal experience, it appears, need not be inscribed within a literal-minded realism; there is even something noble about imagining it privately and sustaining it in faithful memory.

Shanshan, the daughter whose most significant life experience still lies ahead of her in the reform 1980s, can speak quite freely of "souls" in an idiom consistent with antimaterialist traditions like Christianity and romanticism. But her mother, who took part in the revolution and lived a life of duty, service, and communist political correctness, avoids pure idealism even in her most spiritual moments. Both, however, work to open up a space for experience in which they can safely develop personal goals and a sense of their own particularity. Their prospects for realizing such a self—if these embattled collections of worries and wishes can be called that—differ in relation to their distinct historical situations.

Shanshan worries, for example, both about what others will think of her and about discerning her own motives and best interests. The decision she must make to marry or not involves both of these concerns, as she tries to probe her lover's view of her, anticipate criticism from acquaintances if she remains single, and analyze her own feelings: "But oddly enough I myself can't figure out whether to marry him. Because I can't get clear what I really love about him, or what he loves about me" (102; 1). By the end of the story, she has resolved some of this uncertainty in her determination to ignore social pressure and live single, arguing that this could be "a higher form of social life with respect to civilization, cultivation, delightfulness, and more" (122; 15). Speaking now in the first-person plural, as if speaking for her whole generation of young women, she insists that it is worthwhile for "us" to patiently await "that one who calls out to us" rather than rushing into marriage.

The image of a soul mate calling out to one is connected in the story to a line from Thomas Hardy:

> The great English writer Thomas Hardy said that "the call seldom produces the comer" [literally "the one who calls and the one who is called can seldom reply to each other"]. I cannot judge by ordinary moral standards whether they should have loved each other or not. All I want to judge is why didn't they wait for that one who calls out to one's own soul? If only we could all wait for each other, avoiding foolish marriages, such tragic melodramas could be prevented.
>
> When we achieve true Communism, will there still be this kind of situation in which love and marriage part? Since the world is so large, there could still be times when people who call out to each other can receive no reply, so of course this kind of situation could still come about. But that is so tragic! Perhaps by the time we have reached that golden age we will have better ways of avoiding such tragedies. (121; 14)

Perhaps this romantic notion of a fated counterpart (it is arguably an old one in Chinese literature) accomplishes more persuasively than anything else the individuation Shanshan seeks. If she can believe that there is, somewhere in this very large world, one other person whose call is directed specifically to her, she will have the courage to live on alone. This is not the logic of Du Wanxiang and the model worker, even though, like the collective struggle for true communism, it is a commitment to defer fulfillment of a dream. Shanshan's world is one in which sacrifices will be made but only in the service of deeply personal goals. This is no longer the commune, in which people are distinguished from each other by the extent of their selfless and tireless service to the people. Rather, it is a setting in which individuals might find each other and form true marriages of loving souls.

Shanshan's closing words are strongly oriented toward the future. The "higher form of social life with respect to civilization, cultivation, delightfulness, and more" to which she aspires tends to eclipse, in its brilliance, any complicated or painful memories. She faces the future faithful to herself and the memory of her mother, bolstered only by a bourgeois fantasy of the perfect soul mate. Zhong Yu, however, does

not seek any epiphany of self-realization, preferring to maintain continuity in a structure of feeling set up long ago. This requires appro-
priating all of daily life into the private conversation she carries on in
the diary. As Shanshan describes it: "That text [the diary] really didn't
have much that referred to their love; most entries dealt with the mundane things in her life: why one of her essays had been a failure; her
anxieties and doubts about her own talent; why Shanshan (that's me)
was naughty, and whether she should punish her; the fine play she
missed by absent-mindedly mistaking the time on the ticket; how she
got drenched when she went out for a walk and forgot her umbrella.
Her spirit (*jingshen*) was with him day and night, as if they had been
a loving married couple" (115–16; 10). Yet, as Zhong Yu faces her own
failing health and her daughter's uncertainties, she explicitly asserts a
confident and seasoned sense of individual priorities.

> When you're young you don't necessarily understand your own striv-
> ings, your own needs (*xuyaode*). And other people may even push
> you into a marriage. Only after you've grown up a bit and matured
> can you understand what it is you really need. By that time you've
> done a lot of stupid things you regret. . . . Often when I can't sleep at
> night I force myself to recall all the stupid blunders of my youth, just
> to sober myself up. Of course this is very uncomfortable, to the point
> that I often hide my face in the covers for shame, as if there were eyes
> watching me in the dark. But even in these unhappy feelings there is
> a kind of redemptive (*shuzuiside*) pleasure. (106–7; 4)

These comments were not written in the diary but offered to her
daughter as loving (if somewhat indirect) advice at this time of crisis
for the younger woman. Zhong Yu clearly does not invoke her "own
needs" in her everyday life, even in her private diary, but when her
daughter's lifetime happiness might be at stake she is apparently willing to state a choice. It is wiser, she suggests, to know and obey one's
own individual imperatives than to "stupidly" cave in to what other
people want. At the same time, she betrays an inner life in which both
remembering a personal past and taking painful responsibility for it
are sources of a certain pleasure.

For readers of this story in twenty-first century North America, this
point about personal needs and memorious self-consciousness may
appear to be the height of banality. For those who read it in early
reform Beijing, a time and place that offered precious few heroines

beyond the willing workers and victimized peasant girls of stories like "Du Wanxiang" and *The White-Haired Girl*, however, it was quite liberating. But there were, I think, several levels to this reading.

The first level involves identification with the characters. I have been writing of the voices and viewpoints of Shanshan and Zhong Yu as if they were real people. This is, after all, one of the claims and appealing features of realist fiction, that it offers recognizable people and lives to the reader's imagination, inviting identification and imaginative participation. And I have suggested above that Shanshan was a believable person for the late 1970s, while her mother is a somewhat more fantastic (and therefore, perhaps, more attractive) heroine in her steadfast commitment to a secret life of writing throughout the Maoist years. Whatever the differences between these two women, Shanshan's decision in favor of personal autonomy and Zhong Yu's faithful love presented novel possibilities to readers, informing, perhaps, the inner and intimate lives that were becoming (almost) possible for everyone for the first time in several decades. If two realistically depicted characters could experience life in this deeply personal way, why couldn't many more people?

What of "the old cadre," who stands, ramrod straight, at the edge of this story? What possibilities did he offer to an empathetic reading? He is perhaps the least typical reform era character of all. His life has been devoted to work, to Marxist theory and proletarian practice, to a marriage with a politically correct origin. His marriage, in fact, responds quite literally to the collective imperative to privilege the sacrifices of workers in revolution. As the author describes it: "Toward the end of the thirties, when he was doing underground work in Shanghai, an old worker had given his life to shield him, leaving behind a wife and daughter who had no one to turn to. Out of revolutionary vanguardism, deep class feeling, and gratitude to the dead he had unhesitatingly married the daughter" (110; 6). But he also remembers other things. Both of the two snatches of conversation attributed to him in the narrative include the words "I remember" (Shanshan attests even more often that she can't remember things at all, her father among them). On one occasion, the old cadre remembers overhearing that Zhong Yu likes Chekhov, and the other time he recalls seeing Shanshan as a little girl. These are relatively trivial remarks, though to Zhong Yu they are all-important, but they do identify her lover as a man who not only does his duty by the past, officially and publicly remembering the suffering of the masses, but has his own personal stock of everyday memories and commemorations. Thus, the story offers us a firmly Maoist figure who, against all proper discourses, has also been harboring a secret inner life. Perhaps.

Another way of reading the story makes "love" a central character (hence the title). "Love Must Not Be Forgotten" is a good translation for the Chinese title, which nevertheless adopts a slightly different tone: "Ai, Shi Buneng Wangjide" is more literally rendered as "Love, That Which Cannot Be Forgotten." One of the most attractive features of this story and its characters may have been the way in which love in the form of a personal passion that has nothing to do with Maoist politics was centered and revalorized. I suggested above that something happened to the story's narrator, Shanshan; similarly, something happens to the story's main topic, love. The import and gravity of the word *ai* shifts a great deal in the course of the story. First *ai* is that conventional love that Shanshan can interrogate in herself and her ordinary lover ("I can't get clear what I really love about him, or what he loves about me" appears in the opening pages); later it appears in the context of Zhong Yu "loving" to read Chekhov and as a joking reference to readers loving Zhong Yu for her beautiful style. The word *love* is also used in reference to patriotism: *aiguo*, "love of country," a pervasive term in popular usage at the time. This love used in everyday language is transformed in this text into an emotional commitment of such depth that it can barely be mentioned.

Thus, just after the political murder of her lover, Zhong Yu writes in her diary: "I don't believe you were an 'Old Rightist.' You were the finest among those murdered; otherwise how could I have loved you? Now I no longer fear saying those three words" (118; 11–12). The three words in question are *I love you*, but they are not spoken as such in this sentence. Later in the same long passage, however, Zhong Yu writes of one of the few occasions when the lovers were actually together, walking in a small lane. "How we treasured that one 'stroll,' the only one of our lives. We were clearly fearful, afraid of losing control and blurting out those three words that had tormented us for so many years, 'I love you.' Apart from me there is probably no one in the world who would believe that we never even held hands! Much less ever speaking of that!" (119; 12–13). So it appears that those three words never were actually spoken. They are a silence that has become the fetishized center of an entirely private subjective experience.[11]

The story has, then, introduced love of a newly intimate, newly freighted kind into reform China's language and thought. But I am even more interested in the two other words of Zhong Yu's fetishized phrase than I am in love itself: with its sentimental burden of romantic love, this story has smuggled in an "I" and a "you" who are capable of loving. True, the you is largely imagined, and he has almost no voice in the story. But this is no disqualification; after all, passion everywhere may make rather fantastic figures of those we love. The I, on the other hand, emerges as a person who can decide to live true to her own needs and keep faith with another for a very long time. This I is partly imagined, too, no doubt. But it must have been with this kind of imagining that private selves—emotional, memorious, possessed of needs and idiosyncratic experiences—began to appear as the demands of the collective began to recede.

I will return to a different dimension of "Love Must Not Be Forgotten" at the end of this chapter. But first I want to briefly examine that other genre of writing that appeared alongside it, performing a similar kind of social labor and working in a similar way to renovate memory. Like fiction, it, too, produced new kinds of individuals and a new privatization of experience. This is the autobiographical writing of senior Chinese doctors.

As If Protecting a Flame

The faithful continuous self narrated by Zhang Jie existed in a very small space, that of the personal diary and the quiet domestic life. The prominent selves that began to come into existence for Chinese medicine in the early 1980s were adapted to a much more public field, one bustling with clinical, publishing, and research activity. But they shared the same post-Maoist sense of crisis and invested their newfound personal experience with no less passionate intensity.

Chinese medicine had its own Cultural Revolution, one that escaped the worst punishments visited upon intellectuals and scientific experts while participating in the same radical collectivism and emphasis on the mass line that influenced the lives of other skilled specialists. More than one doctor who lived through those years, when talking about the strategic challenges facing institutions of Chinese medicine at the time, has remarked to me that "Red Guards and high cadres got sick, too." In other words, good doctors were needed even by the most antiexpert of political activists. As a result, individual doctors, clinics, and even hospitals had their highly placed protectors.

Because people of all classes continued to get sick, and because the institutions of traditional Chinese medicine (schools, clinics, and hospitals, though no journals or professional associations) continued to function even during the Cultural Revolution, oral transmission of lore about good doctors and treatments did not disappear. But there were few occasions on which anyone "put out his head" (*chutou*) to take responsibility or credit for action beyond the most basic clinical work. Medical authorship and personal medical authority, in particular, had all but disappeared. Journals of traditional medicine ceased publication between 1966 and 1977, and throughout the first thirty years of the People's Republic the most important publications (textbooks, reference works, and annotated classics) were edited and authored by large committees.

As the field began to regroup after the fall of the Gang of Four, various kinds of individually authored or coauthored works began to appear, especially in the journals and newsletters that were being established in record numbers. Attention in such articles turned from the theory and practice of egalitarian health care to technical medical matters. Beginning in 1977, schools and colleges once again demanded up-to-date comprehensive textbooks of traditional medicine, and editing committees set to work producing them, in the same move vigorously resystematizing the field and its canonical knowledge. Laboratory research and controlled clinical trials engaged the attention of the younger faculty in colleges and large hospitals; at the same time, scholars were reconsidering the Chinese medical archive in the framework of an increasingly depoliticized historiography.[12]

In mid-1980, the quarterly *Bulletin of the Shandong College of Traditional Chinese Medicine* began publishing a series of autobiographical essays under the title "Paths of Renowned Senior Chinese Doctors" (Ming Laozhongyi zhi Lu). The journal's editors proposed to include two or three of these personal histories each quarter, seeking to "unearth the expert professional heritage [of Chinese medicine], introduce scholarly and therapeutic experience, . . . salvage precious research materials, and enrich research on medical history." The editors also noted that "the significance [of this project] lies in inspiring future scholarship; we can learn from the ways in which a generation of famous doctors has matured."[13] In keeping with these goals, the essays focused particularly on recalling the formative experiences of study, clinical work, and (occasionally) political involvement of their authors, the "paths" by which the senior doctors (the *laozhongyi*) who had for several decades led the field of traditional medicine had reached their present eminence.

Reader responses to this feature were immediate and extraordinarily positive, catching even the editors by surprise; in each of the next few issues, they published several pages of letters from medical luminaries all over China who lauded the project and offered to participate by writing personal memoirs. Most of the essays that appeared in the Paths series were eventually published in a three-volume anthology that appeared between 1981 and 1985.[14] The editors' preface to volume 1 suggests the special cultural weight this publication project developed by the time the *Bulletin's* autobiographies reached anthology form.

> Because of the passage of time and the ten years of turmoil, the famous scholars of Chinese medicine and renowned senior Chinese doctors who are still alive are few and far between [literally "as rare as stars at dawn"]. Moreover, according to our information, among these some are both weak and ill. . . . Therefore, we have from the very inception of this project cherished a pressing sense of urgency. . . . News [of deaths] has made it impossible for us to rest and has led us to handle the revered authors' manuscripts as if we were protecting a flame. An unspoken imperative urged us to hasten the process of editing, making fair copies, and bringing this volume to the world; rescuing the work and realities of senior Chinese doctor's experience can brook no delays![15]

Ordinary readers seemed to agree about the importance of the project, and these collections became ubiquitous on the bookshelves of Chinese medical practitioners and were widely read by medical students as well, especially the very committed graduate students I knew in Guangzhou in the early 1980s. Moreover, the new biographical genre quickly spread throughout the Chinese medical publishing world. In a literature survey I conducted in 1984, I found that all but one of the major monthly journals of traditional medicine had a regular section devoted to "laozhongyi experience"; most of the essays adopted biographical conventions similar to those of the Paths project.[16]

On the Road

What was it about this kind of essay that appealed to those who worked in the field of Chinese medicine? Many writers advanced justifications of the genre in prose whose style resembled that of the autobiographical essays themselves. For example, Yue Meizhong of Beijing wrote in a second preface to volume 2 as follows.

> I have been bedridden for some time now, and my family often puts a vase of flowers on my desk in the sickroom to make me feel less lonely. The dark green jade plant, the fragrant jasmine, the dignified "gentleman" orchid, the orange kumquats—"flowers fresh and fruits ripe," each with its unique appeal. Still, I have yet to see my most beloved chrysanthemum. I asked my daughter, who said that although she had planted them the necessary conditions were lacking so they didn't do well. I remember in the fifties my daughter would go with me every autumn to look at the chrysanthemums in Jie Garden. At that time, I attended only to appreciating the chrysanthemum's divine appearance but had not yet reflected on how it is grown. Evidently anyone who has an interest in this flower must also know the rare beauty of its growth as well as the conditions necessary for its cultivation. This led me to think of the heritage of Chinese medicine. With the passage of time and the deepening of practice, the work of rescuing and transmitting the scholarly experience of senior Chinese doctors has been emphasized more and more. In the last few years, the medical theories, cases, commentaries, and other scholarly writings of some senior Chinese doctors have been published. Many are private treasures, the results of a lifetime's deliberation. Comparatively speaking, generalizing research work on the therapeutic-scholarly roads and therapeutic-scholarly methods of senior Chinese doctors is not enough, for these [roads and methods] are themselves an organic component of the scholarly experience of senior Chinese doctors. Researching these forebears—asking under what concrete historical conditions they achieved their successes, discussing the accumulation and development of factors beneficial to scholarship and the causes of scholarly weak points, seeking the principles common to their acquisition and use of knowledge—we can help people understand the scholarly experience of senior Chinese doctors more vividly, more deeply, and more fully. The sweetness of eating a honeyed fruit is enhanced by knowledge of its

source. Scholarly works alone cannot always provide for their talented heirs the inspirational function that the experiences and paths of those who went before can. Now, when we are feeling the urgency of solving the problem of Chinese medicine's lack of successors especially keenly, comrades at the Shandong College of Traditional Chinese Medicine, unstinting in their efforts, have collected the scholarly experience of famous senior Chinese doctors throughout the country. . . ; they have thereby made a contribution to the leaders of Chinese medical work, to its educational workers, to Chinese medicine as a whole, and to the generation of young people who intend to take up Chinese medicine as a career. This intention, indeed, can be called noble.[17]

This literally flowery (and fruity) prose makes several points. Overall Yue is concerned to emphasize the nobility of the task of recording the experience of senior doctors like himself. By association, of course, the value of the historical field of Chinese medicine is also being asserted at a time when an official policy of "scientization" was functioning as a mixed blessing for both modernizers and traditionalists in the profession.[18] There is an understandable concern with medical training, given that schools and colleges had taught relatively little medicine during the Cultural Revolution and in 1981 were still scrambling to catch up. And the road or path metaphor for medical experience is quite noticeable.

Yue insists that the experiences of scholarly forebears can serve to guide those young people who are now being trained. I have argued at length elsewhere that a certain notion of experience (jingyan) was quite central to the self-consciousness of the profession of Chinese medicine in the early 1980s.[19] This kind of experience, accumulated by individuals through both practical clinical work and assiduous study of the medical heritage, served many useful purposes as medical work underwent "reform." Experience could legitimate the age hierarchies that partly governed the social life of Chinese medical work units; only the elders who dominated clinics and academic departments could claim the truest wisdom based on the greatest amount of experience. Experience also provided a unifying ground for the very diverse archival materials that were then being reread, and records of even the most bizarre or implausible treatments could be taken seriously as part of the clinical experience recorded in the archive. This notion could also be invoked to explain logical inconsistencies in texts as well as practical discrepancies in the clinical work of different practitioners. If someone had had a good experience with an idiosyncratic approach, it would not be rejected out of hand, no matter how tenuous its connection to the ruling principles of the field.

Perhaps most interesting, *empiricism* (*jingyanzhuyi*) was one of the most valorized terms in national modernization discourses, an imported term that was very much in keeping with the scientizing policy of "seeking truth from facts." *Jingyanzhuyi* literally translated is "experiencism." Mostly unaware of the European intellectual history of empiricism (perhaps fortunately so), Chinese medical people supplied their own understanding of experience and used the term to legitimate the "essential spirit" of Chinese medicine.

Of course, this experience differed from that on which medicine had founded its legitimacy just a few years before. As the first quotation that opens this chapter indicates, up until the late 1970s it was the collective experience of the laboring masses that counted; "the people" had accumulated the "vast treasury" of Chinese medicine and the principal responsibility of its experts lay in getting these riches to them. Much lip service was still being paid to this idea in the mid-1980s, but by the time I began field research at a medical college in Guangzhou in 1982 it had clearly become an empty formula.

Perhaps this Maoist background to the notion of experience informed Yue Meizhong's distinction between "generalizing research work" on the roads and methods of senior Chinese doctors and the project of chronicling of "the roads and methods themselves." He argues that research must turn to the "forebears" and their particular scholarly experience; only by seeking this specificity can we understand the field "more vividly, more deeply, and more fully."

The path metaphor thus neatly addressed both the specificities and the continuities that engaged Chinese medical writers at the time. The word chosen by the series editors, *lu,* is utterly common, used alone and in compounds to both name and refer to streets and roads throughout the Chinese-speaking world. Used metaphorically, it also gestures to a long philosophical heritage in which a slightly grander word for path, road, or way is important—this word is *Dao* (*Tao*), of course. Choosing the somewhat more common word *lu,* the editors emphasized the down-to-earth concreteness of the narratives they collected while also deploying all the metaphorical richness of the Way. The term evokes the particular stories of individual travelers; it suggests idiosyncrasy, contingency, and multiplicity. It can expand to contain all manner of memories; it is made of experiences. The recounting of a path need not be a causal or a moral narrative; nor does it need to pretend to generality, however much its rhetoric may seek to influence readers or resonate with their experiences.

A path, however, is constituted by a traveler. This must be a traveler, moreover, who can remember and select from his or her experiences, who becomes the sole authority on the way he or she has traveled, and who has been transformed along the way.[20] It follows, then, that not only do travelers make paths but paths make travelers, especially in China where there is no tradition of an essential self that struggles to express itself. The experiences recounted by the new medical autobiographers were nothing other than accounts of self. Not surprisingly, many of the authors who contributed to the Paths project chose to work with the path metaphor in their own essays. Titles such as the following are examples: "Paths Are Made by People" (Jin Shoushan), "On the Road of Studying the Prevention and Treatment of Coronary Heart Disease" (Guo Shikui), "My Teacher's and My Medical Paths" (Peng Jingshan), "A Long and Cloudy Road" (Deng Tietao), "Blazing a New Trail" (Wang Pengfei), "Looking Back on My Medical Journey" (Guan Youbo), "An Account of a Backward Look at Fifty Years on the Medical Path" (Gao Shiguo), "Learn from the Virtues of the Hosts of Scholars but Travel Your Own Road" (Qiu Xiaomei), and "The Medical Road I Have Traveled" (Tan Riqiang).[21] All of these roads stretched back in memory to midcentury. Although the essays contain gaps, the roads are presented as if they do not, and all lead toward a future, however clouded.

In the essays, this generous framework was able to accommodate a wide range of topics. Authors described their family and early childhood connections to Chinese medicine, spoke of the many kinds of teaching they had received (all were trained before traditional medical education was nationally institutionalized in the 1950s), penned tributes to honored teachers, and identified works from the medical archive that had been important in their professional development. Most of these experienced doctors chose one or a few exemplary clinical cases to discuss by way of dramatizing an important lesson they had learned. There was also much attention devoted to the uses of the Chinese materia medica and to theories drawn from various canonical works. Some of the essays were very carefully structured and elegantly sprinkled with classical idioms and literary allusions. Others were the straightforward life stories of down-to-earth clinical people. Very few authors made any reference to the political difficulties or challenges they might have experienced during the Maoist years, and the one woman included in the collection makes no issue of her gender. Thus, these very diverse narratives are pure in one respect: they are *medical* autobiographies, designed and intended to advance the cause of traditional medicine as a profession.

I suppose this makes the Paths essays sound very dry indeed, and perhaps they are for readers who were not there at the time. Yet I think we must take seriously the sense of urgency with which the editors went about this task and the warm welcome the essays received when they began to appear. The appeal of these essays undoubtedly had something to do with the fact that this generation of senior Chinese doctors had lived through most of the twentieth century (many were born before the Republican revolution of 1911). Of course, they had witnessed massive social transformations, but it was more important to their essays that they had led the field of Chinese medicine through a period of unprecedented attack (before 1949) and even more unprecedented expansion after Liberation. They were the founders and designers of the forms of medicine and professional life that are now recognized as "traditional medicine" in China. They had taught and supervised a large proportion of the younger doctors who were just then coming into their own as leaders in a new wave of reorganization and expansion. Their writings, however anonymous they sometimes were, had informed the preoccupations and practices of everyone working in the field. In short, they were heroes.

Up until the end of the Cultural Revolution, however, they were heroes without stories. Maoism had provided one master narrative, that of the people. Assimilation of individual lives into this grand communist project offered many personal rewards, not the least of which was an inspiration to join in "the battle against disease" and an admirable role as humble servant of the people. But there is also little doubt that by 1980 this idealistic regime of national and personal sacrifice had suffered fatal blows. The fear of reprisals against those who committed themselves to a theoretical stance or practical course was receding, and there was much highly visible work to be done in retooling Chinese medicine for "market socialism." People were ready to "put out their heads" in a novel way. The autobiographies of senior doctors showed them how.

These life stories grounded medical authority in a rich relationship with history (the accounts of revered teachers and classic texts) and practice (emblematic clinical cases, discoveries about drug use and therapeutic technique). They proffered experience as a comprehensive ground on which all manner of things could be combined, and they valorized individual doctors as the sites at which this (newly privatized) experience could accumulate. This was a vision of the profession that brought readers into a professional imaginary that addressed them as individuals—scholars who had some connection with those senior teachers and writers, professionals who might someday embody the same amount of authority and garner the same explicit respect. And, perhaps most importantly, doctors and their students could come to see themselves as bringing the past glories of scholarly medicine and practical healing back to life through the arts of memory—not only commemorating their elders but memorizing the treasures of the archive, not only remembering their own formative experiences but recalling for students the great developments in the field as a whole. Although texts were very important in preserving the field, the Paths project insisted that people were even more important sites of traditional medicine's precious experience.

There is one problem, however, with a professional culture that revolves around individuals. People die. Hence, great emphasis was placed by the Paths editors on the advanced age of their subjects and on the fact that many were ill or dying, and they decided to devote volume 3 to biographies of recently dead luminaries written by their students and descendants. Thus, something might be salvaged of the extratextual lives of these forebears before living memory faded too much. Perhaps the several kinds of history and memory that can be embodied in an authoritative figure could still be held together under personal names.

The problem of natural attrition eventually led to a decline in the usefulness of this structure of experience, however. Although it was immensely attractive for a while to see the most essential knowledge of the field as something that had accumulated in the lives of individual sages—for one thing, it made a nice contrast to the ultra-rationalization of "Western medicine"—this was in fact an inadequate foundation for a modernizing field. By the later 1980s, a parallel strain of discourse and practice, that of scientific research on Chinese medicine, had gained a great deal of ground. As I write this in 2001, the more personal universe of embodied practice and idiosyncratic experience is still active in some quarters, but it is beginning to look more and more like nostalgia.[22]

I am touched, as I read these life stories, by the hope and optimism they express. These authors tend to be modest in their claims to personal achievements, and some even prefer to emphasize less glorious aspects of their careers. (My personal favorite is the sly essay by Jin Shoushan, "Paths Are Made by People," in which the author characterizes a number of his self-training methods as "stealing" medical knowledge and techniques and locates the origin of his sneaky studies in his bungling of a treatment.) But they all express confidence that these stories have been progressive ones, that all setbacks provided productive lessons, and that their field of Chinese medicine deserves to continue and develop as a world resource. Many are not sure that such a development is likely; Deng Tietao's characterization of Chinese medicine's future as "a long and clouded road" is typical, for example.[23] Although many authors characterized their essays as backward looks, in fact almost all were quite pointedly looking forward. They took their responsibility as guides for youth quite seriously, it seems, and most of them tried to distill some principles from their experience that would translate from the conditions that had produced them to the new and different conditions under which younger people were practicing.

These senior Chinese doctors, in other words, in writing their lives put out their heads as exemplars. Unlike Du Wanxiang, who owed most of her personality to the Maoist tradition of the model worker and was constantly disappearing into the masses, these seniors spoke of specificity, diversity, discrimination, and embodied knowledge. They were not there to be literally emulated but to inspire newly particular, individual careers. These were especially envisioned as careers that could draw on Chinese medicine's huge archive in the service of practical clinical insight. This point is emphasized by what is perhaps the most authoritative of the various prefaces to the *Paths* volumes, that written in 1982 by scholar, historian, and doctor Ren Yingqiu for volume 3.

When Xu Dachun [1693–1771] took up the idea that "In medicine it isn't everybody who can study the literature," he said, "Medicine is a Dao—the reason why the ancient sages revealed the secrets of heaven and earth and took hold of the powers of creation and change (*zaohua*) was to save people from death. The essence of these patterns is as subtly nuanced as [those of] the gods; anyone who is not clever and sensitive to philosophy simply cannot study medicine. . . . The feeling of some illnesses can be conveyed in an instant, but true and false may at one time be hard to distinguish, at another time slow to emerge, and [what makes the difference between] life and death must sometimes be instantly judged—anyone who is not both humble and flexible (*lingbian*) simply cannot study medicine. Illness names number in the thousands, symptoms in the tens of thousands. There are the visceral systems and circulation tracts, the internal doses and external treatments, books of drugs and formulae; in many years, one could not enumerate them—anyone who is not a diligent reader and a good recorder simply cannot study medicine. Further, after the *Inner Canon*, scholarly factions divided, people set themselves up as teachers, there was no lack of biased disputants, and there were plenty of eccentric writings and philistine teachings. Confusedly put forth and unevenly established, these confused and misled people to a hundred different ends; anything might be a mistaken belief, yet whole lives could be committed to them. Anyone who cannot carefully scrutinize to determine the truth simply cannot study medicine. Thus, to be a follower of this Tao one must have exceptional abilities and the knowledge of an erudite scholar as well as being able to reject vulgar things and commit his heart and mind for many years. He must also receive the teachings of masters and at the same time be able to penetrate to the tacit meanings hidden at the heart of the ancient sages." This statement by Xu Dachun has its true aspect in that he says that medical theory is subtle and deep and the ancient classic works are rather difficult to read; the medical literature is indeed vast; it cannot be finished in a short period of reading. From ancient times to the present, each scholar and each school has had differing teachings, so who's right and who's wrong needs to be actively distinguished. This is a reality with which everyone who studies Chinese medicine will be confronted.[24]

The autobiographies of senior Chinese doctors presumably only added to the welter of positions and possibilities offered by the medical archive, and readers would have to select for themselves from many conflicting and contradictory materials. In a clinical field, it could not be otherwise. Consequential decisions about treatment strategies must be made, and the totality of experience can neither be comprehended nor mobilized for particular daily tasks. Thus, the task for a serious doctor becomes one of personal embodiment through both accumulation of experience (in the clinic and the library) and a deep grasp of the essences lurking in that experience. The responsibility to "penetrate to the tacit meanings hidden in the heart of the ancient sages" cannot, these materials suggest, be taught in a few evenings or a few years of bookish study. It is a lifelong quest, and inevitably when a good doctor dies something irrecoverable dies with him.

The writing styles of the essays in *Paths of Renowned Senior Chinese Doctors* reflect a certain naïveté about the capacity of ordinary language to represent a life and its significance. They are presented in chronological order, they note the names of people and books and places, and they draw morals from events as readily as Aesop's fables. Still, the very position of these humble texts in a vast archive, and their deployment in a training process that had its own challenges and traditional practices, suggests that no one believed them to have captured any of the essential things about their revered authors. The path metaphor itself suggests otherwise. After all, the path is not the traveler, and those of us who retrace the traveler's steps will never see or experience quite what he or she did.

Language Crisis

To address the problem of how texts can represent or otherwise address experience, I return to "Love Must Not Be Forgotten." Much of this famous story centers on dilemmas of writing and language. Even beyond the obvious fact that Zhong Yu's diary comprises the central occasion for the narrative, there is hardly a detail in the story that does not address a problem of verbal representation in some respect. It is not only important that Zhong Yu was an author of stories, that she treasured a set of Chekhov's works given her by her lover, and that her lover died as a result of something he said about a theoretical essay. We have also seen that "those three words," the "I love you" that was never spoken between them, form a certain silent center around which her whole life is organized.

Zhang Jie was one of many fiction writers in the early 1980s who wrote in a language that they believed was in crisis.[25] Modern standard Chinese (*baihua*) was a twice-colonized tongue, having suffered first the semicolonial modernizations of the early-twentieth-century vernacular movement[26] and then the ideologically charged idioms of Maoism, which produced a language heavily loaded with both a global and a state political history, some of which these early reform era writers sought to definitively escape.

They were not so naive as to think, however, that they could recover an uncompromised language in which to express experience and meaning. Neither writing nor practice can be purified of the history of discourses; no part of the lived world is innocent of previous representations. As a consequence, any literature that seeks to be both innovative and effective must work toward new forms using the tools and methods of older ones. Zhang Jie and other 1980s writers thus found themselves in an unresolvable dilemma, seeking to make sense of experience through a historically mixed and heavily freighted language and using writing to produce a new (more private, more autonomous) kind of experience.

One way in which these writers dealt with the problem was to thematize language itself, both making fun of and despairing of its limited powers. In some respects, this was a problem of the moment: it was both a source of bitterness and an occasion of much humor that "words" had managed to depart so far from "reality" in the short history of the People's Republic. In B. Michael Frolic's interviews of the late 1970s, for example, urban youths sent down to the countryside hilariously theorized pigs' failure to thrive in terms incongruously derived from Maoist dialectics: "the internal factor (the pig itself) is the main contradiction."[27] In a story by Shen Rong, journalists must admit that the "secret" of one village's economic survival, however exemplary, would not survive their published reports of it.[28] At the optimistic ending of Gu Hua's *Hibiscus Town*, the town's propagandist and ideological activist is denounced as a "god of plague" and sent to an asylum muttering his now clichéd slogans.[29] In Zhang Xianliang's pessimistic *Half of Man Is Woman,* much fear is aroused by the prospect that "Dumbo," a worker driven to mute idiocy by politics, might one day soon begin to speak again.[30] And, as we saw in chapter 2, Lu Wenfu's *The Gourmet* problematizes language itself and questions its efficacy. The dialectical materialist analysis to which Old Gao subjected the food business was seen by some as a pack of lies, but finally it began to appear simply as an exhausted idiom, no longer able to clarify a present or promise a future.[31]

"Love Must Not Be Forgotten," earlier than any of these, gestures toward an interesting position on this problem of language. This aspect of the story opens with Shanshan's disappointment with her suitor, Qiao Lin. Describing with relish his resemblance to a Greek statue, Shanshan at first appears less concerned than her mother with questions of truth and writing; but she analyzes her lover's weaknesses in terms of his inability to articulate anything beyond a sort of binary classification. His shortcomings are summarized in his linguistic limits. Shanshan says,

> Qiao Lin and I have been together for nearly two years, yet I still cannot fathom whether his habit of reticence is because he just dislikes talking or because he has nothing to say. When I decide to test his intelligence and insist on getting his opinion of something or other, he can only utter the kind of words used in kindergarten: he just says "good" or "bad" (*hao, buhao*), and can't rephrase it any other way. Once when I asked, "Qiao Lin, why do you love me?" he thought the question over seriously for about an age, a really long time for him. I could see from the way his normally smooth forehead got all wrinkled that the little grey cells in his handsome head were engaged in a very demanding thought process. I couldn't help feeling pity for him and a little ashamed—it was if I were grilling him with this question. Finally he raised his clear childlike eyes to tell me, "Because you're good." My heart filled with a very profound loneliness. (103; 1–2)

Shanshan's loneliness becomes even more understandable as a failure of language later in the story, when she speculates about what it was her mother had loved about her own lover: "Analyzing it now, it must have been he who had moved Mother's heart with his greatness of spirit. That great spirit came from his mature and steadfast political consciousness, his narrow escapes from death during the revolution, his lively mind, his dedication to his work, his cultivation in literature and the arts. . . . On top of all that, strange to say, he and my mother both liked the oboe" (112–13, 8).[32] A paragon, indeed, the sort of person one could talk with for many years. The fact that the dialogue carried on between these two lovers was quite one-sided might have made it more convenient to sustain. But surely the most important enabling element in this conversation was the fact that both partners loved language and understood its powers. Unlike Qiao Lin, they had much to say but very little opportunity to say it. Zhong Yu, pouring her feelings out in a diary, was not able to make direct references to this illicit relationship. So her diary is fragments of a conversation, not an attempt to describe or characterize her love, her lover, or herself. This central text in "Love Must Not Be Forgotten" does not even begin to realistically represent a coherent world; it simply generates mundane but impassioned language within it.

Neither Shanshan nor Zhong Yu finds anyone with whom to really exchange words. There is a solipsistic quality to their verbal life: they read; one of them, at least, writes; and they dream in a language that articulates a changing reality and an expanding inner life. Both keep faith with the promise of language to map reality. Although life fails them by providing no suitable interlocutor, they do not doubt the value of conversation or the power of writing to depict a shared world.

Although words only falteringly represent reality in the story, they do have certain real powers. Perhaps the most direct efficacy we witness for a text is the effect of Zhong Yu's diary on her daughter. This effect was not intended; Zhong Yu had directed Shanshan to cremate the diary and the treasured set of Chekhov's works with her. As she wrote, then, the older woman anticipated no readers but herself, even as she imagined a fully formed interlocutor in the old cadre. But for Shanshan, who cannot bear to destroy the diary, reading makes all the difference. She even reembodies her mother as she reads the diary: "At first I thought these were raw materials she had jotted down for the things she was writing. They didn't look like stories or reading notes, or a diary, or letters. But after reading the whole thing from beginning to end those fragmentary entries and my fragmentary memory came together to form a nebulous impression. After thinking it over a long time, I finally understood that what I was holding in my hand was not a lifeless, bloodless text but a passionately warm, suffering heart full of love, and I could see how that heart had struggled in its anguished love" (109; 6). Reading the fragments her mother had written only for herself, Shanshan goes beyond the life-less, bloodless text. She even learns something about memory as she imagines her mother's long struggle.[33] Not that the text has encour-aged her to read so much into it, but having lost her mother so re-cently Shanshan is ready to read in a new way, a way that puts some-thing quite warm and alive into her hands.

This capacity of language to stimulate emotions and imagination is referred to elsewhere in the story in a much more mundane ex-change. One of Zhong Yu's writer friends jokes that her essays are so beautifully written that "just reading your works could make anyone fall in love with you" (107; 4). Zhong Yu replies tartly that all they would need to sober them up was one look at her wrinkles and gray hair. Her friend points to the efficacy of her language; Zhong Yu points to its inability to depict what is real.

Of course, this is quite a literal understanding of how language represents. But even at a deeper level of meaning we are left unable to determine what sort of world written language gives us. Perhaps the most touching acknowledgment of this condition in the story appears at the moment of Shanshan's diary-induced decision not to marry: "Every time I read that notebook entitled "Love Must Not Be Forgot-ten" I cannot hold back my own tears. I sob, sob uncontrollably, just as if this miserable and tragic love had been my very own experience. If this was not a tragedy it was a big joke. No matter how beautiful or moving it was, then, I have no wish to repeat it" (121; 14). If this love was not tragedy, it was farce. Which was it? How would one decide? Even Shanshan, informed by her imaginative participation in the emotions lurking within her mother's diary notes, can't work it out. But finally she has little doubt about what (not) to do.

Conclusion

"Love Must Not Be Forgotten" has brought us into that space where ethics and politics both intersect and divide. Shanshan decides what to do more or less on her own, orienting herself toward a future for which she will have to take responsibility. By the end of the story, she has sorted out her values and drawn her life and desires apart from those of moralizing others who might judge her on the basis of more conservative principles. Once she has done so, she begins to speak as if this choice has been made not for herself alone but for many: "I really want to shout out, mind your own business, let us wait patiently, wait for the one who calls to us; even if we wait in vain this is better than a meaningless marriage! Don't worry that the solitary life might become some kind of frightful disaster. Know this: it could be that this is actually a higher form of social life with respect to civilization, cultivation, delightfulness, and more!" (122; 15). This is, I think, a fairly classic ethical resolution. A foundation for an evaluative choice has been found in the self, and this choice has been declared to be generalizable. Crying out now on behalf of a "we," the narrator declares her romantic vision of personal autonomy to be appropriate not just in one situation or for one actor but for many who occupy a wider social, even civilizational, field.

Of course, this apparent choice did not come easily; a great deal of groundwork had to be laid in advance. The self capable of such a choice was a new sort of construct built on the rubble and with some of the tools of Maoist discourse. The fact, for example, that Shanshan envisions a better society and civilization, more cultivation, and more delight *rather than* the achievement of true communism is very interesting. The state and party forms that would sustain the progress from socialism to true communism (wherein the state "withers away") are nowhere to be found in her ethical vision. This young woman, then, "the same age as our People's Republic," divides private ethical choice from the public imperatives that concern the state; she also divides the individual from society with her final passionate cry.

Zhong Yu's situation, and that of her lover, are not so simple, or at least not so readily recognized by those of us who have inherited an Enlightenment division between ethics and politics, private and public, and the individual and society. She and the old cadre apparently had no difficulty seeing in what direction their duty lay. Not only were they unwilling to cause another person pain, thus adhering to a conventional "do unto others" morality, but, perhaps more important, neither doubted the correctness of his original choice to marry without love. Zhong Yu admired her lover for his revolutionary commitment in "unhesitatingly" marrying the daughter of the "old worker" who had died for the revolution. The old cadre is imagined to have seen his marriage devoted to work and children as more trouble free than matches that arise from unreliable passions. The story thus makes it appear that choices were simple in those days; the working class was always right, and the task of reordering an unjust old regime always came first. Individual desires might exist—though without a usable language to express them one wonders just what their mode of existence might have been—but they would always be submerged in the good of the collective.

Zhang Jie in this story uses the figure of Zhong Yu, the good communist, both to craft a private self and to problematize its powers and limits. Her daughter Shanshan bravely and hopefully faces an utterly unimaginable future as an ethical individual (adapted, not accidentally, to a privatizing market economy), but Zhong Yu dwells in duty, love, and (partly) the past. She does not seek the freedom to choose, her only rebellion being her insistence on writing to sustain her imagination. Her situation, as her daughter points out, was either tragic or a farce, and neither is quite what one would wish for a life. But at least her life has the ring of truth about it. Her plausibility is grounded in its moment; she suggests a post–Cultural Revolution private self still constrained by public values but at least inventing a personal past to remember and a personal present to chronicle. Shanshan must have been inspiring for some despite the uncertainty of her future, but I think I have company among Chinese readers in preferring Zhong Yu's (and even her old cadre's) parts of the story.

Zhang Jie presented early reform readers with an ambivalent, irresolvable form of subjectivity and experience. I share her ambivalence, and I am attracted to writing like hers, which refuses to rush to judgment. The fully autonomous self is not, after all, very plausible. And however much it may frame its dilemmas as ethical ones that implicate universal (or universalizable) values, this self cannot come into existence without politics. The value regime that made both Zhong Yu and Shanshan imaginable, that allowed Zhang Jie to push the limits of language while referring constantly to its failings, was still a reflex both of the state politics that changed so drastically after 1976 and the discursive politics that infuses language and everyday practice with powers and limits.

Perhaps this sense of the mutual implication of ethics and politics is what has attracted me for many years to the vision of Chinese medicine I glimpsed in the early 1980s. This vision could not afford to ignore politics, and yet it took form within a classically ethical domain, that of healing. Transformations in public values were very clearly on the professional agenda in the early reform period. And the complexity of this changing situation was addressed very effectively and prominently by those senior doctors who put their personal and scholarly experience on the line and did so in writing. Arguing that the medical archive was far too complex to ever be mobilized in toto, they emphasized the ways in which they had themselves selected from among the riches of the past to provide responsible and effective clinical services. They wrote idiosyncracy but not creation. Drawing from the archive and learning from the unpredictable challenges of everyday clinical life, they crafted principled paths along which to organize their healing and their teaching. Although these processes of selection were carefully depoliticized in the essays, in keeping with the revisionist tenor of the early reform period, they were not seen as free choices. Rather, they were profoundly constrained by past experience, past writing, and the limits of what could actually be recovered in memory and scholarship. This unfreedom is not so different from the ethics that informs any medical practice; faced with a sufferer and armed with methods that could relieve that suffering, doctors seek a good that is relatively clear-cut. It is not so surprising, then, that the *Paths* autobiographers did not aspire to any true autonomy from "society" or even "the state." Instead they tinkered with their positions within a national tradition and a state system of practical institutions.

This may seem a modest task, perhaps a little tedious. Yet there was a huge optimism and excitement alive in the field at the time. When I arrived at the Guangzhou College of Traditional Chinese Medicine in 1982, I saw a great deal of evidence of a revived and newly ambitious field; every aspect of medical work and every college department was expanding, and the recent literature of the field was already massive. A newly reinstated academic and clinical leadership was sharing power with party cadres. The first class admitted on the basis of merit since the mid-1960s was about to graduate, and there were several postgraduate programs thriving on campus. Other changes, quieter ones that could be called rectifications after Mao, were ongoing. One of them involved me.

The adviser to whom I was assigned was historian and philosopher Huang Jitang. The administrator who arranged this relationship hinted that it was an honor for both of us. Professor Huang had recently been rehabilitated—I later learned that he had been denounced as a rightist in 1957—and I was his first designated graduate student. This was thought of as a milestone for him and further proof that his proper status had been restored. On the other hand, he was clearly seen by all on campus as an intellectual treasure. However badly they may have treated him during his many years of political disgrace, people now acted as if no one had ever doubted the superiority of his mind, the depth of his learning, or the integrity of his commitment to traditional medicine. I was expected to learn a great deal from him, and I did.

I learned much too much to chronicle here, in fact. And a great deal of what I learned, the part I value the most, was intangible. Professor Huang helped me with my studies in the classroom, reviewing my notes and elaborating on what teachers (might have) said. He assigned me extra philosophical and historical readings, which I struggled through much more slowly than either of us wished. After a while, he began to comment on his own early studies, which had begun with philosophy in Hong Kong before Liberation and continued with Marxism and the history of medicine after his return to the mainland. We discovered a mutual interest in philosophical pragmatism (He taught me Dewey and I said a few things about Rorty) and a shared love for the vigor of the writing we found in Marx and Mao. He explained to me his own views on how the Taoist canon and medical classics related to each other. We never spoke of the Cultural Revolution.

I have a number of scraps of paper saved from our tutorials; they show snatches of text and numerous single words in both our hands, diagrams that are not helpfully labeled, jotted page numbers referring to the (unrecorded) text we might have been working on at the time. There is even the occasional tea stain. Whatever these marks may have once represented is quite lost to me. But looking at them does help me remember how, working across a rather formidable language barrier (his southern accent and literary allusions gave me difficulty, while my stumbling grammar and limited vocabulary were surely a challenge for him to decode), we came to share a joy in language and its complicated historical accumulations that I, at least, treasured. It's been a long time since those afternoons in Guangzhou, and the experiences I had there are by now as much fantasy as memory. But my scattered notes remind me still that it felt like love.

chapter 5

SEXUAL SCIENCE: THE REPRESENTATION

OF BEHAVIOR

On the face of it at least, our civilization possesses no *ars erotica*. In return, it is undoubtedly the only civilization to practice a *scientia sexualis;* or rather, the only civilization to have developed over the centuries procedures for telling the truth of sex which are geared to a form of knowledge-power strictly opposed to the art of initiations and the masterful secret: I have in mind the confession.
—Michel Foucault

Beginning in the mid-1980s, Chinese modernity began to look a lot more sexy. Several distinct literatures on sex—pornographic novels and magazines, family sexual hygiene manuals, medical sexology, respectable erotic fiction, translations of sexology classics like Havelock Ellis's *Sexual Psychology* and the Kinsey Report, scholarship on ancient Chinese ars erotica, and a new subdiscipline of traditional medicine called *nanke*, "men's medicine"—emerged and flourished in a book market that was no longer directly controlled by the state. Gender differentiation in the surfaces of everyday life—dress, cosmetics, and gestural style—became extreme for a while, particularly among the young, with rococo assemblages of ruffles, ribbons, sequins, and satins mostly on women and leather jackets, cowboy gear, and motorcycle boots mostly on men.[1] In many cities, shops opened where white-coated clerks sell birth control supplies, condoms, herbal aphrodisiacs, skimpy leather clothing, and sexual aids in a matter-of-fact, clinical manner. By the late 1990s, Chinese-made movies had begun to include explicitly filmed sex scenes as a matter of routine. Beijing viewers say that "the sex scene" is now obligatory for films, and even family-oriented television shows make increasingly open references to both marital and nonmarital sex.

The family of a farm wife who also does tailoring on market days poses after changing their clothes for the camera in 1990. She wears a skirt, and her daughter wears a ruffled princess dress that her mother made for her. A few years before she would not have admitted to owning clothes like this. Author photo.

A photo shop that includes makeovers offers sample looks on a signboard outside its door for customers to consider. Author photo, 1990.

At the same time, from the early 1980s on, rates of sexually transmitted disease began to soar and commercial sexual services became widely available. By 1990, specialized clinics for treatment of such diseases and "men's disorders" had appeared, not only in cities but in rural areas. Even the storefront doctors I know who practice medicine in county towns to which few of the new books make their way are beginning to invent or study up on treatments for venereal diseases and sexual functional disorders.[2]

Thus, since the late 1980s there have been many venues for explicit representations of sexual activity. One of them is the national sex survey, one of the main topics of this chapter, which clearly acknowledges the popular explosion of sexual discourse and imagery. Question 8 of the survey's college student questionnaire, for example, lists the following as possible sources of "sexual knowledge": newspapers and magazines, Chinese films and TV, foreign films and TV, literature and the arts, medical and public health literature, and pornographic reading matter. Other questions, notably number 35 of the questionnaire for sex offenders, mention home viewing of videos as well as public theaters, entertainment centers, and "secret video establishments."

These media for consuming sexual knowledge are not equally accessible to all people, but they are very numerous and widespread and their influence extends far beyond the big cities to figure in the street life of rural market towns throughout the rapidly developing parts of China. Often located near train and bus stations, video parlors, for example, tend to show mainstream films during the day—Hong Kong and U.S. action films feature prominently here, along with a few Bombay spectaculars—and offer more sexually explicit fare at night. Respectable people think of these businesses as magnets for undesirables from other areas, and I've been told that no one would risk patronizing such a place (at night anyway) in their own home town. Places through which travelers pass are also prime locations for print media sensationalism, much of which is more interested in violence than sex; it is easier to find sexploitation magazines on sale near train stations than elsewhere in the towns I have visited, but newsstands in residential neighborhoods sometimes keep small and unobtrusive stocks of disreputable publications. Some bookstalls have more pornography hidden in the back, not on display but available on request for any who think—or dare—to ask for it.[3]

A 1991 health magazine,
Friend of Health, has a young
female model on its cover.
This issue also announces
an article on lesbian love.

Although the erotic boom is largely oriented toward heterosexual
sex, publications for gay men and lesbians are intermittently published in Beijing and elsewhere and the sexology literature takes up
homosexuality as a topic with varying degrees of disapproval. Gay
subcultures of a highly fluid kind flourish in a few big cities.[4] In the
spring of 2001, Beijing newspapers reported that the newly published
Chinese Standards for Classification and Diagnosis of Mental Disorders
had deleted homosexuality from its official list of mental disorders.[5]
Masturbation occasions a large amount of concerned discussion,
most of which concludes that this asocial practice is natural but not
very wholesome.

Meanwhile public representations of sexualized commodities
abound. Advertising in reform era China was quick to adopt the strategy of draping a beautiful model across a washing machine, and
many perfectly sober family magazines—about health, interior deco-
ration, sewing—boast cover photos of seductive women in lip gloss
and jewels (and sometimes little else), their ringleted images making
no pretense of connection to the content of the publication. Imported
and domestic films and TV shows are quite explicit about who is sleep-

ing with whom, and the depiction of erotic behavior in these widely distributed media is beginning to resemble the range of possibilities with which we are familiar in the United States.

This apparently sex-obsessed (and commodity- and violence-obsessed) street life possesses in fact more than a resemblance, since so much of it is directly imported to China from the United States.[6] Whatever cultural specificities might be found in urban Chinese everyday life, they cannot be sought in textual materials alone, partly because so many of these resources so closely resemble the books, magazines, films, and television shows that make up North American everyday life. Many media products are translations of U.S. bestsellers and classics, and some bookstores in Beijing carry little besides translations from European languages and Japanese. The sex that is taking the Chinese market by storm, in other words, is precisely that recognizable entity with which we in the Euro-American West have lived for the past hundred years or so.[7]

Or so it seems, though its very multiplicity and commercial energy suggests room for unthought possibilities. In any case, anthropologists are always tempted to consider the local meanings of these globally circulating cultural entities. The history of both pronatalist propaganda in the 1950s and 1960s and birth control campaigns in the 1980s and 1990s in China, for example, suggests that sex must have shifted its significance a number of times even within the latter part of the twentieth century. Once an integral part of a complex in which families ensured continuity and wealth through a complex politics of kinship and marriage, sex changed its functionality when the Maoist state made individual workers and bureaucratic work units the target of so many of its policies. After collectivization in the 1950s, old family strategies were much less emphasized even by the large rural population that had traditionally lived by them, and the reproduction-oriented subjectivities these strategies had fostered also shifted. Sex became a tabooed subject for language, and (as I argued in the preamble to part II) erotic attention turned toward cooperative production for the state. For a while, model mothers were rewarded for building socialism by giving birth to many children in a Maoist logic that tried to translate all the challenges of national development into the correct deployment of more and more human labor. But by the early 1980s China's famous birth control policies began to be implemented in a serious way. As Chinese citizens in many walks of life—farmers who still need family-controlled labor and reproductive capacity, workers whose "iron rice bowl" has been eliminated, white-collar careerists who think more of money than family—have adjusted their desires to new policies and new market conditions, the role of sex in life and experience has been changing rapidly again. As much of the material discussed in these chapters suggests, since the mid-1980s sexuality has emerged as a part of life quite apart from either reproduction or obligations to the state. Sex has become a freestanding topic in a brand new way. Although sexuality in China these days looks more and more like an attribute of bourgeois individuals, a source of private pleasure, and a social force requiring moral surveillance—in other words, quite "normal" by cosmopolitan standards—the very recentness of its appearance as such no doubt gives it a special urgency and charm. Moreover, as I will argue below and have suggested in chapter 4, this naturalization of a cosmopolitan sexuality is also a form of individualization, one that is linked to the unstated assumptions of social science and to other forms of modern knowledge production in China.

It could be argued that the sexy images that are now proliferating are at least as important in conveying a generalized imagination of modernity and wealth as they are in stimulating erotic feeling or educating innocent youth about ways of performing sexuality. Certainly this often seems to be the case where there are domestic displays of (more or less) erotic calendar art. Many rooms for newlyweds in rural compounds, for example, are decorated not only with dowry furniture and fairy lights but with photographic images of nearly nude women surrounded by (though not always wearing) cosmopolitan commodities. The photographic style is *Playboy* magazine; the models nowadays may be either Euro-American or Asian.[8] The message of these images is a complex one that cannot be separated from a number of concurrent concerns of their consumers. Among these are the politics of mate selection and family nuclearization in villages, where most marriages are still arranged; the related politics of family planning policy, which makes the sexuality of couples a semipublic concern; the expressive requirements of marriage rituals, in which everyone inspects the "newlywed bedchamber"; the uses of space in industrializing rural areas where land has only recently been freed from grain production to allow the construction of new housing; the claims of entrepreneurial young farmers to have commercially useful connections to bigger towns and cities; the assertion of generational distinctions that set off the post-Mao generation from its less consumerist parents; and much more. Perhaps all of these elements can be summarized as a kind of "rural development modern" in which sexy calendar art figures as a condensed signifier linking its users to a new and ambitious imaginary. Under these circumstances, it hardly seems useful to see such images as narrowly or directly sexual.[9]

Newlywed bedchambers are not, after all, the only places where pinup photos appear. I have also frequently seen them in the main rooms of houses where meals are eaten, children study, guests are entertained, sewing is done, and family life is lived. They are displayed in exactly the same way as calendar art of fuzzy kittens, dimpled babies, popular music stars, and tulip fields in Holland. In these cases, it is even more obvious that such pictures assert a generalized image of modernity, wealth, and cosmopolitanism.

Beauty is also an issue. This became especially clear to me in a tumble-down restaurant in a Shandong county town where one crumbling wall of the back room (which doubled as a bedroom and family room after hours) was papered with twelve large calendar pages. These glossy color photos depicted a matched set of Asian models wearing fabulous fur coats over very small bikinis and very high heels. In the summer of 1991, I ate in this small establishment often (the proprietor was a good cook and he needed all the business he could get). In the course of my frequent chats with the waitress—who worked there six days a week, returning to her remote village about twice a month to see her five children (a highly illegal number!)—she indicated that these pictures gave her pleasure because they were very beautiful. When I asked her where she wanted to have her own picture taken, she chose to stand before that wall.

We could interpret popular pinup photography as insulting to the dignity of women. And it would not necessarily be a contradiction to report that many women don't perceive this insult. But in trying to understand how the surface sexiness of modern Chinese life affects the desires and gratifications of real people there are, I think, more interesting questions. Such questions might focus on the particular means and processes through which a relatively new account of bodily life, one centering on sexual activity and employing "procedures for telling the truth of sex," actually reaches modern Chinese people: how, in other words, a global revolution in popular culture might alter (or leave untouched or suggest new capacities for) the life of the local body.

Do viewers, for example, turn these images to fantasy account? As men make love with their wives, do they fantasize the Hong Kong, Singapore, or Hollywood woman? Do their wives mind? Do their wives identify with these femininities or fantasize about their corollary masculinities? Do the stiletto heels and fur coats figure in somebody's mind's eye? If so, when? How, in practice, would we know what goes on at this level? Experience of this kind is not, I think, particularly accessible to anthropological research. Perhaps the global poster girls for wealth, modernity, and standardized female beauty are making their way into the hearts of Chinese men and haunting the beds of Chinese couples. But the mere presence of these images on the wall or in the market cannot reveal the nature of their subjective efficacy. Certainly we have to believe that wealth, beauty, and modernity are important elements in the consumption of erotic images because people will tell us as much. Nevertheless, as I will argue below, we cannot quite drain the sex from these images of the modern. Rather, we must presume that for the moment modernity is sexy and explicit representations of sex are modern.

Because it is clear that residents of Beijing, Shandong, Guangzhou, and many other places in China tend to take modernity as an unalloyed good, and because I suspect that erotic experience might be especially vulnerable to authoritative suggestion, I must also presume that things are changing in the life of the body in China and that the commercial dissemination of sexual imagery has something to do with these changes. In other words, I am interested in the powers of the new incitements to desire that have appeared while at the same time I do not wish to attempt an exhaustive representation of that desire. It is part of the argument here that any such attempt would be doomed.

In this chapter, then, I presume that an object called sexuality is coming into being in China in a specific relationship with global modernity. Science, via survey research, mediates this relationship. Thus, in what follows I focus on certain aspects of sexological research and sex education, two new (and closely linked) arenas where the prestige of systematic data collection and analysis, and the authority of cosmopolitan expertise, operate to add reality to particular

formations of desire and practice. In collusion with certain reifi-
cations and reductions typical of the scientific method, the "sexuality"
that is emerging in the Chinese popular cultural mainstream is increasingly naturalized and normalized. History is turning into nature, as Bourdieu has pointed out in other contexts.

Of course, this history is not innocent of politics. Here I will briefly
examine several new projects: survey research on "sexual behavior"
and formal sex education pedagogy directed at the physical body
(routi). In these projects, many of the broad social and political dilemmas of the reform period may be discerned. At the same time, these
new sexualized objects of attention simultaneously produce and oc-
clude the very forms of experience that apparently draw their (and my)
interest. As sexual behavior and the physical body take on authoritative reality in science and pedagogy, experts in these fields also advance the broader civilizing project of national modernization and
bourgeois normalization. This civilizing project attempts to colonize
bodies from a somewhat different angle than most of the popular materials mentioned above. This "official" sex of sociological surveys and
formal sex education is particularly interesting, however, because it
carries the authority of science and the national interest with it.[10]

Scientia Sexualis

Science, like writing, is a representational practice. But it differs from
the fictional realism discussed in chapter 4 in its rigorous insistence
on the independent existence of the reality it represents. In their classic study of the practice of science, Bruno Latour and Steve Woolgar
contend that "the strength of correspondence between objects and
statements about objects stems from the splitting and inversion of a
statement within the laboratory context."[11] This process of splitting
and inversion is lucidly explained by Woolgar in his later introduction
to the field of science studies, Science, the Very Idea.[12] He notes five
steps, or stages, in the process through which science splits off a
seemingly natural object, places it "out there," and inverts its practical relationship with the work of representation. This process of
knowledge production in the laboratory sciences is also discernible in
the sociological research that informs modern sexology in China. Understanding the way in which certain natural objects come into exis-

tence in scientific practice can help us to understand other common objects that are emerging in the reform period. In Woolgar's scheme, the stages of scientific discovery are as follows.

1. First there are documents or "traces." In this case, these would include the classic works of foreign sexology, the epidemiology of sexually transmitted diseases, new statistics on rape, prostitution, pornography, and so on. These documents have already brought into view a domain that is unproblematically identified as sexual, one that is probably both narrower and broader than anyone's personal experience.

2. In the hands of researchers, the various topics of the documents are reorganized and delimited into a new (hypothetical) object, for example, "Chinese sexual behavior." That such an object exists seems plausible from the documents at hand, especially since they contain an image of a sex that is both naturally given for humans and socially and culturally inflected in particular communities. These texts propose universal models of human nature that are produced and assumed in a global discourse on sex. The documents also rely on an internationally recognized social science methodology rather than local impressions and assumptions. Thus, a social science agenda converges with transnational "common sense" about sex to generate a specific object, located in China, for investigation. As any sociologist knows, considerable labor must be devoted to defining the object in question for purposes of consistency and clarity in the research. All the messy eroticism and theoretical debate (about "instincts," for example) must be carved away, and a purified behavioral object must be conceived.

3. In the course of research, the object and the documents (representations or traces) take on an independent existence. They are split from each other in other words. The sex survey to be discussed below, for example, relies on neutral questions (i.e., suggesting no prior evaluation) that will elicit true statements from informants about their previous sexual experience and their preferences. These experiences and preferences are believed to have existed before the survey was administered and to persist unchanged after the survey has been completed; the multiple choice format dictates as much. Thus, the survey instrument must presume that "sexual behavior" (*xing xingwei*) enjoys an existence independent of the instrument's written questions

and the carefully crafted sociological categories from which they are constructed.

4. The natural object thus constituted then generates new documents, which represent it as real. "Chinese sexual behavior" comes to be *reflected* in the results of the survey. The metaphor of the mirror is important; the reflected object, sexual behavior, is out there, at a great enough distance to be visible in all its discreteness in the mirror of the survey report. The mirror itself is a passive and predictable technology for producing an accurate image. Although investigators may admit that there are problems with the reflected image of their hypothetical object—there may be artifacts in the data stemming from the survey's wording, and not all biases and other "methodological horrors" may have been overcome—the significance of the study results from its capacity to give an objective picture of actual behavior.[13] This actual behavior would be "out there" whether the research had been conducted or not.

5, Finally, researchers deny, or forget about, steps 1 through 3. The purification processes by means of which they have posited a distinct domain of Chinese sexual behavior and the various social processes through which they have decided how this domain is to be represented (and what possibilities are to be ignored or deferred) are no longer part of the official history of the project. Instead the object itself is presented as always having existed in nature; at a certain point in Chinese history, it began clamoring for systematic characterization through scientific research. The summary documents from the survey, the sober scientific language that tells the truth of sex, also severely delimit what it can be: Chinese sexual behavior stems from natural biological needs, it is socially controlled, it is affected by knowledge or ignorance, it is rooted in individuals, and so on.

Splitting and inversion, then, are representational practices that naturalize and reify erotic activity into "sexual behavior." The original documents and the associated research practices that have posited the existence of a particular Chinese form of sexual behavior are drawn apart from sex itself. Sexual behavior becomes the nontextual object targeted by certain very special kinds of texts, a survey questionnaire and a series of statistical reports; it is split from its original home in a range of documents and among the many confusions of received knowledge. Then this object is naturalized to the point where it seems to be the source of the simple reflections shown in the new texts that summarize the results of the study.

I suppose it is important to point out at this point that Latour and Woolgar's arguments about the practice of scientific research do not deny the reality or materiality of the objects with which science concerns itself. They simply seek to interrogate the autonomy of such objects from human practice, in other words, their pure naturalness apart from the activity of human knowers. Similarly, I do not deny the reality and materiality of sexual activity in China; on the contrary, my faith in the actuality and possible diversity of erotic life in China informs the concerns of this whole book. It is obvious that Chinese people have managed to reproduce in more or less the usual ways and that they, like the rest of us, have acted at the prompting of desire and found various kinds of pleasure in physical being. As I suggested about Du Wanxiang at the outset of part II, and as I will argue in chapter 6, erotic activity and sexual pleasure may be attached to many situations and gratify many kinds of agents. But this recognition is a different thing from insisting on the importance of clearly defining *sexual behavior,* distinguishing sexual behavior from all manner of "nonsexual" behaviors, and finding an objective way of characterizing the current average state of sexual behavior through social survey research. It is hard for me to believe in such a discrete object even in my own life much less in the lives of people whose private activities I know much less about. *Sexual behavior* is a term that offers a tidy pigeonhole for some kinds of activity while eclipsing many other less orderly but potentially more interesting erotic realities.

But what is disturbing is how quickly one can come to imagine and believe in a delimited sexual domain given the authority and seductiveness of this category. A reader's understanding of his or her own experience might undergo some reorganization even in the period of time it takes to respond to a survey questionnaire or read an article about the science of sex in a magazine. Such alteration might be especially likely if this domain is strongly associated with positive values like modernity, liberation, nature, and science. One starting place for attaining a better understanding of processes of transformation of this kind is an account of the novel discursive objects offered by powerful new discourses. In the remainder of this chapter, then, I discuss the particular character of the sexuality that was "discovered" by the sex survey, consider the relationship of this discovery to normative discourses on "civilization" (*wenming*), and return eventually to that elusive sex that escapes representation.

Imagining Sex

What a field researcher can learn about cultural sexualities is in part imaginary. The things one tries to piece together about other people's sex lives are speculative by their very nature, even, I suspect, for those interviewers who manage to get people talking about sex in ways that go beyond the formulas of popular discourses. Nor are there method-ological rule books for the way this process of imagining should pro-ceed. Certainly any attempt to separate my own memories and desires from my efforts to envision the experience of others would be a doomed enterprise.

But because I suspect (personally) that of all everyday life enjoy-ments sex is perhaps the most contingent—in the sense that condi-tions ranging from material circumstances to bodily states to shifts in emotional climate conspire to make the moment—I have occasion-ally felt able to read events in an erotic direction. The best example of this method (or antimethod) I can recall dates from the winter of 1991 when I was living in central Beijing. One day I had a surprise late morning visit from a friend who had bicycled over from her work unit several miles away. I hadn't expected to see her because I knew that just the afternoon before she had put her mother on a train back to Sichuan. After nine months of sharing a one-room apartment with her mother, who slept on a cot in the entryway, and her kindergarten-age daughter, who, having outgrown her crib, often shared her par-ents' double bed, it seemed the time was ripe for her to enjoy lunch at home alone with her husband. Both of them had long lunch hours, their daughter had recently taken to staying at school during the mid-day break, and Grandma was no longer in residence. So why was my friend visiting me during this prime time? I'll never know, especially since she had no particular business to transact and she only stayed a few minutes.

But it is easy to imagine a playful (or extremely serious) domestic scenario in which this strange errand makes sense. She timed her de-parture from my room so that she would be back about twenty min-utes after her husband arrived home. I suppose during that twenty minutes he must have wondered where she was and whether she planned to come home for lunch at all. Had she, too, identified this time as a special opportunity or was she going to make him wait a few more days? How would she have handled his anxiety or irritation when she returned? Would she feel she had successfully demonstrated that even marital sex is not to be taken for granted? Perhaps a bike ride in the middle of the day has a salutary effect on one's looks, one's relaxation, one's responsiveness so she was at her physical best by the time she got home. On the other hand, maybe her husband had made and was acting on a few coy plans of his own. What those plans might have been and how they may have colored the encounter I never heard. But I am pretty sure that my guest house room and my very proper friendship played a role in a sexual drama that day.

As an ethnographer, I have not gotten much closer to other people's sex than this. Nor do I want to, at least *as* an ethnographer, however far I may go to imagine the pleasure, desire, or private meaning that might charge the observable surfaces of everyday life. But other kinds of scientists are making a very sustained effort to know and inscribe sex, especially Chinese sex. I turn to them now.

The Sex Survey

In 1992, the first major study of sexual behavior in China was published in Shanghai. Authored by Liu Dalin of Shanghai University and an international team of colleagues and entitled *Contemporary Chinese Sexual Culture: Report of the "Sex Civilization" Survey of 20,000 Subjects,* it summarized the results of a nationwide survey of male and female, married and single, young and middle-aged, and rural and urban Chinese.[14] The sociologists who had organized the survey and analyzed its results concluded that their findings were consistent with those found in similar research in other parts of the world. "On the whole," they concluded, "the present survey reveals a picture of 'average' and in part even robust sexual health in China with a few fuzzy spots that need to be cleared up."[15] These "fuzzy spots" resulted in part from limitations in the topics that could be decently addressed by the questionnaire: questions concerning orgasm, for example, were considered too difficult for Chinese respondents with their current "degree of understanding." Moreover, China's large rural population was significantly underrepresented due to their "low level of education, their feudal attitudes, and their conservatism,"

which would have made it especially difficult, we are told, to adminis-
ter the questionnaire.[16]

The survey did indeed avoid collecting very detailed information.
The most concrete and explicit questions concerning sexual practice
appeared in the questionnaire administered to 7,971 married people.
These asked about foreplay (passionate affection, *qin re* in Chinese,
parenthetically defined as kissing, hugging, and humor) and "fash-
ions of sex life" (*xing shenghuo de fangshi*, which was a translation of
the English "sexual position"). There were also questions about satisfaction (*manyi chengdu*) and pleasure (*kuaigan*), but these were not
connected in the questionnaire to particular practices; rather the respondents were asked "in general" about "sex life."[17] Partly because of
the vagueness of the questions, the results of the survey were not easy
to compare to those of surveys conducted in other countries. We don't
know a lot more about what people do in private than we did before,
in fact. Presuming, however, that this *is* the central question in any
study of sexual behavior, the chapter that discusses the findings
among married couples concludes that "many try various ways of en-
hancing sexual pleasure (e.g., different sexual techniques and positions), but they only do so secretly and there is no open agreement
that it is all right."[18]

What are the chief components of sexual behavior as presumed
and articulated by the questionnaire? Apparently it includes the capacity to be stimulated by seeing images of sexual activity, seeing the
other sex nude, chance body contact with the opposite sex, talking
about sex, "dating," and dancing. These are the choices, along with "at
leisure" and "other," that are offered to high school students on the
questionnaire. Sexual behavior for high school students also includes
masturbation (both sexes) and ejaculation, and respondents are asked
in one question whether they have had sexual intercourse. The survey
went into more detail with older groups, offering them the chance to
answer questions about masturbation and mutual masturbation
(specifying either the same or the opposite sex), fantasies and dreams,
use of aphrodisiacs, becoming sexually stimulated in inappropriate
situations (torture, rape, with children, and so on), and degree of nudity during sexual intercourse. (Full nudity, the report informs us, is
more progressive.) There were also questions about foreplay and timing of marital sexual intercourse as well as whether the role played
was active or passive. Adult respondents were even asked to report the

frequency of heterosexual or homosexual hugging, kissing, genital fondling, coitus, genital-anal and genital-oral contact, and which of three feelings—enjoyment, feeling offended, not minding—was experienced. (For many, this questionnaire must have been an education in itself!) Whatever responses to the most specific questions may have been collected, the more intimate details about sexual activity were not reported in the published findings.[19] A few secrets are still being kept it seems.

These behavioral questions are not the only ones the survey addresses. All the surveys inquire into socioeconomic background and family relationships, sometimes even adding an interesting question on material circumstances. The married couples' questionnaire, for example, asks about the effectiveness of the sound insulation and the presence or absence of other family members in the marital bedroom. A majority of married respondents claimed inadequate privacy but a high degree of "sexual satisfaction" nevertheless. There are also at least as many questions on attitudes toward sexual issues as there are on sexual behavior.

The findings of the study are much too complicated to summarize here, and in any case I am not centrally interested in the sorts of facts the survey collected, which fall under headings "Chinese sexual behavior" and "attitudes." The vicissitudes of desire and the unpredictable conditions that cultivate it are notoriously hard to capture in a questionnaire. But it is worth noting that the professional sexologists were most surprised at the "low" rates (by Western standards) of masturbation and sexual intercourse in the college-age group. The Chinese investigators also frequently return, in their discussion, to what they perceive to be a high state of ignorance and confusion found in all sorts of respondents.[20] Despite the overall normality found at the level of behavior, more sex education of the enlightened modern kind is, they argue, badly needed.

Research as National Pedagogy

This is the overall message of the study, which is not surprising since the impetus to conduct it mostly arose from the pioneering sex education work of several Shanghai agencies. An appendix to the national survey gives a brief history of sex education in modern China.[21] The story it tells makes it very clear that the 1980s emergence of formal sexology and school pedagogy about sex in China was a result of a collaborative effort between city schools and several professional associations of sociologists and psychologists.[22] Like other scientific research in China, the knowledge produced by the survey was meant to be as useful as possible as soon as possible.

This attitude toward the task of sexological research was not born in the research process itself. The Chinese name for the survey project and the title of its final report clearly indicate that national progress and development are and always were the goal. Recall that the survey was known as the National Sex Civilization (wenming) Survey, and the summary report of findings was lengthily entitled *Contemporary Chinese Sexual Culture: Report of the "Sex Civilization" Survey on 20,000 Subjects (Zhongguo Dangdai Xing Wenhua: Zhongguo Liangwan Lie "Xing Wenming" Diaocha Baogao)*. The invocation in these titles of "culture" (*wenhua*) and "civilization" (wenming, also translated at times as "civility") places the project firmly within the scope of national development ideology. As Ann Anagnost pointed out in her important discussion of the relationship between these terms, "wenhua is the highly contested ground on which a national culture must be reconstituted in the project of moving toward wenming, a state of civility that is closely identified with the advanced industrial cultures of Asia and the west."[23] In her careful characterization of wenming (civilization) in particular, Anagnost emphasizes the way in which the term's obsession with modernity and cultural quality figures the state of the Chinese people as one of chronic lack. In relation, for example, to the domain of sexuality, the people are relatively ignorant, backward, conservative, and repressed. The discourses of wenming—and they are legion, ranging from elite social theory generated in Chinese government think tanks to neighborhood cleanup campaigns and the everyday chat of those who are affected by them—assume and seek to remedy the shortcomings of the general population. As Anagnost points out, "this concern with low quality constructs the necessity for a national pedagogy."[24] In reform China, research and intervention in the name of progress are seldom distinct.

This point was not lost on the survey's twenty thousand respondents. The social and national agenda of the survey were emphasized in the short preface to the questionnaire, which was presumably read by or to all twenty thousand participants: "Sex is a major component of human life, having an intimate connection to the healthful development of youth, the happiness and harmony of married couples, and the stability and cohesiveness of society. Because society has for so long produced (*shixing*) sexual inhibitions, as well as for various other reasons, at present there are many problems with respect to sex. We are undertaking this research in order to understand this situation and explore ways to resolve the contradictions. The significance of this research to social development is very great, and we request your help and support."[25] Until very recently, social research in the PRC has always been undertaken by the state; the word for survey, *diaocha*, is strongly associated with revolutionary mobilization. This prefatory statement was, moreover, signed by the National "Sex Civilization Survey" Core Leading Group, the very name of which recalls many earlier mass campaigns and their "leading groups." And the language of the statement itself invokes the broad collective concern of the state with "resolving the contradictions"—a Maoist phrase if ever there was one—that could interfere with sound social development.

Thus, the domain of propriety and civic duty within which talk about sex would proceed was made very clear at the outset. As they confessed their personal business by ticking off multiple choice boxes or responding to the questions of official interviewers, high school students, college students, married couples (urban and rural), and sex offenders were supposed to feel that they were contributing to the welfare and development of their nation and society. Perhaps they were also expected to drop any sexual (or political!) inhibitions that would interfere with full and honest disclosure to their inquiring visitors. After all, the research group had noble goals; it not only sought to learn about sexual behavior but to understand and intervene in the many problems that bedevil society "with respect to sex."

The final report of the research was even clearer in asserting the interdependence of representing sexual behavior and intervening in it.[26] I quote the report at length here, partly because this paragraph was only briefly summarized in the English-language edition and partly because it so elegantly expresses the researchers' views on their social responsibilities.

> Through theoretical analysis of the survey, we arrive at conclusions and viewpoints in order to achieve guidance for social life. In his first report, Kinsey said: "In this report our main purpose is to explain

what people are doing; it certainly does not touch on what they ought to do, nor does it judge people for what they do. Our report simply reveals the sexual behavior of American males, and is certainly not the kind of research with the usual messages about 'moral' or 'immoral' males and their behavior." For the time being, we don't wish to criticize Kinsey or decide whether he was able to sustain this kind of pure objectivity, this neutrality; we only wish to point out that generally speaking scientific research should always have its practical value and social purposes. Since human sexual behavior has its social component, it follows that [this social dimension] is also very important. Since Kinsey also said that the road to human sexual liberation (shifang) depends on the influence of social culture and social environment, we seek to research what kind of social culture and social environment could enable the development of a healthy human sexuality as well as researching what kind of sexual attitudes and models of sexual behavior will facilitate progress in the development of society. Therefore, we must insist on a certain tendency toward identifying the problems, promoting some things while opposing others, and so on. Only in this way can scientific research provide a firm foundation for policy in the government sector; only in this way can it lead the people and promote social progress. In present-day social life, there are many ethical points of view, and it would be very difficult for us to sustain a position of perfect neutrality or reach a unanimous conclusion on matters of sex. But what we can do is: vigorously face problems on the basis of the highest state of current developments while not rigidly adhering to the present situation; drawing on objective data, venture some tentative opinions while avoiding arbitrariness and subjectivity in drawing conclusions; and instruct in an enlightened, responsible [literally "leaderly"], and above all effective way. The views expressed in our various survey research reports are not absolute truth; they are just exploratory footprints placed one after another along the path to truth.[27]

We will return to truth—and footprints, too—at the end of this chapter. But first it is important to understand this particular joining of objective scientific ideals and sober didactic responsibilities. Where sex is concerned, this is not an unfamiliar conjuncture, of course. But here it has certain specific characteristics that need to be understood in the context of modern Chinese life.

Health is one of the core values around which this statement turns (the other one is progress). Health is a difficult goal to argue with in a country that has known such debilitating poverty, but it has never been easy to define, especially since most experts prefer to find a positive definition that goes beyond the mere absence of disease.[28] Even undefined, the word has played an important role in the politics and public life of the People's Republic since the 1950s.[29] Although it probably has a much longer genealogy in Chinese popular culture, in the People's Republic the unassailable goal of health has been used to justify a great deal of normative propaganda and numerous means of regulating everyday life. And it has been internalized as an experiential virtue by a great many Chinese people, who can justify anything from quiet sitting to swimming in frozen lakes as "good for the health." (The experiential and political dimensions of health are explored elsewhere in this volume, especially in chapters 1 and 6.)

Where sex is concerned, however, states of health could be quite various and distinctions between good and ill sexual health could be markedly subjective. Some married couples or college students may not agree, for example, that full nudity during sexual intercourse is obviously the most wholesome and progressive approach. Reported low rates of masturbation or "sexual interest" among secondary school students may or may not be healthy. Perhaps this is one reason why objective research is necessary, to determine what is normal and what behaviors usually lead to "robust sexual health." As a coherent representation of sexual normality begins to emerge from worldwide and local research, it is necessary, even in the face of rather tentative scientific conclusions, for the experts to accept responsibility for "the guidance of social life." Some things must be promoted while others are opposed. Chinese sexological science has no choice but to declare authoritatively the nature of sexual health even though some of the details must await further research.

Given the "fuzzy spots" in this survey, and its admitted "biases," it remains difficult to know what people actually do or feel in private. The mirror image of an autonomous reality that a scientific method should offer to us remains hard to read in experiential terms, but even on the basis of this imperfect knowledge (the researchers argued) we must proceed with the important work of enlightened sex education. Even though Chinese sexual behavior, when described, "reveals a picture of 'average' and in part even robust sexual health," the urgency of bringing sex into the domain of civic discourse is undiminished. Certainly the fuzzy spots must be cleared up for sexology; this goes without saying for a science that values knowledge for its own sake. But there are also many dangers attendant upon leaving the population mired in sexual ignorance.

The actual extent of this "ignorance" is unknown, although the national survey made a (methodologically flawed) effort to assess it. For years, popular anecdotes and rumors circulated among medical people and educators about young married couples who had no idea how to proceed sexually, and as sex discourse became more general in the 1990s these condescending stories made their way into popular periodicals. Such rumors encourage well-educated urbanites and professionals to believe that China's general population is unusually ignorant, inhibited, and backward. The people not only need to engage in sexual behavior (for their health, their happiness, and social solidarity), but they need to learn how. As formal sex education programs expand beyond the big cities and popular sexual health manuals proliferate as a mass genre of literature, a certain modern sexual imaginary can be expected to gain a foothold not only in public discourses but in private expectations, not only in formal knowledge but in personal action.

Sex Ed

The sexual body envisioned by the national sex survey is Chinese in that it is unusually backward and repressed and transnational in that it is much like the body studied by Havelock Ellis, Alfred Kinsey, and Masters and Johnson. In this frame, a universal biological sexuality lurks beneath a thick layer of local oppression. When the sex experts turn to the task of sex education, they tend to address this body: a discrete individual standing in opposition to society while receiving its influences, a bearer of natural needs who, once liberated, is capable of gratifying his or her normal desires through "sexual behavior." This is in many respects a recent body, specific to a particular Euro-American bourgeois imaginary. The extent to which this body, which was generated in nineteenth- and twentieth-century medical and social science discourses ranging from utilitarianism to Freudianism, is actually lived even in the West remains an open question, however.[30] When we examine the translation of this understanding of bodies into historical and discursive environments that differ dramatically from those that invented it, the reality and universality of this natural body become even more problematic. I doubt that these versions of the bourgeois individual can be fully realized outside their natural habitats (and these may be very restricted, indeed). Consequently, I read the Chinese sex education literature as a form of cultural imperialism. It is an attempt to impose a relatively alien way of organizing intimate experience and private relationships in the name of modernity and (arguably) in the service of a consumer economy. These ideas and images are not (yet) common sense for Chinese readers—this is the nature of the people's "backwardness"—and I am not sure that they are likely to become so. But if this "naturally" sexual individual doesn't take, it will not be for lack of trying on the part of educators, publishers, and booksellers.

The sexual civilization survey would be a useful tool in advancing this image of sex, as it presumably can adapt the scientific object known as sexual behavior to Chinese conditions. Sex surveys on behaviors and attitudes and even the physiological research of Masters and Johnson do not objectively supply a very full picture of sex life, however. And it is life that must be reached by means of education, especially education of such a morally freighted kind. Pedagogy must go beyond what is objectively known (and even what is objectively known about American and European sexuality) and propagate a full imaginary of wholesome, modern, responsible sexuality.

In the new genre of Chinese works that aim to educate the populace about sex, this broad imaginary is fairly evident. The knowledge invoked is monochromatic even though its genres vary, ranging from high school textbooks to homely advice for newlyweds, medical self-care manuals, and technical surveys of formal sexological knowledge. Perhaps most obviously this body is a physical frame that can be characterized in detail by anatomy and physiology. Most of the official sex education books begin with and devote most of their space to sexual physiology.[31] After the biological facts (so calming in their authoritative universality and neutral objectivity) are laid out, the textbooks can turn to the somewhat more anxious domain of "sexual psychology."

Rather than focus on the ways in which the reproductive physiological body is presented in the Chinese sources, a body that differs very little from the one presented in our own sex education classes, I will focus on the propagation of a sexual psychology in these sources.

Although there are still many familiar elements in these discourses, the relative newness of this approach to personal life in China has imparted a certain insistent tone, and even at times a narrow dogmatism, to the texts that teach it. This effort reminds us of how much work is involved in producing the proper modern subjectivity; although the texts insist that they are simply encouraging the responsible expression of a sexual nature that has always been there, their anxiety to teach readers how this sexuality might work belies its naturalness.

A widely distributed 1989 book for a general readership, *Sex Education,* by Hong et al., will serve as my main example. Apparently presuming some basic biological knowledge about the structure and functioning of the human body on the part of its readers, the book plunges straight into psychological issues. After opening chapters that pedantically assert the importance of a responsible, enlightened, and scientific attitude toward sex, the book turns to "sex psychology and sex role." This chapter strongly advocates seeing sexual behavior as (mostly) psychologically determined. It divides "the psychological phenomenon" of sex into the conceptual categories of sexual desire, sexual love, sexual behavior, sexual deviance, and functional disorders. I reproduce and discuss some of these definitions below. Although many books don't bother to systematically define these basic terms, the definitions provided are consistent with other sources and the content and tenor of these extracts is quite typical of the field.[32]

> *Sexual desire* can be regarded as a kind of human urge (*yuqiu*) or need (*xuyao*); it is a psychological phenomenon. That it is not a purely physiological phenomenon can be seen from its obvious social character. Human sexual desire is strongly controlled by cultural attitudes. For example, modern males are not usually able to conceive desire for their biological sisters, no matter how beautiful and attractive the latter may be. Even the occurrence and intensity of a husband's desire for his wife is necessarily influenced by spiritual factors such as the state of knowledge in his time and place, emotional background, and the regulation of consciousness. In the 1940s, there were those who thought that sexual desire was produced by hormonal secretions, and today there are still some who hold this view. But in reality it's not like that. In Northern Europe, someone studied several hundred cases of people who had been castrated (for com-

mitting serious sex crimes) and discovered that, though some of them had lost their desire for sex, there were others in whom sexual desire was clearly still present, and for some individuals it was even stronger.

Unlike some other sources, this text makes a distinction between the physiological and psychological elements of desire in order to make its point about the importance of "psychological phenomena." This distinction is common in the sex education sources, though usually in a simple additive manner. Desire is a matter of *both* body and mind. The most authoritative (and the reform period's earliest) book-length discussion of "sexual knowledge," in speaking of puberty and adolescence, for example, sees desire as a normal concomitant of maturation and advocates physiological and psychological education to help young people understand it.[33]

One interesting aspect of the passage quoted above is the presumption that desire resides in individuals (though only males are explicitly mentioned) and turns naturally toward individuals of the opposite sex. While "social factors" such as an incest taboo and physical alterations such as surgery can affect object choice and the degree of sexual desire, there is apparently no need to suggest that desire might range more widely over possible objects or that it might be diffused beyond the individual body and mind. Desire in these texts is not uncoupled from a strictly defined concept of sexual behavior. And sexual behavior is pretty narrow.

Sexual behavior can be divided into the series of actions taken and the experience (*tiyan*) of feelings in the mind while in the process of making love (*zuo ai*). With regard to the series of actions, these can be seen as conscious human activities; they are under the control of the acting person's psychological activity at the time. Sexual behavior has instinctual elements, but it cannot be reduced to instinct alone. Engels said, "We simply cannot avoid this situation, whatever moves men to activity must go through men's brains. Even eating and drinking arise from hunger and thirst, which pass through the perceptions of the brain, and by the same token the satisfaction and cessation of hunger and thirst must also go through the perceptions of the brain." Like eating and drinking, sexual behavior must pass through the human brain and manifest itself via the control and regulation of psychological activity. Whether the individual at a given time manifests sexual behavior, what fashion of sexual behavior it is, and even the inner experience of sexual behavior are all under the control of many kinds of psychological factors such as cultural concepts, attitudes toward sexual behavior, individual habits, feelings for and attitudes toward the sexual partner, and so on. As for the intense inner feelings experienced during sexual behavior, it goes without saying that this is an even more psychological activity; in the absence of such emotional experience, perhaps it would be difficult to initiate or complete sexual behavior. (40–41)

Many of the ruling assumptions of Chinese (and transnational) sexology and sex education are visible in this extract. Even in its effort to assert the primacy of the psychological in the domain of sexuality, this argument makes a clear divide between body and mind and re-asserts the reality of both. This is even accomplished at the level of paragraph structure, as the discussion first takes up a "series of actions" and then returns, fleetingly, to "the intense inner feelings experienced." Any straightforward body-mind divide remains problematic, however, even for contemporary Chinese discourse. This point is easy to argue for classical literature, philosophy, medicine, and art.[34] But even now, even in discourses that have been profoundly colonized by the distinctions underpinning Marxism, Christianity, orientalism, and all manner of other "Western" modes of thought, modern Chinese language (and hence, modern Chinese experience) does not take kindly to distinguishing mind from body. Only in the kind of clotted social scientific prose I have translated here are there enough technical neologisms and loanwords available to attempt it.[35]

It is also interesting in this definition of *sexual behavior* that the activity in question is not actually defined and the vague imported term *making love* is preferred to anything more clinical, such as sexual intercourse (*xingjiao*), or, as some foreign investigators would have it, behavior leading to orgasm. In any case, it seems unlikely that these writers would place many kinds of intense visceral experience— erotic dreams, intense solitary or group exercise, the epiphanies of political rallies, verbal badinage and flirtation, shared manual labor, reading erotica, performing well before an audience, and so on— within the range of the term. Perhaps most of us would disqualify these activities as well. But what interests me is the certainty of the definition achieved in this modern Chinese prose. In suggesting that everybody knows what sexual behavior and "making love" are and that our only question would be whether or not it is "psychologically" caused, the authors impose a vision of normality that may or may not be in accord with the common sense of their readers.

But lest we become too complacent about the self-evidence of sexual behavior, there is sexual deviance to consider.

Sexual deviance (xing biantai) designates forms of sexual behavior and sexual desire that depart from the normal. The term normal denotes forms held in common by the greatest number of people in society. Therefore, it is hard to avoid a certain elasticity in the line between the normal and the deviant. There are many types of sexual deviance such as sadism, masochism, exhibitionism, cross-dressing, homosexuality, and so on. Although the causes of sexual deviance are complicated, psychological factors are very important. Research on homosexuality, for example, has shown that in an early stage of childhood there is a period of gender confirmation that concerns whether one is male or female. If a small boy cannot smoothly complete this process and manifest clear-cut gender behavior, and if his parents cannot intervene at the right time, then this boy might in the future develop homosexual tendencies. The confirmation of a child's personal gender (ziwo xingbie) is undoubtedly a psychological process, primarily a process of psychological knowledge. Thus, we can see the role of psychological factors in sexual deviance. (41–42)

The inclusion of homosexual behavior among the deviations listed is intentional. As a footnote to this passage explains: "In recent years some foreign sexologists have ceased to view homosexuality as deviant. Some American states have gone so far as to permit the marriage of homosexual lovers. But we think that [sexual] love for the same sex and feelings of sexual indifference to the opposite sex are in the final analysis inconsistent with nature. It is no wonder their numbers are so small in the general population. If it were otherwise, this would produce a serious social problem in the future because homosexuality cannot reproduce the younger generation" (41). This is a view that is shared, in print at least, by other sexologists in China, and most sources go on at greater length on the subject of homosexual maladjustment, criminality, immaturity, promiscuity, and so on. They also propose therapies for the cure of homosexuality and denounce its antisocial character as unnatural because it is nonreproductive. Perhaps this official position on a common form of "sexual behavior" illustrates more clearly than some of the less openly judgmental American approaches just where the danger of a commitment to the notion of "nature" lies. If only potentially reproductive sex is "consistent with nature," then "deviations" of many kinds could multiply inside and outside of the bedroom. This kind of normalizing discourse is alarming, not least because it encourages official intervention in private lives by scientific experts and various other enforcers of "natural" propriety.

But there is another note struck in the passage that impresses me as even more troubling. In speaking of the confirmation of a child's personal gender, the term *ziwo xingbie* ("self" plus "sex difference") is used. This is very likely a translation of the term *gender identity*. The translation is awkward; there are no readily available terms in modern Chinese for a psychological notion of identity. That deep core of self-hood—how we know who we are—was not a feature of premodern Chinese discourses. It was a troubled and unresolved issue in the modernizing cultural discourses of the Republican period (1911–49).[36] All such individualistic obsessions were quite thoroughly eclipsed, in discourse at least, during the Maoist period in favor of collective identifications. I have not found it easy to convey to Chinese friends, even those who are well versed in the globalizing social sciences, our North American concerns with fixing personal identity or expressing an essential self. (Actually, I've found it a relief not to have to make an issue of these culture-bound concerns!) In the extract above, the author gets around the shortage of useful Chinese concepts by making sure there is no doubt that a psychosocial process is at issue: proper gender identity must be "confirmed" (*queren*) in the course of sexual development.

What troubles me is the possibility that "Chinese modernity" will appropriate all the central essentialisms of bourgeois individualism. Identity discourse has proven immensely attractive in North America, not only in psychology, popular and theoretical, but in anthropology and cultural studies. As a result, there has been a corresponding recent effort in these latter disciplines either to define the concept away from its more essentialist forms or to displace it from the center of our concerns.[37] My own work has attempted to do without the concept of a stable core of the self altogether, in the perhaps vain hope that (even modern, postcolonial, cosmopolitan) experience in China can be thought about without centering individual identity. Sexual identity in particular, that privileged touchstone of psychological stability and coherence, impresses me (as it did Foucault) as a highly contingent product of specific discursive developments in European and North American medicine and psychosocial sciences; it is a concept, moreover, that encourages unfortunate rigidities of thought and social practice.[38] For an anthropologist to see the formation of sexual identity as a universal problem, discernible everywhere, would be ethnocentric. The normalization of sexual practice, however, demands the attention of any ethnographer who attends to the powers of discourse in a shrinking mass media world.

In my reading of the Chinese sex education literature, the remark above about confirming personal gender is the bit of text that comes closest to much more verbose North American effusions on the subject of sexual identity. Most Chinese works in the field of sex education do not center identity issues in this way, preferring to talk about gender roles. Roles are easily understood as systems of socially appropriate behavior that can be studied and performed by kids who understandably need a little practice acting like men or women. This sober sociological approach to sexual maturation is quite consistent with the recent history of sexual appearances with which I opened this chapter. After the concerted gender neutrality of the Maoist style, Chinese people of all ages (re)learned how to dress and act the part of their sex. Although this was seen by some reform era Chinese feminists as a refreshing pleasure and a kind of liberation from the hypocritical domination of an ideology that claimed gender equality while ignoring many of the needs of women, it was not, I think, experienced as a deep psychological liberation.[39] People were not freed to express their essential selves; rather, they embarked with pleasure on the play of sexual differences. It was this play, perhaps, that cried out most clearly for normalization by the experts.

The Repressive Hypothesis

In *The History of Sexuality, Volume 1,* Foucault identifies the familiar argument of "the repressive hypothesis." For years, he notes, we presumed that our natural sexual expressions had long been repressed by a regime of hypocrisy and silence; a puritanical society external to the individual made it impossible to express natural sexual urges either in practice or in honest, straightforward speech. The repressive hypothesis itself was the occasion of a huge linguistic effusion, however, speaking endlessly of sex while adopting a proper sociological code for its various practices. This order of discourse, which placed sex at the center of experience, is constitutive of the discourse of sexology wherever it may appear. Natural sex, made up of needs and drives, influenced by society but subject to self-control, is the object of this science. This object has been awaiting discovery beneath the layers of hypocritical taboo imposed by backward social regimes—waiting to be discovered and to be spoken of. Liu Dalin, the leading investigator of the national sex survey, expressed the situation concisely.

> From the 1980s forward, as China undertook a drastic program of reform and adopted a policy of openness, Western culture and ancient Chinese culture were much more broadly disseminated. These made everything seem fresh and new and widened the field of vision. Thought and attitudes underwent continuous development and transformation. The development of a commodity economy raised the standard of living of the people, and their social contacts widened, leading to the production of many new needs (*xuqiu*). Thus, more and more people liberated themselves from the confines of traditional thinking and the illusion that they could avoid "eating the smoke of ordinary fires" (*shi renjian yanhuo*). They began to face reality, to simultaneously pursue and create realistic life joys. True love, a satisfying marriage, and a healthy and harmonious sex life are gradually coming to form a dominant motif in the symphony of life. The young yearn for it, and middle-aged and elderly people yearn for it, too. The heavy curtains shrouding the mysteries of sex are gradually being opened. The attitude that "talk of sex only encourages lust" (*tan xing se bian*) is gradually disappearing.[40]

In some respects, this paragraph is classic sexology. The mysteries of sex have been there all along, waiting behind bed curtains for popular and scientific discovery. In the study in which this paragraph appears, a discrete (if sometimes "fuzzy") object is being characterized at length, objectively. The process of splitting and inversion through which such an object is created is both evident in extracts like this and denied throughout the text. The social production of this scientific fact is, in other words, an open secret.

On one hand, new needs are being produced by radical social and cultural change. On the other, the satisfaction of these needs is the true path to a "realistic" life. Implicitly but unmistakably, the era prior to the 1980s, the Maoist era, is cast as unrealistic, unnatural, and confining. Yet apparently the yearnings for a good sex life shared by young, middle-aged, and elderly people are new. Were these same people unnatural during the Maoist period because their yearnings were different? Is it plausible that such a large population for such a long time—nearly four decades—could have denied nature in themselves and their everyday lives?

This statement suggests as much, especially with its idiom, awkward in English, about "eating the smoke of ordinary fires." The phrase refers to a willingness to settle down, deal with things as they are, and seek satisfaction in the everyday, the here and now. In this context, its use embodies a comment on "the illusion" that there might be some other, less earthbound approach to life. This illusion, so recently abandoned, was the Chinese Communist program that caught people up in vast collective goals, set them to work building Chinese socialism and a classless society, and taught them that the meaning of life derived from a beautiful, egalitarian, but ever-receding future. This was a future, moreover, that could not be achieved in truth until it had been achieved for all of China, if not for the whole world. In those days, these authors suggest, people tried to eat the smoke of illusory, ideological, transcendent fires. Whatever satisfactions may have been available in that life (and I have suggested that there were many), the attempt to live as an extraordinary collectivity cannot have been as sexually satisfying (the author suggests) as the new private lives of reform China. Once people thought they could defer private indulgence until the revolution was complete; now they are turning with relief to the joys of "ordinary" life.

And—so the reform era story goes—sex has been there all along, waiting for them. But they'll need some help in figuring it out since sex is still a constrained and confused domain. Old fears may persist (the sexologists tell us), and people may worry that speaking of sex will unleash all manner of socially disruptive forces; they may still think that "talk of sex only encourages lust." Sexual science, of course, must insist that these fears are illusory. Only by bringing what is natural into the bright light of objective investigation, only by applying all the modern and cosmopolitan scientific methods of comparing, generalizing, averaging, and normalizing sexual behavior, only by preparing the nation's young people with true knowledge for responsible behavior, and only with all this frantic talking, writing, publishing, and teaching can we be freed of the illusions, political and personal, of a dark past.

Clearly, the verbose habits and indiscreet interests of a modern scientia sexualis are beginning to extend into China. These practices may, as Foucault has pointed out, function as a kind of erotic art in their own right. Educating people into the sexual possibilities that are listed in the questionnaire and itemized in sex education texts as well as encouraging them to explore new connections between speaking and other bodily activities—after all, talk of sex *might* encourage lust—could be an erotic practice in itself. Whatever areas of silence and secrecy may have been maintained in the past, for whatever reasons and with whatever associated incitements to desire and expansions of pleasure or misery, they are now open to invasion by public and scientific discourses.

Reading the extract by Liu Dalin charitably, in appreciation of its humanistic spirit, we can see the expansion of sex discourses as not necessarily a bad thing. If better sex education, a more nuanced understanding of sexual life in China on the part of the sex experts, and a selective opening of the bed curtains can lead to more "realistic life joys" for people, it would be churlish indeed to criticize further. But I still wonder. Thinking, for example, of my friend who may have used a bicycle ride and a late arrival home as a kind of flirtation, I wonder what help sexology can be to her. No amount of wholesome coitus-centered theory about normal sex is going to get her and her family a larger apartment, nor will it provide more leisure and private time in her and her husband's busy lives. I rather hope, moreover, that a narrowing of the idea of the erotic would not drain the playful exchanges I witnessed between this wife and husband—while cooking, helping me with language, playing with their daughter—of all specifically erotic joy. In fact, I think these friends are safe from corruption by the new national concerns with sexual propriety. But their daughter, growing up in a very different environment from the one that formed them, might never understand how they took such mysterious joy in such tiny, inconclusive acts.

And speaking of inconclusive acts, it seems important to recall that Liu Dalin and his sex research colleagues were engaged in an everyday life of their own, one that must see the production of authoritative and complete knowledge, even about something as common as sex, as an endlessly deferred goal. Recall, for example, the statement they felt compelled to make in the preface to the sex survey report. In comparing their research with the Kinsey Report, and anticipating professional (and perhaps official Chinese government) criticism, they modestly pointed out that "the views expressed in our various survey research reports are not absolute truth; they are just exploratory footprints placed one after another along the path to truth." I love this word *footprints*. After sexual behavior and natural needs have been so clearly inscribed in the footprints decoded one after another by the sexologists, we are left to silently imagine the unspeakable creature that, leaving these traces in the road, has escaped.

chapter 6

ARS EROTICA

Years ago King Bao of Chu and I, Song Yu, traveled to the platform at Dream-cloud Lake to view the Gao Tang Hall. All within was cloudy qi, but the fog suddenly lifted and swept upward, its moving visage changing every moment, ceaselessly shifting, never for a moment stable. The king asked me, "What qi is this?"

I replied, "These are called dawn clouds."

"And what are dawn clouds?" asked the king.

"When of old a former king was enjoying a tour to Gao Tang," I told him, "he fell asleep while resting during the day. In his dream, a maiden spoke to him, saying, 'I am a daughter of Mount Wu, a visitor here. I heard you were traveling in Gao Tang, and I want to share your mat and pillow.' The king joyfully did as she asked. But she departed then, saying in farewell, 'You will find me beneath the yang platform on the sunny slopes of Mount Wu, at its steepest incline; at sunrise, I am the dawn clouds, at dusk I am rain, dawn after dawn, dusk after dusk.'"

This quote from a very ancient prose poem is used to open one of the many recent books published in China on the classical Chinese erotic arts.[1] The author of this 1993 compendium, Luo Dunren, says that the text is the earliest reference to sexual intercourse in Chinese literature and also the origin of a convention, still used today, that refers to the sex act as "clouds and rain" (*yunyu*). The poem's images of clouds drifting and swirling among mountain peaks that are one moment visible and the next obscured, its picture of unstable foggy qi that briefly resolves into an evening shower, also impress me as useful for beginning a discussion of the ancient Chinese bedchamber arts. But my purposes are different from those of Luo Dunren; while he sought to sort out and explain in modern terms a collection of classic texts, some of them over two millennia old, I wish to focus on the modern uses of these texts. The reform era vogue for publications on ancient Chinese sex lore itself presents a complex cultural scene—"its moving visage changing every moment, ceaselessly shifting, never for a moment stable."

Sex (including sexual fantasy) is a part of a complex lived embodiment that is necessarily contingent on its historical moment. Neither sexual intercourse nor reading about sex are merely expressions of natural functions belonging to biological bodies. Rather, our experiences of these activities are entangled with all manner of other elements in our lives. Discourses and practices intersect at the site of the body, ordering and disordering, generating, articulating, and occluding many levels of experience. These discourses and practices are global and local, casual and specialized, titillating and pedantic; they collaborate to constitute our desires and limit our imaginations. Even in the midst of a contemporary glut of more or less salacious imagery, only a few of the discursive formations that pervade our everyday lives touch on sexuality explicitly. Nevertheless, their ever-shifting intersections and persistent fragments produce the conditions under which sexual desires and gratifications can surprise us in the midst of the most mundane things.

So much goes unspoken that the task of studying everyday sensual life becomes difficult indeed. It is unusual enough to catch people in the act of articulating any of the dimensions of their lives that are taken for granted. Habitus is not easily collected in interviews. But when the topic is sex, in all its heavily freighted commonness, this difficulty is multiplied. The intrepid researchers discussed in chapter 5 were willing, apparently, to ask direct questions about sex in administering their structured (and state-sponsored) survey. I am not. I have instead approached this topic mostly by reading, taking popular texts as resources for everyday material life that cannot ultimately be held apart from embodied experiences of desires, events, social relations, written and graphic discourses, and more.

Fortunately, there has been no shortage of reading matter. Since the mid-1980s, classical Chinese writings on the erotic arts have become more readily available to Chinese readers than ever before in history.[2] One author, writing in 1991, reported that in the less than ten years since the early 1980s there had been ninety new studies of some aspect of sexuality in China; he counted twenty-three of these as concerning the "ancient Chinese bedchamber arts." He also noted the formation of many local sexology research associations and a number of specialized journals.[3] Since then, many more works that draw on the corpus of materials called the bedchamber arts (*fangzhong shu, fangshi*) have appeared. A collection of short articles and abstracts published in 1994, for example, entitled *Chinese Traditional Sex Medicine,* includes 369 items of which 145 are devoted to readings of the arts of the bedchamber. These and many other such works are available in local bookstores and market stalls in big cities and even some smaller towns; the managers of these outlets tell me that works devoted to the ancient sexual texts are good sellers.

It is in keeping with the shifting and unreliable nature of sex, perhaps, that the bedchamber arts texts have been turned to many purposes by many authors.[4] The scholarly and pedagogical agenda evident in these texts overlap, intersect, conflict, and feed on each other. They are nationalist, religious, economic, eugenic, therapeutic, moralistic, feminist, anthropological, prurient, modernizing, orientalist, aesthetic, governmental, muckraking, hedonistic, scientific, pedagogical, and practical. Sometimes, but rarely, they are all of these things at once. All of the studies of the bedchamber arts draw on the same small but interesting collection of ancient texts, and almost all make a distinction between an earlier period characterized by "life nurturing" (yang sheng) techniques and a later period known for the "inner alchemy" of Taoist longevity practices.[5] Moral repressiveness is said to have increased as the centuries passed. These few generalizations form the common ground held by modern commentators, and I will say more about these approaches in what follows.[6] But the lessons that authors and editors seek to draw from this shared archive are not easy to summarize.

As I read the recent commentaries and analyses published in the People's Republic on China's heritage of sexual lore, I am most struck by the ambivalence and inconclusiveness of this literature. Historians who hesitate to moralize nevertheless employ analytical categories infused with an anxious propriety; *husband and wife* (*fuqi* or *fufu*), for example, is substituted where *male and female* or *lord and concubine(s)* would be more accurate terms for the historical categories. Medical sexologists look for scientifically justifiable therapies while reporting in a neutral tone the physiological impossibilities of an ancient "inner alchemy." Male authors who enjoy the patriarchal emphasis in many of the ancient works struggle manfully to find some note of gender equality in the archive, turning a technical interest in female arousal into an ethical commitment to women's happiness.

In some cases, the only solution to the interpretive challenge of this body of historical sources has been a fragmentary eclecticism. Anecdotes from fictional literature, excerpts from ancient books on technique, discussions of previous analytic works of the modern era— all of these are scattered through the pages of many recent works, sometimes linked by no semblance of an overarching argument. As I was reading this corpus of modern works, I began to feel that the sexual desires recorded in the classic books were far outnumbered by the scholarly and didactic desires at work in the modern readings (editing, annotating, publishing, analyzing) of these books. Many of these scholarly desires remain tacit in the contradictions and cross-purposes of the texts, though I believe that readers are capable of both perceiving and sharing at least some of them.

This multiplicity of views and cacophony of interpretations have forced me to examine my own purposes even more closely than usual. Although I take as my occasion the reform era revival of a Chinese ars erotica literature, I do not aim simply to report the contents of it. Rather, I ask what gratifications the new books and articles on the historical archive, all published cheaply in Chinese, offered to the particular consumers they reached in 1990s urban China. Understanding the coherence of these writings, along with the conditions under which they are now being consumed, allows a privileged access to a modern Chinese imaginary of bodily life. As I argued in the introduction and have shown throughout this book, a shared material world links writers (and editors, archivists, and so on) and readers in a historically specific formation of textual legibility and practical appropriateness. Many positions may be staked out and defended, but all must assume a certain common terrain where language makes sense, actions can be imagined and mimicked, and bodily life of a certain kind can be presumed. This terrain is culturally and historically specific.

The readers to whom these books are addressed, for example, are the heirs of a Maoist formation in which all private desires and most ancient arts were banished from discourse. Whatever interest such readers might have in their remote forefathers' approaches to the private life of the inner chambers, then, will be refracted through a sense of novelty and transgression. The pleasures offered by books about sex, whatever they may be, are heightened by the consciousness that only a few years ago they would have been entirely illicit, even unimaginable. Moreover, Chinese urbanites today are bombarded with a global popular culture and consumer economy that places sex at the center of just about everything. This newly eroticized public landscape can be read in many ways, but it is clear that for the time being in China the most readily available sexual images speak of capitalist, bourgeois modernity as much or more than they do of erotic practice. It should thus be clear that the introduction of private desires, far from depoliticizing everyday life, invokes new "liberal" political values while occluding the collective politics of Maoism.

The globalization of sexual modernity, far from banishing local specificities, invites for many in China a constant comparison of traditional Chinese ideas and objects with their foreign, Western, or American "equivalents." As Appadurai has made clear, global processes often produce a heightened sense of local cultures.[7] The bedchamber arts, like Chinese medicine, are easily appropriated to this mode of cultural consumption. And, finally, the material constraints of private life are changing fast. Urban development and booming economic growth are producing a vast increase in smaller nuclear families with more disposable income that live apart from senior relatives and in larger apartments. Members of an emerging middle class have more space for private activities but perhaps less time to indulge in them as they pursue success in the competitive economies of the big cities. These conditions, among others, combine to frame a discursive locale that can be analyzed for its significance to a specifically situated readership.

Thus, I begin by asking: what is there to read, how do texts "expect" to be read, and what possible variations in reading do they offer? This question of reading—its charms and its powers in a given historical place and time—is only one of many possible anthropological approaches to understanding cultural life.[8] But in the case of the ars erotica literature it leads readily to deeper questions concerning historically specific cultivations of embodiment. What kinds of bodies are solicited by the texts that became available in the reform period? What social and cultural environment have these bodies arisen from or responded to? What past do they wish to remember? What future do they hope for or fear? What pleasures do they take for granted and what other pleasures do they seek? Most important, perhaps, how do the texts themselves work subtle transformations on the lives of bodies?

Answers to these questions are not readily available for whole communities of people, much less whole nations the size of China, especially if we keep embodiment—which tends to be mute—at the center of our concerns. Yet, given that literatures are cultural collaborations among writers and readers and must take a great deal for granted as common ground, I think these questions remain good ones to guide a method of reading for embodiment.

The ancient texts on the arts of the inner chambers, like those of medicine dating from the same period, speak directly and in detail of active, enjoying, and suffering human bodies. Some of the gratifications of reading these books are amazingly immediate, considering the millennia of history and the cultural and linguistic divides that separate us (twenty-first-century readers) from the authors and compilers of these texts. Their descriptions of sexual activities, in exact detail and using a (sometimes) beautiful classical language, evoke an eerily familiar world of bodily practice.[9] Even the minor labor of picturing the scenes described, a work we do with any reading, deposits the reader in a rather steamy and seductive "bedchamber" environment. At the same time, the texts have a certain curiosity value, as the ancient works presume a physiology and social order that are exotic to modern readers. Neither large patrifocal households with numerous concubines and servants, for instance, nor semen that travels up the spine to collect in the brain are part of everyday reality in the twenty-first century. This unfamiliarity only adds to the fascinations of a literature that invokes and presumes such formations.[10]

As a reader, I am as responsive as anyone to the charms of bedchamber arts texts, both their intimate familiarity and their startling exoticisms. The fantasies and curiosities developed in the course of reading the texts must vary a great deal among readers, especially, perhaps, by gender; still, it is worth reflecting on the reason for their broad appeal. In this corpus, we have very explicit representations of body practices, and they seem oddly familiar, or at least possible, as recipes for bodily practices we ourselves use or could adopt. Unlike some well-known scholars of the Chinese ars erotica—more of them than are willing to admit it, I think—I myself do not wish to mine these materials for particular techniques that would add variety to my own or my readers' sexual habits. This is partly because the most obvious form of sexual embodiment encouraged by these texts is quite markedly male, a point I will develop below. But the odd familiarity and quirky charm of these texts are apparent even for a female reader like me. I thus seek an approach that will acknowledge the readily translated, and possibly universal, erotic appeal of these texts while insisting on their historical specificity *and* the specificity of their present-day consumption in China.

Unlike personal life histories of the kind discussed in chapter 4 or academic critiques like that undertaken in chapter 5, there are few conventional chronologies or sequences for telling the life of the sexual body. Thus, I have found it particularly difficult in this chapter to adopt a step by step argument that can represent this cultural specificity, a "reform Chinese sexual/practical body." My strategy instead is to introduce what at first may appear to be a rather miscellaneous series of topics, all derived from the literature on Chinese sex, as background to some more general observations about writing, reading, and embodiment. These topics range from the most common word for sex to questions of archaeological nationalism and Chinese medical physiology. They will touch on a few technicalities and speculate about some personal motives, widely shared agendas, and common experiences. Eventually, these topics, all circling about the hydra-headed mythical entity known as sex, will crystallize a vision of the pleasures offered by China's past to Chinese bodies in the reform era.

Once this shifting, "clouds and rain" visage has been sketched, it will be possible to return once again to a consideration of the reasons for, and the limits of, talking and writing about (not just sexual) experience. As in the last few chapters, I will consider the ethics of representation not by making broad judgments about how sex should be represented but by suggesting that an understanding of representation as action in everyday worlds of embodied practice opens an inevitably ethical domain. Although ancient texts are decidedly sexist and inegalitarian, can they, perhaps, be read against their patriarchal grain? Nationalist agendas are clearly active in the recovery of a literary "Chinese" past; should nations be taken to own—and therefore to

enjoy privileged authority about—ancient heritages of bodily practice? Sex in the twenty-first century is inseparable from morality and
propriety; what are the good or ill effects on readers' subjectivity of an
insistent moralist tone in writing about "natural" feelings? Given that
representations are effective in the construction of real, embodied
worlds, questions like these are opened for debate.

Xing: *Cosmic Sex, Inherent Nature?*

In modern Chinese, the most commonly used word corresponding to
the English word *sex* is *xing*. Like *sex,* it not only stands alone but appears in many compounds: *xingjiao* (sexual intercourse); *xingbie* (gender); *xingyu* (sexual desire); *xing xingwei* (sexual behavior); and
xingqiguan (sex organs). Both noun and adjective, it can be translated
as "sex," "sexual," "sexuality," and sometimes "gender." Its ease of use
is increased by the fact that the divide between social gender and natural sex that informs our careful sex-gender distinction is not particularly pertinent to common usage in modern Chinese. Even so, the
relatively neat correspondence between the denotative domain covered by *xing* and that covered by *sex* is convenient for modern sociological research. The national sex survey discussed in chapter 5, for
example, had no difficulties with the term and never bothered to
define it, either in the report or the questionnaire. In the English
translation of the study, *sex* presented itself as a useful and flexible
equivalent. The authors assumed that the import of these terms
would be clear to all their modern respondents and readers in both
languages.

One hundred years, or perhaps only fifty years, earlier, this self-
evidence would not have been possible. When scholarship turns to an
earlier period of writing about sexual activity, the tidy (colonized)
equivalence of xing and sex gets very complicated. First of all, there is
no classical evidence that this word *xing* ever meant "sex" before the
twentieth century. In the canonical texts of the period that are most
focused on by the modern bedchamber scholars, *xing* is understood
to refer to a certain innate or characteristic tendency of things. The
Encyclopedic Dictionary of the Chinese Language, published by the Academia Sinica (Taiwan) in 1973, for example, supplies classical sources
that illustrate the following meanings:

1. The heavenly endowment in humans; the *Book of Rites* (1st c. B.C.E.), for example, states that "What heaven has decreed is called xing."
2. The substance of things, or their most basic character; examples are given from the *Zuo Zhuan* and Mencius (both works prior to the 3rd c. B.C.E.), among others.
3. Life, fate, or the span of life; the example from the *Zuo Zhuan* is "[He] cannot protect his xing."
4. Life, as in the *Zuo Zhuan*'s remark, "The people enjoy their life."
5. Body, glossed as such in *Abundant Dew on the Spring and Autumn Annals* (2nd c. B.C.E.).
6. Beauty, appearance; here the authority is the 2nd c. B.C.E. *Book of the Prince of Huainan.*
7. The five phases, the "natural" order of classification by which the ancient world related the things of the world to each other.

In addition to these, classical authority is provided for several technical uses of the term *xing* in Buddhist texts. But the only definition approaching the modern sense of the word as referring to sex—"the types of male and female are xing, for example, male xing, female xing"—is given without a single classical source. Moreover, in this carefully worded definition, *xing* is still best translated as "character" or "inherent tendency."

In modern Chinese, xing still refers in some contexts to the idea of innate character: the word for personal temperament, *xingge*, for example, or for material qualities, *xingzhi*. The word has also come to function as a suffix for compound words, roughly translatable as "-ity," or "-ness." Thus "modernity," for example, can be expressed as *xiandaixing*, and "effectiveness" is sometimes referred to as *xiaoguoxing*. The usage is not especially elegant, but it comes in handy when one is translating works or ideas from Western social science; a suffix like this is useful, for example, when one is speaking or writing of distinctions between modernism and modernity.[11] Thus, the "inherent tendency" meaning of the word has here been extended to provide a grammatical fragment translatable as "the quality of being ——— ."

Let's return for a moment to the implications of the ancient sense of the word *xing* for modern research on the bedchamber arts. Joseph Needham, in speaking of "nature" or the ancient concept of "self-so-ness" (*ziran*), translates a wonderful passage from the *Huainanzi* (*Book of the Prince of Huainan*, 2d c. B.C.E.) that makes the classical understanding of *xing* abundantly clear.

> He who conforms to the course of the Tao [Dao], following the spontaneous (*ziran*) processes of Heaven and Earth, finds it easy to manage the whole world. Thus it was that Yu the great was able to engineer the canals by obeying the water and letting it guide him (*yin shui yi wei shi*). Likewise Shen Nong, in the sowing of seed, attended to germination and let it teach him. Water plants root in water, trees in earth; birds fly in the air, and beasts prowl on the ground; crocodiles and dragons live in the water, tigers and leopards dwell in mountains—such is their inherent tendency (*xing*). Pieces of wood when rubbed together generate heat, metal subjected to fire melts, wheels revolve, scooped-out things float. All things have their inherent tendencies (*ziran zhi shi*) . . . thus all things are so by themselves (*wanwu gu yi ziran*).[12]

What is especially appealing about this passage is that things reveal their inherent natures in the course of their characteristic activity and in intimate relation to, and even participation with, other things. In this classical vision, it is not static visible structures like those that interested Linnaeus, for example, that distinguish entities most essentially from each other; rather, it is differences in the characteristic activities of all things. The freestanding individual essences of some Western philosophical traditions are nowhere to be found.

When, armed with this classical vision of inherent tendencies toward forms of activity and relationship, we turn to modern writing on *xing*, we find what at first looks like a hopeless muddle. No one denies that the word *xing* also means something besides sex. The best evidence of this fact is that every scholar repeatedly quotes a line from the *Mencius* (ca. 2d c. B.C.E.), felicitously translated by D. C. Lau as "appetite for food and sex is nature" (*shi se xing ye*).[13] In this line, the word for sex is *se*, not *xing*; *xing* is translated by Lau as "nature." In the same modern contexts in which this line is quoted, however, numerous other texts of the same period are cited. In them, *xing* is taken to refer to sex. Yet this always involves a certain forcing of the original texts; the notion of inherent tendency still works better when glossing the word in its earliest appearances, even when these are taken out of context and marshaled to support a discussion of modern sexuality.

One particularly dense example of this presentist rereading of the classical archive appears in an annotated collection of bedchamber arts texts edited by Song Shugong and published in 1991 and 1993 by the China Medical Sciences Press. This commentary is not content to allow *xing* to refer to inherent natures; rather, these natures must be sexual.

> People generally presume that the *sex* (*xing*) in *sexology* (*xingxue*) is the modern term, but in fact the term had already appeared in the Zhou and Qin periods [11th c. B.C.E.–2d c. B.C.E.]. The *Analytical Dictionary of Characters* by Xu Shen says: "Xing is human yang qi. Xing is the good. . . ." Duan Yucai annotates this as follows: "Dong Zhongshu said 'Xing is the substance of life,' what is called the most basic substance." [This and all other texts cited herein date from before the second or third century C.E.] The idea of this is that xing is the basic substance of the human body and human life, and its substantial quality is yang (*yangxing*). This word is often used together with the word for sentiment or emotion (*qing*), and if we look up *qing*, the *Analytical Dictionary* defines it as "that which human yang qi desires. . . ." Wang Chong in his *Discourses Weighed in the Balance* comments: "The great framework of heaven is one yin and one yang; the great framework of man is one qing and one xing. Xing is born of yang, qing is born of yin. Yin qi is vulgar (*bi*), yang qi is fine (*ren*), and I say that what is good about xing is its yang manifestations, what is bad about xing is its yin manifestations." Duan Yucai comments: "Dong Zhongshu said, 'Qing is human desire, and what humans desire is [also] called qing. Qing must be controlled and regulated.'" We can also cite the *Classic of Filial Piety*, which says: "Xing is born of yang, and principle must control it; qing is born of yin to permeate consciousness." Moreover, the *Record of Rites* says: "What are the human feelings (qing)? Joy, anger, grief, fear, love, hate, and desire, the seven capacities that are not learned."
>
> The idea of these texts is that qing is an instinctual desire that exists in man's bodily life and its substantial quality is yin (*yinxing*). The movement of feelings of desire must induce the movement of life's most basic substance, xing; in other words, if yin moves then yang must respond accordingly. These are things that we can know and do without any training, but if they are to differentiate humans from the birds and the beasts they must be regulated; thus, we pursue matters

of sex, intercourse, and reproduction under the ritually regulated
forms of marriage and the family. These activities are within the domain investigated by sexology, and because they are things that take
place in rooms the ancients called them bedchamber arts.[14]

This author seems to me to be guilty of a rather aggressive overreading. All of the snippets of text quoted (all of which can be found in a
good etymological dictionary so one doubts whether context has been
taken into account) can be read as the comments of philosophers exploring the implications for earthly human life of a yin-yang theory of
cosmic form and process. The terms are abstract, and the active polarity of yin and yang apply to much more than the bedchamber life
of concrete male and female humans. Even the words here translated
as "desire" (yu, yuwang) are used in a broader sense than the sexual.
It is well known that the general problem of human desires, read as
excessive emotional attachment to the world, was one that exercised
philosophers of the time.

The strategy adopted by this text, that of finding classical authority
for a modern scientific discipline, sexology, and its preferred objects
(drives, sexual behavior, and so on), is typical of modern Chinese
scholarship not only in the bedchamber arts but in the research that
chronicles the history of medicine and other national traditions.
Among historians there is a large investment in finding evidence
in the Chinese past, preferably the very remote past, for the prior invention of many elements of modernity. This is a familiar formation
in developing world nationalisms, and I will return to it several times
in what follows.[15] Here we need only note the nationalism involved in
Song Shugong's interpretive implication: the science of sex, he asserts, was founded not by Sigmund Freud and Havelock Ellis but by
Chinese philosophers writing before the birth of Christ.

For moderns, then, xing means character or substance, and it also
means sex. Because the canonical texts from the classical age of Chinese civilization often discuss the ramifications of a cosmology polar-
ized and linked through the yin-yang pair, it is not difficult to read
these ancient materials as strongly gendered and sexualized. There
are, of course, texts contemporary with these that explicitly and concretely discuss bedroom practice, but they are few. How much more
satisfying it is to the modern sexologist, perhaps, to discover in the extensively studied philosophical canon that his (we are talking about

male authors here) national ancestors had a sexual theory of nature and humanity. Xing thus comes to mean both nature and sex at once.

This discovery, in the course of rereading a rich and ambiguous archive, is not just Chinese nationalist; it is markedly twentieth century. The universal man we are given in this process is one whose "most basic substance" is sexual. Moreover, the very universe in which he lives is modeled on (what is taken to be) the sexual duality of human beings. This is a natural sexual duality, a "heavenly endowment" that can be neither learned nor altered.

The ancient texts could be read otherwise, of course. Perhaps when they speak of xing and qing they are referring to characteristics and desires that are quite general, incorporating the sexual as only one of many aspects of human life. Placed in an abstract yin-yang dynamic, such texts can be read to expand our ways of imagining cosmic generativity. A yin-yang universe is one that is self-activating, dynamic, and ever transforming. It invites a scholarship more attentive to qualities of change and patterns of influence than to the determination of causes or fixed essences. All of this has been discussed in the rich scholarship of the worldwide sinological humanities. But when historians appropriate these texts for the history of sex their reading is narrow. The philosophical canon appears to be taken hostage by the modern category of sex itself. Male-female sexual intercourse becomes a narrowing and overliteral metaphor and model for one of the world's richest archives of ancient cosmological thought.

I find this literalism asensual, rationalistic, heterosexist, unimaginative, and ultimately quite discouraging. But I nevertheless must acknowledge a certain New Age charm in the idea that sexual union might be modeled on and chartered by the rhythms of "nature" itself. This is not the clash, cooperation, or intercourse of selfish instinctual drives borne by discrete individuals; rather, the yin-yang image suggests a pattern of natural generativity that governs or authorizes the activity of sexual intercourse itself. In this vision, men and women join in sex not as slaves to their biological needs but as expressions of a natural process that exceeds their individual bodies, their relationship, and even local conditions. A sexual process governed by the intimate reciprocities of yin and yang would be cosmic indeed!

As I imagine the implications of this sexualized yin-yang vision appropriated from millennia-old texts, though, I can't help wondering whether contemporary Chinese sexologists have confronted the difference between a scientific sexology involving biologically driven individuals and a cosmology and metaphysics that take the relational logic of yin-yang processes seriously. The original texts now being re-published almost require attention to the latter, while many of the commentaries written in the last decade seem determined only to see the former. Thus, the new bedchamber arts compilations, as a reading experience, are quite hybrid: in these sources, science, history, biology and classical philosophy are invoked side by side, as if they naturally supported each other. But perhaps fantasy does not require that these different visions be sorted out?

In any case, the hybrid prose of the modern scholarship of the bedchamber seems to support more ways of imagining sex than the scientific and the antiquarian, inviting the constitution of an embodiment with many facets. I now want to contemplate some of those facets by providing more background on the current bedchamber arts vogue.

Mawangdui: The Pleasures of the Han

In 1973, a large collection of early Han dynasty (206 B.C.E.–220 C.E.) texts was excavated at Mawangdui in Hunan Province. This very rich library of philosophical, historical, and technical works, easily dated and in good condition, in one stroke permanently altered the landscape of classical Chinese historical studies. Previously some of the works unearthed had only been known through references to them in bibliographies and histories. Other texts found at the site were identifiable as precursors of books that were compiled much later, so it became possible to understand the genesis of canonical literature in more accurate historical terms.

Scholars around the world are still exploring the ways in which these materials alter the historical visage of the formative periods of Han Chinese civilization. Mawangdui and some smaller subsequent finds have left classical historians in a permanent state of excitement about what archaeology might turn up next. (A Japanese student of the history of medicine who was my classmate in Guangzhou in the early 1980s visited only one site as a tourist during his long stay in China, and that was Mawangdui. Getting there was a great challenge, as it is not on any tourist routes. After his return, my friend proudly showed me a snapshot of himself standing in the featureless field where the tomb had been found and excavated.) Partly because these early records of systematic thought in China appear to be so internally consistent and technically developed, historians now dream of much earlier, more fragmentary texts that would take them closer to the primitive origins of various East Asian knowledge traditions.

Perhaps if there had been no Mawangdui there would now be less attention paid to the Chinese bedchamber archive. Before the 1970s, the ars erotica classics studied by a handful of Japanese, Chinese, and European scholars dated from the Sui (581–618 C.E.) and Tang (618–907 C.E.) dynasties, almost a millennium later than the Han sources found at Mawangdui. Moreover, the most ancient fragments available from the Sui-Tang corpus had been preserved in a Japanese collection that was only published in reconstructed form, by a conservative Chinese nationalist scholar named Ye Dehui, in 1903. If contemporary discussions of this history are any guide, moreover, before the 1980s the most respected scholars of Chinese sex lore, even in China, were foreigners: Robert van Gulik, Henri Maspero, and Joseph Needham. Several authors writing in the 1980s and 1990s have pointed out that before Mawangdui it would have been difficult even for native Chinese scholars to improve much on the histories written by these authors.

From the point of view of a nationalist historiography, then, this was a pretty corrupted archive. Recall that Mawangdui was excavated three years before the 1976 death of Mao Zedong. Prior to that time, and even before Liberation in 1949, the tasks of history were especially heavily freighted with ideological agendas. Not only was the topic of the bedchamber arts interpretable as appealing only to bourgeois individualists, its origins were "feudal" and its chief afficionados were foreigners. The involvement of the despised Japanese in preserving the pre-1970s archive could not have added much to its luster, either.

Mawangdui, however, located as it was in the classical golden age of Chinese civilization, was well positioned to place the history of sexuality in China within the new nationalist historiographies that emerged after Mao. For at least the decade of the 1980s, and to some extent up to the present, historians concentrated on crafting a new grand narrative, replacing the universalist and internationalist agenda of Communist historiography with a history of the nation and people of China that emphasized the rise (and in some cases the decline) of a single great civilization. In these projects, the earliest textual sources enjoyed the privileges accorded to pristine origins.

It was also important that these newfound historical records enabled scholars to posit a particularly close relationship between the history of medicine and the history of sexuality. Among the texts found were previously unknown medical works and several texts that are now taken to be the original versions of the earliest items in the Sui-Tang bedchamber archive. Of the medical works, one known as "The Ten Questions" speaks simultaneously of metaphysics, medicine, and sexual practice and others provide herbal formulas for the treatment of sex-related disorders. Thus, in scholarship both in China and abroad this group of texts has generally been considered together, and for two decades historians of ancient medicine have been exploring the implications for prehistory of this strong evidence that Chinese medicine and sex lore have a common origin.

The close linkage between erotic manuals and medical works turned out to be fortuitous for those who, beginning in the late 1980s, sought to legitimate the scientific study of sexuality along with formal sex education. Their rhetoric of legitimation could draw not only on a nationalist argument (sexcraft is Chinese) and an argument from origins (sexcraft is ancient) but on the assertion that the bedchamber arts were conceived from their inception as methods of elevating health and thus serving the people. Although traditional Chinese medicine faced its own crises of legitimation in the twentieth century, apologists for the indigenous Chinese sciences have found that skeptics do not like to argue with the ideal of health. Ancient medical texts may have been seen by many modernizers as unscientific, but they were always seen as respectable history and a noble component of Chinese civilization, aspects of which could and would be shown, even by the most rigorous scientific standards, to have value for human health.

The bedchamber texts themselves are concerned with health, but they are also very explicit descriptions of the "paired practices" of the inner chambers.[16] A naive reading would suggest that these texts belonged in the category of pornography, long known and denounced in China as "yellow literature." Thus, the earnest scholarly sobriety of the commentaries sometimes seems a little forced. This distinction between modern commentaries, which insist on the centrality of health concerns, and ancient texts, which also had other agenda, is consistent with the concern among modern editors to insert this corpus into legitimate history, legitimate health care, even legitimate science.

Consider, for example, the odd reduction to the scientific achieved in this editorial introduction to the Mawangdui text "Uniting Yin and Yang."

> The texts collected in the book discuss matters of the conjoining of yin and yang in terms of male and female sexual intercourse, such as the ten movements, the ten postures, the ten refinements, the eight movements, the ten exhaustions, and other activities of [sexual] connection; they also take the positions and activities of animals as models and metaphors for techniques of connection. The text emphasizes the life-nurturing and healthful Dao of combining the bedchamber arts with [the breath control and meditation disciplines of] *qigong* and *daoyin*. Because the text was produced on the basis of very detailed observations, it allows us to raise questions about the responses of the female genital area during sexual intercourse. Doubtless these points had an enlightening effect for medical sexologists in later times.

This is all very proper. Health promotion is central, and the scientific character of the text's "very detailed observations" is also noted. In the text itself, which follows immediately upon this modern introduction, the much broader framework and lavish results of these observations make rather a contrast. Clearly, they are about something more than "the responses of the female genital area during intercourse."

> This is the method for uniting yin and yang.

> Clasp her hands and cross over to the outside of her wrists; stroke the elbow chambers; Go beside the armpits; move up to the stove frame; go to the neck region; stroke the receiving basket; cover the encircling ring; descend to the broken basin; pass over the sweet wine ford; cross the bounding sea; ascend Mount Constancy; enter the dark gate; and mount the coital sinew.

> By breathing in the vitality of her jing essence and elevating it within [oneself], one can live forever and be coeval with heaven and earth. The "coital sinew" is the coital channel within the dark gate. If one is able to lay hold of and stroke it, this causes both bodies to be pleasurably nourished and joyfully radiant in a wonderful way.[17]

It is a text full of puzzling names and phrases, but evocative nonetheless! And this is only the beginning. The text then turns immediately to "the Dao of dalliance," in which the "signs of the five desires" in the female partner are described (face flushing, nipples hardening, tongue quality changing, genitals moistening, throat drying with the swallowing of saliva). After these signs have been observed, the male is advised to mount his partner and begin performing the ten movements, the ten postures, and the ten refinements. When "qi has extended to the ancestral gate," it is time to employ the eight movements while remaining alert so as to avoid the ten exhaustions. All of these numerically specified techniques are named in the text, referred to with yet more poetic names (the ten postures, for example, include such terms as *roaming tiger, dragonflies,* and *fishes gobbling*), and are linked to patterns of response that indicate when a particular technique should be employed. In keeping with the androcentric character of "Uniting Yin and Yang," then, the male is taught how to read his partner's activity by listening for "the five sounds": "When she holds her breath, it means that she is experiencing inner urgency. When she pants, it means that she feels intense joy. When she moans, it means that the 'jade pod' has penetrated and the pleasure begins. When she exhales, it means that the sweetness is intense. When she grits her teeth and her body quivers it means she wants the man to continue for a long time." [18] Finally, the ten exhaustions are signs of damage to the male system stemming from excessive indulgence in orgasm. This is not the same thing as indulgence in sexual activity itself, as elsewhere in the same text the male is advised that numerous "arousals" without orgasm can lead to spiritual illumination and even immortality. I will return to this argument below.

Some of the techniques and observations discussed here appear to be unique to the Chinese bedchamber arts archive; others must be part of oral lore, or at least mute experience, in many historical and cultural settings. As pointed out above, texts like these are fascinating, stimulating, and possibly even practical for many kinds of readers.

I am most interested, however, in what they are for modern Chinese readers. And in this I think the editors' interests, reductionist and prim as they are, remain an important guide. What matters to these scholars, as we have seen, is the health-promoting and scientific aspects of the bedchamber texts. The ancient authenticity of the texts is also a significant framing emphasis for them. Of course, one could argue that these emphases are merely a rhetorical frame being used to legitimate a covert prurient interest in the texts. But I think there is a certain passion even in the rhetoric of propriety. We saw that the linguistic muddle that afflicts the modern word *xing* (sex, character) may have a semantic importance in that it makes sexuality an innate essence of the human, a thought that did not need to be argued in Chinese letters before the twentieth century. Similarly, there might be a very contemporary consciousness involved in reading ancient sex manuals as specifically healthful, scientific, and nationalist. In other words, the body that enjoys *this* sex is strong (in that illness and death are kept at bay), truth bearing (the essential scientific character of the world's earliest sexological knowledge promises as much), and above all *Chinese,* continuing a tradition of bedchamber practices that is both ancient and national. In other words, a technique for the private life of the inner chambers can perhaps be experienced as a very immediate way of being Chinese.

Nurturing Life

Of the Mawangdui texts directly concerned with sex, "Uniting Yin and Yang" is the most purely technical. "The Ten Questions" and "The Discourse on the Highest Dao under Heaven" refer to the same techniques but place them more fully in the context of broader philosophical and medical arguments. Because of this broad contextualization, all the bedchamber arts can be classed among the techniques that "nurture life" (yang sheng). This is a point the editors like to make as often as possible.

Yang sheng is the term that has long been used to embrace the canonical works of medicine. Thus, when sexology and sex education began to emerge in the 1980s the decades of rhetorical work, spanning the twentieth century, that had served to historically frame and legitimate the traditional medical archive could be directly appropriated in the interest of legitimating the bedchamber classics. The bedchamber texts found at Mawangdui took their place within the domain of serious scholarship not simply because they were old but because of their association with the ancient sciences of the body already institutionalized as traditional chinese medicine.[19] The healing arts and those of the inner chambers could both be seen as part of the "highest Dao," which ensured long life, wholesome reproduction, and enjoyable self-cultivation.

Yang sheng is the broadest heading under which the traditional medical arts are classified. The category can and does also include the traditions of the martial arts, meditation disciplines associated with religious movements, and the erotic arts. And it can easily be extended to music, calligraphy, and other aesthetic traditions that involve the body of the artist in a creative discipline. Nurturance of life also fits well with a Confucian philosophical interest in the self-cultivation of the superior man (*zixiu*). The term has even survived many changes in national health politics: within the framework of socialist medical policy, which until the end of the 1970s emphasized primary and preventive care delivered by "barefoot" paramedics, theorists of traditional medicine could highlight the "preventive emphasis" implicit in the yang sheng tradition. Twenty years later, as health care was being rapidly commodified, all manner of skills and disciplines could be retailed as yang sheng approaches to improving the quality of (bourgeois) life. Thus, the term has survived great changes in health policy and historiographic practice.

The notion of life nurturance offers a certain resistance to the global order of medical and scientific categories. When contemporary practitioners of the traditional technical arts claim that their practice is a form of life nurturance, they reject modern disciplinary divisions and institutional orders. Claiming holism, national civilization, and a positive understanding of health that goes beyond the absence of disease, yang sheng advocates claim a diverse set of activist, productive, bodily practices. Such practices—*taiji*, qigong, herbal tonics, fan dancing, year-round swimming, mountain climbing, and even the bedroom arts—are not only conceptualized as keeping disease at bay; they are also meant to produce experiences of embodiment that are pleasurable, comforting, and stable.[20] Although people who are ailing or experiencing declining health often take up yang sheng hobbies, many say that even after their complaints are alleviated they keep them up because these activities make them feel better in general. At the same time, they may recruit their friends and relatives to join them in a specialized group and begin to invest in special costumes, equipment, and books that help them improve their practice.

The modern scope of the yang sheng category is well illustrated by

the structure and strategy of a 1996 book intended for a general audience called *Yang sheng Jing* (*Classic of Life Nurturance*).²¹ This little
tome is titled as if it were a modern edition of an ancient text, although there is no such text in the premodern archive. It takes its
place as one of a series, the Five Little Classics. (The other volumes
are the *Classic of Being an Official*, the *Classic of Tactics*, the *Classic of
Enjoyment*, and the *Classic of Doing Business*.) Each is a compilation of
selected extracts from various ancient works, with each extract accompanied by a helpful gloss in modern vernacular Chinese. The
Yang sheng Jing organizes its textual tidbits into five sections: (1) Nurturing Life through Regulation of the Heart-Mind, (2) Nurturing Life
in Accordance with the Seasons, (3) Nurturing Life with Food and
Drink, (4) Nurturing Life in Habits of Everyday Life, and (5) Nurturing Life in the Bedchamber. A brief preface justifies the structure in
terms of its usefulness: a book like this is both more accessible to the
average reader than the classics themselves and organized to provide
advice for the common challenges of maintaining a wholesome style
of life.

As this self-help book indicates, the bedchamber arts make their
own contribution to yang sheng. Most of the classic texts argue that
long life results from correct stewardship of bodily resources, especially the crucial substance jing or seminal essence. This is both a sexual and a medical idea. A modern version of it is evident in the introduction that opens one "bedchamber medicine" text: ²²

> Bedchamber matters are a human instinct, part of the requirements
> of normal physiology. A harmonious and moderate bedchamber life
> is not only an important element in the feelings between husband
> and wife; it also contributes to the physical and mental health of both
> partners. Doctors both ancient and modern had clear teachings on
> this point. The *Secrets of the Jade Chamber*, for example, says: "Male
> and female complete each other just as Heaven and Earth give birth
> to each other. Heaven and Earth have attained the Way of intercourse;
> there is order in their eternal copulation. If humans lose the Way of
> intercourse and gradually cease engaging in it, this can be a damag-
> ing thing, but [for those who] learn and practice the art of yin and
> yang this is the Way of not dying." This argues for an emphasis on
> the nurturance of life through the bedchamber arts because they can
> be used to avoid injury due to sexual exhaustion. Clinically, there are

not a few examples of illnesses arising from immoderation in the bedroom. Therefore, a grasp of the methods of life nurturance through the bedchamber arts has a rich positive significance for improving the feelings between husband and wife, for raising the quality of life, and even for extending the life span to a healthy old age.

This is an appropriately modern opening, one that emphasizes moderation and responsibility in rather vague terms. Unlike some sex education texts, however, which adopt a similar tone derived from the global discourses of psychological and sociological sexology, this book bases its advice on a traditional medicine physiology. Hence, it turns immediately to introducing techniques and defining terms that are more familiar in the world of Chinese medicine than in that of cosmopolitan sexological research.

> 1. *The method of regulating desire to conserve jing.*
> *Desire* refers to sexual desire or the general concept of desire; *jing* refers to jing-qi [i.e., physiological jing essence] or the seminal essence of sex. *Regulating desire to conserve jing* is a term for practices that control sexual desire, conserve and nourish jing and qi, and reabsorb seminal essence. The meaning of *jing* in Chinese medicine is rather broad; it refers not only to male semen but more broadly to a fundamental substance that constitutes and maintains the living activity of the human body. The inception of human life stems from jing, it is due to jing that bodies take form, and it is jing of the yin type that nourishes bodies. Thus it is that the *Divine Pivot* says: "When a human is being born, first to be formed is jing; if jing has formed, the brain and marrow can emerge, the bones can be dry, the circulation tracts can channel [substances], the muscles can be firm, the flesh can form surfaces, the skin can be tight, and the hair can grow." The *Plain Questions* says, "Jing is the root of the body."

The text immediately establishes the ambiguity of this central term *jing*. Because this word could easily be taken to mean semen in all contexts (this is the error with which recent commentators charge Joseph Needham in his reading of the bedchamber classics), the broader physiological sense of the term must be explained.[23] Importantly, this definitional move makes it clear that both male and female bodies rely on a continuous production of jing for their organic life.[24] When one reads further in the bedchamber classics, this broad understanding of jing helps a lot. It accords with the mutual production of jing in coitus, the recirculation of jing in the body when ejaculation is interrupted, and the ability to add to one's own stores of jing by receiving the jing produced by another. If jing is "the clouds and the rain" of bodily life, its generality is easy to understand, as is the relation of transformability that exists between desires and acts, between palpable semen and the flow of bodily energies. A grasp of the dynamic physiology of Chinese medicine thus makes some of the anomalies that have exercised modern commentators on the bedchamber texts much less puzzling.

Moreover, this understanding of jing as foundational to physiological life (and therefore less easily replaced than other body substances such as qi and vitality [shen]) entails a conservative approach to preventive medicine. This need for conservation is immediately addressed by the same bedchamber medicine text, which states: "If jing of the yin type plentifully fills out the frame, then the functions of the organ systems flourish and the body is robust, seldom falling ill. If yin jing is rashly excreted, depleted, or weakened, then the functions of the organ systems are debilitated and the body becomes feeble, ages prematurely, and is often ill." Because jing is so intimately connected to health and (though this is seldom pointed out) more subject to permanent depletion than other body substances, every effort must be made to prevent its loss through "rash" excretion in sex. The "regulated" sexual hygiene that is recommended has more to recommend it, however, than the deferred rewards of rational stewardship; it also promises the positive pleasures of a body replete with energy and nourishment in the present.

> The regulation of desire can protect jing. The body that controls sexual desire enjoys a peaceful spirit, an inner store of yin jing, and a state of surplus that nourishes the whole bodily frame. One approach is not to think of desire, thus preventing internal damage to yin jing; a second approach is not to initiate sexual activity (yang shi) in order to avoid the rash excretion of yin jing in mutual passion. . . . The Ming period medical scholar Zhang Jiebin held that "desire must not be overindulged. If desire is blindly obeyed, then jing will be exhausted, and you must not exhaust jing. Exhaustion of jing causes true qi to scatter. This must not be allowed to happen because jing gives rise to qi and qi gives rise to vitality (shen); [these substances]

nourish and protect the whole body. Thus, he who would best nurture life must conserve his jing: if jing flourishes qi flourishes, if qi flourishes vitality is full and complete, when vitality is complete the body is robust, when the body is robust illnesses are few, and when vitality and qi are firm and strong in old age you can still enjoy the benefits of good health. All of this is rooted in jing." Obviously, the regulation of desire to conserve jing is intimately linked to the health of the human body, and the person who excels in the nurturance of life must regulate his desire to conserve his jing so that he can enjoy flourishing vital qi and a healthy body.

Apparently, Zhang Jiebin could be read in a way that would offend certain modern emphases of sex education. It will be recalled from chapter 5 that these include an interest in modern liberation from the strictures of feudal society; no one wants to urge celibacy or undue prudishness, it appears. Thus, the passage I have been quoting concludes with the caveat: "It should be pointed out that bedchamber matters are a physiological phenomenon of human reproduction and maturation and sexual desire is a normal human emotion. The so-called regulation of desire to conserve jing is not about forbidding desire or keeping all semen from being excreted; rather, it is about regulating desire and reabsorbing yin jing within limits in the context of normal physiology."

From the point of view of twenty-first-century American common-sense understandings of desire and embodiment, which are informed in part by writings on sex as diverse as those of Wilhelm Reich, Herbert Marcuse, and Masters and Johnson, this emphasis on regulation of desire may seem a little odd. If sexual feelings are so "normal" (I can hear my students asking), then why do they need to be so attentively and technically regulated?

One could answer this question with reference to public proprieties in a still conservative state. Policymakers have good reason to fear the public health problems and family instabilities that might be driven by a Western-style sexual hedonism. (Indeed, one interesting class of urban myth at the moment involves rumors of new millionaires who keep numerous concubines, each in her own apartment, for their sexual convenience.) So it would not be surprising if the government exercised what remains of its censorship powers to ensure that publications on any aspect of sex speak constantly of self-control.

But, as the text discussed here suggests, an appeal to self-regulation as a means of increasing gratification runs deep in the Chinese medical canon: "Heaven and Earth have attained the Way of intercourse; there is order in their eternal copulation." Yang sheng is all about the disciplines that would have to be adopted to achieve a bodily state that can be reliably satisfying both now and in the future. Longevity is certainly a goal, but enjoyment of a wholesome, vigorous embodiment right now is also promised by these texts. Jing, for example, is essential to the production of qi and vitality, and it is these that make it possible to feel energetic, to focus one's energies on the tasks at hand, to experience the appetites and enjoy their satisfaction, and to engage pleasurably with others. (It is no accident that the bedchamber texts promise that multiple engagements with few ejaculations can, among other things, sharpen one's vision and hearing and make one's voice clear. These are relational resources par excellence.) Unlike most other essential bodily substances, jing can be excreted in palpable amounts, especially by the male, and (also unlike qi, blood, fluids, and vitality) it is not easily replenished even with all the tonics available in Chinese medicine. Jing depletion would leave a sufferer without the healthy surplus of basic resources he or she needs to rise—generously, enthusiastically, and creatively—to the challenges of everyday life.

From the point of view of traditional medicine, then, the use of the bedchamber arts to achieve a well-nurtured life must revolve around the management of an economy of bodily substances, especially jing. In the modern books on "traditional sex medicine," writers and editors tend to emphasize sexual moderation and (as above) control of desire. One of the illness syndromes that these clinically oriented scholars are prepared to treat, for example, is "sexual exhaustion," and many other syndromes are also reported that stem from the depletion of jing and its host, the Kidney Visceral System. Moderation can be justified in traditional medical terms as a form of jing preservation, and in this respect contemporary advice is consistent with medical knowledge both ancient and modern.

In the classical sources on which the modern sex medicine authorities draw, however, limits to the frequency of sexual intercourse and avoidance of desire are not exactly recommended. Apparently, the earliest Chinese culture of sexual practice saw no virtue in abstention from sexual activity or even restriction of its frequency. The entire cosmos runs on the intimate relations of forces classified as yin and yang; why would men and women wish to remove themselves from this dynamic? Moreover, sexual activity produces physiological jing and renders it more active and productive within the body. It follows that the man who seeks to live long and well should have sex often. Because it is very important not to lose jing, however, one of the key techniques advocated by the very earliest bedchamber sources (and continued for centuries as an increasingly esoteric Daoist inner alchemy) was the prevention of ejaculation.[25] (The texts especially emphasized control of male ejaculation, though Wile has discussed some parallel techniques in the much later "women's solo meditation texts" he has translated.)[26] Jing that is stimulated into heightened activity through sexual activity can be reabsorbed, thereby adding to the strength and inner resources of the disciplined lover. Moreover, some classic writers suggested that males can collect and benefit from jing emitted by women in orgasm. It follows, then, that the ideal bedchamber arts lover would draw on multiple partners and practice his longevity arts very frequently indeed, for "One arousal without orgasm makes the eyes and ears sharp and bright. Two and the voice is clear. Three and the skin is radiant. Four and the back and flanks are strong. Five and the buttocks and thighs become muscular. Six and the watercourse flows. Seven and the whole body becomes sturdy and strong. Eight and the pores glow. Nine and one achieves spiritual illumination. Ten and the whole body endures."[27] Rhetoric like this may once have promoted the actual practice of sexual techniques that had a social place in large patrifocal polygamous households as well as — who knows?— positive effects on the health of a few men. But few experts today advocate this kind of sexual performance. In fact, they downplay these "feudal" features of the texts in their own prose.

Nevertheless, the original texts are there, full of athletic suggestions that are made crystal clear in helpful commentaries and footnotes. Some of these writings suggest changes of partners in midstream, and others advocate the choice of childless young women, "well-covered with flesh," as partners who offer particularly nourishing jing for male collection. The techniques recommended would require of a man an almost limitless capacity to achieve erection, considerable stamina, and (from a modern North American viewpoint) rather extraordinary self-control as ejaculation approaches. It would also be convenient to have a ready supply of willing (and very patient) partners. Grounded in a Chinese medical physiology that many find both intellectually and experientially persuasive, this classical image of the superior man whose bedtime prowess both expresses and increases his power and virtue must be quite intriguing for contemporary Chinese readers.[28] Even if not a single reader actually attempts to mobilize this sort of health regime in his or her own bedroom, many people probably believe that others are doing so. As I pointed out above, modern commentators are careful not to advocate sexual practices that might disrupt families or exploit minors. But they do nothing to disable an emerging image of a modern hypermasculine sensualist: a superlover with special expertise in techniques and disciplines that both express and increase "Chinese" superiority.

Impotence and Capitalism

I have argued thus far that some of the emerging discourses on sexuality are strongly oriented toward Chineseness, in effect transporting nationalist fantasies even into the (real or imagined) intimate space of the bedroom. I am not alone in linking nationalism and sexuality in China, however; writers in reform China have frequently used sexual elements in narratives that address contemporary dilemmas of the Chinese nation. Many of these have, however, tended to focus on the libertine's troubled twin, the impotent husband.

In recent years impotence has become an "epidemic of signification" in China.[29] Its appearance has paralleled the rise of the sex education movement discussed in chapter 5. This is one of the disorders that educators and sexologists hope will be alleviated by greater doses of open discussion and sound, scientifically based advice. Many new books in the 1990s self-health genre, for example, advising families and newlyweds about good relationships and healthy practices, addressed the possibility of impotence becoming a problem. While remaining much vaguer than the bedchamber arts classics on the subject of procedures, they advocate sensitivity on the part of wives and patience on the part of husbands. Occasional impotence, they argue, is normal, no cause for alarm, and usually manageable with a few changes in attitude and a little self-control.

At the same time that a scientific light was being thrown on this subject, the disease itself seems to have become very popular. At some point in the late 1980s, for example, advertising flyers for clinics

A clinic that treats male impotence, premature ejaculation, sexually transmitted diseases, and various skin disorders advertises by way of flyers pasted to telephone poles and compound walls. This one promises esoteric prescriptions and treatment by specialists. Author photo, 1997.

specializing in sexual disorders began to appear everywhere. Glued to telephone poles, in public toilets, and on dumpsters and compound walls, these flyers are pervasive in cities and even find their way to villages far from the clinics concerned.[30] Prominent among the conditions named in these flyers is impotence (yangwei). Although much of the business in these private clinics involves the treatment with antibiotics of sexually transmitted diseases, yangwei sufferers are also prominently targeted in the advertising.

Prior to the release of Viagra, which has made as big a splash in China as it has in the United States, there were a great many treatments for impotence, ranging from surgical implants to mechanical stimulators and aphrodisiacs. As the sex vogue gained ground in the late 1980s, discussion of these treatments began to appear in periodicals of many kinds and in readily available self-help and family health books. Beginning in 1985, a new subdiscipline of Chinese medicine, *nanke,* or "men's medicine," was organized. Committees of interested clinicians began to produce textbooks and research reports. Practitioners of Chinese medicine who had long been quietly treating men with "obstacles to sexual function" added *nanke* to their list of specialties and began holding specialist clinics. (Although the clinics that advertise on utility poles and those of mainstream traditional medicine are not the same, they certainly share reading lists and techniques to some extent.) Traditional Chinese medical treatments for yangwei proliferated. Witness the titles of a few of the forty-three abstracts devoted to impotence in a recent "traditional sex medicine" anthology: "Report on Treatment of Sixty Cases of Impotence Using 'Strong-Heart Equilibrium Liquor,'" "Clinical Insights from Treating Eighty-Three Cases of Impotence Using My Own Preparation of Red Ant–Centipede Powder," "Clinical Insights from Treating Thirty-Four Cases of Impotence of the Deficient Kidney Jing Type Using 'Former Han Life-Nurturing Essence,'" and "Analysis of Eight Hundred Cases of Kidney Depletion Impotence."[31] The last title is especially noteworthy, as the abstract reports on research conducted in a single hospital on a subset of the full array of impotence patients seen. Although details are scanty in this short report, the authors claim that they selected only those eight hundred patients who were suffering from a certain type of impotence (there are at least two other common types), and they also noted that all of the patients had been diagnosed in Western medicine clinics as suffering from impotence of a "psychological" type.

Thus, there is some evidence to suggest that the disease of impotence is both more common than it was a few decades ago and more commonly seeing the (clinical) light of day in treatment settings. What is more interesting for my argument, however, is the increasing popular *visibility* of the male who suffers from "obstacles to sexual function." Certainly this popular culture figure must inform anxieties and expectations in ways that could not have been imagined even in the recent past. Moreover, his visibility is not confined to advertising, traditional medicine, and the self-health literature. He plays an important role in literature and journalism as well.

One of the earliest appearances of the disorder in reform era fiction, for example, was in Zhang Xianliang's famous and very popular novel *Half of Man Is Woman* (1987).[32] In this story, the protagonist, a political prisoner serving out his term on a remote labor reform farm, is impotent until he plays a heroic role in saving a nearby village from floodwaters. Only after this act of service to the people is he able to consummate his marriage to a fellow prisoner, a former sex worker. Thus, he gains his manhood within a Maoist formation of collective labor as a direct consequence of an act that makes him (the equivalent of) a model worker. Shortly thereafter, however, he achieves an individual and personal transcendence partly through his sexual mastery over his (suddenly weak and dependent) wife. He eventually leaves her for a career of political activism in a coastal city. One presumes that he would not have had the strength or the courage to join the overheated economic and political life of the mid-1980s city unless he had gotten over being "half a man."

This novel uses impotence to neatly mark a national transition in the 1980s; the allegory of the impotent but then increasingly empowered individual is easily mapped over the situation of China as a nation. Even though the national political culture has changed since then, the trope of impotence has remained attractive. In a much more recent film, for example, Wu Ming's *Frozen* (1997), which fictionally chronicles the anomie and despair of young Beijing performance artists, one artist's middle-aged brother-in-law is impotent; clearly, he stands in for the Maoist-trained generation, which is better suited for a bygone collectivism and bureaucracy than for the market economy of the 1990s. The film suggests that members of this generation have values and commitments, unlike their nihilist children and younger siblings, but now they see no way to act on them or even to achieve a meaningful life in the competition and greed of reform era culture.

My favorite example of impotence in fiction, however, is the 1994 film *Ermo,* directed by Zhou Xiaowen. In this comedy of the new rural entrepreneurism, Ermo's (the protagonist's) husband is impotent. He is a retired Communist cadre, formerly the village head and a man of some consequence; everyone in the village still calls him Chief, which irritates him. Now that everyone must do business to live, the Chief's only skills, those of a bureaucrat, are useless. He takes second place to his wife's efficient (but endless) commodity production—she makes noodles—and his neighbor Blindman's superior access—he owns a truck—to the urban distribution networks through which Ermo can make a profit. Of course, Ermo and Blindman have an affair, sexually consummating the all-important relationship between commodity producer and distributor. (According to my farming acquaintances, this relationship is one of the key elements of rural economic success in China these days; it is also one of the most difficult for rural people to organize.) The Chief eventually (and briefly) recovers some of his practical power, for once Ermo has managed to buy the biggest television in the county his organizational skills are needed to provide enough seating for everyone in the village to enjoy the national New Year's show. But the film's ending promises no resolution to the chronic contradictions of Ermo's situation. She is married to a useless past, but the future that Blindman tries to offer is corrupted by his eagerness to make her his dependent. Outside of Ermo's troubled home she sees only lonely competition and relationships based on the exchange of cash.

In this film, objects are used brilliantly as allegory. The television, for example, brings global banality right into Ermo's rural house by way of an antenna made from her noodle ladle; here an older local mode of production—noodles always have a local character in China—is appropriated to the service of a universal form of consumption. The big wooden noodle press, operated at night to the point of exhaustion by Ermo, acts as a displacement for the sexual intercourse that is not happening elsewhere in the compound. The most the Chief can do about this displacement is sip Chinese medicine, a nationalist therapy for a disabled former servant of the nation. Ermo sells her blood at the hospital. Arguing that it is not so different from any other commodity, she seeks to produce more for sale by drinking bowls of saltwater. The proprieties of commercial relations of production are clear to her: she's willing to sell an adulterated product, watered-down blood, but never to receive money for no product at all. Thus, she rejects Blindman's love when she discovers that he has been slipping funds to her indirectly through an arrangement with a short-term employer.

One scene involving novel commodities speaks especially well to the themes of this chapter. In a guesthouse room, Ermo and Blindman compare recent purchases. She has bought a flashy brassiere to impress him, and he has bought her a case of antiwrinkle cream. She removes her shirt to show her new look; he lathers thick white goo on her shoulders and arms in clownishly vast quantities. The scene is classically edited as a figuration of sexual intercourse: in the hotel room, which they have clandestinely entered separately, a broken mirror reflects the woman's lovely face. If the scene weren't so ridiculous, it would be erotic. But it is ridiculous, and this is partly because of Blindman's overeager and overabundant use of the cream. This rural entrepreneur may know how to produce money, but he remains "backward" in the ways of the worldly consumer. Clearly, in keeping with his willingness to spend the money he makes with his truck, he is not a man to conserve his seminal essence in a long-term bed-chamber arts project of health and strength. In fact, as he spreads the goo on Ermo's skin he speaks only of its utility in preserving the more superficial aspects of her beauty. The life-nurturing disciplines of traditional China are not the point here, clearly; not even a classical capitalist strategy of reinvestment of profits appears to be important.

The sexual-economic relations depicted in this scene figure China's rapid plunge into global modernity. A thoroughly modern Ermo can increasingly be perceived as trapped between an impotent old husband and a profligate new lover, neither of whom offers her a viable alternative to the unending labor of domestic production and petty commerce. If we cared to seek a national allegory here, the scene and the film as a whole could be read as a denunciation of the failures of the past and the banality of the future for a China that has committed itself at every level, even the most domestic, to millennial capitalist relations of production. Impotence in this domain is serious indeed.

From Model Worker to Model Lover

Perhaps the fantasy male of the bedchamber arts, with his multiple engagements and many strategies of accumulating and reinvesting seminal essence, offers for some a counter to this depressing scenario. In fact, it need not only be men who enjoy imagining this patriarchal source of lasting strength, filial responsibility, and global competitiveness. The image invokes a systematic domestic order centered on the father and drawing on rules of filial practice that are rooted deep in Chinese history. The filial order does not exclude or (necessarily) exploit women, children, servants, and other dependents; rather, it places them in an asymmetrical system of mutual responsibilities in which they can demand that seniors and leaders meet their proper needs. (Propriety, however, is not normally open to negotiation.) When filiality is translated into sexual practice, the woman of the bedchamber arts scenario can expect exquisite attention to her desires and a great many techniques for gratifying them. But it is the male who determines the overall purpose of the encounter and who reaps the long-term benefit of his carefully crafted disciplines.[33]

The image is simultaneously economic and erotic. This model lover invests domestic product in the well-understood infrastructure of the Chinese medical body. He calculates his activities of exchange (a literal translation of *xingjiao*, sexual intercourse, would be" sex/ natures exchange") in a disciplined practice that both builds his own resources and keeps his partner(s) loyal or at least dependent on him. He expends/excretes resources only when he can afford it (or when his surplus is becoming burdensome) and on occasions when this expenditure will increase his pool of useful dependents. He plans for long-term strength while guaranteeing a few basic satisfactions in the present.

This is a superman, largely imaginary. Like Lei Feng the model soldier (recall the preamble to part I), he raises the bar for the performance of everyday life duties to a level that seems inconsistent with contemporary conditions and human limitations. These exemplars may never have been at home anywhere. But the bedchamber worker presented to the modern reader is different from the model soldier in several important respects. Even beyond the fact that Lei Feng was a creature of a state propaganda apparatus, and known to everyone, while the lord of the bedchamber must be sought out and partly interpreted from difficult texts by historically inclined consumers, these two supermen figure a vast difference between the Maoist and reform eras.

Maoist models like Lei Feng served the people in a national collective; the system of resource management in which their great or small labors made sense and had efficacy was nationally organized under the leadership of the party. Reform era models of the bedchamber arts can be nationalist (drawing on ancient Chinese lore) without being collectivist; their nighttime labors are oriented only toward their personal welfare and that of their families. Moreover, the achievement of a bedchamber arts form of productivity requires very skilled labor indeed. But the work that Lei Feng and his fellow soldiers did—he was the leader of a motor pool brigade—demanded fairly minimal skills that were shared by many. Lei Feng was Red; the bedchamber sensualist is expert. Although in some quarters the battle rages on, there is no doubt which side has emerged victorious from China's midcentury battle between Communists and technocrats.

Although Lei Feng was supposed to have argued that labor for the people is its own reward (and we saw this made explicit in the other story of a model worker, Du Wanxiang, which introduced part II), the kind of work he did was tiring, thankless, and undertaken in the company of mute and resistant objects. Bedchamber labors, on the other hand, offer immediate rewards and are driven by personal appetites. Boiled down to its national-cultural minimum, this contrast makes sense as a shift from one party-approved slogan to another: "Serve the People" was replaced in the 1980s with "To Get Rich Is Glorious."[34] The Maoist worker expected no thanks but the gratification of seeing conditions slowly improve for the poor. The reform era lover works only when it is in his or her own interest.

This contrast adds a further cultural and historical dimension to the popularity and prominence of the bedchamber arts corpus in late 1980s and 1990s China. Surely part of the appeal of these works is that they are not at all like Maoist discourse. They are like other postsocialist formations discussed in this book, enjoyable in contrast to what went before. The new moralisms are different, as was suggested in my discussion of sex education in chapter 5. Commentators on the bedchamber arts valorize the monogamous bourgeois husband and wife who can be envisioned using ancient Chinese techniques to increase their love for each other, to extend their years of health and enjoyment, and to produce a single healthy child. Although this proper modern reading is not especially consistent with the original texts with which it is juxtaposed, it at least offers the transgressive thrill of advocating something other than selfless labor for the collective. One of the many pleasures of these texts is that in them the selfless spirit of Lei Feng is nowhere to be found.

The sexual-economic ideals that link sex and the economic in the reform era are just that, ideals. In *Ermo*, for example, we have seen the cost for women of a regime that valorizes "getting rich." Zhou Xiaowen's critical comedy suggests that Ermo's new earning power cannot offer her a more satisfactory life in a rapidly expanding consumer regime. In parallel with the working woman's domestic and sexual disappointments, we might also suspect that there are disappointments in store for the modern male who gets too involved in the bedchamber arts literature. I am reminded of a remark made by a medical colleague of mine after I had described to him some of my research on impotence and culture in China. Commenting on the possibility that sexual impotence is increasing in China, he said that it is hard to understand "the numerator" in any statement of rates of cases because in a disorder like this "the denominator keeps changing."[35] In other words, as expectations rise the position of the bar between normality and dysfunction is likely to change in ways that have great consequences for people's happiness. This dilemma is not, of course, solely Chinese.

Representation and Ethics

These observations have finally brought us into the domain of the ethics of representation that I promised at the beginning of this chapter. In the rather miscellaneous topics discussed above, I have assembled an image of the modern bedchamber arts body: this is a historically civilized, Chinese-nationalist, life-nurturing and jing-conserving, potentially impotent (and thus anxious), thoroughly post-Maoist male. This body is, in other words, a creature of the reform era. He reflects patriotically on his country's long history of civilization while carefully forgetting certain recent decades, he admires the superior understanding of bodies and pleasures evident in the writings of his national forefathers, he orients the disciplines of everyday life to conservation and prudent expenditure of scarce resources (or wishes he could), and his goals extend to the requirements of his immediate family but not far beyond.

I do not know if any such person exists in today's China, but I know many people who think such men are everywhere. Some commentators in China, recalling a Maoist collectivist ethics or longing for some new form of altruism, deplore the selfishness of this new bourgeois and his female counterparts. I have found it easy to engage middle-aged people in irritable conversations about how selfish everyone is these days and how much morality has been forgotten since the end of the Maoist era. I have also talked with many younger people, both rural and urban, workers and students, who are attracted to Christianity; they say it offers an ideal of moral goodness not available in the Chinese tradition. The appeal of the Falungong religious movement, which was banned in the summer of 1999, also derives at least in part from its emphasis on "truth, goodness, tolerance" (*zhen shan ren*).

A film released in China in 1997, *Days of Leaving Lei Feng*, typifies this disquiet about the ungenerous tendencies of the new middle class. It is a film with the fingerprints of the state all over it, and its moral imagination does not extend past that of the old Maoist rheto-

ric. The story follows the adventures of a relatively luckless but idealistic truck driver who had inadvertently caused Lei Feng's death in
1962. Although he carries on the tradition of selfless service he
learned from his friend and group leader Lei Feng, he keeps running
into corrupt and selfish people who interfere. The bad characters in
the 1990s segment of the film are all entrepreneurs, who drive expensive cars and dress in the height of fashion. The angel of mercy
who eventually rescues the hero and his son from a breakdown in a
remote area also has old ties to Lei Feng, and she is training young
people to carry on (what she takes to be) his teachings of "love" and
"offering a helping hand." Perhaps it is significant that the final
scenes, in which this teacher's army of cheerful students turns up on
bicycles wheeled through the long grass of a frozen swamp, are filmi-
cally handled like a dream sequence. The dream is revolutionary romanticism; for better or for worse, in the 1990s it fails to persuade.

I am very sympathetic to the popular critique of bourgeois selfishness, of course, and I love talking with my Chinese acquaintances
about these problems and the virtues of the past. One of the rewards
of these conversations for me has been the discovery (also discussed
in part I) that some in China are deliberately remembering the Maoist
past in a new way, finding virtues in the social life of a period that a
decade or so ago could only be denounced as error and excess. This is
not anything like the historiography preferred by the new sexologists
and their antiquarian colleagues who edit the bedchamber arts. For
these scholars, history is either dissolved into human sexual nature
(see chapter 5), becoming a long boring story of feudal repression of
natural instincts (or, more properly, repression of a natural desire to
speak of sex), or it disappears in the concept of Chinese civilization, a
timeless structure of sensibilities and deep insights that must be distinguished from the cultures of all other nations. By skipping over the
radically transformative first three decades of the People's Republic
and denying the historical force of twentieth-century revolutions and
their roots in colonial and imperial formations, this historiography
denies the specificity of the present. It offers rewards, perhaps, to nationalist readers who need to find Chinese superiority in historical
eras prior to the "humiliations" of the nineteenth and twentieth centuries, and it articulates well with existing structures of knowledge
and scholarly practice in the sinological humanities and cultural an-
thropologies practiced in Europe and North America. Wherever they

may appear, historiographies betray history itself when they privilege the abstractions of either nature or culture (or, as is usual, both) over empirical attention to the discourses and practices that make the real conditions of life. More important for the modern Chinese readers whose preferences and resources have been the main concern of this chapter, a nature-culture historiography does not, in my view, offer a practical ground on which the problems of today can be realistically addressed.

Collective remembering of any kind requires and produces re-presentation; every recasting of history in the service of new values involves a certain amount of rewriting of reality. This axiom of contemporary cultural studies has a methodological corollary: all forms of rewriting can be read for the new social values they entail. However innocent or commonsensical new literary genres may appear, and however divorced from the contestations of political and social change, we can tease out the basic social interests they serve through a political and ethical reading. Sometimes, however, this involves coming to terms with our own deeply embodied commitments to "common sense." As a generation of scholars in cultural studies has argued and demonstrated, common sense is everywhere suffused with specific ideological commitments. The example provided by the current chapter is almost too predictable: the naturalness of the sexual relations figured in both the original bedchamber texts and stuffy modern commentaries relies on all too common asymmetries in heterosexual relations both here and in China, both now and in the remote past. These texts excite people whose fantasies (and memories and desires) are comfortable with male-directed sexual activity. This may have been a very common characteristic of sexual activity in many places and times throughout history. But by allowing it to charm and even arouse us we may be forgetting that it is not the only natural possibility.

Thus, the bedchamber arts revival, the rewriting of certain ancient texts as national treasures of health and enjoyment, demonstrates how "the body" can have a "common sense" that hides politics within it. This is especially pertinent in the politics of gender. We are all trained from an early age in accordance with sex/gender regimes. At least in my experience, our desires are not particularly obedient to the careful gender politics we craft for ourselves as adults. However much we may believe in gender equality and work to make our practical lives more egalitarian, the subtle appeal of the old reliable asymmetries may reach us at levels that are untouched by our public commitments. Yet it would be a mistake to see our various and unpredictable fantasies and pleasures as wild, instinctual, or natural forces that collide with the rules and regulations we read in books, talk about publicly, and accept cognitively. Both our "natural" desires and the "cultural" ethical constraints to which we subject them are produced on the complex terrain of social practice. We may find many resemblances between an ancient corpus of life-nurturing, rulership-cultivating, eugenically effective writings on the life of the bedchamber and our own fantasies and practices. But these similarities are more a testimony to the powers and limitations of our socially constituted carnal imaginations than they are evidence of a unitary human nature.

The resemblances and appeal of these texts may also be a depressing testimony to the stubbornness of patriarchy. From the beginning of this project, I have felt uncomfortable in joining the international ranks of the male historians of the ancient Chinese ars erotica.[36] This is not because the heritage is a shameful one in any respect; the scholarship has often been exemplary, even thrilling in its thoroughness, sensitivity, and breadth. But in picking up these previous studies I have not been able to avoid wondering about the motives and situations of the scholars who have produced them. While admiring van Gulik's social history, Needham's linkages of sex lore to Chinese scientific traditions, Wile's charming writing and his addition of the "women's solo meditation texts" to the archive, and the philological seriousness of the Chinese scholars, one notes that there is a certain suspect intensity in their empiricist rhetoric. They unearth and offer these texts in accessible form simply because they are there, and— here the repressive hypothesis kicks in—these sources must no longer be hidden behind the bed curtains. Sex, too, is a legitimate part of history, they suggest, and only a backward prudishness has prevented the insertion of this crucial aspect of human discourse into the acknowledged historical record. It is apparently not pertinent to the progress they envision that these erotic arts focus on one kind of artist, and he is male.

Debates about morality and the place of women have not been absent from these histories, however; van Gulik, for example, reports in the introduction to his second, more widely read study that Needham had chastised him for suggesting that the Daoist tradition included sexual "vampirism." [37] Both scholars noted the relative absence of an erotics of cruelty, and both were concerned to determine whether or not certain practices of inner alchemy were exploitative of women. Needham insisted that they were not because of the ample evidence of sensitivity to women's sexual needs. Neither scholar, however, sought to challenge the gendered organization of power in the texts or to read against the grain in search of a less uneven distribution of powers.

Chinese scholars, overseen by a state apparatus that still officially concerns itself with women's rights, have been more willing to undertake moralistic readings, and, as I have argued, these sometimes stand in marked contrast to the ancient texts they are meant to elucidate. Yet with all their bourgeois stuffiness these moralisms have certain virtues; the commentators are quite explicit about acknowledging and preventing the possibility that the contemporary re-presentation of the bedchamber arts could lead to socially irresponsible exploitation of women and children. They presume—correctly, I think—that writing has the power to produce what it describes, so scholars must reflect on the social implications of even their most realistic narratives (e.g., empiricist history). In keeping with a long-standing state cultural policy, there is little scholarship in China that even claims to be value free. Historians write history in the understanding that the representation of the past is always an ethical project. Since gender inequality is a question of power, it is also a political one.

The gender politics of even the most ethical bedchamber commentaries, Chinese and Euro-American alike, still participates, of course, in a distinctly paternalistic logic. Male lovers are praised for devoting their arts to delivering female pleasure, and proprieties are invoked that will protect women from abuse by the men who remain in charge. Taken together, this twentieth-century discourse on Chinese sex manages to produce a very nuanced and articulate image of masculinity. Predictably, though, the female remains in the shade, unarticulated as such, accorded little agency, and holding powers that can only operate outside the domain of the protocols for bedchamber practice. The "woman" of this "natural," "common-sense" sexual ethics has not enough distinct presence to put her own preferences on the twenty-first-century agenda.

This does not mean, of course, that concrete historical women have not been getting their way at least some of the time. If the pathways of desire and improvisation exceed the imagination of what is written—and who is to say they do not?—it is also possible to hope for nonpatriarchal, nonheterosexist appropriations of texts. The ancient works written in classical Chinese invite, in fact, a much greater diversity of readings than their modern versions do, especially the modern versions translated into Western languages. Classical Chinese language has few gendered pronouns, and most sentences take the form of a predicate (sometimes preceded by a "topic") without a subject or explicit agent. English, of course, very frequently requires a grammatical agent as the subject of a predicate, and this agent is usually explicitly gendered. Although the English translators of the bedchamber arts writings have been correct in presuming a heterosexual emphasis in the texts, and thus in supplying the gender specificity demanded by English with the use of the pronouns *he* and *she*, this move reduces the ambiguity of the original texts. It would not be easy to retranslate the texts in a way that is less compulsory about male agency and heterosexuality, but it is easy to *read* them in a broader spirit.

Whatever the potentials of the original texts, there is little doubt that twentieth-century scholars have treated the bedchamber arts texts as instances of an ancient discourse on natural sexuality. In doing so, they have elided whatever differences may have inhabited the texts on bedchamber practices in different historical periods and they have allowed the patriarchal forms of this literature to pass as natural. At the same time, the revival of this literature in China has coupled erotic desire to an anti-Maoist interest in "Confucian" filial social relations that make a virtue of inequality while valorizing a national distinctiveness in a static and ahistorical discourse on civilization. In my opinion, all of these tendencies are problems that should be addressed by conscientious scholars who realize that their work is never really value free. At present, the function of the bedchamber arts texts is to couple a naturalized desire to the nation and patriarchy through the reliable delivery of pleasure. This is not an elite conspiracy against the people; it is the highly contradictory common sense in which we are all to some extent inevitably entangled, bodies and all.

In the Bedchamber

In conclusion, I want to advance, finally, my own favorite fantasy regarding the bedcraft classics, hoping to return them to a domain of use that may be both less nationalist and less orientalist than some other contemporary uses. My fantasy depends on the discovery by scholars, as they sifted through poetry and fictional prose works looking for materials reflecting sex life in history, that these works were sometimes used as bedside manuals. One of the most famous scenes comes from an early Qing period novel, *The Carnal Prayer Mat,* in which a libertine husband, Vesperus, uses a pillow book with pictures and text to persuade his overrefined bride that their nighttime repertoire needs to be expanded.

> Pulling up an easy chair, he sat down and drew her onto his lap, then opened the album and showed it to her picture by picture. . . . Vesperus told Jade Scent to try to imagine herself in the place of the people depicted and to concentrate on their expressions so that she could imitate them later on. While she looked at the pictures, he read out the comments:
>
> Picture Number One: the Releasing the Butterfly in Search of Fragrance Position. [Here ensues a description of an early stage of intercourse in which the lovers' bodies are poised atop a Lake Tai rock. Four other positions in increasing degrees of passion follow.]
>
> By the time Jade Scent reached this [fifth] page, her sexual desires were fully aroused and could no longer be held in check. Vesperus turned the page and was about to show her the next picture when she pushed the book away and stood up.
>
> "A fine book this is!" she exclaimed. "It makes one uncomfortable just to look at it. Read it yourself if you want to. I'm going to lie down." [38]

From this point, the two lovers combine emulation of positions from the book with innovations that are "apparently . . . even beyond the album's powers to depict."

Particularly when books are put to use in private contexts, as they are here, no one really expects them to be comprehensive representations of reality and there is nothing compulsory about the manner of their reading. Just as modern libertines are free to ignore the careful moralistic framing provided by contemporary editors and indulge whatever imperial fantasies their partners will cooperate in, lazy lovers can read rigorous ancient bedcraft techniques more as stimulation than as a list of rules and requirements. There is not any particular reason why users of these pillow books couldn't also ignore the heterosexual presumptions of the texts. And one certainly hopes that the asymmetry between the male who orchestrates the encounter in the interest of his health, freely using up women who are encouraged to expend their precious jing, is not as attractive to moderns as it appears to have been a millennium or so ago.

What kinds of relationships would accommodate the diverse and practical use of bedchamber texts in the contemporary world? Vesperus and Jade Scent, in the wider context of *The Carnal Prayer Mat*, do not offer much of a model despite the delicious humor about sex and gender relations that lightens the pages of this classic novel. For one thing, Vesperus is a thoroughgoing cad and Jade Scent loses her distinctive erudition along with her scruples in her quest for sensual pleasure. But it is interesting that these two pleasure seekers did not rely solely on their natural impulses to guide them. They turned to history, finding in the text—I hope—more inspiration than constraint, treating the past—it appears—more as resource than guide.

HAILING HISTORICAL BODIES

This book has traced bodies and pleasures through a few sites that span twenty years of vast social change in China. I have tried to show how carnal life has responded to the political in a country where the significance of politics has been altered profoundly but has not diminished. I have insisted on the embodied nature of reading and the generative power of texts. At the same time, I have taken Chinese realist writers and filmmakers as partners in ethnography, giving considerable weight to their analyses of reform era dilemmas in the People's Republic. I therefore want to close the book with a reading of one last text, one that exemplifies much of the political and embodied ambivalence of popular culture in contemporary China. This text—an advertising image—marks how much has changed and heralds a more delight-full future while at the same time addressing a habitus that was forged in a now banished collectivist everyday life.

WALKING IN BEIJING during a short visit in May of 2000, and distracted as usual by all manner of advertising, signage, and public notices, I was startled one morning to see a fresh image of Lei Feng. The model soldier's uniformed figure had suddenly appeared at taxi stands and busy corners throughout the downtown area, beaming from large posters mounted in chrome-framed and glass-fronted cases. The posters announced a new health information web site, www.999.com. The web site was sponsored by Sanjiu, one of China's biggest drug companies, and the sign turned out to be part of an extensive and expensive ad campaign being conducted throughout Beijing. It promised "a new concept in digital health" and included web pages like "Information Center," "All About Health," "Hot Topics," "Finding a Doctor," "Sexual Relations," "Health Club," "New Beauty Line," and "On-line Shopping Mall." In strong contrast to this

The renovated Lei Feng advertising a drug company Web site in the
year 2000. Author photo.

up-to-date Internet language, Lei Feng's image was rendered in classic socialist realist fashion. His green uniform was set off by a bright red sash and rosette indicating his status as an officially designated model, his figure and features were clearly outlined, and his face displayed the usual rosy glow. Toward the bottom of the frame, a slogan appeared: "One person on the Web, health for the whole family" (*yiren shang wang, quan jia jiankang*). The slogan echoes a motto from the Lei Feng campaigns of the 1960s: "One person in the army, glory for the whole family."

My first reaction to this unusual apparition was to marvel at the cleverness of the advertising ploy it embodied. In it, a large pharmaceutical corporation had appropriated an icon of socialist state power and the mass political movement, transferring it wholesale into the neoliberal environment of the Chinese free market. The campaign juxtaposed a morally serious nationalist collectivism and the indiscriminate diffusion of the World Wide Web; it offered a local and historically resonant body, that of the model soldier, alongside the transnational and modern images of fashion models that inhabit nearby billboards and posters. A Lei Feng encased in chrome and glass, and offering easy access to the individual desideratum of "health," is quite different from the old Lei Feng, whose very body exhorted the people to extra effort in the service of building socialism. And yet the new image invokes that older world powerfully and immediately.

The posters are not, after all, directed toward people like me. The imagined consumer of Sanjiu's new Web-based services is a Beijinger who remembers Lei Feng and may once have even been persuaded to emulate him, perhaps at some personal cost. One can imagine the first impression the new Lei Feng produces in this consumer. Is there a new government campaign? Are they reviving Lei Feng once again? Is some serious public duty being propagated here? Immediately the answer is clear—this is only a perfectly casual and private pleasure being offered, the chance to check a Web site for "Hot Topics" in health and beauty, sex and medicines. What a relief, yet what an unforgettable experience: for a split second the Maoist past is here again, only to reveal itself as the harbinger of a capitalist middle-class future. If one person in the family uses this Web site, everyone can have access to the latest in health news and products; any problem that shopping can solve will henceforth be fixed with the click of a mouse.

This publicity campaign conforms to advertising gospel. It draws attention, sticks in the memory, and addresses the person the consumer would like to become. Now that every salaried family has a refrigerator and color TV, the home computer is becoming a favorite appliance need. Many workplaces now offer opportunities for employees (one member of each family, I guess) to surf the Web; Internet cafes are proliferating as well. Everyone can contemplate going on-line. Moreover, adequate medical care is not easy to find, so this advertisement suggests that for those whose lifestyle affords them access to a computer health will be within much easier reach. In Lei Feng's smiling image, a vision of bourgeois ease and convenience is coupled with the good taste of people who can smile at their national past. In the substitution of advertising for political campaigns, the model soldier becomes an icon not of state demands but of a consuming personal future.

The future in which computers will be ordinary and health will be easy is here made to draw on a Chinese past. The great appeal of the image itself—Lei Feng's happy smile, his direct gaze, the vibrant red and green coloring, the huge honorific rosette positioned right at the center of his chest marked by the X of the sash—does not fade after the modern high-tech message of the text is perceived. This model soldier, beyond all irony, still invokes some of the same virtues he once did; for many of those to whom this campaign was directed, he embodies health itself. Lei Feng's was the body that labored with pleasure, gave unstintingly, learned with enthusiasm, and knew no doubts. Who wouldn't want to live like that, even today? Even as collectivist forms recede, the model of health and virtue that was adapted to the socialist world retains its appeal.

Certainly it is significant that Lei Feng is forever young, and many aging Chinese now facing health problems were young along with him. Whatever nostalgia contemporary consumers may have for more carefree childhoods or less competitive times can be evoked by this fresh face and blooming silk rosette. Insofar as he is read as an exemplar of state goals, moreover, Lei Feng is also Chinese. Unlike the sleekly clothed (or unclothed) models on other billboards, images that proclaim Beijing's enthusiastic participation in transnational culture, Lei Feng invokes a specifically local referent. Those who did not live that history would not recognize him since his identity is dependent on the familiar rhythms of the slogan, "One person on the Web, health for the whole family."

The Lei Feng of this poster is no fashion plate, but he still manages to reach embodied middle-aged, middle-class Beijing consumers. He is their youth, but he is also their future. No longer (as in his photographs) gazing beyond the frame at a rosy communist utopia, he makes direct eye contact with the viewer. Individual to individual, the model soldier marked with an X hails the citizen who realizes that health, as well as morals and wealth, is very much one's own responsibility. Yet Lei Feng cannot help but suggest that some generous collective vision might still count. With Lei Feng as your guide to the World Wide Web, perhaps, you can link up with altruistic corporations, which make it their business to ensure your personal health. At the same time, you and your family can recover something of that moment when there was glory for all to be found in the service of one person. Playing on the logic of the model, an advertising agency has found a way to invoke a postsocialist habitus beyond the predictable formulas of "modernization" or "transition to capitalism." But for how long will Lei Feng be able to model the healthy, responsible, Chinese body? How much longer will a very local form of pleasure be available in the text of his portrait?

This is essentially a historiographic question. What kind of history is required if we wish to find the rhythms of bodies as they learn and change, desire and age beneath and within the clamor of public debate? Does writing give us access only to "minds" or can it be read for a vision of the material existence of writers and readers? What is it we ethnographers learn when we join others as participants and observers in everyday lives previously unfamiliar to us? Must we historians and anthropologists reconsider our own carnal existence, not only as eaters and sexual beings but as readers and writers, if we are to come honestly to terms with the embodied realities of social change? Was Mencius right to see "appetites," after all this historicization, as "natural"?

This book has tried to answer these questions by example. I am quite attracted to the idea that appetites are a common ground that I can share with the people I have known in China as well as with the readers of this book; perhaps this category also joins my readers with people in China. I hope to have demonstrated, however, that the objects of all our desires, and thus the character of those desires, are thoroughly contingent. Our palates, which salivate for pork rinds or deep-fried scorpions, our imaginations, which are erotically piqued by highly variable charms in other people—the content of these forms of experience is hard to predict. This is, of course, where Mencius, or Gaozi, went wrong: one can declare eating and sex to be natural, but little can be taken for granted about what eating and sex *are* in any particular place and time. The details, however, are less important than the process of identifying with appetite itself. The eating of dog can be troubling for those who see dogs only as pets, but we can nevertheless understand how deprivation heightens desire; ancient erotic writing may translate awkwardly to specific modernities, but its direct appeal to the senses remains powerful. Carnal metaphors address real bodies.

REAL BODIES? Can I speak of real bodies when all I have to draw on are texts, notes, images, and a few sentimentalized memories? The "problem" of the reality of bodies across temporal and cultural divides is analogous to the problem of translation: to render the history congealed in a text in another language is impossible, yet it is done all the time. One way or another, sensitively or crudely, the world's people have read each other's literature, eaten and enjoyed each other's food, found pleasure in each other's bodies, and had each other's children. I have not so much described these encounters as tried to materialize a version of such an encounter in a narrative of my own. I have tried, in other words, to simultaneously hail the body of the reader while exploring the embodied practices of a certain time and place. And I have tried to both invoke and detotalize that time and place—"late twentieth-century China"—by rendering it in terms that speculate about very local but very common experience.

This is a matter of making connections. The reality of the body "in" the text is a problem for an anthropology of meaning and a theory that sees language as primarily referential. Perhaps it seems to us that bodies are always outside of the textual—and thus cannot really be spoken of—because we insist on reading textual reference as metaphoric and representational (words standing for things) rather than metonymic and historical. In a broadly metonymic approach to the uses of language, however, words connect with other words and other things. Words and texts are, after all, perfectly respectable things in their own right. They have a material existence, they have an efficacy, and they make things happen. The power of words to generate experience is by now unarguable; as a consequence, wherever reading and writing are going on bodies are also present.

Thus, it is impossible for me to read the new image of Lei Feng as merely a good joke on advertising aesthetics or a play on the local history of propaganda techniques. Rather, I think the sudden reappearance of the model soldier on the streets of Beijing invokes forms of embodiment—that is, citizens—that still know how to read models with their hands, feet, hearts, minds, and stomachs. The jolt that must have accompanied the first glimpse of the new posters for those city dwellers was a reminder not only that big capital is taking the place of the state but that there was a time when the state offered youth, sincerity, and optimism within an altruistic project. With all of its disappointments, this vision both promised and for a time delivered healthier bodies, bodies more connected to a coherent collective, bodies that could take pleasure in the ordinary things of a shared life.

Some years ago I visited a friend in the house where my best friend Ellen had lived when we were all children. It was summer, and as I stepped out the back door the smell of a jasmine in bloom struck me like a very personal blow. The jasmine plant was old and lush; it had already been flourishing more than thirty years before when I had spent long summer afternoons in that back yard. In the moment of smelling that aroma, I suddenly remembered how I had felt in that very spot long before: how much I had feared Ellen's occasional anger, how hurt I was when she moved away, how childishly anxious I was that I might similarly lose my family. In the space of a second, past experience came back to me with a force it may never have had when I was small. I thought I had forgotten what it was like to be eight years old, but something in me remembered all too well and not pleasantly. That jasmine slipped its flavor beneath all of my carefully constructed adulthood, my standard account of a happy childhood and an adored best friend, to bring back a body that, trembling and sweating, for a moment could not move in the miserable awareness of fear and helpless love.

I do not think that Lei Feng's image as offered by the Sanjiu Corporation would have produced quite such an extreme response in Beijingers in the summer of 2000. But it, too, hailed a remembered, embodied, and therefore far from lost self. There are contemporary Chinese thinkers—Lu Wenfu, Mo Yan, Zhang Jie, and Zhou Xiaowen

have been heard from in these pages—who wonder whether the reform era can offer any substitute for the simple but undeniable pleasures of socialism. As their readers search for some new collective
vision, one more compatible with global neoliberal capitalism, I cannot help wondering with them.

Introduction

1 Although my focus here is Chinese philosophy, I would argue that a similar argumentative form, which casts the appetites in a supporting role to
deeper questions, has been characteristic of much mainstream philosophy
written in European languages. (Twentieth-century phenomenology is perhaps the most notable exception to this tendency.) Consequently, I here refer to philosophy in general rather than specifying Chinese philosophy. The
problem is not confined to the systematic thought of premodern China.

2 For the sake of consistency, I use Lau's translations here, although there are
many differences of opinion about the best way to render the gnomic prose
of the *Mencius* and other texts of the early Confucian canon into English
(Lau 1970: 160–70). The Chinese text I consult is Zhu Xi [12th c.] 1987:
465–82.

3 The tradition of anthropological description that produces detailed images
of unfamiliar lifeways is very long and begins with the earliest field ethnographers. Two influential articles that take the material surfaces of everyday
life even more seriously than our forefathers did are Terence Turner, "The
Social Skin" (1980), and Pierre Bourdieu, "The Kabyle House" (1990).

4 Lau interpolates the word *appetites* in his translation to make the "food and
sex" (*shi se*) more parallel with human notions of benevolence and rightness. I find this a legitimate and helpful translation strategy. But Gaozi/
Mencius himself may not have meant to naturalize the appetites as much
as the eating and drinking itself. Either way, the problem of social and cultural variation presents itself.

5 Some American scholars date the reform period from 1978 (when Deng
Xiaoping's economic policies gained full Chinese Communist Party support) to 1989, the date of the Tiananmen incident. Chinese writers are
more likely to emphasize 1992, the date of Deng Xiaoping's tour of southern cities, as the turning point that brought a certain closure to the moderate policies of the reform era proper and ushered in a less controlled form

of capitalist development that moved at a more rapid pace. For purposes of the present study, however, because reform economic policies continue to be an important aspect of everyday life and the marks of Maoist socialism in mundane discourse and practice continue to show, I am less concerned to set an end to the post-Maoist "reform" period. Moreover, most of the materials and experiences discussed here date from the 1980s, well within the reform period by any reckoning.

6 See Anagnost 1997: 75–97 for a discussion of public civility campaigns.

7 The body is just one of the vast, overly abstract categories I am reluctant to theorize in these pages. Two others that have been the concern of many ethnographies recently are agency and power. These latter notions have been well and classically discussed by Bruno Latour (and many others in science studies) and Michel Foucault, respectively (see, e.g., Latour 1993 and Foucault 1978). These relatively more theoretical accounts are important precisely because they call for historical and social research into the empirical forms that agency (beyond individual humans) and power (beyond its institutional forms) have taken. The present study seeks to provide just such an empirical account, historicizing embodiment while taking a great deal for granted about disseminated agency and capillary power.

8 Mary Douglas (1966, 1970) wrote classic symbolic analyses of the body. On the processual body, see, for example, Maurice Merleau-Ponty, *The Phenomenology of Perception* (1962). Despite some brilliant writing that chips away at the notion of the given individual body as the necessary foundation of experience, Merleau-Ponty did not succeed in overcoming the stasis and ahistoricism of this approach to embodiment. See Csordas 1994 and Ots 1994 for phenomenological approaches that continue this tradition.

9 For ethnographies that have made embodiment an issue in their accounts, see Comaroff 1985, Munn 1986, Feldman 1991, Seremetakis 1991, and Weiss 1996. For ethnographies that successfully resist the tendency of the genre to localize and exoticize its topic, see Tsing 1993 and Stewart 1996.

10 The term *out of the way* is borrowed from Anna Tsing's *In the Realm of the Diamond Queen* (1993). This marvelous ethnography itself goes a long way toward showing how the most local of studies can have the most global of implications.

11 Arjun Appadurai has argued for the value of a cosmopolitan ethnography that takes the role of a transnational media more seriously in the production of cultural imaginations (1996: 52–56). On the subject of itinerant ethnography, see Schein 2000: 28.

12 Recent ethnographies of China include important works by Anagnost (1997), Kipnis (1997), Litzinger (2000), Rofel (1999a), Schein (2000), and Yan (1996). One of the more valuable journalistic works to appear recently

is Zha 1995, and see review articles by Kong (1999) and Zarrow (1999) for discussions of the autobiography literature published in English.

13 Tucker [1972] 1978: 171.

14 Ibid.: 154 (italics mine).

15 Ibid.: 87.

16 Ibid.: 89.

17 The tentativeness of this sentence is deliberate. A dualistic theory of reference and an ideal-material divide are inherent to the English language, and I cannot claim to have overcome this deep tendency with any consistent success. I hope, however, that the effort will be clear at times.

18 The notion of habitus and the definitional quotes are from Pierre Bourdieu's most frequently cited exploration of the concept in chapter 2 of *Outline of a Theory of Practice* (1977, 72–95). Perhaps the fullest brief definition he provides in that chapter states that "the habitus is an endless capacity to engender products—thought, perception, expressions, action—whose limits are set by the historically and socially situated conditions of its production" (95). I consider some notion of habitus to be essential for materialist ethnography and the anthropology of the body, but readers of Bourdieu will note that I have avoided using his word *system*, which suggests more coherence and unity than I am willing to presume. At times, moreover, his language implies a greater importance for the limits to imagination and practical possibility than I am willing to acknowledge, having seen so much change in Chinese everyday life. Still, it is important to acknowledge that Bourdieu has been uncompromising in his insistence on theorizing beyond the modernist dilemmas of freedom and necessity. I believe his very rich and demanding notion of practice succeeds in moving beyond the old dualisms of anthropology, and I attempt to live up to this theorization here.

19 Readers will no doubt find a great deal of abstraction in the pages that follow. But the kind of abstractions I seek to avoid are those that social science has deployed as categories that rule the structure of research: social structure, the economy, culture, mind, and so on. For useful critiques, see Sayer 1987 and Laclau 1990.

20 By far the most extended and interesting exploration of the notion of disposition for a China scholar is François Jullien's *The Propensity of Things* (1995), a book-length study of the Chinese word *shi* (disposition, configuration, array of forces, tendency) in classical philosophy.

21 My own participation in modern Chinese life dates from 1982, when I began an eighteen-month period of research (and class auditing and English teaching) at the Guangzhou College of Traditional Chinese Medicine. Since then, I have spent two years as a resident of Beijing, working with scholars and doctors of Chinese medicine, and six summers and shorter

visits in Zouping County (Shandong Province) and Beijing. Since about 1991, I have been collecting materials on popular culture and discussing them with various friends and acquaintances in Beijing and Shandong and with Chinese speakers in Chapel Hill, North Carolina.

22 Corrigan and Sayer 1985.

23 Some journalistic accounts of the revolution of the 1940s have rightly become classic sources, but they arguably overstated the rapidity of change in China as a whole since these reporters mostly wrote from areas of intense party and army activity. See, for example, Snow 1957; and Hinton 1966. The recent emphasis on rapid social change in the "discos and democracy" style of journalism has focused on fairly superficial changes and has vastly oversimplified popular reactions against the Maoist past. See, for example, Schell 1989 and Kristof and WuDunn 1995.

24 For comments on the famine, see Becker 1996, Riskin 1987, and Yang 1996.

25 Li [1985] 1991.

26 Bourdieu 1977: 78.

27 Geertz 1973: 412–53.

28 For discussions of the critical role ethnography has played, see Marcus and Fischer 1986 and Clifford 1988.

29 The notion of an ethnography of reading is consistent with this point (see Boyarin 1993). An important historical treatment of the efficacy of readings of a certain early form of ethnography can be found in Liu 1995, especially her chapter on Lu Xun and the missionary writer Arthur Smith (45–76).

30 Fredric Jameson has written on "Third World literature" as national allegory (1986). He was famously critiqued for this by Aijaz Ahmad (1992: 95–122).

31 See Landsberger 1995 for "revolutionary romanticism" and examples of these posters.

32 Barthes 1986: 146.

33 Ibid.: 148.

34 Ibid.: 144.

35 Ibid.: 145.

36 Ibid.: 144.

37 Anderson 1990: 37.

38 Ibid.: 32. I will suggest in my discussion in chapter 4 of an early reform period novella, Love Must Not Be Forgotten, that this "polarization" has been an active project for modern Chinese literature. It has not been possible in Chinese literature to presume a "natural" individual capable of opposing "external" social demands; rather, it has been necessary to invent this figure through some sometimes tortuous styles of writing. See, for example, "Miss Sophia's Diary," by Ding Ling, in Barlow 1989: 49–81.

39 For historical studies of the May Fourth generation of writers, see Anderson 1990, Lee 1973, Prusek 1980, and Schwarcz 1986.

40 See Wang 1996 for a full critical exploration of the literatures of the 1980s.

41 An exemplary project in this respect, closely related to my own in that it mostly addresses early Chinese texts, is that of Shigehisa Kuriyama, who argues—first in his study of pulse lore (1987) and then in his recent book (1999)—that a central question for the historian is: if the human body has been relatively invariant throughout recorded history, how is it that medicine can have a history? In other words, because medicine has varied so much, we can presume that the bodies it has addressed have been less stable, less "given," than was once supposed.

42 Here I refer especially to biomedical institutions in the United States and traditional medical institutions in China. The situation may be quite different for both biomedicine and the so-called alternative medicines in countries where there is a viable national health system.

43 Hence there has been a recent turn by medical anthropologists to the problem of suffering, which some are treating as a ground of comparison, if not a humanistic turn away from the uncritical adoption of medical agendas (e.g., compliance and efficacy of treatments) by anthropologists. See Kleinman et al. 1997, Kleinman 1988, and Good 1994.

44 Nanjing College of Chinese Medicine 1979.

45 Consider, for example, a 1993 film produced in China, Zhao Le (Pleasure Seeking or Looking for Fun), directed by Ning Ying. Under this pleasure-focused title, the film examines the adventures of a group of hobbyists, mostly old men, who sing opera in the Temple of Heaven Park. The title is both ironic and affectionate; it names a simple pleasure of the elderly—singing opera—with the same term that is constantly on the lips of Beijing's most consumption-obsessed nouveau riche young people.

46 Rabinow 1984: 82.

47 Ibid.: 83.

48 Ibid.: 76.

Preamble to Part I: Lei Feng, Tireless Servant of the People

1 Geertz 1973: 93–94.

2 Bennett 1976.

3 Anonymous [1963] 1990 (unpaginated).

4 Some argue that the death, too, was convenient (Tung and Evans 1976: 162). Lei Feng's story, his writings, and his ubiquitous fur-hatted image were either invented or appropriated at a time, the early 1960s, when "emulation campaigns" were taking on particular importance as a political strategy (Houn 1973: 117; Ahn 1976; Bennett 1976; Meisner 1986: 294–

95). Ahn has argued that methods of ideological education that emphasized taking "advanced" national models as guides for local practice were
developed and perfected in the PLA around this time. As the importance of
the military increased in the power struggles that led to the Cultural Revolution, the army's preferred methods of social control and political education spread far beyond the confines of its own institutions (Ahn 1976).

5   See Ebrey 1981: 386–87.

6   *Diary of Lei Feng* (Anonymous 1963: 15). Unless otherwise noted, all translations from Chinese texts are my own.

7   Ibid.: 74.

8   For an interesting comment on public ownership of agricultural produce
and the strategies imagined to evade some of the less convenient features
of this system, see Shen Rong's brilliant story "The Secret of Crown Prince
Village" (Shen [1982] 1987a).

9   These tendencies are particularly noted in a memoir published in English
just at the close of the Cultural Revolution period (Tung and Evans 1976).
The sarcasm is hard to miss: "During a bus ride . . . he would begin by
scrubbing the floor of the bus and cleaning it up generally. Next, he would
read the newspaper aloud to his fellow passengers. Thereafter he would
lead a lively ideological discussion to raise the political level of the passengers. He would end with stories concerning the glorious leadership of
Chairman Mao. For the rest of the trip he would tend babies or nurse the
ill or aged" (161).

10 Images of Lei Feng bearing the memory of his moral vision continued to
appear throughout the 1980s and 1990s. As recently as the summer of
2000, Lei Feng portraits accompanied by Chairman Mao's calligraphy were
being repainted on publicly owned walls in Beijing. Key dates in Communist Party or People's Liberation Army history are still (in 2001) marked by
Lei Feng fairs where soldiers offer haircuts, bike repairs, knife sharpening,
and health checkups free of charge. In chapter 6, I discuss a 1997 film in
which the image of Lei Feng is used to exemplify these values, and in the
conclusion I discuss an ironic recent advertising campaign featuring Lei
Feng's image in an entirely new (yet highly reminiscent) context.

11 A great many collective canteens have in fact been privatized, their proprie-
tors taking out contracts with the work unit administration to hand over a
percentage of the profits or tender a flat annual fee, in exchange for price
increases and control over the business. In addition to offering better cooking and more varied menus, these privatized dining halls have often renovated the vast spaces they inherited by adding small banquet rooms and
specialized subkitchens. This kind of reform adds conviviality to convenience for those who can afford the higher prices.

12 On banquet etiquette and allied theories of social relations, see Yang 1994,

Kipnis 1997, and Yan 1996. I will return to the practice, and the critique, of banquets below.

13 James Hevia and I have argued elsewhere that the uses of the word *culture* in Chinese studies tend to be especially idealist, referring more often than not to a tacit presumption that culture occupies a stratum above the level of social, economic, or biological structures (Farquhar and Hevia 1993). Hence I use the term somewhat ironically here, especially since I devote so much space in this study to that undeniably "cultural" domain, literature.

14 The operations of guanxi have been well studied by recent ethnographers of China. See Yang 1994, Kipnis 1997, and Yan 1996 for studies that focus on this term and its social importance.

15 Both of these foods are even more complicated than I have made them here. Many claim to especially crave the crusty part of the rice left along the edges of the pot, so it, too, is a desired food, though not one that is prepared on purpose. Lichees are a local delicacy in Guangzhou and other far southern parts of China and are difficult to grow elsewhere. Until a better highway system was built during the late 1980s and 1990s, enabling a much larger trucking industry, it was nearly impossible to get fresh lichees in northern areas. A certain emperor is even said to have once arranged for a sort of pony express from the south to deliver the fruit to his favorite concubine in the northern capital. So there is (or was in 1983) a strong sense of elite privilege attached to lichees in the popular imagination.

16 See Chang 1977 and Anderson 1988 for anthropological studies of food in Chinese culture. Food is mentioned as central to Chinese culture in Farb and Armelagos 1980: 191–95. Gang Yue's masterful study of food in Chinese literature (1999, chap. 9) discusses the issues surrounding a tendency in Asian American literature to associate Chineseness with eating.

Chapter 1: Medicinal Meals

1 See Good 1994: chap. 2 for a more comprehensive picture of the field of medical anthropology, with a slightly different orientation, than I indicate here.

2 See Hall 1986 and Hebdige 1979: 5–19 on the unity of ideology and common sense.

3 See Lisa Rofel's comments on masculinity in her study of the television soap opera *Yearnings* (1994).

4 Below I explore some of the connections that are being made between these domains, especially with reference to certain crises of masculinity in 1980s and 1990s China. For these highly political, though often intimate, problems, use of the term *yangwei* for impotence is very suggestive.

5 See Scheper-Hughes and Lock 1987, which proposes the categories of "the

body politic" and "the social body" as rubrics for the investigation of broad collective bodies. In their paper these categories are suggestive but methodologically not entirely clear.

6 Williams 1973.

7 Anderson 1988: 188; Anderson and Anderson 1977: 368–69; Chang 1977: 9; Farb and Armelagos 1980: 191–95; Kleinman 1980: 275–77; Lai 1984: 12–14; Lu 1986; Simoons 1991: 15–26.

8 Examples of some recent books on therapeutic cuisine are Zhuang 1995, Shen et al. 1998, Xie and Yang 2000, and Shang 1998.

9 Davis 2000.

10 Shen et al. 1998. The title of this work, *Siji Bushen Shishan,* is difficult to translate. Literally rendered, it goes something like this: meals to nourish and improve the functioning of the body and self over the course of the four seasons. See Ames 1993 and Elvin 1989 for discussions of the word *shen* glossed as "body-self" or "body-person." It is also worth noting that the verb *bu* is difficult to translate since even the Chinese glosses are only able to define it in terms of itself; all the terms used here as equivalents also include *bu* as part of the compound word.

11 See Furth and Chen 1992 for field research on popular ideas about women's aging in Taiwan. It should be pointed out that Chinese medicine as it is taught nowadays in the People's Republic does not extensively theorize death, nor has it developed an influential notion of dying as a medically interesting process. The definition of *death* as it was taught to me in the early 1980s in medical school classes was the complete and final divergence of the body's yang qi from its yin qi.

12 See, for example, Shang 1998.

13 Hence there was a sense of scandal when, as a result of the publication in Taiwan of an unauthorized biography of Mao Zedong, it became evident that high cadres around the chairman had long been feasting on delicacies, even at the height of the national famine. See Li 1994, in which it is claimed that Mao eschewed meat after the extent of the disaster became clear to him.

14 Deborah Davis (2000) suggests that consumers' habits may be more differentiated along gender and generational lines than along obvious social-economic class lines. Certainly the consumption patterns observable in China seem to demand a rather situational definition of what constitutes a social class, and gender and generation are indeed important factors influencing consumption patterns, as the studies in the Davis volume show.

15 Page numbers refer first to the English translation (1969) and then to *Le Cru et le Cuit* (1964). I have slightly altered the translations.

16 A philosophical study inspired by Lévi-Strauss's structuralism, José Gil's *Metamorphoses of the Body* (1998), has gone far toward recharging signs

with sensory and bodily force while preserving, minimally, the dualist logic of a semiotic approach. As Gil points out, his strategy differs markedly from that of ethnography, and it is mainly for this reason that I have chosen not to draw on it here.

17 It is worth noting for American readers that the word *mind*, or *mental patterns*, often found in the standard English translation of *Le Cru et le Cuit*, is a translation of the French *esprit*.

18 This particular use of the term *mediate* is indebted to that of Bruno Latour, who developed it especially clearly in *We Have Never Been Modern* (1993).

19 See Munn 1986 for her use of the Peircean notion of qualisigns in this connection. Weiss (1996) also attends to semiotic qualities in his ethnography. For approaches to the anthropology of the senses, see Howes 1991, Classen 1993, and Seremetakis 1994, and see the excellent discussion by Pels (1998: 101–2) of theoretical issues in the study of sensuous social life.

20 For theoretical work on translation that is very suggestive for contemporary anthropology, see Arteaga 1994; Derrida 1974; Graham 1985; Lefevere 1992; Niranjana 1992; Rafael 1988; Sakai 1997; Simon 1996; Spivak 1993: 179–200; and Steiner 1975.

21 The notion of tendency may seem vague here, though it is quite clear in Chinese. For a very rich explanation of why this is so, see Jullien 1995.

22 All Chinese personal names, with the exception of authors' names cited in the normal manner, are pseudonyms.

23 People who eat often in restaurants in China will note that this insistence is not unusual. But Sarah and I had been in town for a while, working on separate research projects, and were by now old hands at eating out. Although we each got to know many people in the course of our research, few of them were accustomed to or in a position to pay for restaurant meals, so we relied on each other for dinner companionship. We routinely insisted on sitting in the open, more public front areas of restaurants, partly for the lighter and more spacious surroundings and partly to maximize opportunities to chat with others. This was not an option at the Yao Shan Restaurant, however.

Our sequestering was not due to embarrassment over associating with foreigners as far as I was able to tell. In general, I was welcomed by the doctors and other businesspeople I dealt with in this town, and people were proud to claim me (an odd foreigner) as an acquaintance.

24 Mr. Wu, the restauranteur, had studied Chinese medicine in a three-year health school and later taken some correspondence courses. Both he and his brother claimed to belong to the fifth generation of medical specialists in their family. The drugs in question were ginseng, astragalus, schisandra, hawthorn fruit, chrysanthemum, fennel, and Asiatic cornelian cherry.

25 Throughout the book I mark technical terms in Chinese medicine by capi-

talizing them to remind readers that they do not refer to the same entities that the English word presumes. *Qi* and *jing* are exceptions, since they are not English words. In the case of terms like this, I add English words to serve not as translations but mnemonics (as in qi energy and jing essence). For definitions and more adequate translations of these terms, see Sivin 1987.

26 For a series of studies of structural changes in this county, see Walder 1998.

27 The optimum location and time of year for collecting each drug is meticulously noted in the many encyclopedic reference works on materia medica. Such dictionary entries also refer the reader to previous literatures in which material on the drug can be found, many of them quite ancient. See, for example, Jiangsu College of New Medicine 1997. Marta Hanson has begun to explore the significance of locality in the properties of medicines historically (1998).

28 Yue 1999: 150–83. In this brilliant recent study, entitled *The Mouth That Begs: Hunger, Cannibalism, and the Politics of Orality in Modern China*, Gang Yue has comprehensively explored the poetics and politics of "alimentary discourse" in twentieth-century Chinese literature, linking the orality of eating to that of language and the mundane incorporation of food to the "cannibal" practices of society. I became aware of Yue's research after I had already written on the theme of eating (Farquhar 1995a), but on reading his early drafts I was immediately humbled to learn of both the broad scope of alimentary discourse in modern China and the power of this writing (along with Yue's readings) to address contemporary Chinese situations.

29 See Anagnost 1997: 27–38, on *suku*, the institution of speaking bitterness in Maoism. Interestingly, as reform prosperity accelerates in eastern China, I find that many are too young to plausibly claim personal *chiku*, and this term is now very often used to refer to one's parents' trials during times of national upheaval. As I will suggest, the existence of suffering in a local history still serves to legitimate a personal politics for some speakers through identification with senior generations.

30 On the other hand, the commercially available infusions that I have taken are mild flavored and rather comforting. Presumably, patent medicine manufacturers try to avoid driving off customers with repellant products; they package the nastier-tasting herbals in capsules and boluses that can be swallowed without tasting. But everyone also knows that patent medicines are not as effective as customized prescriptions for stubborn complaints.

31 See Porkert 1976, Sivin 1987, and Farquhar 1994 for extended studies of the functional logic of Chinese medicine.

32 Chengdu College of Chinese Medicine 1978: 7.

33 The Upper, Lower, and Middle Jiao, sometimes translated as the "Three

Burners," are classified together as a visceral system in Chinese medicine. The standard modern accounts present them as the three spatial regions of the functional body especially responsible for managing the movement of fluids.

34 See, for example, Keys 1976, Hyatt 1978, Li 1974, and National Academy of Sciences 1975; exceptions are Porkert 1976: 193; Sivin 1987: 181–82; and Farquhar 1994.

35 See, for example, Taussig 1980 and Kleinman 1988.

36 Liu 1982: 206–7; Hou 1981: 119–20; Guangzhou College of Chinese Medicine 1982: 88.

37 This question in a broader form has strongly influenced the history of science in China. Joseph Needham's monumental *Science and Civilization in China* has been devoted to explaining why modern science *failed to develop* there, and many historians of science working in the PRC have followed his lead (see Li et al. 1982). Needham's project has many virtues, but it has not been able to respond to recent sociological and historical work that relativizes science and shows its intimate dependence on Western social developments.

38 Farquhar 1987, 1991, 1992.

39 I do not here consider the domain of acupuncture in traditional Chinese medicine. As for the complexities of herbal medicine that are outside the scope of this volume, I have elsewhere studied the practices and logics that mediate in modern clinical work between presenting illnesses and the administration of herbal therapies (Farquhar 1994). Ted Kaptchuk has presented the basic logics of Chinese medical diagnosis in an accessible form (1983). Others have explored the rich theoretical and scientific heritage of Chinese medical texts, which record considerations far beyond symptoms and herbal medicines (Porkert 1974, Sivin 1987, Unschuld 1985, Needham and Lu 1980).

40 Like everything else, increasingly commodified Chinese medical services and products are becoming differentially available to the comfortable. Chinese medicine is not yet a luxury of the very rich, but its use does require a certain expenditure and a degree of control over one's daily life that many (e.g., migrant workers and residents of underdeveloped rural areas) don't enjoy. As China's economy has "opened," traditional medical commodities have become a significant export.

41 I have here focused on aspects of clinical work that are, as far as I've been able to tell in ten years of intermittent fieldwork, nearly invariant across the whole range of medical services known in China under the heading "traditional Chinese medicine" (*zhongyi*). Since my original field research, more detailed accounts of variations in traditional medicine practice in China

have begun to appear. See, for example, Scheid, forthcoming; and Hsü 1999. Work in progress by Eric Karchmer, Yan Jianhua, and I will report the results of extended interviews with practitioners about variations in practice and their implications for Chinese medical theory.

42 I defer to a later discussion the newly important role of an "ancient" logic of "cultivation of life" and a popular culture of health-seeking preventive practices. These forms of lore and self-care have a significant relationship with the world of Chinese medicine, but they extend far beyond it as well (see chapter 6).

43 See, for example, Beijing College of Chinese Medicine 1978: 83.

44 For my unconventional use of *sign* and *symptom* here, see Yoshida 1987: 210–14, which discusses various approaches to defining the usage of the English words *sign* and *symptom* in biomedicine. He indicates the centrality of a distinction between the objective (signs) and subjective (symptoms) for most usages. This distinction is not useful for Chinese concepts of sign and symptom; rather, these terms, when they are distinguished, reflect differences in the level of medical abstractness in a clinical encounter that is a play of mingled subjectivities (see Farquhar 1994).

45 See Farquhar 1994 for a fuller discussion.

46 Arthur and Joan Kleinman report a case of neurasthenia in which the patient not only altered her regime of food and medicine but involved the whole family over a period of years (1985: 463–66). This is not at all an atypical scenario, as case histories published in China suggest.

Chapter 2: A Feast for the Mind

1 The epigraph is quoted in Solomon 1975: 53. The original editorial by Liu Youliang appeared in Red Flag 1970: 2.

2 In making this argument, and in this chapter in general, I draw on Solomon 1975, especially chapter 3, and Yue 1999. Solomon's survey of images of oral consumption in Maoist discourses gathers many of the figures that have remained important in Chinese popular memory since his study appeared. One of his contributions is to link the East Asian cold war imagery of nations as tigers—paper or otherwise—to the capacity to dominate by swallowing competing powers. As an observer sympathetic to the Chinese revolution who published before the death of Mao and the rewriting of history that began with the arrest of the Gang of Four, Solomon has provided for me a unique window into the daily life of the Maoist period. Yue's reading of alimentary discourse in Chinese literature includes attention to cannibalistic imagery and problems of speech; thus, it seeks a deeper level of analysis, specifically a more Freudian analysis, than I do. I think he very

successfully demonstrates the conflation of eating, speaking, and dominating through consumption in twentieth-century Chinese discourses.

3 See Meisner 1986 for the history of rural mobilization that many historians take to be the secret of Communist Party success in the 1940s.

4 Mao 1971: 30, 71; Solomon 1975: 46.

5 But see Gang Yue's discussion of the "hunger artist" writing of the 1930s (1999).

6 See Yang 1996.

7 This is evident from various biographical and autobiographical accounts. Even those that seek to expose the corruption and love of luxury among China's socialist leaders note how difficult it was even for the privileged to get enough food of any kind during this period. Mao Zedong is said to have given up eating meat in a gesture of solidarity with the people (Li Zhisui 1994: 40).

8 See Anagnost 1997: 27–38.

9 See Rofel 1994. Everything from all eras of film and television is now being broadcast, offering all manner of ideological positions. Cultural Revolution model operas compete with Japanese cartoons, Shaoxing opera goes up against nature shows, infomercials for exercise machines run against anti-Guomindang military dramas, and speeches by members of the Central Committee hold the attention of some even though MTV is on all day. "Propaganda" can no longer be easily periodized, and it seems that nothing has really disappeared.

10 Most historians of the People's Republic trace the emergence of the Great Proletarian Cultural Revolution to leadership struggles stemming from the great famine of 1958–61. Although the political activity that erupted as the full scope of the famine slowly became clear at the top levels of the party was hidden from public view, it could also be called a kind of revolution or at least a rebellion against Mao that backfired.

11 For works of this kind that have appeared in English, see Feng 1991, 1996; Liu 1983; and Zhang Xinxin 1987. The personal memoir as a genre of Chinese medical writing will be considered in chapter 5.

12 Although the reporters who collected these populist stories sometimes got in hot water—Liu Binyan is the best-known example in the United States—as state employees who reported to policy-sensitive editors, they cannot be considered to have been collecting narratives that were entirely free of state agendas. I will return to this issue in my discussion of *Hibiscus Town*. Both Jing Wang (1996) and Zha Jianying (1995) argue that much of the apparently transgressive writing of the 1980s was actually very much in accord with official policy about the history of the Cultural Revolution.

13 See Meserve and Meserve 1970.

14 Quoted passages are from He et al. 1945. The opera has been translated as *The White-Haired Girl, an Opera in Five Acts,* by Yang and Yang (1954), but the translations here are my own.

15 This is not subtle or nuanced writing, even in the original Chinese. But, although the images used in the opera were simplistic, the political reversal they represented in the 1940s apparently pleased audiences. In fact, the authors insist in a preface that many of the details of the libretto were provided by groups of peasants, workers, and soldiers who commented on early versions of the opera (He et al. 1945: 1–7).

16 This extract is taken from the Yang and Yang translation of 1954, not the 1945 version of *Bai Mao Nü* cited above (one of the only copies of the opera in the original Chinese available in the United States). The 1954 text I have quoted differs markedly from the concluding aria of the 1945 opera in that it emphasizes class struggle much more strongly. I presume that the Yangs worked from a later version of this frequently revised and always politically correct work.

17 The well-known novel of the 1950s, *Linhai Xueyuan,* translated as *Tracks in the Snowy Forest* (Qu 1962), for example, treats feeding the people oppressed by holdout landlords in the early land reform period as a feature of military strategy. In this relentless work, trainloads of grain are juxtaposed with flying bits of grenade-exploded bodies in a series of military maneuvers in the snowy Northeastern Province.

18 A similar reversal is noted by Gang Yue in his discussion of Wang Ruowang's *Hunger Trilogy:* "This ambivalence toward revolution displays the dilemma faced by many revolutionary writers, who feel betrayed by the Party yet unable to disown their own past. Since his revolutionary struggle ineluctably constitutes who he is, the author must paradoxically turn the whole structure of *yiku sitian* upside-down. That is, the reader is asked to read his text as recalling past sweetness (his participation in the revolution) and thinking over present bitterness (the tragic failure of the revolution)" (1999: 168).

19 The book could be classified as both scar literature and an early example of roots literature. See Wang 1996.

20 See Mo 2000: 57. Also see Wang 1996: 159–62, for comments on the social and political importance of fictional literature. *Furong Zhen* was an immensely popular novel in China in the early 1980s.

21 Gu 1981: 158. The extract is my own translation, but see the English version (1983) for a full translation. In my translations, I have tried to preserve all of the food and body imagery of the original, sometimes at the cost of fluency in English.

22 This was a catchphrase propagated by the central government in countless official venues between 1979 and the mid-1980s.

23 The long passage discussed here is from Gu 1981: 166–67.

24 Ibid.: 194.

25 Ibid.: 158.

26 Ibid.: 230–31.

27 This return to a more virtuous and straightforward socialism is even noted in the book. When Yuyin learns that her husband has been rehabilitated, she sputters in hysterical surprise, "My God, the Communist Party has come back, the new society has not disappeared, it seems its policies have also returned!" (ibid.: 229).

28 See Khan and Riskin 1998 for information on increasing economic inequality in reform China.

29 *Hibiscus Town* also incorporates interesting concerns with clothing (the rags that emblematize the bitterness of the old society) and housing (the stilt house that links the old society to the Maoist state and the fine brick house bought with Yuyin's entrepreneurial wealth).

30 Gu 1981: 196.

31 Ibid.: 231.

32 *Asceto-Marxism* is Gang Yue's term (1999).

33 Gu 1981: 166.

34 Lu [1982] 1986. Page numbers cited in the text are all from this Chinese edition. Translations are mine.

35 Gang Yue calls this the third voice of the text, which he sees as underdeveloped in the story (1999: 182–83). He approached this question of the third voice as follows: "Through the two characters' narrative entanglement, a third voice will come to the fore to identify neither. While it oscillates between the two to weave their interplay into a social history, the third voice also ironizes itself when it has to face the ambiguous picture it has created. In this way, the author has created a shadow of himself in the narrator just as the gourmet has haunted the narrator like a specter. The path of this third consciousness marks the author's travel from faith to irony. His faith, no matter how lofty it was, must ride on the hungry tide of everchanging history" (175). On the question of eating well, see Derrida [1989] 1991; I will return to his remarks in chapter 3.

36 See Wang 1996: 137–94, for an illuminating discussion of literary debates and schools in the 1980s. See also Yue 1999 for an extended reflection on the career of the unstable opposition between ideology and aesthetics in twentieth-century Chinese literature. Chinese medicine also developed a brief and limited interest in aesthetics in the mid-1980s (see Wang 1989). On *The Gourmet*, in particular, Gang Yue notes:

> "The Gourmet" offers a compelling example of how a politically compulsive semiosis [in Maoism] traverses the oral space of eating and how

eating's political overreading has [in the reform period] turned oral pleasure into an aesthetic resistance. Lu's novella further complicates the total politicization of food in the P.R.C. by tracing it to the "origin" of food's
political systematization in . . . pre-1949 China. The pathological overreading in post-1949 China thus is historicized as an end effect of a
justifiable cure for the existing social disease. Reflecting a social history
of food consumption, the text describes a rare picture of socialism as it
existed for a Marxist reading that must address a whole set of ethical issues concerning desire, pleasure, and consumption. (1999: 174)

Yue's reading of Lu's story is thus almost as ambivalent as the story itself.
People cannot but be moved by starvation and inequality, especially when
these problems appear on the terrifyingly grand scale we associate with
China's war-torn midcentury. Nor can we entirely repudiate the justifiable
efforts of the Chinese Communist Party to alter the deeply rooted social
practices that produced hunger and inequality, even when this involved the
penetration of the reforming state into the very heart of thought and everyday carnal existence. Writing from the perspective of the post-Mao period,
Yue is able to see the revolution of foodways sought by the party and its
propaganda apparatus as "a politically compulsive semiosis" and a "pathological overreading." And he appreciates the creativity of the "aesthetic resistance" that emerged in the 1980s. But he still insists on the seriousness
and idealism of the original intentions of the revolution to feed the people
and eliminate the exploitation of workers by a leisure class.

37 Gu Hua is less nuanced than Lu Wenfu in that he uncritically naturalizes a divide between the material and the ideological. Various versions of
this dualism were both invoked and resisted by many other authors. Especially as the 1980s wore on, however, many of them avoided naturalizing
any simple material-ideological divide, seeking instead to remove writing,
meaning, and life from the political domain through an aestheticizing
style. Writers identified as members of schools such as the misty poets, the
roots-seeking novelists, and the Experimentalists all found ways to recast
the lingua franca of modern China (*putonghua*) that had been thoroughly
dominated by "the Mao style" for decades. See Wang 1996.

Chapter 3: Excess and Deficiency

1 Derrida [1989] 1991: 115.
2 One well-known source for these claims is the problematic biography
of Mao Zedong written by his "personal physician," Li Zhisui (1994).
The book is still banned in China, but a Taiwan edition circulated widely on
the mainland in the mid-1990s and at that time there was much talk of the

problems it presented. Although the fact of privileged overconsumption while the masses were starving was entirely consistent with reform era expectations and critiques (corruption was the major focus of public complaints and critiques), many were concerned about the ways in which this memoir would or should alter their perception of Chairman Mao's historical meaning. It is common among readers I've spoken with in China to see the book and its author as untrustworthy and politically motivated. I share this view, but a certain part of the book's message has been successfully conveyed anyway. It is probable that shortages were never evenly distributed over China's population; there have always been privileged exploiters among the masses.

3 Marx [1844] 1972: 160.

4 Ibid.

5 This passage is excerpted from a version of a 1919 manifesto that appeared in the first issue of the journal *Xiangjiang Pinglun* and from several subsequent articles published in the same year. This text was painstakingly assembled (and translated) by Stuart Schram (1969: 162–64) from secondary resources published in Beijing that I have not been able to locate.

6 See Hinton 1966: 174–75 for the classic account of land reform.

7 Reading Mao's works chronologically however, one can note several important tendencies, one being an increasing emphasis on class struggle and the demonization of enemies and another being an increasingly abstract and jargon-ridden prose. His work gained an administrative component that had not concerned the young revolutionary of 1919; in this increasingly predominant voice, the future and its glories began to fade from view. The conflation of material wealth and true communism was continued, however, in various popular discourses and encouraged by the propaganda apparatus of the later Cultural Revolution period.

8 Schram 1969: 350.

9 Mo 1997: 96.

10 Jun Wang, personal communication.

11 See the introduction for a discussion of the anthropological uses of realistic genres.

12 Mo [1992] 2000. See also Yue 1999: 262–87; and Yang Xiaobin 1998.

13 Mo 1997.

14 This is a reference to a comment by Lu Xun; see Rae Yang 1997.

15 The comparison of people with animals is one of the ruling tropes of the essay. This is the sort of corrosive materialist viewpoint that characterizes Mo Yan's works and no doubt makes him hard for the more refined critics to swallow.

16 Deng 1988: 177.

17 I discussed the logic of eight-rubrics classification in *Knowing Practice* (1994: 76–85).

18 Deng 1988: 177.

19 This example is based on a five-phases logic of the relations of influence among the visceral systems. In this system, Heart is classified with other substances and functions in the fire category, while Kidney is classified with other substances and functions in the water category. Some physiological functions can be understood, in shorthand, to reflect Kidney water controlling Heart fire.

20 For a fascinating historical exploration of the climatic logic that may have informed some of this thinking in Chinese medicine, see Kuriyama 1994.

21 Yin and Zhang 1989: 210.

22 The category of psychology is not particularly well fitted to the way Chinese medical people think, as can be inferred from this discussion. Thus far, the category has provided a rubric for gathering Chinese medical material relating to the emotions and conditions like neurasthenia (*shenjing shuairuo*), but it has not really reorganized Chinese medical perception into a clear mind-body divide.

23 This point was clarified for me by conversations with Dr. Yang Runsheng in Zouping, Shandong, and Dr. Wang Jun in Chapel Hill, North Carolina.

24 Mo [1992] 2000. I have here used Goldblatt's translation, which is based on a 1992 edition of *Jiu Guo* published in Taiwan. The Chinese edition I have consulted is *Ming Ding Guo* (*The Republic of Drunkenness*), which was published in Beijing in 1995 and appears to differ solely in its title from the text Goldblatt used.

25 I do not here intend a summary of the rhetorical aims or satirical achievements of *The Republic of Wine*. One aspect of Mo Yan's project that I cannot take up here is a great concern with writing itself that is brilliantly explored in the novel.

26 Kipnis's discussion of banqueting in rural Shandong is detailed and useful (1997). Mayfair Yang has analyzed some of the exchange logics involved in banqueting in the 1990s at a more general level (1994).

27 This fieldwork was supported by the U.S. National Academy of Sciences through the Committee on Scholarly Exchange with China. At that time, there was still considerable concern about "access" to sociological and historical records in China's rural areas, so the academy negotiated a relationship with the Shandong Provincial and Zouping County governments to allow groups of U.S. researchers to pursue long-term projects in the county. This fieldwork was both assisted and marked, then, by official government support. For the kind of work I was pursuing on medicine (a field not strongly marked as political), this relationship was very productive. Insofar

as the role of state agencies in providing and regulating medicine was one of my interests, it was a rare opportunity.

28 Kipnis 1997: 185.

29 See Xin Liu's discussion of matchmaking in rural Shaanxi for some context (2000: 71–75).

30 Kipnis 1997: 53.

31 Ann Anagnost has noted the positive glow that accompanies the "little triumphs" of social maneuvering; she sees the operations of *guanxixue* (the art of social relationships), especially in the hands of its virtuosos, as having "a certain entertainment value that can be 'subversive' to the proper locus, communicating the pleasures of negotiating successfully around the constraints of a system" (1997: 65). Mayfair Yang (1994) has emphasized the practice of guanxixue as resistance most strongly, but she has a tendency to dichotomize the field in which resistance operates, seeing a somewhat reified state at one pole and an idealized people at the other.

32 For theoretical works that have contributed to undermining the Enlightenment foundations of ethics and epistemology, see Smith 1988, Laclau and Mouffe 1985, Lyotard 1984, and Latour and Woolgar ([1979] 1986).

33 An exception to this tendency to depoliticize pleasure and experience has been a strain in feminism exemplified most classically in Vance [1984] 1992.

34 Chengdu College of Chinese Medicine 1978: 7.

35 I have not always stayed in clinics long enough to personally witness many return visits on the part of patients with these problems. But case histories, with their careful itemization of symptoms for each visit, have filled in a lot of the stories for me even when I observed a patient only one time.

36 I base this example on interviews conducted in Shandong in the early 1990s. This was an area in which the village I knew best was known to be agriculturally wealthy and to enjoy skilled and responsible leadership. Some villages nearby were much more impoverished, however. The strategic situation I outline here was explained to me when I noticed that many brides marrying into the village had come from these much poorer villages. Of course, the motives of the relatively wealthy are interesting in such a situation as well; there was also a tendency toward village endogamy, as families attempted to keep under local control their well-organized system of wheat production, which served as a wealth base for many more diverse and far-flung economic relationships. See also Harrell and Davis 1993.

37 Derrida [1989] 1991: 115.

38 Ibid.: 114.

39 Ibid.: 115.

Preamble to Part II: Du Wanxiang, the Rosy Glow
of the Good Communist

1 I here rely heavily on Tani Barlow's translation of the story and her analysis of Ding Ling's life and works (1989: 1–45, 329–54). The Chinese-language version of the story I have consulted is Ding 1988.

2 Barlow 1989: 335; Ding 1988: 254.

3 Barlow 1989: 345; Ding 1988: 264.

4 Daughter of the people was one of many clichés used to refer to model women in the first decades of the communist regime.

5 Barlow 1989: 347; Ding 1988: 266.

6 The story "Du Wanxiang" appears to be a simple example of Maoist social-ist realism only at first glance. Barlow has placed it thoughtfully within the whole corpus of its author Ding Ling's work and shown the complexity of the political (and gender) history to which the story responds brilliantly. Nevertheless, it is much more indebted to the literary tradition of the first decades of the People's Republic than to the personalistic and depoliticiz-ing literatures that followed it in the 1980s, and it serves as a clarifying example in the periodization I am attempting in this study.

7 Barlow 1989: 354; Ding 1988: 273–74.

8 Throughout part II, I will purposely mix references to love and sex. In this project, I am more concerned to clarify what sex is than what love is, but I wish to insist that only by seeing them as closely linked issues can we be-gin to recover some of the eroticism of everyday life. I am not here exam-ining the special domains of, for example, sex work for pay, singles bars, or abusive marriages, topics in which a confusion of sex with love might be seen as mistaken or even offensive.

Chapter 4: Writing the Self

1 The epigraphs are from Zhou et al. (1981–85: 1:1).

2 Throughout this chapter, I often write of experience as though it were a self-evident thing or at least a capacious natural category that can just as easily accommodate a fantasy love affair as it can hold an elderly clinician's accu-mulated expertise. As I argued in the introduction, however, I consider ex-perience to be a very slippery concept. For senior Chinese doctors in the early 1980s, it was invoked to provide a ground of personal authority; for fiction readers a year or so earlier, it was interiorized to charter a private subjectivity. Although it is sometimes convenient for whole discourses to write as if experience were a simple reality, we have seen that they can at the same time acknowledge that the relationship between experience and writing is a problematic one. Even the fact, for example, that Chinese- and

English-language usage should be similar in this respect is a highly contingent historical curiosity. As some historians and literary scholars have
argued, moreover, and as Zhang Jie realizes in her short story, efforts to
read texts (even oral texts) as if they transparently reported experience are
naive at best.

3 Jing Wang 1996: 32–36, quoting Dai Houying, discusses the particular
forms of "humanism" that informed the early reform emergence of "a
fictional persona 'made of flesh and blood, love and hatred, a being full of
emotions and desires with a capacity for contemplation.'" The Dai Houying novel *Ren a Ren* appeared in 1985.

4 Outside of the scar literature, many other late 1970s and early 1980s stories present the Cultural Revolution in this light. One particularly amusing
story, "Ten Years Deducted," by Shen Rong ([1983] 1987b), pokes fun at the
tendency to remove the Cultural Revolution from history, as if it were a long
nightmare and nothing else. The story chronicles the fantasies and plans
of a group of office workers who hear a rumor that because of the errors of
the recent past ten years will be officially deducted from everyone's age.

5 Scar literature has been extensively presented elsewhere. Although it undoubtedly played its part in putting the individual on the agenda, especially
via a certain populist romance with humanism that was counterposed to
the ideological dogmatism of the Maoist period, I will not consider it here.
In this chapter, I am more interested in literary gestures that present a
more complicated picture of the past and look toward the future with a less
simplistic optimism. For translations of scar literature, see Link 1983, 1984.

6 Scholars of the May Fourth movement in literature have explored the forms
of individualism and sexuality that were invented and written in the Republican period. See, for example, Anderson 1990, Lee 1973, Prusek 1980,
and Schwarcz 1986. See also Barlow's discussion of the work of Ding Ling
and her story "Miss Sophia's Diary" (1989: 1–45).

7 Zhang Jie, "Biographical Note: My Boat" (1987: 223–27).

8 See the works cited in note 6 as well as Gunn 1991 and Zhang Xudong
1995.

9 Page citations to the Chinese edition (1980) and the English translation
(1987) of Zhang Jie's novella are given in that order.

10 I have discussed *ling* at some length as part of the compound *linghuo*, which
is often used in Chinese medicine (1994). See also Feuchtwang 1992 for
comments on the ling of gods.

11 There are other fetishes in the story as well, for example, the full set of
Chekhov's works given to Zhong Yu by her lover and the small lane where
she walks in all weathers.

12 An interesting intermediate point between the radical class-oriented politics of the Maoist period and the market orientations of the later 1980s was

visible in the short-lived field of "natural dialectics." Specialists in this field, following Engels, undertook a materialist history of Chinese medicine, referring to resources as diverse as the Chinese medical classics, Marx and Marxists, and Western historians and philosophers of science such as Kuhn and Popper. See Farquhar 1995b for a discussion.

13 *Shandong Zhongyixueyuan Xuebao* 1980.

14 Zhou et al. 1981–85.

15 Ibid.: 1:1.

16 This convention of medical publishing is not completely novel, though it was never so widespread before the 1980s. Dong Demao, whose autobiography appeared in volume 2, claims to have initiated the practice of publishing laudatory essays on the lives and significance of renowned laozhongyi in a journal he published in the early 1940s. But these earlier essays focus less on the personal histories of their subjects and more on the medical significance of their successful cases and preferred techniques.

17 Zhou et al. 1981–85: 2:1.

18 See Farquhar 1995c.

19 Farquhar 1994.

20 These particular points hold regardless of gender, so I have included both male and female pronouns. It is worth noting, however, that there is only one essay by or about a woman in the three volumes of *Paths*.

21 The first three titles are in volume 1; the rest are in volume 2. Volume 3 is devoted to biographical essays on the generation of recently deceased famous teachers of Chinese medicine, and the titles were all built around their names.

22 See Scheid (forthcoming) for a detailed account of the play of seniority and power in a much more recent field of Chinese medical practice. The contrasts with the early 1980s as I observed them are quite marked.

23 See my discussion of Deng Tietao's essay in "Re-writing Traditional Medicine in Post-Maoist China" (1995c).

24 Zhou et al. 1981–85: 3: 2–3.

25 See Wang 1996: 313–14, for a discussion of the language crisis in the mid-1980s. She discusses the persuasive argument of Li Tuo that this crisis reached its height, and began to see some real solutions, in the mid-1980s with the *xungen* (roots-seeking) and experimentalist schools of writing. I think the post-Maoist problem of language can be found earlier in the literature of the early reform period, but this is perhaps mainly because the most fundamental problems of how language represents experience are constitutive of realist genres. Any serious writer seeking to both describe and propose a plausible world must face the powers and inadequacies of language.

26 See Liu 1995.

27 Frolic 1980: 11.

28 Shen [1982] 1987a.

29 Gu 1981, 1983.

30 Zhang Xianliang 1988.

31 A more recent commentator on the cultural transformations of the Maoist period and after has noted the depth at which changes in language practice, many of them mandated by the party, brought about changes in experience. Yang Dongping in a 1994 essay points out that "after Liberation . . . the dialect of the leadership became the official and standard dialect and this language was adopted as soon as one left the cradle." Particularly pertinent to the concerns of this chapter, he describes how a new social asceticism altered the terms and reduced the sense of intimacy associated with love and marriage: "Within this new discursive formation, love and marriage were perceived as 'personal matters,' but really they were framed by a structure that organized and systematized them" ([1994] 1998: 167).

32 The Chinese word for oboe would be literally translated as "double reed pipe," not a strange image at all for metaphorically inclined lovers. A reference is also being made here to a common phrase characterizing a profound friendship, *tongyin*, or "[hearing the] same music."

33 Note that the word used for struggle here, *zhengzha*, is not the same as that used for struggle (*douzheng*) in political writing such as that in this chapter's first epigraph.

Chapter 5: Sexual Science

1 This highly visible aspect of street life was particularly noticeable in the mid- to late 1980s in the conservative north; it developed earlier in the southern cities of Shanghai and Guangzhou. But by 1987, when I was working in the Shandong countryside, various forms of gender-marked fashion had become quite popular even in county seats far from the big cities. In villages, however, the strict unisex dress codes required by farm labor and a lingering Maoist morality were still dominant. One young wife I knew had made herself a skirt, which she wore at home in the evening; when she was required to dash outside in it to bring the cow into its courtyard stall, she hoped no one would see her wearing this scandalous clothing.

2 See Dutton 1998: 131–32, for a brief but suggestive comment on the sexualization of reform Chinese life. On storefront doctors, see Farquhar 1996.

3 See Tani Barlow's forthcoming work on "smut" in Beijing and Shanghai. My observations here are indebted to pleasurable afternoons spent sharing Tani's quest for disreputable literature.

4 See Rofel 1999b.

5 Feng 2001.

6 Michael Dutton in *Streetlife China* (1998) has taken such a rich cultural studies approach to Chinese popular culture and everyday life that the term *street life* has come to mean almost as much in Chinese cultural studies as *culture* and *society*.

7 Foucault 1978. To note that this "sex" is recognizable is not to say that the calendars, videos, advertisements, porn films, and so on are made in the United States or elsewhere outside China. Many, perhaps most, such products are produced in China but on models closely copied from "the developed world." The models and actors may be Chinese, but the image being sought is a kind of borrowed modernity.

8 See Schein 1994.

9 See Louisa Schein's important work on the play of images of modernity among Miao villagers and townspeople of Guizhou Province (2000). She has done much to nuance our understanding of the relationship between modernities and sexualities in contemporary China. Other important studies of notions of modernity in China are Anagnost 1997, Litzinger 2000, and Rofel 1999a.

10 On the prestige of science in twentieth-century China, see Kwok 1965, Wang 1995, and Simon and Goldman 1989.

11 Latour and Woolgar 1986: 77. The language of splitting and inversion is also used in psychoanalysis. Although I am not interested in pursuing a psychoanalytic interpretive frame here, it is particularly useful to be reminded of the psychic processes of splitting and inversion when turning one's attention to research in social psychology. The entities produced in sociological and psychological research are perhaps particularly seductive because they can articulate knowledge production processes with psychic production processes through the same "logical" procedures.

12 Woolgar 1988: 68–69.

13 *Methodological horrors* is Woolgar's term (ibid.: 30–38). Regarding this question of an objective picture, note Woolgar's definition of *representation* as "the means by which we generate images (reflections, representations, reports) of the object 'out there.'" And he points out that "representation is axiomatic not just to science but to all practices which trade upon an objectivist epistemology, in short, to all activities which claim to capture some feature beyond the activity itself" (30).

14 The title of the Chinese edition (Liu et al. 1992) translates as *Contemporary Chinese Sexual Culture: Report of the "Sex Civilization" Survey on 20,000 Subjects*. The title of the American translation omitted questions of culture and civilization in favor of behavior: *Sexual Behavior in Modern China: Report on the Nationwide Survey of 20,000 Men and Women* (Ng and Haeberle 1997).

In these two editions, there were significant differences in prefatory comments and the phrasing of discussions of the findings. Hence I tend to cite
them separately here.

15 Liu et al. 1992: 6; Ng and Haeberle 1997: 12. Here I quote the English version since the sentence in question comes from Haeberle's introduction,
which I presume was translated from his English into Chinese for the 1992
publication.

16 Liu et al. 1992: 7.

17 Ibid.: 816–18.

18 Ibid.: 403.

19 One suspects that there was very low compliance with the more invasive
questions. Most of the adult questionnaires were filled out personally in
writing by the selected respondents rather than being administered by
(possibly insistent) interviewers.

20 This object ignorance, too, could be suspected of being produced by the
questionnaire, which has some of those particularly annoying kinds of
questions that ask what you "know" about —— (homosexuality, parturi-
tion, menses, and so on). Respondents can be forgiven for wondering why
they are asked about these technical terms since they clearly already know
what these things are.

21 Liu et al. 1992: 838–59; Ng and Haeberle 1997: 553–64.

22 Social sciences such as sociology and psychology had only recently reconstituted themselves as academic professions after the end of the Cultural
Revolution.

23 Anagnost 1997: 79.

24 Ibid.: 78.

25 Liu et al. 1992: 774.

26 The notion that science both represents and intervenes is discussed at
length by Ian Hacking (1983). Although in this book he concerns himself
mainly with the history of laboratory research, some of the philosophical
and historical problems he discusses pertain to social research as well.

27 Liu et al. 1992: 6–7.

28 See Lock 1980 for an ethnographic consideration of definitions of *health* in
Japan and by the World Health Organization.

29 See Lampton 1977 for some early material on this subject.

30 Literature on the body in history has proliferated in recent years. For emblematic studies, see Feher 1989.

31 See appendix 2 of Ng and Haeberle 1997 (561) for a tabular summary of the
contents of the four major official sex education textbooks for middle
school students.

32 Hong et al. 1989: 40–41. The quote from Engels in the passage on sexual

behavior is from a Chinese edition of the collected works of Marx and Engels (1972: 228).

33 Ruan 1988: 101.

34 See, for example, Ames 1993, Jullien 1995, and the articles in Zito and Barlow 1994.

35 Even so, the authors slightly undermine their distinction between psychology and physiology by using the word *tiyan* for "inner psychological experience." This compound is made up of a word for "body," *ti*, and a word
meaning "to test or examine," *yan*. Thus, it could be more literally, if rather
clumsily, translated as "to embody through experience." The ontological
specificity of the psychological slips away here.

36 Ding Ling's important story "Miss Sophia's Diary" makes this quite clear.
See Barlow 1989: 49–81.

37 See, for example, Hall and du Gay 1996, Henriques et al. [1984] 1998, Holland et al. 1998, and Smith 1988.

38 See Butler 1990.

39 For the views of one Chinese feminist, see Meng 1993.

40 Liu et al. 1992: 11.

Chapter 6: Ars Erotica

1 Song Yu, "Prose Poem at Gao Tang," a Warring States Period (475 B.C.E.–
221 B.C.E.) text cited in Luo 1993: 3.

2 Of course, it is also important that the number of Chinese readers is greater
today than it has ever been, especially since the institutionalization of an effective national education system with the establishment of the People's Republic. The texts I will refer to most often in this chapter, those that have
been revived since the mid-1980s in a scholarship of the ars erotica, were
not originally written for a broad readership. Although little is known about
book circulation in the earliest period (3d. c. B.C.E. to the 3d c. C.E.), for most
of the history of these works it seems likely that a few copies circulated privately among elite collectors and temple or monastery collections.

3 Song 1991: 3.

4 Edward Said (1978) has shown how classic humanities and social science
studies of the Middle East generated an "Orient" that had more to do with
a Euro-American commitment to an East-West divide reflecting politically
charged differences than it did to any particular histories or social practices
occurring in the areas studied. Most of his insights are just as pertinent to
East Asian as to Middle Eastern studies, and they certainly apply to the central Western scholarship on the Chinese ars erotica.

5 The best and most recent overview and compilation of these ancient texts

in English is Wile 1992.

6 They share this common ground, incidentally, with the major works in English, that is, those of Needham (1954–: vols. 2 and 5), van Gulik (1961), and Wile (1992).

7 Appadurai 1996.

8 Boyarin 1993.

9 The texts I have collected and examined in bookstores, all published since 1980, include few pictures. This is partly a result of publishing economics (pictures are more expensive) and partly a way of sustaining a scholarly air that will deflect the attention of official censors.

10 This chapter will not be able to attempt any truly historical reading of the classical bedchamber texts. The works themselves are very complex and demand very careful contextualization in the other literature and the social history of the times in which they were written. There are two important aspects of many of the texts that I will almost completely ignore here: one involves techniques for the production of high-quality children, a theme that is almost as important as the (currently much more emphasized) longevity arts of the bedchamber; the other is the art of rulership, which I suspect frames the earliest texts, those that appeared prior to a postclassical appropriation of the bedchamber arts by Daoist alchemists. Charlotte Furth has pointed out this latter possibility in her critique of van Gulik's reading of these texts (1994); see also Roger Ames's extensive study of rulership in classical Chinese philosophy (1994).

11 This grammatical usage appears to have been borrowed from modern Japanese. See Liu 1995: 348, app. E.

12 Needham 1954–: 2:51. The translation has been slightly modified to avoid Needham's tendency to overuse the word *nature*.

13 Lau 1970: 161. As was pointed out in the introduction, this line appears in a context in which *xing* clearly means "inherent nature."

14 Song 1991: 1–2.

15 See Anderson 1991, Chatterjee 1993, and Sakai 1997.

16 *Paired practices* is Wile's term for *shuang xiu* (1992).

17 Fan et al. 1997: 19–20; Wile 1992: 78. In this extract and those that follow, I adhere closely to Wile's translations of the classic works. Although he provides explanations for the terms in quotation marks in his footnotes, they are rather more tentative and markedly different from those provided by the Chinese scholars who have edited these texts. In the text just cited, for example, the Chinese editors prefer to name acupuncture points that correspond to the places figured in these poetic phrases; Wile names body parts, and his interpretation gets the male lover to the female genital area a lot sooner than the interpretations of Fan et al.

18 Fan et al. 1997: 22–23; Wile 1992: 79.

19 "Traditional chinese medicine" is the official English translation of *zhongyi*, the term used for indigenous medicine in the classical tradition in the People's Republic.

20 The recent emergence of the Falungong movement, which unites Buddhist ideas with qigong practice, suggests that this embodiment might offer itself as ethical as well. Falungong practitioners, I am told, claim that their beliefs emphasize tolerance and generosity toward others.

21 Yan Deliang et al. 1996.

22 Cao et al. 1992: 1–2.

23 On the meaning of *jing*, see, for example, Wile 1992.

24 In fact, some bedchamber texts hold that women produce seminal jing (in the narrow sense of the term) in sexual activity just as men do. So bodies of both sexes can be seen as equivalent in producing and relying on both the palpable substance of seminal essence and the physiological substance, jing, that transforms itself into qi and vitality.

25 See Needham 1954–, vol. 5, on forms of alchemy.

26 These are nineteenth- and twentieth-century texts, although they may reflect a much older tradition of practices used by Buddhist nuns and other women who devoted their lives to meditation practices. See Wile 1992.

27 Ibid.: 78; Fan et al. 1997: 21.

28 The nature of the power and virtue envisioned by the ancient texts is a complicated matter. There are many discussions of this question in the classic sinological humanities; one well-known example is Arthur Waley's *The Way and Its Power* (1934). A recent work that has brilliantly reread the Confucian canon with reference to one word for power, *shi*, is Jullien 1995. See also Zito 1997 for very suggestive explorations of imperial power and its nature and scope in eighteenth-century China. Although works like these suggest that the ideas of personal and political power encoded in contemporary Chinese-language texts may be somewhat different from those we find in English writing, so much has changed since the classic sources were written that it would be a mistake to speculate idly. The topic deserves an ethnographic and discursive study of its own.

29 I here borrow Paula Treichler's term from her article on AIDS as "an epidemic of signification" (1987). Impotence may also be an epidemic in the more classical sense, but given that no official or other reliable statistics are kept it is very difficult to know the extent of the spread of disease itself.

30 Friends have told me that the broad range of any given clinic's advertising makes sense because they need to reach faraway clients more than those who are nearby; everyone insists that people seeking such services would never go to a nearby clinic.

31 This anthology included seventy-four abstracts on sexual dysfunction, of

which forty-three were more or less centrally concerned with the treatment of impotence. See Kang and Cui 1994.

32 For an English translation, see Zhang Xianliang 1988.

33 There are exceptions to these rules, of course. Wile (1992) makes a valiant effort to find the gender-sensitive countercurrents in the patriarchal bed-chamber arts. Moreover, my discussion of filial domestic orders here refers only to the idealized relations between the husband-father and his wife or wives, children, and other dependents. See Cao Xueqin's *Story of the Stone* (1979) or Ba Jin's *Family* (1972) for classic novelistic explorations of the play of real power in large traditional families.

34 The other reform era slogan that has been important from the 1980s to the present is "Seek Truth from Facts." This policy is cited by historians to jus-tify their historical investigations in the national heritage of medical and bedchamber texts.

35 Stuart Bondurant, personal communication, spring 1998.

36 I can hardly presume to have added to a field that has included historians like Tamba Yasuyori (10th c. C.E.), Ye Dehui (1864–1927), Robert van Gu-lik, Joseph Needham, Douglas Wile, Liu Dalin, and the groups of scholars that have been working in China since 1985. I cannot even, like Charlotte Furth, mount a feminist critique on empiricist historical grounds since I have not systematically studied the discursive environments in which the bedchamber classics were produced. My purposes are anthropological and seek to grasp the historicity of the texts in their present incarnation.

37 van Gulik 1961: xiii.

38 Li 1990: 47–51.

Ahmad, Aijaz. 1992. *In Theory: Classes, Nations, Literatures*. London: Verso.

Ahn, Byung-Joon. 1976. *Chinese Politics and the Cultural Revolution: Dynamics of Policy Processes*. Seattle: University of Washington Press.

Ames, Roger. 1993. The Meaning of Body in Classical Chinese Philosophy. In *Self as Body in Asian Theory and Practice*, ed. Thomas P. Kasulis, 157–77. Albany: State University of New York Press.

———. 1994. *The Art of Rulership: A Study of Ancient Chinese Political Thought*. Albany: State University of New York Press.

Anagnost, Ann. 1997. *National Past-Times: Narrative, Representation, and Power in Modern China*. Durham: Duke University Press.

Anderson, Benedict. 1991. *Imagined Communities: Reflections on the Origin and Spread of Nationalism*. New York: Verso.

Anderson, Eugene N. 1988. *The Food of China*. New Haven: Yale University Press.

———, and Marja L. Anderson. 1977. Modern China: South. In *Food in Chinese Culture*, ed. K. C. Chang, 317–82. New Haven: Yale University Press.

Anderson, Marston. 1990. *The Limits of Realism: Chinese Fiction in the Revolutionary Period*. Berkeley: University of California Press.

Anonymous. 1963. *Lei Feng Riji, 1959–1962*. (Diary of Lei Feng, 1959–62). Beijing: People's Liberation Army Literature and Arts Press.

Anonymous. [1963] 1990. *Laodong Renmin de Hao Erzi Lei Feng* (Lei Feng, Good Son of the Working People). Beijing: China Children and Youth Press.

Appadurai, Arjun. 1996. *Modernity at Large: Cultural Dimensions of Globalization*. Minneapolis: University of Minnesota Press.

Arteaga, Alfred, ed. 1994. *An Other Tongue: Nation and Ethnicity in the Linguistic Borderlands*. Durham: Duke University Press.

Ba Jin [Pa Chin]. 1972. *Family*. Garden City, NY: Anchor.

Barlow, Tani E. 1989. *I Myself Am a Woman: Selected Writings of Ding Ling*. Boston: Beacon.

Barthes, Roland. 1986. "The Reality Effect." In *The Rustle of Language*. Trans. Richard Howard. New York: Hill and Wang.

Becker, Jasper. 1996. *Hungry Ghosts: China's Secret Famine*. London: J. Murray.

Beijing College of Chinese Medicine, ed. 1978. *Zhongyixue Jichu* (Foundations of Chinese Medicine). Shanghai: Shanghai Science and Technology Press.

Bennett, Gordon. 1976. *Yundong: Mass Campaigns in Chinese Communist Leadership*. Berkeley: Center for Chinese Studies, University of California.

Berg, Marc, and Annemarie Mol, eds., 1998. *Differences in Medicine: Unraveling Practices, Techniques, and Bodies*. Durham: Duke University Press.

Bourdieu, Pierre. 1977. *Outline of a Theory of Practice*. Cambridge: Cambridge University Press.

———. 1990. "The Kabyle House." In *The Logic of Practice*, 271–83. Stanford: Stanford University Press.

Boyarin, Jonathan, ed. 1993. *The Ethnography of Reading*. Berkeley: University of California Press.

Butler, Judith. 1990. *Gender Trouble: Feminism and the Subversion of Identity*. New York: Routledge.

Cao Hongxin, Mao Dexi, and Ma Zhongxue. 1992. *Zhongyi Fangshi Yangsheng yu Xing Gongneng Zhangai Tiaozhi* (Life Nurturance through the Chinese Medical Bedchamber Arts and the Treatment and Management of Sexual Dysfunction). Jinan: Shandong Science and Technology Press.

Cao Xueqin. 1979. *Story of the Stone: A Chinese Novel in Five Volumes*. Trans. David Hawkes. Bloomington: Indiana University Press.

Chang, Kwang-Chih, ed. 1977. *Food in Chinese Culture: Anthropological and Historical Perspectives*. New Haven: Yale University Press.

Chatterjee, Partha. 1993. *The Nation and Its Fragments: Colonial and Postcolonial Histories*. Princeton: Princeton University Press.

Chengdu College of Chinese Medicine. 1978. *Zhongyaoxue* (Chinese Pharmacy). Shanghai: Shanghai Science and Technology Press.

Classen, Constance. 1993. *Worlds of Sense: Exploring the Senses in History and across Cultures*. New York: Routledge.

Clifford, James. 1988. On Ethnographic Authority. In *The Predicament of Culture: Twentieth-Century Ethnography, Literature, and Art*. Cambridge: Harvard University Press.

Comaroff, Jean. 1985. *Body of Power, Spirit of Resistance: The Culture and History of a South African People*. Chicago: University of Chicago Press.

———, and Peter Maguire. 1981. Ambiguity and the Search for Meaning: Childhood Leukemia in the Modern Clinical Context. *Social Science and Medicine* 15B:115–23.

Corrigan, Philip, and Derek Sayer. 1985. *The Great Arch: English State Formation as Cultural Revolution*. London: Blackwell.

Csordas, Thomas. 1994. *The Sacred Self: A Cultural Phenomenology of Sacred*

Healing. Berkeley: University of California Press.

Davis, Deborah S. 2000. *The Consumer Revolution in Urban China.* Berkeley: University of California Press.

Deng Tietao, ed. 1988. *Shiyong Zhongyi Zhenduanxue* (Practical Diagnosis in Chinese Medicine). Shanghai: Shanghai Science and Technology Press.

Derrida, Jacques. 1974. White Mythology, *New Literary History* 4, no. 11: 5–74.

———. [1989] 1991. "Eating Well" or the Calculation of the Subject: An Interview with Jacques Derrida. Trans. Peter Connor and Avital Ronell. In *Who Comes After the Subject?* ed. Eduardo Cadava, Peter Connor, and Jean-Luc Nancy, 96–119. New York: Routledge.

Ding Ling. 1988. *Ding Ling Daibiao Zuo* (Representative Works of Ding Ling). Zhengzhou: Yellow River Literature and Arts Press.

Douglas, Mary. 1966. *Purity and Danger.* New York: Praeger.

———. 1970. *Natural Symbols.* New York: Pantheon.

Dutton, Michael. 1998. *Streetlife China.* Cambridge: Cambridge University Press.

Ebrey, Patricia, ed. 1981. *Chinese Civilization and Society: A Sourcebook.* New York: Free Press.

Editing Committee of the Encyclopedic Dictionary of the Chinese Language. 1973. *Zhongwen Dacidian* (Encyclopedic Dictionary of the Chinese Language). Taipei: Institute of Chinese Culture, Academia Sinica.

Elvin, Mark. 1989. Tales of *Shen* and *Xin:* Body-Person and Heart-Mind in China during the Last 150 Years. In *Fragments for a History of the Human Body, Part Two,* ed. Michel Feher, 266–349. New York: Zone.

Fan Youping, Yang Fang, Cheng Jiaxiang, and Wang Dapeng, eds. 1997. *Zhonghua Xingxue Guanzhi: Zhonghua Xing Yixue Zhenxian Jicheng* (An Overview of Chinese Sexology: Collected Essential Literature of Chinese Sex Medicine). Guangzhou: Guangdong People's Press.

Farb, Peter, and George Armelagos. 1980. *Consuming Passions: Anthropology of Eating.* Boston: Houghton Mifflin.

Farmer, Paul. 1988. Bad Blood, Spoiled Milk: Bodily Fluids as Moral Barometers in Rural Haiti. *American Ethnologist* 15, no. 1: 62–83.

Farquhar, Judith. 1987. Problems of Knowledge in Contemporary Chinese Medical Discourse. *Social Science and Medicine* 24, no. 12: 1013–21.

———. 1991. Objects, Processes, and Female Infertility in Chinese Medicine. *Medical Anthropology Quarterly* (n.s.) 5, no. 4: 370–99.

———. 1992. Time and Text: Approaching Contemporary Chinese Medicine through Analysis of a Case. In *Paths of Asian Medical Knowledge,* ed. Charles Leslie and Allan Young, 62–73. Berkeley: University of California Press.

———. 1994. *Knowing Practice: The Clinical Encounter of Chinese Medicine.* Boulder: Westview.

———. 1995a. Eating Chinese Medicine. *Cultural Anthropology* 9, no. 4: 471–97.

———. 1995b. History and the Evanescent: A Problem from Cultural Anthropology. *Asian Medicine Newsletter* (n.s.) no. 5: 1, 8–9.

———. 1995c. Rewriting Chinese Medicine in Post-Mao China. In *Knowledge and the Scholarly Medical Traditions*, ed. Don Bates, 251–76. Cambridge: Cambridge University Press.

———. 1996. Market Magic: Getting Rich and Getting Personal in Medicine after Mao. *American Ethnologist* 23, no. 2: 239–57.

———, and James Hevia. 1993. The Concept of Culture in Post-war American Historiography of China. *positions* 1, no. 2: 486–525.

Feher, Michel. 1989. *Fragments for a History of the Human Body.* 3 vols. New York: Zone.

Feldman, Allen. 1991. *Formations of Violence: The Narrative of the Body and Political Terror in Northern Ireland.* Chicago: University of Chicago Press.

Feng Jicai. 1991. *Voices From the Whirlwind: An Oral History of the Chinese Cultural Revolution.* New York: Pantheon Books.

———. 1996. *Ten Years of Madness: Oral Histories of China's Cultural Revolution.* San Francisco: China Books and Periodicals.

Feng Qihua. 2001. More Tolerance for Homosexuals. *China Daily*, April 20, 4.

Feuchtwang, Stephan. 1992. *The Imperial Metaphor: Popular Religion in China.* London: Routledge.

Fine Arts Collection Section, PRC State Council. 1976. *Peasant Paintings from Huhsien County.* Beijing: People's Fine Arts Publishing House.

Finkler, Kaja. 1991. *Physicians at Work, Patients in Pain: Biomedical Practice and Patient Response in Mexico.* Boulder: Westview.

Foucault, Michel. 1978. *The History of Sexuality.* Vol. 1. New York: Pantheon.

Frolic, B. Michael. 1980. *Mao's People: Sixteen Portraits of Life in Revolutionary China.* Cambridge: Harvard University Press.

Furth, Charlotte. 1994. Rethinking van Gulik: Sexuality and Reproduction in Traditional Chinese Medicine. In *Engendering China: Women, Culture, and the State*, ed. Christina K. Gilmartin et al., 125–46. Cambridge: Harvard University Press.

———, and Chen Shu-yueh. 1992. Chinese Medicine and the Anthropology of Menstruation in Contemporary Taiwan. *Medical Anthropology Quarterly* (n.s.) 6, no. 1: 27–48.

Geertz, Clifford. 1973. *The Interpretation of Cultures.* New York: Basic Books.

Gil, José. 1998. *The Metamorphoses of the Body.* Minneapolis: University of Minnesota Press.

Good, Byron J. 1994. *Medicine, Rationality, and Experience: An Anthropological Perspective.* New York: Cambridge University Press.

Gordon, Deborah R. 1988. Tenacious Assumptions in Western Medicine. In *Biomedicine Examined*, ed. Margaret Lock and Deborah Gordon, 19–42. Boston: Kluwer Academic.

Graham, Joseph F., ed. 1985. *Difference in Translation*. Ithaca: Cornell University Press.

Gu Hua. 1981. *Furong Zhen* (Hibiscus Town). *Dangdai* 1:157–231.

Gu Hua. 1983. *A Small Town Called Hibiscus*. Trans. Gladys Yang. Beijing: International Bookstore.

Guangzhou College of Chinese Medicine, Dialectics of Nature Research Section, ed. 1982. *Ziliao Huibian* (Collected Teaching Materials). Vol. 2. Manuscript.

Gunn, Edward. 1991. *Rewriting Chinese: Style and Innovation in Twentieth-Century Chinese Prose*. Stanford: Stanford University Press.

Hacking, Ian. 1983. *Representing and Intervening: Introductory Topics in the Philosophy of Natural Science*. Cambridge: Cambridge University Press.

Hall, Stuart. 1986. The Problem of Ideology: Marxism without Guarantees. *Journal of Communication Inquiry* 10, no. 2: 28–44.

———, and Paul duGay. 1996. *Questions of Cultural Identity*. London: Sage.

Hanson, Marta. 1998. Robust Northerners and Delicate Southerners: The Nineteenth Century Invention of a Southern Medical Tradition. *positions* 6, no. 3: 515–50.

Harrell, Stevan, and Deborah Davis, eds. 1993. *Chinese Families in the Post-Mao Era*. Berkeley: University of California Press.

He Jingzhi et al., eds. 1945. *Bai Mao Nü* (The White-Haired Girl). Shanghai: Yellow River Press. Translated and edited by Yang Hsien-yi and Gladys Yang. Beijing: Foreign Languages Press, 1954.

He Jingzhi. 1954. *The White-Haired Girl: An Opera in Five Acts*. Trans. Gladys Yang and Yang Xianyi. Beijing: Foreign Languages Press.

Hebdige, Dick. 1979. *Subculture: The Meaning of Style*. New York: Methuen.

Henriques, Julian, Wendy Holloway, Cathy Urwin, Couze Venn, and Valerie Walkerdine. [1984] 1998. *Changing the Subject: Psychology, Social Regulation, and Subjectivity*. London: Routledge.

Hinton, William. 1966. *Fanshen: A Documentary of Revolution in a Chinese Village*. New York: Vintage.

Holland, Dorothy, William Lachicotte Jr., Debra Skinner, and Carole Cain. 1998. *Identity and Agency in Cultural Worlds*. Cambridge: Cambridge University Press.

Hong Jiahe, Sha You, and Fu Anqiu. 1989. *Xingde Jiaoyu* (Sex Education). Shanghai: Shanghai Peoples Press.

Hou Can. 1981. *Yixue Kexue Yanjiu Rumen* (Introduction to Research in Medical Science). Shanghai: Shanghai Science and Technology Press.

Houn, Franklin W. 1973. *A Short History of Chinese Communism*. New York: Prentice-Hall.

Howes, David, 1991. *The Varieties of Sensory Experience: A Sourcebook in the Anthropology of the Senses*. Toronto: University of Toronto Press.

Hsü, Elisabeth. 1999. *The Transmission of Chinese Medicine*. Cambridge: Cambridge University Press.

Hyatt, Richard. 1978. *Chinese Herbal Medicine: Ancient Art and Modern Science*. New York: Schocken.

Jameson, Fredric. 1986. Third World Literature in the Era of Multinational Capital. *Social Text* no. 15: 65–88.

Jiangsu College of New Medicine, ed. 1977. *Zhongyao Dacidian* (Unabridged Dictionary of Chinese Materia Medica). 3 vols. Shanghai: Shanghai People's Press.

Jullien, François. 1995. *The Propensity of Things: Toward a History of Efficacy in China*. New York: Zone.

Kang Lisheng and Cui Meng, eds. 1994. *Zhongguo Chuantong Xing Yixue* (Chinese Traditional Sex Medicine). Beijing: China Medical Sciences Press.

Kaptchuk, Ted J. 1983. *The Web That Has No Weaver: Understanding Chinese Medicine*. New York: Congdon and Weed.

Keys, John D. 1976. *Chinese Herbs: Their Botany, Chemistry, and Pharmacodynamics*. Rutland, VT: Tuttle.

Khan, Azizur, and Carl Riskin. 1998. Income and Inequality in China: Composition, Distribution, and Growth of Household Income, 1988–1995. *China Quarterly*, no. 154: 221–53.

Kipnis, Andrew. 1997. *Producing Guanxi: Sentiment, Self, and Subculture in a North China Village*. Durham: Duke University Press.

Kleinman, Arthur. 1980. *Patients and Healers in the Context of Culture: An Exploration of the Borderland between Anthropology, Medicine, and Psychiatry*. Berkeley: University of California Press.

———. 1988. *The Illness Narratives: Suffering, Healing, and the Human Condition*. New York: Basic Books.

———, and Joan Kleinman. 1985. Somatization: The Interconnections in Chinese Society among Culture, Depressive Experience, and the Meanings of Pain. In *Culture and Depression: Studies in the Anthropology and Cross-Cultural Psychiatry of Affect and Disorder*, ed. Arthur Kleinman and Byron Good, Berkeley: University of California Press.

Kleinman, Arthur, Veena Das, and Margaret Lock, eds. 1997. *Social Suffering*. Berkeley: University of California Press.

Kong Shuyu. 1999. Swan and Spider Eater in Problematic Memoirs of the Cultural Revolution. *positions* 7, no. 1: 239–52.

Kristof, Nicholas, and Sheryl WuDunn. 1995. *China Wakes: The Struggle for the Soul of a Rising Power*. New York: Vintage.

Kuriyama, Shigehisa. 1987. Pulse Diagnosis in the Greek and Chinese Traditions. In *History of Diagnostics: Proceedings of the 9th International Symposium on the Comparative History of Medicine East and West*, ed. Yosio Kawakita, pp. 43–67. Osaka: Taniguchi Foundation.

————. 1994. The Imagination of Winds and the Development of the Chinese Conception of the Body. In *Body, Subject, and Power in China*, ed. Angela Zito and Tani Barlow, 23–41. Chicago: University of Chicago Press.

————. 1999. *The Expressiveness of the Body and the Divergence of Greek and Chinese Medicine*. New York: Zone.

Kwok, D. W. Y. 1965. *Scientism in Chinese Thought*. New Haven: Yale University Press.

Laclau, Ernesto. 1990. The Impossibility of Society. In *New Reflections on the Revolution of Our Time*, 89–92. London: Verso.

Laclau, Ernesto, and Chantal Mouffe. 1985. *Hegemony and Socialist Strategy: Towards a Radical Democratic Politics*. London: Verso Books.

Lai, T. C. 1984. *At the Chinese Table*. Hong Kong: Oxford University Press.

Lampton, David M. 1977. *The Politics of Medicine in China: The Policy Process, 1949–1977*. Boulder: Westview.

Landsberger, Stefan. 1995. *Chinese Propaganda Posters: From Revolution to Modernization*. Armonk, NY: M. E. Sharpe.

Latour, Bruno. 1993. *We Have Never Been Modern*. Cambridge: Harvard University Press.

————, and Steve Woolgar. [1979] 1986. *Laboratory Life: The Construction of Scientific Facts*. Princeton: Princeton University Press.

Lau, D. C., trans. 1970. *Mencius*. Harmondsworth: Penguin.

Lee, Leo Ou-fan. 1973. *The Romantic Generation of Modern Chinese Writers*. Cambridge: Harvard University Press.

Lefevere, Andre, ed. 1992. *Translation/History/Culture: A Sourcebook*. New York: Routledge.

Lévi-Strauss, Claude. 1963. The Effectiveness of Symbols. In *Structural Anthropology*, 186–205. New York: Basic Books.

————. 1964. *Le Cru and le Cuit*. Paris: Plon.

————. 1969. *The Raw and the Cooked*. New York: Harper and Row.

Li, C. P. 1974. *Chinese Herbal Medicine*. Washington, DC: U.S. Department of Health, Education, and Welfare.

Li Guohao, Zhang Mengwen, and Cao Tianqin, eds. 1982. *Explorations in the History of Science and Technology in China*. Shanghai: Shanghai Chinese Classics Publishing Co.

Li Tuo. [1985] 1991. *Jintian* (Today Literary Magazine) 3, no. 4: 59–73.

Li Yu. 1990. *The Carnal Prayer Mat*. Trans. Patrick Hanan. Honolulu: University of Hawai'i Press.

Li Zhisui. 1994. *The Private Life of Chairman Mao*. Trans. Tai Hung-Chao. New York: Random House.

Lindenbaum, Shirley, and Margaret Lock, eds. 1993. *Knowledge, Power, and Practice: The Anthropology of Medicine and Everyday Life*. Berkeley: University of California Press.

Link, E. Perry, ed. 1983. *Stubborn Weeds: Popular and Controversial Chinese Literature after the Cultural Revolution*. Bloomington: Indiana University Press.

————, 1984. *Roses and Thorns: The Second Blooming of the Hundred Flowers in Chinese Fiction*. Berkeley: University of California Press.

Litzinger, Ralph. 2000. *Other Chinas: The Yao and the Politics of National Belonging*. Durham: Duke University Press.

Liu Binyan. 1983. *People Or Monsters? And Other Stories and Reportage from China After Mao*. Bloomington: Indiana University Press.

Liu Changlin. 1982. *Neijingde Zhexue he Zhongyixuede Fangfa* (The Philosophy of the *Inner Canon* and the Methodology of Chinese Medicine). Beijing: Science Press.

Liu Dalin, Ng Manlun, Zhou Liping, and E. J. Haeberle, eds. 1992. *Zhongguo Dangdai Xing Wenhua: Zhongguo Liangwan Lie "Xing Wenming" Diaocha Baogao* (Contemporary Chinese Sexual Culture: Report of the "Sex Civilization" Survey on 20,000 Subjects). Shanghai: Sanlian Bookstore Press.

Liu, Lydia H. 1995. *Translingual Practice: Literature, National Culture, and Translated Modernity*. Stanford: Stanford University Press.

Liu, Xin. 2000. *In One's Own Shadow: An Ethnographic Account of the Condition of Post-reform Rural China*. Berkeley: University of California Press.

Lock, Margaret. 1980. *East Asian Medicine in Urban Japan*. Berkeley: University of California Press.

————. 1993. *Encounters with Aging: Mythologies of Menopause in Japan and North America*. Berkeley: University of California Press.

Lu, Henry C. 1986. *The Chinese System of Food Cures: Prevention and Remedies*. New York: Sterling.

Lu Wenfu. [1982] 1986. *Meishijia* (The Gourmet). In *Lu Wenfu Ji* (Collected Works of Lu Wenfu), 1–85. Fuzhou: Straits Cultural Press. Translated by Yu Fanqin as *The Gourmet*. In *A World of Dreams*, 121–214. Beijing: Chinese Literature Press, 1986.

Luo Dunren. 1993. *Zhongguo Gudai Fangshi Yangsheng Jicheng* (Collected Works of Ancient Chinese Life-Nurturing Bedchamber Arts). Tibet: Tibet People's Press.

Lyotard, Jean-François. 1984. *The Post-Modern Condition: A Report on Knowledge*. Minneapolis: University of Minnesota Press.

Mao Zedong. 1971. *Selected Readings from the Works of Mao Tsetung*. Beijing: Foreign Languages Press.

Marcus, George, and Michael Fischer. 1986. *Anthropology as Cultural Critique: An Experimental Moment in the Human Sciences*. Chicago: University of Chicago Press.

Marx, Karl. [1844] 1972. The German Ideology. In *The Marx-Engels Reader*, 2d ed., ed. Robert C. Tucker, 146–200. New York: Norton.

————, and Frederick Engels. 1972. *Makesi Engesi Xuan Ji* (Selected Works of Marx and Engels). Vol. 4. Beijing: People's Press.

Meisner, Maurice. 1986. *Mao's China and After: A History of the People's Republic*. New York: Free Press.

Meng, Yue. 1993. Female Images and National Myth. In *Gender Politics in Modern China*, ed. Tani Barlow, 118–36. Durham: Duke University Press.

Merleau-Ponty, Maurice. 1962. *The Phenomenology of Perception*. Atlantic Highlands, NJ: Humanities Press.

Meserve, Walter J., and Ruth I. Meserve, eds. 1970. *Modern Drama from Communist China*. New York: New York University Press.

Mo Yan. 1995. *Ming Ding Guo* (The Republic of Drunkenness). Beijing: Authors Press.

————. 1997. Wangbuliao Chi (I Can't Forget Eating). *Tianya* 5:92–96.

————. [1992] 2000. *The Republic of Wine*. Trans. Howard Goldblatt. New York: Arcade.

————. 2000. *The Republic of Wine*, by Mo Yan: Interview with the Author. Interviewer Noël Dutrait. *China Perspectives* 29 (May–June): 57–62.

Munn, Nancy. 1986. *The Fame of Gawa: A Symbolic Study of Value Transformation in a Massim (Papua New Guinea) Society*. New York: Cambridge University Press.

Nanjing College of Chinese Medicine. 1979. *Nanjing Jiaoshiben* (Annotated Canon of Problems). Nanjing: Nanjing College of Chinese Medicine.

National Academy of Sciences. 1975. *Herbal Pharmacology in the People's Republic of China: A Trip Report of the American Herbal Pharmacology Delegation*. Washington, DC: National Academy of Sciences.

Needham, Joseph. 1954–. *Science and Civilization in China*. Various volumes. Cambridge: Cambridge University Press.

————, and Lu Gwei-djen. 1980. *Celestial Lancets: A History and Rationale of Acupuncture and Moxa*. Cambridge: Cambridge University Press.

Ng, Man-lun, and Erwin J. Haeberle. 1997. *Sexual Behavior in Modern China: Report on the Nationwide Survey of 20,000 Men and Women*. New York: Continuum.

Niranjana, Tejaswini. 1992. *Siting Translation: History, Post-structuralism, and the Colonial Context*. Berkeley: University of California Press.

Ots, Thomas. 1994. The Silenced Body, The Expressive *Leib*: The Dialectic of Mind and Life in Chinese Cathartic Healing. In *Embodiment and Experience*, ed. Thomas J. Csordas, 116–36. New York: Cambridge University Press.

Pels, Peter. 1998. The Spirit of Matter: On Fetish, Rarity, Fact, and Fancy. In *Border Fetishisms: Material Objects in Unstable Spaces*, ed. Patricia Spyer, 91–121. New York: Routledge.

Porkert, Manfred. 1974. *The Theoretical Foundatons of Chinese Medicine: Systems of Correspondence.* Cambridge: MIT Press.

Prusek, Jaroslav. 1980. *The Lyrical and the Epic: Studies of Modern Chinese Writers.* Bloomington: Indiana University Press.

Qu Bo. 1962. *Tracks in the Snowy Forest.* Beijing: Foreign Languages Press.

Rabinow, Paul, ed. 1984. *The Foucault Reader.* New York: Pantheon.

Rafael, Vicente. 1988. *Contracting Colonialism: Translation and Christian Conversion in Tagalog Society under Early Spanish Rule.* Ithaca: Cornell University Press.

Riskin, Carl. 1987. *Feeding China: The Experience since 1949.* Helsinki: World Institute for Development Economic Research of the United Nations University.

Rofel, Lisa. 1994. "Yearnings": Televisual Love and Melodramatic Politics in Contemporary China. *American Ethnologist* 21:700–22.

———. 1999a. *Other Modernities: Gendered Yearnings in China after Socialism.* Berkeley: University of California Press.

———. 1999b. Qualities of Desire: Imagining Gay Identities in China. *Gay and Lesbian Quarterly* 5, no. 4: 451–74.

Ruan Fangfu. 1988. *Xing Zhishi Shouce* (Handbook of Sexual Knowledge). Beijing: People's Health Press.

Said, Edward W. 1978. *Orientalism.* New York: Pantheon.

Sakai, Naoki. 1997. *Translation and Subjectivity: On "Japan" and Cultural Nationalism.* Minneapolis: University of Minnesota Press.

Saunders, Barry F. 2001. *CT Suite: The Work of Diagnosis in the Age of Virtual Cutting.* Ph.D. diss., University of North Carolina.

Sayer, Derek. 1987. *The Violence of Abstraction: The Analytic Foundations of Historical Materialism.* London: Blackwell.

Scheid, Volker. Forthcoming. *Plurality and Synthesis in Chinese Medicine.* Durham: Duke University Press.

Schein, Louisa. 1994. The Consumption of Color and the Politics of White Skin in Post-Mao China. *Social Text* 41 (winter): 141–64.

———. 2000. *Minority Rules: The Miao and the Feminine in China's Cultural Politics.* Durham: Duke University Press.

Schell, Orville. 1989. *Discos and Democracy: China in the Throes of Reform.* New York: Anchor.

Scheper-Hughes, Nancy, and Margaret Lock. 1987. The Mindful Body: A Prolegomenon to Future Work in Medical Anthropology. *Medical Anthropology Quarterly* (n.s.) 1, no. 1: 6–41.

Schram, Stuart. 1969. *The Political Thought of Mao Tse-tung.* Rev. ed. New York: Praeger.

Schwarcz, Vera. 1986. *The Chinese Enlightenment: Intellectuals and the Legacy of the May 4th Movement.* Berkeley: University of California Press.

Seremetakis, C. Nadia. 1991. *The Last Word: Women, Death, and Divination in*

Inner Mani. Chicago: University of Chicago Press.

———. 1994. *The Senses Still: Perception and Memory as Material Culture in Modernity*. Chicago: University of Chicago Press.

Shandong Zhongyixueyuan Xuebao (Bulletin of the Shandong College of Traditional Chinese Medicine). 1980. Cover text. *Bulletin of the Shandong College of Traditional Chinese Medicine*, no. 2.

Shang Guanfeng. 1998. *Gongting Canyin yu Yangsheng* (Chinese Imperial Cuisine and Eating Secrets). Beijing: Panda Books and Chinese Literature Press.

Shen Rong. [1982] 1987a. The Secret of Crown Prince Village. In *At Middle Age*, 237–342. Beijing: Chinese Literature Press.

———. [1983] 1987b. Ten Years Deducted. In *At Middle Age*, 343–64. Beijing: Chinese Literature Press.

Shen Yingsen, Zhao Changying, and Meng Hui. 1998. *Siji Bushen Shishan* (Seasonal Meals for Body Bolstering). Guangzhou: Guangdong Science and Technology Press.

Simon, Denis F., and Merle Goldman. 1989. *Science and Technology in Post-Mao China*. Cambridge: Council on East Asian Studies, Harvard University.

Simon, Sherry. 1996. *Gender in Translation: Cultural Identity and the Politics of Transmission*. New York: Routledge.

Simoons, Frederick J. 1991. *Food in China: A Cultural and Historical Inquiry*. Boca Raton, FL: CRC Press.

Sivin, Nathan. 1987. *Traditional Medicine in Contemporary China*. Ann Arbor: Center for Chinese Studies, University of Michigan.

Smith, Paul. 1988. *Discerning the Subject*. Minneapolis: University of Minnesota Press.

Snow, Edgar. 1957. *Random Notes on Red China, 1936–1945*. Cambridge: Harvard University Press.

Solomon, Richard H. 1975. *A Revolution Is Not a Dinner Party: A Feast of Images of the Maoist Transformation of China*. Garden City, NY: Anchor.

Song Shugong, ed. 1991. *Zhongguo Gudai Fangshi Yangsheng Jiyao* (Anthology of Essential Works of the Ancient Chinese Life-Nurturing Arts of the Bedchamber). Beijing: China Medical Science Press.

Spivak, Gayatri. 1993. *Outside in the Teaching Machine*. New York: Routledge.

Steiner, George. 1975. *After Babel: Aspects of Language and Translation*. London: Oxford University Press.

Stewart, Kathleen. 1996. *A Space on the Side of the Road: Cultural Poetics in an "Other" America*. Princton: Princeton University Press.

Taussig, Michael. 1980. Reification and the Consciousness of the Patient. *Social Science and Medicine* 14B:3–13.

Treichler, Paula. 1987. AIDS, Homophobia, and Medical Discourse: An Epidemic of Signification. *Cultural Studies* 3, no. 1: 263–305.

Tsing, Anna Lowenhaupt. 1993. *In the Realm of the Diamond Queen: Marginality in an Out-of-the-Way Place*. Princeton: Princeton University Press.

Tucker, Robert C. [1972] 1978. *The Marx Engels Reader*. New York: W. W. Norton and Co.

Tung, Chi-ping, and Humphrey Evans. 1976. *The Thought Revolution*. New York: Coward-McCann.

Turner, Terence. 1980. The Social Skin. In *Not Work Alone: A Cross-Cultural View of Activities Superfluous to Survival*, ed. Roger Lewin and Jeremy Cherfas, 112–40. Beverly Hills: Sage.

Turner, Victor. 1967. An Ndembu Doctor in Practice. In *The Forest of Symbols*, 359–93. Ithaca: Cornell University Press.

Unschuld, Paul. 1985. *Medicine in China: A History of Ideas*. Berkeley: University of California Press.

Vance, Carole, ed. [1984] 1992. *Pleasure and Danger: Exploring Female Sexuality*. London: Pandora Books.

van Gulik, Robert. 1961. *Sexual Life in Ancient China: A Preliminary Survey of Chinese Sex and Society from ca. 1500 B.C. till 1644 A.D.* New York: Barnes and Noble.

Walder, Andrew, ed. 1998. *Zouping in Transition: The Process of Reform in Rural North China*. Cambridge: Harvard University Press.

Waley, Arthur. 1934. *The Way and Its Power: A Study of the Tao Te Ching and Its Place in Chinese Thought*. London: Allen and Unwin.

Wang, Hui. 1995. The Fate of "Mr. Science" in China: The Concept of Science and Its Application in Modern Chinese Thought. *positions* 3, no. 1: 1–68.

Wang, Jing. 1996. *High Culture Fever: Politics, Aesthetics, and Ideology in Deng's China*. Berkeley: University of California Press.

Wang, Xudong. 1989. *Zhongyi Meixue* [Aesthetics of Chinese Medicine]. Nanjing: Dongnan University Press.

Weiss, Brad. 1996. *The Making and Unmaking of the Haya Lived World: Consumption, Commodification, and Everyday Practice*. Durham: Duke University Press.

Wile, Douglas. 1992. *Art of the Bedchamber: The Chinese Sexual Yoga Classics, Including Women's Solo Meditation Texts*. Albany: State University of New York Press.

Williams, Raymond. 1973. *The Country and the City*. New York: Oxford University Press.

Woolgar, Steve. 1988. *Science, the Very Idea*. Chichester: Ellis Horwood.

Xie, Chunsheng, and Yang Liuzhu, eds. 2000. *Xiandai Jiating Zibu Yaoshan* (Nourishing Medicinal Meals for the Modern Family). Beijing: Scientific and Technical Documents Publishing House.

Yan Deliang, Ma Ming, and Zhang Jinrong, eds. 1996. *Yangsheng Jing* (Classic of Life Nurturance). Wuhan: Hubei Peoples Press.

Yan, Yunxiang. 1996. *The Flow of Gifts: Reciprocity and Social Networks in a Chinese Village*. Stanford: Stanford University Press.

Yang, Dali L. 1996. *Calamity and Reform in China: State, Rural Society, and Institutional Change since the Great Leap Famine*. Stanford: Stanford University Press.

Yang Dongping. [1994] 1998. Revolutionary Culture and Language. In *Streetlife China*, ed. Michael Dutton, 165–69. Cambridge: Cambridge University Press.

Yang, Mayfair Mei-Hui. 1994. *Gifts, Banquets, and the Art of Social Relationships in China*. Ithaca: Cornell University Press.

Yang, Rae. 1997. *Spider Eaters: A Memoir*. Berkeley: University of California Press.

Yang, Xiaobin. 1998. The Republic of Wine: An Extravaganza of Decline. *positions* 6, no. 1: 7–31.

Yin Huihe, and Zhang Bona, eds. 1989. *Zhongyi Jichu Lilun* (Fundamental Theories of Chinese Medicine). Beijing: People's Health Press.

Yoshida, Tadashi. 1987. Some Problems in the Analysis of Manifestations of Sickness. In *History of Diagnostics*, ed. Kawakita Yosio, 210–14. Osaka: Taniguchi Foundation.

Yue, Gang. 1999. *The Mouth That Begs: Hunger, Cannibalism, and the Politics of Eating in Modern China*. Durham: Duke University Press.

Zarrow, Peter. 1999. Meanings of China's Cultural Revolution: Memoirs of Exile. *positions* 7, no. 1: 165–91.

Zha Jianying. 1995. *China Pop: How Soap Operas, Tabloids, and Bestsellers Are Transforming a Culture*. New York: New Press.

Zhang Jie. 1980. *Ai, Shi Buneng Wangjide* (Love Must Not Be Forgotten). Guangzhou: Guangdong People's Press.

———. 1987. *Love Must Not Be Forgotten*. Trans. Gladys Yang. Beijing: Panda.

Zhang Xianliang. 1987. *Nanrende Yiban shi Nüren* (Half of Man Is Woman). Hong Kong: Ming Chuang Press.

Zhang Xianliang. 1988. *Half of Man Is Woman*. Trans. Martha Avery. London: Viking.

Zhang Xinxin. 1987. *Chinese Lives: An Oral History of Contemporary China*. New York: Pantheon Books.

Zhang, Xudong. 1997. *Chinese Modernism in the Era of Reforms: Cultural Fever, Avant-Garde Fiction, and the New Chinese Cinema*. Durham: Duke University Press.

Zhou Fengwu, Zhang Jiwen, and Cong Lin, eds. 1981–85. *Ming Laozhongyi zhi Lu* (Paths of Renowned Senior Chinese Doctors). 3 vols. Jinan: Shandong Science and Technology Press.

Zhu Xi, ed. *Sishu Jizhu* (The Annotated Four Books). [12th c.] 1987. Punctuated by Chen Shuguo. Changsha: Yuelu Book Club.

Zhuang Lixing, ed. 1995. *Zhongyi Shiliao* (Nutritional Therapy in Chinese Medicine). Guangzhou: Guangdong Tourism Press.

Zito, Angela. 1997. *Of Body and Brush: Grand Sacrifice as Text/Performance in Eighteenth Century China.* Chicago: University of Chicago Press.

Zito, Angela, and Tani Barlow, eds. 1994. *Body, Subject, and Power in China.* Chicago: University of Chicago Press.

Anagnost, Ann, 227, 311 n.31
Authorship, 22, 191, 196–97
Autobiography, 6, 31, 84, 86, 175, 180, 190, 192, 196, 198, 201, 208, 314 n.16

Banquets, 10, 15–16, 30, 59, 62, 96, 108, 112, 114, 122–23, 135, 137, 144–53, 160, 161
Bedchamber arts (*fangshu*) literature. *See* Erotic arts or bedchamber arts (*fangshu*) literature
Biomedicine, 25, 53, 64, 67, 150, 156, 199, 297 n.42
Bitterness (*ku*), 61–63, 82, 84–90, 95–96, 98, 107, 135, 157, 179, 302 n.29, 306 n.18
Bodies, body, or embodiment, 3, 5–11, 13, 17, 20, 24–29, 32–33, 48–49, 57, 65, 67, 69, 75–77, 90, 103, 108, 115–19, 124, 137, 140, 143, 147, 152, 156–57, 161–62, 169–70, 199, 201, 204–5, 218, 231–32, 244, 246–50, 256, 261–62, 265–67, 275, 277, 279, 282, 285, 287, 289–91, 294 n.7, 299 n.5, 318 n.35
Bolstering (*bu*) therapies, 51–53, 55, 60, 129, 300 n.10
Bourdieu, Pierre, 8–9, 17, 219, 295 n.18

Carnal Prayer Mat, The (Li Yu), 283–84
Chinese Communist Party (CCP), 3, 10–11, 37–39, 48, 80, 84–85, 90, 96–97, 126, 128, 154, 167, 169, 180, 182, 240, 275, 307 n.27
Chinese medical pharmacy. *See* Materia medica (*bencao*) or Chinese medical pharmacy
Chinese medicine: traditional, 19, 25–31, 41–43, 49, 52–55, 58–59, 64–76, 119, 123–24, 136–43, 150, 155–58, 160–63, 176–77, 191–201, 247–48, 258, 261–62, 264–65, 267–71, 273, 275, 297 n.42, 300 n.11, 303 nn. 39–41, 313 n.12
Civilization (*wenming*), 223, 227, 262, 277–78, 282, 316 n.14
Clothing, 15, 99, 103, 154, 307 n.29, 315 n.1
Collective canteens, 14, 39, 41, 50, 54, 94–95, 97, 100, 298 n.11
Collectivism or collective forms, 11, 16, 39, 40–41, 54, 83, 86, 125, 170–71, 174, 195, 237, 271–72, 275–77, 285, 287–89, 291–92
Commensality, 53–55, 87, 93, 101, 106, 111, 123, 146, 152
Common sense, 2, 47, 48, 64, 137, 153, 163, 279, 281–82

Consumerism, 3, 15, 26, 41, 49, 81, 98, 112–13, 117, 134–36, 145, 160, 217, 232, 246–47, 273, 288–89, 300 n.14

Contemporary Chinese Sexual Culture: Report of the "Sex Civilization" Survey of 20,000 Subjects (Liu Dalin et al.), 31, 213, 219–22, 224–32, 239, 241–42, 250, 317 n.19

Cuisine, 44, 50, 51, 54

Cultural Revolution. *See* Great Proletarian Cultural Revolution

Days of Leaving Lei Feng (film), 277

Deficiency. *See* Excess and deficiency

Deng Xiaoping, 12, 15, 80, 94

Depletion (*xu*) and repletion (*shi*), 122–24, 129, 132, 136–43, 155, 158, 161

Depoliticization, 84, 90, 100–101, 116, 123, 191, 208, 247

Derrida, Jacques, 121, 123–24, 153, 162

Desires or desire, 2, 28, 118–19, 171, 183, 207, 217, 222–26, 231–34, 244, 246–47, 253–55, 260, 264–67, 274, 280, 283, 289–90

"Du Wanxiang" (Ding Ling), 30, 167–71, 186, 188, 199, 222, 275

Ellis, Havelock, 211, 231, 254

Embodiment. *See* Bodies, body, or embodiment

Engels, Frederick, 234, 313 n.12

Ermo (film by Zhou Xiaowen), 18, 272–74, 276

Erotic arts or bedchamber arts (*fangshu*) literature, 31, 243–68, 274–83, 318 n.4, 319 n.10

Ethics, 80, 113, 124, 136, 145, 152–53, 160, 162, 176, 205–8, 246, 249, 277–82, 307 n.36

Ethnographic method, 5, 9–10, 17–25, 32–33, 57

Everyday life, 1–3, 7–11, 15, 17, 23–27, 30, 42–43, 47–48, 84, 90–91, 93, 99, 110, 124, 135, 137, 143, 156, 173, 187, 240–41, 244, 249, 263, 267, 275, 277, 289, 291, 312 n.8

Excess and deficiency, 121–26, 128–38, 141–46, 151, 153–63

Experience, as topic of ethnography, 1–3, 5, 8–10, 25, 27, 29, 32–33, 47–49, 52, 55–58, 61–67, 69–71, 74, 76, 81–82, 90, 106, 108, 116, 119, 122–23, 137, 143–44, 154, 156–57, 163, 175–80, 182–83, 185, 190, 192–96, 198, 201–2, 207–8, 218–19, 222–23, 230, 235, 239, 249, 260, 262, 290–91, 312 n.2

Expertise or experts, 32, 108, 177, 180, 190, 275

Famine, 12, 16, 29, 37, 44, 82–83, 94–95, 97, 102, 111, 122, 130–32, 135–36, 154, 159, 163, 305 n.10

Filiality, 274, 282, 321 n.33

Flavors, in food and medicine, 27, 29, 56–57, 59, 62, 63–66, 73–76, 119, 143, 156, 163

Foucault, Michel, 7, 8, 32, 238, 241, 294 n.7

Frozen (film by Wu Ming), 272

Gluttony, 79, 113, 119, 122, 129, 133–36, 154, 163

Gourmet, The (Lu Wenfu), 13, 30, 81, 105–19, 136, 154, 162, 203, 307 n.36

Great Leap Forward (1958–1960), 11–12, 82, 92, 127, 159

Great Proletarian Cultural Revolution, 12, 16, 39, 80, 82, 88, 98,

109, 114, 159, 176, 178–80, 183, 190–91, 197, 207, 209, 305 n.10, 313 n.4

Guanxi, or social relating, 43, 145–52, 311 n.31

Gu Hua, 90, 93–95, 101–2, 105, 116, 143, 202, 308 n.37

Habitus, 8–9, 17, 27, 61, 106, 136–37, 160, 163, 171, 244, 285, 289, 295 n.18

Half of Man Is Woman (Zhang Xianliang), 18, 203, 271

Health, 28, 51, 96, 123, 142, 154, 157, 229–30, 258–69, 274, 276, 279, 284, 287–89, 291

Hibiscus Town (Gu Hua), 13, 18, 29, 80–81, 83–84, 89–105, 110, 113, 116–17, 119, 130, 137, 154, 160, 202

Homosexuality, 214, 236–37

Hunger, 10, 29, 38, 79, 81–87, 92, 94–95, 110, 115, 129–37, 157, 163, 305 n.7

"I Can't Forget Eating" (Mo Yan), 129–37, 158

Individualism, 3, 22–24, 26, 39, 171, 176, 186, 216, 232, 237, 313 n.6

Jiang Qing, 12, 179

Kinsey Report, The (Alfred Kinsey), 211, 228–29, 231, 242

Kipnis, Andrew, 146–47, 151

Language crisis, 13, 180, 201–5, 207, 314 n.25, 315 n.31

Lei Feng, 23, 30, 37–41, 44, 54, 75, 275–78, 285–91, 297 n.4, 298 nn. 9, 10

Liu Dalin, 224, 239, 241, 321 n.36

Love Must Not Be Forgotten (Zhang Jie), 13, 18, 31, 177–90, 201–7, 296 n.38

Lu Wenfu, 18, 30, 105–6, 110, 113, 115–17, 121, 136, 143–44, 203, 291, 308 n.37

Maoism as a cultural formation, 3, 10, 13, 15–17, 23, 29, 30–31, 37–41, 54, 77, 79, 82, 84–85, 89–90, 93, 98, 113, 116, 118, 127, 154, 158–60, 169–70, 177, 179, 189–90, 195, 197, 199, 202, 206, 208, 215, 228, 245, 271–72, 276–78, 287, 302 n.29, 308 n.37, 315 n.31

Maoist period (1949–c.1985), 20, 24, 83, 102, 122, 126, 128–129, 159, 173, 237, 240, 275–78, 304 n.2

Mao Zedong, 6, 10, 12, 19, 24, 37, 39–40, 79–80, 103, 125, 127, 145, 154, 160, 168, 178–79, 182, 208–9, 259, 300 n.13, 308 n.2, 309 n.7

Markets, 14, 49–50, 92–93, 98–104, 128, 160, 176

Marx, Karl, 6–8, 25, 124, 209

Masters, William, and Virginia Johnson, 231–32, 266

Materialism, 6–9, 64, 101–2, 175, 185, 290–91, 310 n.25

Materia medica (bencao) or Chinese medical pharmacy, 26, 47, 58, 61, 63, 65–66, 68, 73, 197, 302 n.27

Mawangdui manuscripts, 256–61

May Fourth movement, 22, 24, 182, 313 n.6

Mencius, 1, 5, 28, 251–52, 289–90, 293 nn. 2, 4

Model theatricals (yangbanxi), 23, 80, 85–86, 88, 91

Mo Yan, 18, 30, 123, 126–31, 134–35, 143–45, 152–53, 158, 160, 163, 291, 309 n.15, 310 n.25

Nationalism, 19, 24, 31, 32, 79, 97, 116, 155, 169–70, 249, 254–55, 257–58, 261–62, 269, 273, 275, 277–79, 282–83, 287
Needham, Joseph, 251, 257, 264, 280–81, 303 n.37, 321 n.36
Nurturance of life (*yang sheng*), 27, 51, 245, 259, 261–63, 266–67, 274, 277, 280, 304 n.42

Parks, public, 14, 173
Patent medicines (*zhongchengyao*), 69, 302 n.30
Paths of Renowned Senior Chinese Doctors (Zhou Fengwu et al.), 177, 180, 190–201, 208, 314 nn. 20, 21
People's Liberation Army (PLA), 37, 39–40, 126–27, 133–34, 297 n.4
Pleasure, 26–28, 57, 66, 76, 81, 87, 96, 106–9, 113–16, 119, 122, 131, 135, 142–46, 153–54, 170–71, 187, 206, 216–17, 222, 224–25, 247, 249, 260, 262, 265, 267, 276–77, 279, 281–82, 284–85, 287–92, 297 n.45, 311 n.31
Privatization, 12, 90, 155, 160, 171, 179, 190, 198, 298 n.11
Propaganda posters, 20–23, 154

Reading, 5–6, 8–9, 17–25, 39–40, 53, 113, 115, 117, 182, 184, 189, 204–5, 222, 244, 246–49, 256, 260, 279, 282–83, 285, 289–91, 296 n.29, 318 n.2
Realism, 18–24, 90, 107, 171, 176, 182, 185, 188, 204–5, 219, 281, 285, 314 n.25
Red Guards, 12, 16, 103–4, 116, 190

Repletion. *See* Depletion (*xu*) and repletion (*shi*)
Representation, 7, 13, 17, 22, 24, 176, 180, 201–2, 204–5, 216, 218–21, 223, 228, 230, 249, 277–83, 290, 316 n.13
Republican Period (1911–1949), 22, 82–83, 85, 89–90, 97, 104, 117–18, 179, 237
Republic of Wine, The (Mo Yan), 129, 144–45, 153
Restaurants, 42, 50–51, 59, 91, 106, 111–12, 114–15, 118, 134, 149, 301 n.23
Revolutionary romanticism, 20, 23, 154, 182, 278

Self-health (*ziwo baojian*) literature, 26, 51, 269–71
Senior Chinese doctors (*laozhongyi*), 175–77, 180, 190, 192–99, 201, 208, 312 n.2
Sex education, 31, 218–19, 226–27, 230–38, 241, 258, 261, 264, 269, 276
Sexology or sexual science, 211, 218, 226–27, 230, 235, 239–41, 245, 253–55, 258, 261, 269, 278
Sex survey. See *Contemporary Chinese Sexual Culture*
Sexual impotence (*yangwei*), 48, 269–74, 276–77, 320 nn. 29, 31
Sexuality, as a discursive topic, 31, 170–71, 211, 216, 218–19, 222–23, 231, 245, 250, 252, 269
Sexual psychology, 232–38
Socialist realism, 23, 182, 287, 312 n.6
Surplus, 124–26, 133–34, 157, 161, 265, 275
Sweetness (*tian*), 88–90, 95, 100, 107, 157

Traditional Chinese medicine. *See* Chinese medicine: traditional

Translation, 57, 67, 282, 290, 319 n.17

van Gulik, Robert, 257, 280–81, 321 n.36

Visceral systems, 59, 60, 138–41, 156, 158, 161–62, 200, 267, 302 n.33, 310 n.19

Western medicine. *See* Biomedicine

White-Haired Girl, The (He Jingzhi et al.), 23, 29, 80–81, 83, 93, 104, 110, 117, 119, 122–23, 188, 306 nn. 15–16

White liquor (*baijiu*), 147–48, 152

Wile, Douglas, 268, 280, 321 nn. 33, 36

Woolgar, Steve, 219–20, 222

Work units (*danwei*), 11, 13–14, 41, 43, 50, 111, 133, 171–74

Writing, 7, 8, 18, 24, 121, 137, 176, 178, 180, 182–84, 188, 196, 201–4, 207–8, 219, 243, 252, 279, 281, 289, 291, 310 n.25, 312 n.2

Yang sheng. See Nurturance of life (*yang sheng*)

Ye Dehui, 257, 321 n.36

Yin-yang relationship and polar dynamic, 48, 52, 58, 75, 96, 105, 138, 253–55, 259, 263, 268, 300 n.11

Yue, Gang, 62, 304 n.2, 307 n.36

Zhang Jie, 18, 31, 178–81, 190, 202, 207, 291, 312 n.2

Zhou Xiaowen, 18, 272, 276, 291

Judith Farquhar is Professor of Anthropology at the
University of North Carolina, Chapel Hill. She is the
author of *Knowing Practice: The Clinical Encounter of
Chinese Medicine.*

Library of Congress Cataloging-in-Publication Data
Farquhar, Judith.
Appetites : food and sex in post-socialist China /
Judith Farquhar.
p. cm.—(Body, commodity, text)
Includes bibliographical references and index.
ISBN 0-8223-2906-9 (cloth : alk. paper)
ISBN 0-8223-2921-2 (pbk. : alk. paper)
1. Body, Human—Social aspects—China.
2. Food habits—China. 3. Sex customs—China.
4. Medicine—China. 5. China—Social conditions—
1976– I. Title. II. Series.
GT497.C6 F37 2002
394.1'0951—dc21   2001054710